The Complete Guide To Racetrack Betting

David K. Rosenthal

LIBERTY PUBLISHING COMPANY
Cockeysville, Maryland

Third printing: May, 1987

Published by:
Liberty Publishing Company, Inc.
50 Scott Adam Road
Cockeysville, Maryland 21030

Library of Congress #85-81321
ISBN 0-89709-144-2

Publisher's Note

Although great care has been taken to present factual and accurate information, both Liberty Publishing Company, Inc. and The Daily Racing Form, Inc. do not assume responsibility for the methodology and/or the accuracy of the material presented herein. Moreover, both publishers and the author will not be responsible for any resulting losses or profits in the past, present, or future.

Manufactured USA

To My Mom

Contents

Introduction 3

Traits of a Successful Horse Player 7

Why do some bettors make money while others fail?

Pari-mutuel Betting 23

Serious bettors should know how the system works.

The Track from the Inside 31

Horses are living creatures. The bettor should recognize them as such and know something about the people who own, train and ride them.

Handicapping Techniques 73

Most successful bettors have an edge: they know how to read between the lines, recognize a track bias, understand trip handicapping, and can adjust speed figures.

At the Betting Window 101

Proper money management, the *Maximum Bet* concept, exotic wagering, and several examples from three popular North American racetracks.

Acknowledgements 162

Index 163

Introduction

At seventeen, when I first discovered that a "double" was not just a two base hit, my father went out of his way to explain to me that only one out of twenty people win at the racetrack on a given day. He was right. Statistics indicate that 95% of racegoers will lose and that only 2% of the bettors will win consistently and over the long run. These are professional horse players who earn their living at the track. I thought I possessed above average intelligence and if there were people who won consistently, why couldn't I be one of them? What was their secret?

There was only one place to find out—at the track. Once there, it became obvious to me why so many people lost. Most of them were handicapping the public handicappers instead of the horses. Although there are many fine public handicappers, they operate at severe disadvantages. Newspapers and tout sheets have deadlines that must be met before the latest scratches, jockey switches, equipment changes and weather conditions are known. More importantly, they cannot instruct the public on betting—what type of bet and how much to bet. Betting is at least 50% of the battle and it is often the most overlooked detail.

Incredibly, a great percentage of horse players didn't even consider the horses' past performances. No wonder they lost. How can anyone expect to win consistently by blindly taking the advice of others, randomly picking names, or by going on hunches? Even more astounding, after these people lost, they would cry that the race was fixed, the jockey stiffed the horse, or the horse would have won "if this" or "if that."

I then read nearly every book printed on the fundamentals of handicapping. The only firm conclusion, it seemed, was that experts could not agree.

Upon closer examination though, it became apparent that my skills as a handicapper were good, but I could be ranked among the world's ten worst bettors. Then I met Rich Hallahan. He provided my missing key to handicapping—how to read between the lines. Rich was an avid racing fan when I met him at Union College in Schenectady, New York. Today he is a civil engineer, married with two children, and the owner of Golden Cross Farms. Golden Cross is a racing and breeding operation with over thirty horses. With Rich's input, I became a terrific handicapper.

But then, my moment of truth came. After giving many lectures to me (to no avail), my father decided that we should go to the track and split our bets. My dad doesn't drink and dislikes gambling. He couldn't understand how he could have sired a son who loved to bet on horses (I guess breeding isn't perfect in humans either). By going to the track with me, my dad thought he'd lose ten or twenty dollars and teach his son a valuable lesson. After losing, all arguments would cease. I was under the gun! It's hard enough to win on any specific day (as opposed to the long run) but now I had to do it as a two-dollar bettor. If betting two dollars was bad, what would my father say about betting ten dollars, or twenty dollars, or more?

The first exacta race came. We had to pick the first two finishers in exact order. My dad gave me two dollars to bet the exacta. I asked for two more to reverse it and protect ourselves in case my second choice beat my top pick. The two bets cost a total of four dollars. If our first ticket won, we would split almost $300.00. My dad handed me the money, thinking he would have a better chance of seeing it again if it fell from his wallet on a street in Manhattan.

At the top of the stretch my first choice had three lengths on my second selection, which had four lengths on the field! Judging by the fractions, their positions, the jockeys' hold on the horses, and so on, I saw no way for us to lose. I turned to watch the expression on my dad's face. In mid-stretch, he too realized we were going to win, and then it happened. In split seconds his face kept changing from delight at winning the money to disappointment in teaching his son this valuable lesson. He didn't know whether to root for or against our horses. Finally just before the wire, one last contortion, then my father proved he was human and started yelling out encouragement to cheer our horses to victory. In retrospect he claims it was more pride than winning the money. After we collected, I turned to him and said, "See dad, they're giving money away here!" My father still wasn't a believer, but there was peace in the house once again.

Although my dad understood I was good at picking winners, he never realized what a struggle betting was for me. It was not uncommon for me to have five or six winners on the card and arrive home with only a small profit. After many years, I finally saw the light. How easy it was. Why didn't I know how to bet before? Since Rich didn't know how to bet either, I had to find out for myself—the hard way. After blowing the bet many, many times, after coming home a loser when I should have won big, and after much soul searching, I finally learned how to do it! Sure I would lose races again, but never, absolutely never, would I make a bad bet. Betting is an art. It is this knowledge that I now pass along with the hope that others will also find joy in solving an intricate puzzle and make money by so doing.

This book is dedicated to teaching people not just to pick winners, but more importantly, how to make money at the racetrack. What follows is an explanation of what it takes to become a good bettor and a consistent winner. The reader will learn a little about self-analysis and about his or her chances of success, the pari-mutuel system, the track from the inside (based on my experiences as a groom and an owner), a few fundamentals and advanced handicapping techniques, and, most importantly, how to become a shrewd money manager. I'm sure this will lead to more enjoyment and success at the racetrack.

Examples used to illustrate points throughout the book are samples of everyday situations, all from a few years ago. Nothing has changed. Odds at post time and jockey switches are noted left or above the horse's past performance lines. If no jockey is listed, the horse was ridden by the same rider it had last time out. To further illustrate that the examples chosen are not unique, three different racetracks have been selected—Aqueduct in New York, Louisiana Downs in Louisiana and Penn National in Pennsylvania. They are representative of the different sized tracks in the country—large, medium and small (i.e. based on daily attendance and the quality of racing). In this book, those with daily attendance greater than 15,000 are considered large, between 5000 and 15,000 medium, and less than 5000 small. Aqueduct is one of the biggest tracks in the country based on attendance, mutuel handle and level of competition. Louisiana Downs also has an attendance roughly between 10,000 and 12,000 but the quality of racing is not as good as New York's. Penn National has an attendance of roughly 5000 and races $2500 claimers. The differences and subtleties between different sized tracks will be fully explained. These tracks were chosen to prove that by combining sound reasoning, knowledge, hard work, discipline and objectivity, the reader can win at any track in the country. The examples at the end of this book are everyday race situations which will tie all of the previous concepts together. The more time and effort put forth going through the examples, the greater the chances of success at the racetrack. Betting successfully means examining your own strengths and weaknesses and improving on both. Winning is hard work. Winning big and consistently is even more work. There are no short cuts. The reader must decide on the goals and how much effort and time to commit. One thing is for sure: the rewards can be enormous.

Traits of the Successful Horse Player

My buddy Mitch got 800 in Math (a perfect score) on the College Entrance Exams—the S.A.T.'s He is now a computer consultant for one of the largest banks in America and earns a well above average income. Mitch is very bright, but he is a terrible horse player and will probably never become a good one—even if he reads and re-reads this book.

Thirteen years ago, we tried to create a computerized handicapping program. It wasn't very sophisticated because we had more of an interest than a background. After receiving my M.B.A. from Duke University, we again tried to design the ultimate handicapping program. At Duke, I had taken a course in New Venture Management. Students had to write a business prospectus and present it to a board of entrepreneurs, each of whom was a multimillionaire. While other students designed plans to build large corporations, my prospectus was concerned with marketing a computerized tout sheet. Members of the board told me that my project was among the best they had seen and encouraged me to pursue it. One even took out his check book, offering to become the first investor! So, Mitch and I worked together to get more realistic cost estimates and so forth. To design such a system, I had to help Mitch understand handicapping so that he could make the computer do the selections.

Months later, Mitch showed me sophisticated flow charts and estimated that the data base would require 6 or 7 million bytes of storage. Programming would take a year to a year and a half in man hours. The estimated cost was $750,000! Now, I really think I could create a successful program, but maintaining the data base, the program, and the initial cost would not make it feasible. Also, there was the possibility that after all was said and done, the program still might not work—so we abandoned the project.

The point here is that Mitch now understands handicapping but he is still a chronic loser at the track. Once he walks through those gates, something strange happens. All of his plans are thrown out the window. On the way to the track Mitch swears he will make a certain bet. At the track he never does. Going home, he'll tell me, "I was going to bet this" or "I should have done that."

Three years ago we drove to the track together to watch our horse run. The ride took fifty minutes to an hour. "Mitch, you're my friend but I hate going to the track with you because you always lose. Tonight why don't you listen to me for once? Stop being stubborn. I know you think of me as a friend and not a serious handicapper, because we grew up together. But I'm a professional handicapper. I have to be better than you. You know I don't win all the time but I also don't lose every time as you do. Why don't you listen to me tonight?" Mitch was quick to agree—but I know Mitch. The rest of the ride he promised over and over again to follow my advice.

Finally, we're at the windows, just in time for the third race triple (selecting three horses in exact order). "Mitch will you listen to me?" "Yes," he said. I made my bet and turned around to Mitch, who was on line behind me and said: "Mitch, bet the one and six with everything." (i.e. 1–6–2, 1–6–3, 1–6–4, 1–6–5, etc.). He gave me a nod and smiled. He exuded the confidence that comes from knowing he's got it! As I walked away, Mitch approached the window. Then that strange thing happened. I hear Mitch saying to the pari-mutuel clerk, "Let me have $30.00 on the #4 horse to win!" (By the way, the official order of finish was 1–6–4 paying over $400.) Afterwards, Mitch said that he was "going to" and that he "should have."

Serious betting at the racetrack is not for everyone. Based on my experience, I've noticed that people who win big and win consistently share certain traits which will be described shortly. The more of these traits you possess or develop, the greater your chances of winning.

Before all else, though, think in terms of *guidelines* rather than *rules*. Guidelines are helpful because they offer a foundation upon which to build. Rules don't provide the necessary flexibility. Things change at the racetrack. Horses are living creatures and, therefore, a dynamic system. They race and train into and out of form. They get injured. Trainers make equipment changes. Horses get claimed and are improved or worsened. Trainers and jockeys are only human. The weather changes constantly and so does the track condition. The wind shifts. It starts to rain after the fifth race—or it begins to snow. The handicapper can make all of his selections at home, apply all of the fundamentals, but when he enters the track, scratches, jockey switches, overweights, equipment changes and the undeniable pressures, anxieties and excitement of betting all become factors. The successful horse player does not simply follow strict rules. No one I know has made a fortune in so doing.

Horse players are therefore faced with the challenge of putting together many little pieces to solve the big puzzle. Those who do it successfully seem to have this much in common:

1. Above-average intelligence
2. An enjoyment and skill of solving problems
3. Dedication
4. Good or outstanding memories
5. Knowledge
6. Objectivity
7. Discipline
8. Money management ability
9. Math skills
10. Confidence

1. *Above-average intelligence*

The handicapper must have the intelligence necessary to "read between the lines." There are so many variables at the racetrack, so many factors—and they never remain the same. This is part of the fun and the challenge of betting. Naturally, the selection process itself requires reasoning and the application of logic. The question "Why did the trainer enter this particular horse in this particular race?" must always be answered. To read between the lines to answer this question demands a capacity for deduction. Sometimes the answer is obvious. Often, however, it is not. There is a certain enjoyment in discovering a not-so-obvious answer. Find the key that others will overlook! For example, on today, February 5:

***Roger's Pass** — B. c. 4, by Connaught—Varena, by Huntercombe — $12,500 — Br.—Bricken R (Eng) — Tr.—Puentes Gilbert — 117
Own.—Garren M M

	Lifetime					
	19 1 1 0	1983	4	0	0	0	$660
	$12,480	1982	4	0	0	0	
		Turf	1	0	1	0	$3,960

29Jan83- 1Aqu	fst	1¼	⊡:49⅘	1:41⅘	2:09⅘	Clm 10000	2	6	5^{11}	$5^{6\frac12}$	$4^{7\frac12}$	$4^{8\frac34}$	Brown T A		117	21.50	61-20	YoursToCommnd$108^{2\frac34}$VerblDul$112^{1\frac34}$CommnchBrv$106^{3\frac34}$	Even try	7
15Jan83- 1Aqu	my	1½	⊡:48⅗	2:07⅗	2:33⅘	Hcp 16000s	6	7	8^{35}	9^{18}	8^{22}	8^{23}	Belmonte J E		109	53.00	59-22	Gallant Gentleman112^{4}TribalPrince$105^{\frac34}$Philanthropic127^{1}	Outrun	9
9Jan83- 3Aqu	fst	1¼	⊡:49⅘	1:41⅘	2:07⅘	Clm 14000	4	8	7^{16}	8^{9}	7^{12}	7^{11}	Belmonte J E[10]		103	*1.80e	68-17	Sonny Booth 114^{hd} Perfect Bidder 110^{2} Atop It All 119^{2}	Outrun	8
3Jan83- 2Aqu	fst	1⁷⁰	⊡:48⅕	1:13⅕	1:43⅘	Clm 20000	6	8	8^{15}	9^{20}	9^{26}	9^{31}	Davis R J	b	108	49.30	52-25	No Heir $117^{6\frac34}$ Red Hot and Cole$106^{7\frac34}$Mr.Nicefield115^{hd}	Far back	9
23Dec82- 2Aqu	fst	1⅛	⊡:49	1:14⅘	1:55	Clm 14000	1	9	9^{14}	9^{14}	9^{17}	9^{19}	Migliore R	b	113	5.20e	52-27	Sonny Booth 108^{1} In the Process $117^{5\frac34}$ SinghBoldly$112^{2\frac34}$	Outrun	11
9Dec82- 5Aqu	fst	1$\frac{1}{16}$	⊡:48⅗	1:14⅗	1:48⅗	Clm 18000	2	6	6^{11}	8^{13}	7^{18}	7^{23}	Migliore R	b	113	41.90	48-30	Righteous Anger $117^{4\frac12}$QuicksilverLuck110^{6}ArdentBid$117^{\frac34}$	Outrun	8
3Dec82- 3Aqu	my	6f	⊡:22⅘	:46⅕	1:11⅕	Clm 20000	8	10	11^{12}	11^{18}	11^{22}	11^{21}	Santiago A	b	113	22.10e	67-13	Jef Fix 117^{2} Pruner's Intention $108^{3\frac34}$ Shore Leave $119^{2\frac34}$	Outrun	11
3Jan82- 3Aqu	fst	1⁷⁰	⊡:48⅗	1:14	1:44⅘	Clm 30000	6	7	7^{17}	7^{17}	7^{16}	5^{14}	Migliore R	b	117	10.90	65-19	Fried Grits $119^{6\frac12}$ Jet Voyage $117^{1\frac34}$ Heres Anthony 117^{nk}	Outrun	7
19Dec81- 7Aqu	fst	1⅛	⊡:50	1:15	1:53⅗	Alw 17000	2	5	$5^{3\frac12}$	$7^{7\frac12}$	7^{21}	7^{22}	Migliore R	b	117	42.10	57-17	Gauley 117^{4} Jason The Racer 117^{hd} Class Hero 117^{3}	Outrun	7
7Dec81- 7Aqu	fst	1$\frac{1}{16}$	⊡:47⅘	1:12⅗	1:46⅗	Alw 17000	12	11	11^{13}	12^{16}	11^{19}	11^{20}	Saumell L	b	117	62.60	62-16	Wolfie'sRascal$117^{3\frac12}$ClassHero117^{hd}MortgageMn$117^{1\frac34}$	Slow start	12

LATEST WORKOUTS Jan 26 Bel tr.t 4f fst :50⅘ b   Jan 20 Bel tr.t 3f fst :37⅘ b   Dec 29 Bel tr.t 4f fst :50⅕ b   Dec 21 Bel tr.t 4f fst :49⅘ b

Roger's Pass follows an old theory about a horse "giving notice." He hasn't run first, second, or third in at least two years and then suddenly shows improvement. He is giving notice that he is "on the improve" and if he improves more today, he could win. Usually a horse that gives notice seems to do so out of the blue. In this case, there seems to be a logical explanation. In 1981, Roger's Pass was an allowance horse in New York. He even raced against a top New York horse, Wolfie's Rascal. Because he'd been raced so lightly and was laid off for eleven months (January to December, 1982) and because he had dropped down the claiming ladder, it is a safe assumption that something had happened to Roger's Pass—perhaps an injury. Until his last race Roger's

Pass hadn't been within eleven lengths of a winner. His last race wasn't that impressive either, except for the comment "Even try" rather than "Outrun" or "Far back." The trainer, Gilbert Puentes, is shrewd, especially with claimers. He, too, noticed an improved effort and raised the horse in class despite being beaten by 8¼ lengths. What makes this horse playable? The not-so-obvious answer is that Roger's Pass probably improved because Puentes was able to race and train him three times in eleven days, (a feat his assumed injury wouldn't have allowed), race him on January 29th (when he improved) and then bring him right back this day, February 5th. By reading between the lines one can begin to see him rounding into form. Puentes has. Additionally, the rest of the field was weak. To bet the ranch on this horse wouldn't be wise, but at 22–1, Roger's Pass is hard to resist entirely.

2. *Problem solvers that like a challenge*

This is a particular type of intelligence. People who are good problem solvers enjoy the challenge of knowing that in front of them are all, or almost all, of the pieces to a puzzle and that if they apply their skills properly the solution can be found.

No two horses and no two races are ever the same. This is the challenge. This is the fun of handicapping. There is a certain satisfaction in correctly fitting the pieces together. The more the horse player enjoys the challenge, the better the results. Personally, I can remember many, many times waiting at the local candy store at night for the *Daily Racing Form* to be delivered for the next day's races. Most days I can't wait to open up the *Form* to see which horses are racing and to solve the puzzles. Also, I know that I don't do as well on the days when I'm tired, hassled, or just not psyched. Recognizing this helps at the windows. On these days, betting must be more conservative.

3. *Dedication*

Handicapping and going to the racetrack day after day for a month or two or three at a time can eventually be like going to a regular job. The horse player, if he wants, can take a day off or miss the first couple of races. There is no boss to reprimand him. There is no deadline to meet, no order to fill. Casual race goers can win, but it is folly to assume that they can win as much and as often as everyday players. This is not to say that everyone should go to the track all of the time. However, the once a month player will improve his performance by going to the track once a week and the weekly player will increase his chances of success by visiting the track daily. Professional gamblers go daily. This is not stated to discourage or encourage my readers, but rather to insure that their expectations and goals are realistic. This in turn, leads to enjoyment at the track.

The serious handicapper doesn't want to miss any race, even one that isn't being bet. A horse in trouble today might pay a big price next week. Maybe something new will be learned. After every losing race, the smart bettor goes back to the *Form* to figure out why a particular horse won or what pattern the winning trainer followed. Every loss is a learning experience. The answer many times is simply racing luck. But not always. In this manner, the intelligent player accumulates more sophisticated techniques. Maybe it becomes obvious that Nijinski II's do well on the turf; that Lucien Lauren is winning with first time starters; that the Bagdads do well on Aqueduct's sloppy inner dirt track; that speed is winning today; or that only inside speed is winning today; or that the Never Bend's do unusually well as first time starters, etc. Only hard work and dedication can really uncover all of these factors.

Dedication also means putting in 100% effort. To be in the top 2% means only casual drinking at the track. No girlfriends or wives. No distractions. I don't expect many to follow this advice, but it will help. Without a total commitment something may be overlooked, perhaps only a little something. But that might make all the difference to the serious player.

4. *Good or outstanding memories*

A poor memory is a real disadvantage. It means things must always be written down and organized. Personally, I keep a notebook for trip handicapping (more on that later). Writing will help a great deal, but it's just not the same as a good memory. For example, one rainy afternoon look at the sires of all the winners. The next rainy afternoon do the same thing. The second time a Riva Ridge (i.e. a horse by Riva Ridge) wins, the player with a good memory says to himself, "Hey, last week a Riva Ridge also won in the slop." The third time it might be worth looking for Riva Ridges *before* the race. Even if that next Riva Ridge doesn't win, it may do well. If it does better than expected because of the off-track, horsemen say that it steps up on an off-track. Some horses, like Nijinski II's, step up on the turf. With a good memory, the horse player can pick up on these and similar handicapping techniques.

On February 6, Imaromeo stepped up in class to defeat $25,000 claimers after destroying $12,500 claimers on January 30.

Imaromeo — Own.—Brookfield Farm — $25,000 — Dk. b. or br. h. 6, by Gallant Romeo—Irealize, by Chieftain — Br.—Isaacs H Z (Ky) — Tr.—Kelly Edward I — 117

Lifetime								
30 6 1 6	1983	3	1	0	1	$8,400
$69,860	1982	9	2	1	0	$19,220
	Turf	2	0	0	0	

30Jan83- 5Aqu	fst	1⅛	:48⅘	1:13⅖	1:52⅕	Clm 12500	1	1	1hd	1hd	14	15¾	Santagata N	b 117	3.20	85-20	Imaromeo 1175¾ Indigo Star 1084 Axe The Fool 1177	Ridden Out	9
27Jan83- 5Aqu	fst	6f	:22⅘	:46⅕	1:11⅘	Clm 20000	14	11	1311	1314	129¾	108¼	Santagata N	b 117	19.20	77-19	SirSizzlingNhoc113noBusyHlrous1141¾SwssConncton117hd	Outrun	14
12Jan83- 9Aqu	fst	6f	:23⅗	:47⅕	1:12⅗	Clm 18000	8	5	63½	45	47	32	Santagata N	b 117	8.30	80-19	Busy Hilarious 1122 Cool Corn 112hd Imaromeo 1172½	Rallied	12
31Dec82- 9Aqu	fst	6f	:23⅗	:47⅘	1:12⅘ 3↑	Clm 12500	2	7	41	2½	2½	22	Santiago A	b 119	*1.90	80-25	SirSizzlingNehoc1172Imromo1196CountrAttck1171	Best of others	9
27Dec82- 2Aqu	fst	6f	:23⅗	:47⅕	1:12⅗ 3↑	Clm 20000	9	8	55	54½	76¾	76¾	Santiago A	b 117	4.70	75-22	Abelardo 117nk Moon Glider 1174½ Psychosis 113no	No factor	9
17Dec82- 3Aqu	my	6f	:23⅘	:48⅘	1:13⅗ 3↑	Clm 10000	3	6	2hd	33	21½	15	Santiago A	b 117	4.80	76-31	Imaromeo 1175 Big Sport 1081 Ironical 113½	Driving	9
3Dec82- 9Aqu	my	6f	:22⅗	:45⅗	1:11⅕ 3↑	Clm 25000	4	1	913	924	936	960	Hernandez R	b 117	10.70	28-13	Riva'sMagic1142¾Rapido'sRepeat1173WorthyPiper1191¾	Far back	10
9May82- 5Aqu	fm	1$\frac{1}{16}$ T	:48⅘	1:13⅗	1:44	Clm 45000	1	5	55	97	710	812	Santiago A	b 113	14.40	73-13	Deedee's Deal 1171 Freon 1172½ Surf Club 113¾	Tired	10
29Apr82- 5Aqu	fst	1	:48⅕	1:13⅗	1:38⅗	Clm 35000	1	6	32	41¾	3½	1½	Santiago A	b 117	10.50	73-22	Imaromeo 117½ Funny R. J. 113¾ Laddy's Luck 108hd	Driving	8
18Feb82- 5Aqu	fst	6f	:23	:46⅗	1:11⅕	Clm 40000	8	7	78	76½	86½	88	Santiago A	b 117	17.80	79-22	Infinite Saga 117nk Self Pressured 1171 RaiseABuck1171½	Outrun	11

LATEST WORKOUTS Jan 23 Bel tr.t 4f fst :51⅘ b

On February 9, Axe the Fool was entered against $16,000 claimers.

CORDERO 2:1

Axe The Fool — B. g. 5, by Hatchet Man—Time To Turn, by Turn-To — $16,000 — Br.—Lin-Drake Farm (Fla) — Tr.—DeBonis Robert — Own.—Chasringg Stable — 117

Lifetime 27 7 6 4 $120,620 — 1983 2 0 0 1 $1,320 — 1981 14 4 4 3 $78,260 — Turf 3 0 0 0

30Jan83- 5Aqu	fst	1⅛	⊡:48⅘	1:13⅖	1:52⅕	Clm 12500	9	2	2hd	2hd	24	39¾	Smith A Jr	b 117	2.80e	75-20	Imaromeo 1175¾ Indigo Star 1084 Axe The Fool 1177	Weakened	9
23Jan83- 9Aqu	sly	6f	⊡:23	:47⅗	1:12⅘	Clm 16000	3	—	—	—	—	927	Miranda J	b 117	*1.50	53-26	Duck Key Taurian 1179 In the Process 1083 SixthCavalry1082	Fog	9
29Dec81- 8Lrl	fst	7f	:23⅖	:47	1:26⅕	3↑ Alw 11500	4	1	32½	43¾	42¾	38½	Krone J A5	b 109	*1.00	73-34	El Punchero 1141¼ Majestic Song 1095 AxeTheFool1093	Ret. sore	6
10Dec81- 8Lrl	fst	1 1/16	:47⅕	1:12⅖	1:44⅖	3↑ Alw 12000	1	1	1½	1hd	22½	23¼	Daniels W H	b 113	*1.20	93-25	Issue Joined 1163¼ Axe The Fool 1131¾ El Punchero1095	2nd best	10
26Nov81- 2Aqu	fst	1	:46⅘	1:12⅗	1:37⅖	Clm 45000	8	9	95	42	1½	14¾	Avalon W AIII5	b 112	*1.50	79-21	AxeTheFool1124¾NativeGroogle1132¼KingBelgin1142¾	Ridden out	13
7Nov81- 5Aqu	fst	1	:46⅘	1:11⅘	1:37⅖	Clm 75000	6	1	1hd	1hd	2½	2nk	MacBeth D	b 112	4.70	79-22	MainStem117nkAxeTheFool1122¾RahwayII116¾	Stumbled, bore in	8
19Sep81- 2Bel	my	1	:45⅗	1:10⅕	1:36⅕	3↑ Clm 75000	6	5	3½	1½	2½	21¾	Molina V H5	b 101	*3.00	85-13	Southerner 1181¾ Axe The Fool 1013¾ Adam's Pet 112hd	2nd best	7
10Sep81- 8Med	fst	1 1/16	:48⅘	1:12⅗	1:44⅗	Clm 40000	1	1	1½	11	12½	14	Martens G	b 119	*.90	86-19	Axe The Fool 1194 Savage Moment 1163¼ Recant 11615	Driving	5
22Aug81- 4Sar	fst	1⅛	:46	1:11	1:49	Clm 45000	4	2	1½	12½	1½	21¼	Migliore R5	b 108	*1.80 D	89-11	Citizen Doe 1171¼ D Axe The Fool 1088¾ KingBelgian1172	Bore in	6
22Aug81-Disqualified and placed third																			
8Aug81- 3Sar	fst	1 3/16	:49	1:13⅘	1:58⅗	Clm c-35000	5	1	11	11	12	12½	Maple E	b 117	*1.50	81-13	Axe The Fool 1172¼ Larking's Run 117hd OldHoward1142¼	Driving	7

LATEST WORKOUTS Jan 7 Bel tr.t 3f my :38⅖ b Dec 31 Bel tr.t 5f fst 1:04 b Dec 23 Bel tr.t 3f fst :38 b Dec 9 Bel tr.t 3f fst :40 b

After not racing for over a year, Axe The Fool was sent off as the 3:2 favorite on January 23rd and was nowhere to be seen. The trainer, Robert DeBonis, dropped him to $12,500 claimers on January 30th. In that race, Axe The Fool hooked up in a speed duel with Imaromeo. REMEMBER now, Imaromeo stepped up to $25,000 claimers and won just three days ago. The race on January 30th is a key race. When two or three or more losers from the same race come back and win their next race, the race is said to be a key race. This horse improved that day and gave notice (after a tightener when the New York crowd bet him down to 3:2) and today is being raised to only $16,000 claimers, not $25,000. Axe The Fool is a once-classy horse regaining his form with a jockey switch to Angel Cordero. Although these are important factors, the key here is remembering Imaromeo's victory three days before. The Aqueduct crowd did. They bet Axe The Fool down to 2:1. He didn't disappoint.

If ever there was a key race, The Land of Opportunity Futurity, July 29, 1983, was it. This race is for Arkansas breds only, run at Louisiana Downs. There is no two year old racing at Arkansas's only thoroughbred track, Oaklawn Park, because the meet runs too early in the two year old's career—usually from mid-February to mid-April. There is a $500 entry fee to pass the box and an additional $500 fee to start in this Futurity. Therefore, owners paying $1,000 are doing so because the trainer believes the horse has potential. The losers of this race later entered maiden races and look what happened:

Gap Opening

Ninth in the Futurity, wins his next start on August 16th and pays $66.40.

Gap Opening Ch. c. 2, by Natoge—Swift Queen, by Dead [illegible]
Br.—Davis & Al Sowayel (Ark) 1983 2 M 0 0
Own.—Davis T 120 Tr.—Breashear Bill
Lifetime 2 0 0 0
29Jly83-8LaD 6f :22³ :46 1:12 ft 23 114 4¾ 6¾ 9¹⁶ 9¹⁷ WtdDE³ Ⓢ Opportunity [illegible]-21 Lrn'sPrncss,FstAndRcy,J.A.'sUntd 13
15Jly83-8LaD 6f :22² :47² 1:15 sl 15 109⁵ 6⁴¾ 6³½ 7⁸ 7⁹¼ Hiett K¹¹ Aw11[illegible] [illegible]-32 SecrtMountin,Mc'sMrTibb,Dr.Syn 12
Jly 24 LaD 5f ft 1:02 b Jly 8 LaD 3f ft :36² b Jly 6 LaD 5f m 1:03¹ hg

Bubbly Stuff

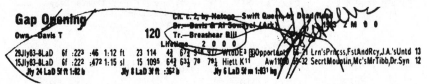

An alibi while finishing fourth in the Futurity, *she* wins next time on August 17th paying $4.20.

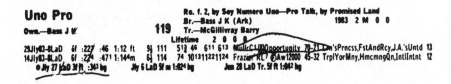

Bubbly Stuff Dk. b. or br. f. 2, by Loco Kid—Olivers Orphan, by Hempen
Br.—Johnston E C Jr (Ark) 1983 1 M 0 0 $2,310
Own.—Johnston E C Jr 119 Tr.—Brennan Terry
Lifetime 1 0 0 0 $2,310
29Jly83-8LaD 6f :22³ :46 1:12 ft 4 109 10⁷¾ 8⁹¼ 4⁷½ 4⁷½ MrKM⁷ Ⓢ Opportunity 75-21 Lrn'sPrncss,FstAndRcy,J.A.'sUntd 13
29Jly83—Forced back at the start
Aug 10 LaD 5f ft 1:02² b Jly 21 LaD 6f ft 1:15 b Jly 12 LaD Tr. 6f ft 1:14³ hg Jly 4 LaD 4f ft :48 b

Uno Pro

Sixth in the Futurity, *she* wins next time paying $8.00.

Uno Pro Ro. f. 2, by Soy Numero Uno—Pro Talk, by Promised Land
Br.—Bass J K (Ark) 1983 2 M 0 0
Own.—Bass J K 119 Tr.—McGillivray Barry
Lifetime 2 0 0 0
29Jly83-8LaD 6f :22⁷ :46 1:12 ft 9¾ 111 5¹¾ 4⁶ 6¹¹ 6¹³ MullrC1[illegible] Ⓢ Opportunity 70-21 Lrn'sPrncss,FstAndRcy,J.A.'sUntd 13
14Jly83-8LaD 6f :22⁴ :47¹ 1:14⁴m 6¾ 114 7⁴ 10¹³11²²11²⁴ Frazier RL⁷ Ⓕ Aw12000 45-32 TrplYorMny,HmcmngQn,IntlIntnt 12
● Jly 27 LaD 3f ft :34³ hg Jly 6 LaD 5f m 1:02⁴ hg Jun 28 LaD Tr. 5f ft 1:04² hg

Fast And Racy

Went head and head for the lead in the Futurity to just miss by a head running second. *She* wins next time on August 25th paying a remarkable $3.80.

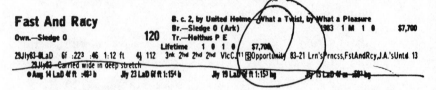

Fast And Racy
B. c. 2, by United Holme—What a Twist, by What a Pleasure
Br.—Sledge O (Ark) 1983 1 M 1 0 $7,700
Own.—Sledge O 120 Tr.—Holthus P E
Lifetime 1 0 1 0 $7,700
29Jly83-8LaD 6f :22^{3} :46 1:12 ft 4$\frac{1}{2}$ 112 3^{nk} 2^{hd} 2^{hd} 2^{hd} VlcCJ^{11} Ⓢ Opportunity 83-21 Lrn'sPrncss,FstAndRcy,J.A.'sUntd 13
29Jly83—Carried wide in deep stretch
●Aug 14 LaD 4f ft :48^{3} b Jly 23 LaD 6f ft 1:15^{4} b Jly 19 LaD 6f ft 1:15^{3} hg Jly 15 LaD 4f sy :50^{3} bg

Zinov's First

Tenth in the Futurity, on August 24th *she* faces another Futurity horse (Uno Pro) and loses. The next time, on September 16th with no Futurity losers in the field, *she* wins and pays $9.40.

Zinov's First
Ch. f. 2, by Zinov—Mini Skinny, by Walter Raleigh
Br.—Hinshaw J E (Ark) 1983 4 M 0 0 $540
Own.—Tempo Stable 119 Tr.—Walker Charles W
Lifetime 4 0 0 0 $540
24Aug83-1LaD 6f :22^{3} :46^{2} 1:12^{1}ft 28 119 74$\frac{3}{4}$ 5^{4} 4^{7} 49$\frac{1}{2}$ Ardoin R^{8} Ⓕ Mdn 72-20 UnoPro,MyHulAngel,BettrYourslf 12
29Jly83-8LaD 6f :22^{3} :46 1:12 ft 47 113 61$\frac{3}{4}$ 57$\frac{1}{2}$ 10^{16} 10^{17} ArdnR^{4} Ⓢ Opportunity 66-21 Lrn'sPrncss,FstAndRcy,J.A.'sUntd 13
14Jly83-8LaD 6f :22^{4} :47^{1} 1:14^{4}m 19 114 3^{2} 71$\frac{1}{2}$ 8^{12} 8^{12} Whited DE^{6} Ⓕ Aw12000 57-32 TrplYorMny,HmcmngQn,IntlIntnt 12
27Apr83-3LaD 4$\frac{1}{2}$f :22^{3} :47^{2} :53^{4}ft 7$\frac{1}{2}$ 119 3 3^{4} 67$\frac{1}{2}$ 11^{13} Ardoin R^{7} Ⓕ Mdn 78-09 HappyRibot,MadSusn,BetTheLine 11
Aug 21 LaD 3f ft :36^{4} b Jly 24 LaD 5f ft 1:02^{3} b

J. A.'s United

Third in the Futurity at 82:1 he hooks up in a speed duel on September 5th—an alibi. Next time, on September 28th, he wins paying $5.00.

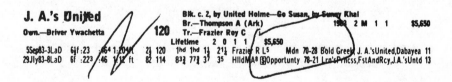

J. A.'s United
Blk. c. 2, by United Holme—Go Susan, by Sunny Khal
Br.—Thompson A (Ark) 1983 2 M 1 1 $5,650
Own.—Driver Ywachetta 120 Tr.—Frazier Roy C
Lifetime 2 0 1 1 $5,650
5Sep83-3LaD 6$\frac{1}{2}$f :23 :46^{4} 1:20^{4}ft 2$\frac{1}{2}$ 120 1^{hd} 1^{hd} 1$\frac{1}{2}$ 21$\frac{1}{4}$ Frazier R L^{5} Mdn 70-28 Bold Greek, J. A.'sUnited,Dabayea 11
29Jly83-8LaD 6f :22^{3} :46 1:12 ft 82 114 83$\frac{3}{4}$ 77$\frac{3}{4}$ 3^{7} 3^{5} HlldMA^{8} Ⓢ Opportunty 78-21 Lrn'sPrncss,FstAndRcy,J.A.'sUntd 13

The word "she" is noted to emphasize that these fillies faced males in the Futurity.

Six losers in the Futurity soon became winners. If you're at Louisiana Downs after the Futurity, may I suggest betting the losers of the Futurity their next time out?

Without a good memory, the handicapper must go to the results charts to find the winners, and then go back to the past performances and circle the winner's name in the race before the win. This process must be repeated every day for every race. If the past performances of one race indicate two or three or more horses with their names circled, that race is a key race. In other words, without good recall, winning requires much more work.

Another common example where memory helps is a horse that runs second in a maiden race. If the winner steps up into allowance company and wins big, it is obvious that the second place maiden was beaten by a real giant. When handicapping maidens that have run before, always look to see who beat whom and try to remember how the winner performed its next time out. With my memory, I can recall how impressive the second place finisher actually was. Speed or class figures by themselves cannot do this analysis justice.

Memory helps in so many ways, so many times. The first time I truly recognized its importance was on a day with Rich Hallahan at Saratoga Harness. Two horses had seemingly equal ability. They were hard to separate—both front runners that had won cutting almost equal fractions last time out at Green Mountain in Vermont. Rich said, "You're right, they should finish one, two—but see this horse? I was at Green Mountain and there was a *blizzard* when he ran his race!" Rich was right! That horse won easily, beating the other by 8 lengths. Perhaps Rich was exaggerating, but, obviously its last effort was much superior to that of the other. The program had listed the track condition for each horse's last race as fast. There was no mention of a "blizzard." A good memory can pay big dividends.

5. *Knowledge*

This point is obvious. It's tough to do well at anything, especially over a long period of time, if you do not know what you're doing. The more important question is "How do I obtain this knowledge?" There are many books that deal with the fundamentals, but it also requires work. The examples in this book not only teach fundamentals, but also encourage the reader to think. I also suggest the *Blood Horse* and the *Thoroughbred Record* magazines. And much can be learned from the articles in the *Daily Racing Form*. If you are lucky, maybe you will find someone like Rich who is knowledgeable, patient, and willing to teach you.

6. *Objectivity*

Just like everyone else, I have my favorite jockeys and horses. Unfortunately, they don't win because they're my favorites. If number 5 wins three times in a row, it doesn't mean number 5 won't win again—and it doesn't mean it will. It may indicate a track bias, but beyond that, nothing.

To be totally objective is difficult. It takes lots of practice. Objectivity is definitely one of the most important traits of successful horse players. Lacking some traits can be overcome. When it comes to handicapping, I try to be like the Tibetian Monk or Star Trek's Mr. Spock with no emotion. Of course, when I spot a horse that I think will win at a price (i.e. a longshot) I can get excited and just can't wait to bet it. However, I never force winners. I never prejudge a race and I never give in (almost never) to gut feelings. There is nothing wrong with the two-dollar bettor playing names, numbers, or hunches if he enjoys doing so. However, his purpose in going to the track just isn't the same as mine.

The technique to insure objectivity is simple. Handicap the entire card in one sitting. Check and double check each horse during this sitting. At an extreme, write a little explanation next to the horse of why he should be crossed off—why it can't possibly win—or cross it off so that its past performance lines can't be read again even if you wanted to. This originated in my early days of betting when I would go to the track, forget why the horse couldn't win, bet it, and then realize why it was crossed off in the first place (after it lost, of course).

After this, put the program down and walk away for an hour or two. Then, handicap it again. Try to remember how you felt the first time. Were you psyched? Alert? Confident? Tired? Did things click? Try to examine yourself. Usually, with this second pass you may realize that you convinced yourself that a certain horse would win. Correct any mistakes or omissions. Finally, put the program down again and check it the next morning *before* going to the track.

Some races you *know* are right. They just click. Give me the same past performances a year from now and I'll come up with the same selection. Some are highly competitive and past experience tells you to watch out for these—that you're forcing a bet. Almost always in that second or third pass you are much more objective. You become more conservative with those races that are less certain. However, with races that you like, you will gain more confidence. There will be a winner each race—but that doesn't mean you must bet all of them or the same amount on each one.

7. *Discipline*

Discipline, discipline, discipline. This word can't be said often enough. I can't tell you how many times I've said it to myself at the race track—usually after it was too late. Discipline, discipline, discipline. No matter how much most people plan ahead, once they pass the admission gate their plans change. Money isn't really money any more. It becomes +20 or −45 on top of the program, not +$20 or −$45 but +20 and −45. Only after leaving the track does a dollar sign appear. The −45 is nothing during the fifth race. During the last race, however, the −45 becomes a bigger number. It starts to become real. After leaving, the race goer starts thinking that he could have taken someone out for a nice dinner for $45 or he might have bought something. To most people, money isn't money at the race track. Almost everyone rationalizes when they lose. "Well, I had a good time." "I almost hit the triple." "So what, it's only money."

Some people start off the day betting $10. After they're up, let's say $100, they bet $20 or $30 a race. By the seventh race they're even again. The bet should be $10. Right? Not to most people—because now they are used to betting $20 or $30 a shot. Discipline, discipline, discipline.

Discipline also means knowing yourself, not only in handicapping, but also at the windows. Sometimes everything is crystal clear. You can forecast exactly how a race will be run, where each horse will be at each pole and each fraction, and sure enough it comes true. Other times it's an effort to think.

The same is true for money management. If any horse loses because of racing luck it's okay because the breaks will even out. But when I mess up the bet even if I win, I'm still not happy. In college, my friend Pete Zabawsky used to go to the racetrack with me frequently. He knew what a horse looked like, but beyond that, nothing about handicapping or betting. Pete, however, used to know me better than I knew myself. He is an excellent listener. During those times when handicapping a race came easy, Pete would bet with me, and sometimes even more than I would bet. The other times, he would decrease his bet. Sometimes, while listening to me talk about a race, he understood my concern for another horse, and played not only my selection, but also placed a saver on the other horse. A saver is a bet an intelligent horse player makes to break even if his primary pick loses. More than once he left the track winning more than me or losing less. Pete derived much pleasure from this—beating me at my own game, especially when he knew nothing about it.

One of the toughest things at the track is admitting to yourself that you're having a bad day, that you're the one at fault. Get to know your strengths and weaknesses. Are you a good handicapper but a lousy gambler? Well, what are you going to do about it?

8. *Money management*

A major theme of this book is money management. It is that important. Like most people, I found it to be one of the most difficult things to learn. Handicapping was fun. Money management was work.

Just like any investment, be it land or stocks or something less sophisticated such as purchasing a television or a stereo, betting requires careful consideration. The chapter, "At the Betting Window," describes proper money management in detail. Becoming a good bettor is an effort, but a necessary one.

9. *Math skills*

No one has to be a genius in arithmetic to win playing the ponies. But let's face it—calculating speed, pace, class, etc., involves numbers. For people not adept or out of practice in this area, it can take 5 or 10 times as long. Sometimes it becomes boring or tedious. Expending too much mental energy here may result in no longer having the edge to read between the lines and to sort out the factors. Enjoyment soon becomes work. If math isn't your forte, be aware of it and try to compensate. This is, however, probably the least important of the ten traits in this chapter.

10. *Confidence*

Confidence is important to success in any area of endeavor. Good horse players are very confident, even cocky. They never, never look at the selections of others. To tell them that so and so picked a certain horse in the newspaper is an insult. You can't talk these people off a horse unless you point out an obvious mistake. They can't be convinced that *any* horse is the better animal (until after the race).

With all the pressures and anxieties at the racetrack it is understandable why people can be shaken. Losing is a lousy feeling. To be successful you must believe in yourself and your abilities.

In my early days, I remember going to the track with Pete and maybe being a bit too cocky. One day, my best bet was in the last race and I really loved the selection. I assured Pete that our victory was guaranteed. In fact, we stood next to the cashier's window to be first in line to beat the traffic home. With the race just about to go off, the cashier asked for my ticket, thinking, naturally, that we were standing there to cash a previous winning ticket. To this I replied, "Can you wait about a minute and twelve seconds?" With age, the cockiness has disappeared, but the confidence remains. Yes, the horse did win easily.

The Fundamentals of Pari-mutuel Betting

Every legal bet in North America, on track or off, is based on the pari-mutuel concept, named for its roots in Paris, France. It is easy to understand. Simply put, before the race begins, money is taken from the total pool to pay the state, the track, the purses, the overhead and the Breeders' Fund, in most states. The money deducted prior to the race is termed the "takeout." In New York, for win, place and show betting, it is 17%. Of this, the state gets 5%, the New York Racing Association gets 8.5% to pay its employees' salaries, electricity, overhead, etc., 3% goes into purses, and 0.5% goes into the Breeders' Fund. The Breeders' Fund encourages quality breeding in each state. This is done by increasing the size of the purses for races restricted to state-breds. This purse money comes from the takeout. In other words, a maiden race for New York state-bred carries a larger purse than a race open to all maidens, even though the quality of state-breds is generally less. In New York, too, daily doubles, exactas and quinellas have a 17% takeout. However, triples have a 25% takeout, of which 7.5% goes to the state, 13% to the New York Racing Association, 4% for purses and 0.5% to the Breeders' Fund. In other words, the bettor is not betting against the racetrack, the patron is actually betting against the person standing next to him. The more bet on a particular horse relative to the others in the race, the lower his odds will be.

Betting to Win—In placing this type of wager, you are trying to select which horse will finish the race first.

Example of Win Calculation

Total win pool—	$1000
Amount bet on number one—	$100

With a 17% takeout, even though a thousand dollars was bet in the total pool, only $830 can be divided among the winners ($1000 × 17% = $170 taken out). If number one wins, there is $730 of losing money to be divided ($830 − $100). Therefore, the odds on this horse, number one, are 7.3:1 ($730 ÷ $100). In this example, for every dollar bet, there is a profit of $7.30. A two dollar bet, therefore, means a profit of $14.60 ($7.30 × 2). When collecting, you will receive $16.60—your original $2 plus the profit. As another example, 8:5 means that if you bet $5 you will make a profit of $8. If this horse wins, you collect $13 ($8 + $5). A two dollar bet on an 8:5 shot returns 2/5 of $13 or $5.20. The reader can make the calculation independently or use the following table:

Odds and Their Payoffs (based on a $2 bet)

1:9	$ 2.20	7:2	$ 9.00
1:5	$ 2.40	4:1	$10.00
2:5	$ 2.80	9:2	$11.00
1:2	$ 3.00	5:1	$12.00
3:5	$ 3.20	6:1	$14.00
4:5	$ 3.60	7:1	$16.00
1:1	$ 4.00	8:1	$18.00
6:5	$ 4.40	9:1	$20.00
7:5	$ 4.80	10:1	$22.00
3:2	$ 5.00	15:1	$32.00
8:5	$ 5.20	20:1	$42.00
9:5	$ 5.60	25:1	$52.00
2:1	$ 6.00	30:1	$62.00
5:2	$ 7.00	40:1	$82.00
3:1	$ 8.00	50:1	$102.00

Betting to Place—Wagering to place means betting that your selection will run either first or second. The payoff is unaffected by the horse finishing first or second, as long as he finishes in the top two.

An example of place calculation:

Total place pool—	$1000
Amount bet on number one—	$100
Amount bet on number two—	$200

Suppose that numbers one and two both run first or second (it doesn't matter what order, since a place bet means you are gambling that the horse will run first or second).

Calculations: $1000 (total bet) − $170 (the takeout) = $830.

$830 − $100 (successful bets on number one) − $200 (successful bets on number two) = $530 remaining to be divided.

Since there are two place winners we must split the $530 in half. $530 ÷ 2 = $265.

Now, $265 ÷ $100 = 2.65:1 and $265 ÷ $200 = 1.325:1. Therefore, a place ticket cashed on horse number one will mathematically return $7.30 ($2.65 profit for each $1). Since we bet $2, there is a profit of $5.30 plus the original $2 ($7.30). A place ticket on horse number two will mathematically return $4.65. That is, $1.32½ of profit for each $1 bet × $2 = $2.65 plus the original $2 ($4.65). Notice that the more money bet on a horse the less it will pay (i.e. the lower its odds will be). Place usually pays less than win, because the amount of money left to be divided is split in half. There is less losing money per ticket.

The final item to note here is breakage. Winning prices are rounded down to the nearest $.20. A horse that should mathematically return $4.39 and a horse that should mathematically return $4.21 will both pay $4.20 after the breakage is taken out. A horse, however, must return a minimum of $2.10. When it figures mathematically to pay less, the track must make up the difference, and a minus pool is said to exist. These situations are rare, but do happen when great horses run. Because of breakage, the track prefers favorites to win, not long shots. The horse that figures to pay $4.27 will mean getting $.07 from many more tickets than the horse that pays $104.27. In the prior place betting example, horse number one will return $7.20 and horse number two will return $4.60. Millions and millions of dollars are made each year by the race track in breakage. At off-track betting in New York, a 5% surcharge is taken out in addition to the takeout. If you bet horse number one there, which paid $7.20 at the track, after the 5% ($0.36) is taken out, the horse mathematically returns $6.84. However, this, too, is rounded down to the lowest $.20, so it returns $6.80. Therefore, at off-track betting in New York, not only are you charged a 5% surcharge but you are charged double breakage. This is a big issue of concern and debate with off-track betting. Some justify it by telling the bettor that he saves on gas money, and parking and admissions. That's why it's worth his while to pay off-track betting's overhead with the 5% surcharge and the double breakage. To most small players it may be worth the convenience. They are not concerned about some more change taken out of their winnings. However, it is a concern to large bettors.

An example of show calculation:

Total show pool—	$1000
Amount bet on horse number one—	$100
Amount bet on horse number two—	$200
Amount bet on horse number three—	$300

Betting to show—Show means betting that your horse will run either first, second or third. The payout is not affected by the horse running first, second or third, as long as it runs in the top three. Let's assume numbers one, two and three all finish in the top three.

Calculations: $1000 (total amount bet) – $170 (the takeout) = $830. Thus, $830 – $600 (successful bets) = $230 remaining to be divided. Now we must split $230 into three, because there were three winning bets. $230 ÷ 3 = $76.66. Now $76.66 ÷ $100 = .77:1 and $76.66 ÷ $200 = .383:1 and $76.66 ÷ $300 = .256:1. Therefore, a show ticket on number one returns $3.54 ($.77 × 2 plus the original $2). The show ticket on number two returns $2.77 ($.383 × 2 plus the original $2). A show ticket on number three returns $2.51 ($.256 × 2 plus the original $2). After breakage, horse number one pays $3.40, horse number two pays $2.60 and horse number three returns $2.40. Show usually pays less than place because there are more tickets to be cashed on show and, therefore, less losing money per ticket.

To make odds calculations easy for the racing patron, racetracks have an odds board, commonly called a tote board, to reflect win payoffs. Almost always there is a direct correlation between the favorite in the win pool and the favorite in the place pool and the favorite in the show pool. If number one has the most money bet on it to win, usually number one also has the most money bet on it to place and to show, but not always. Some modern tote boards display a range for place and show prices too. In other words, a horse that is 4:1, which will pay $10 to win, may pay for example, between $4 to place and $6 to place, and between $2.80 to show and $4.20 to show, depending on what other horses finish second and third. If a long shot places, there will be less bet on it to place and, therefore, the place price on the 4:1 shot will be higher. There is more losing money to go around. If the favorite places, besides the 4:1 shot, the odds board will show that there will be $4 returned on a place bet on the 4:1 shot. This is another disadvantage of betting to place. Even if your horse runs first or second you're absolutely dependent on how much is bet on the other horse that runs first or second. The same can be said for show betting, except, even worse than that, you're dependent on two other horses that run first, second or third. *A common misconception at the race track is betting a 30:1 shot to show, expecting a huge return.* If the first two favorites also show, the return might only be $4 to show or less! But more on this later.

In addition to the tote board, most tracks have television monitors to make it even more convenient for the patron to see the odds. These are usually found throughout the track, even in the dining rooms. Besides win payoffs, place payoffs and show payoffs, these monitors will also show the exacta prices and the daily double prices.

Daily Doubles—The daily double means selecting the winners in two consecutive races, usually races one and two, or any other two designated races on the card. On the monitor, the top line indicates the daily double payoffs with horse #1 in the first race and each of the others in the second race. The next line or flash indicates the daily double payoffs with horse #2 in the first race and each horse in the second race, and so on.

Exactas—An exacta or perfecta means correctly predicting the first and second place horses in exact order. The payoffs for exactas can also be seen on TV monitors in a similar manner. The top line will indicate the payoffs if horse #1 wins and all combinations with the other horses for second place. The next line or flash will be if #2 wins with each of the others second, and so on.

Quinellas—Quinella means betting the first and second place horses, but not their exact order. So, by betting a one-and-two quinella and it comes in one-and-two or two-and-one you're a winner. Naturally, there will be many more winning tickets with quinellas because there are fewer possible combinations. Usually a quinella pays less than an exacta. TV monitors also indicate quinella payoffs.

Triples or trifectas means betting the first three finishers in exact order. Because there are so many possibilities playing triples, racetracks don't have monitors indicating the expected payoffs (only the size of the pools). These payoffs can only be estimated by making a direct correlation between the odds on your horses, and what triples usually pay when horses with those odds finish first, second, and third.

Pick Six Betting—This means betting the winners of six consecutive races. This is perhaps the most exotic "exotic." An exotic wager is any time you have to pick more than one horse. Exactas, doubles, triples and quinellas are all exotics. The pick six is now one of the newer and more popular exotic wagers. (And there will certainly be other exotics in the future—twin triples, and so on.) At most tracks, the bettor fills out a card with his pick 6 selections. The pari-mutuel clerk enters this card into his machine which prints out the ticket. Anyone who picks all six winners wins the entire pool, or shares it if anyone else has all six winners, too. If there isn't a winner, then the race track pays out to those people who had correctly predicted the most number of winners. They split 50% of the pool, and 50% is carried over to the next day. Therefore, if no one picks all six winners the pool keeps building up. It's not uncommon for a big race track like Santa Anita to have a pick six payoff of over $100,000 for a $1 bet. If no one has five of six winners, the track will pay off four of six winners, three of six winners and so on.

In this chapter each type of wager has been defined. When to make each type of wager, and how much to bet on each type of wager, are covered fully in the chapter, "At the Betting Window."

The last fundamental to be covered in this chapter is the "morning line." This is usually determined by the racing secretary or official track odds-maker. It is indicated in the racetrack's program next to the horse's number. Under the number will be the odds—2:1, 3:1, 8:1, 10:1, etc. This is really one person's educated guess to which horse will be the favorite and how the others compare. It is a carry-over from the days in which bookmakers were legalized and posted their own odds. Before pari-mutuel betting came into being, the public would shop around for the best odds with the different legal bookmakers at the different tracks. Interestingly enough, the more that was bet on a horse, the lower the bookmaker would make the odds for the next person. Often one person would be able to bet a horse at 5:1 while the next person could only get 3:1 odds. And it worked the other way too. If no one was betting a horse, the bookmaker would increase the odds. It was a forerunner to the pari-mutuel system. The morning line is used by the ignorant public to get an idea of the prices that horses will pay, if they're lucky enough to choose the right name or number. Horses that are 3:1 in the morning line can go off at 4:5 or 5:2 or anything else, for that matter. The betting odds, once again, are determined by how much is bet on a particular horse, and how much is bet on the other horses. The morning line is only a guide and has nothing to do with the betting odds that reflect pay off prices.

The Track from the Inside

Mary C. stood in her stall just smacking her lips together, making sound like bubbles bursting. Having only been a groom at Saratoga Harness a few short weeks, I knew nothing about the care and training of horses. I wanted to learn as much as possible, even seemingly insignificant details. So I asked Neal Shapiro, my trainer, the reason for this behavior. He responded that Mary C. had done this before and her owner, a sweet little old lady, rewarded her with a carrot. (Neal, by the way, was a silver and a bronze medalist in the equestrian events in the 1972 Munich Olympic games. He never did understand how a guy with an M.B.A. could enjoy mucking out stalls!) Playing with her lips was Mary C.'s way of begging for carrots. Additionally, Neal told me that this homebred was racing over its head, but her owner didn't want to risk losing her pet by dropping it down to a more competitive level in the claiming ranks.

Down at the other end of the barn the "Big Mare" (as she was known) started kicking her stable door. I was told to ignore it, because she was doing it to get attention. Evidently, the Big Mare had once been yelled at for such actions. Believing that negative attention was better than no attention she kept up her act until finally someone screamed at her again.

One horse that I rubbed (groomed) was a two year old who hadn't been to the races (i.e. never raced). At the beginning he would try to nip me. One day I noticed that he tried nipping everyone else, but not me. He got to know me and I him. In the morning, when I'd walk into his stall the first time he'd get a little excited. Naturally, getting struck or kicked was of some concern to me. Other grooms reassured me "Don't worry, Dave, he just feels good."

Early one morning, even before I walked into his stall, I took one look at him and turned to the trainer to tell him that my horse was ill. Having grown up in the streets of Brooklyn with such limited experience, this diagnosis was viewed with some degree of skepticism. Nevertheless, it had to be checked out. Neal took out a horse thermometer (which is probably a foot long) and taught me its proper use. Unfortunately, my horse had a little fever.

The point to these stories is that horses are living creatures. They are individuals and should be treated as such. They think, learn, and react to their environment and the people and the other horses around them. Many things happen to a horse before, during and after a race. These animals are not just names and numbers on a piece of paper called *The Daily Racing Form*. Some handicappers treat horses only as statistics on paper and this is absolutely wrong.

At an early age, the horse's life changes from play to work. Saddles and jockeys do not come naturally. Neither does the regimen of training. The stress of racing and the pounding frail legs take can cause injuries, much like any other athletic training program.

Trainers are well versed in the individuality of horses and bettors must also be. My background as a groom and an owner will give the reader a behind-the-scenes insight into the horse itself and the people that surround it—the trainers, jockeys and owners. In the end, the handicapper should determine why a particular horse is in a particular race. Understanding the animal itself and the informal system at the racetrack will provide the reader with a big edge over the other bettors. With this knowledge, it will be easier to read between the lines to solve the puzzle.

Here are five major areas of importance:

1. "Heart" and "class"

2. Trainers
   —Conditioning
   —Claiming horses
   —Equipment

3. Jockeys

4. Breeding
   —Off tracks (e.g. sloppy)
   —First-time starters
   —Distance

5. Horses are living creatures
   —Injuries
   —"Loose on the lead"
   —Maturing horses
   —Sour horses
   —Early speed *vs.* closers

Heart and Class

Heart—Horsemen always talk about a horse's heart. Hollywood makes movies about it—an old Walter Brennan picture named "Kentucky" comes to mind. In it Walter Brennan is forced to sell one of his two horses to a man with whom he is feuding. Being more shrewd than everyone else, and against all odds, he keeps the one that seems to have less potential. Why? Because it has "The Look of Eagles" (i.e., heart). Of course, this horse beats the other in the climactic big race.

Heart, basically, is the will to win. The will to overcome all sorts of duress. The good horses possess it. It's part of the horse's internal make up that allows it to maximize its potential.

Long ago, it had been established that horses know they are in competition. Red Smith's classic story about a horse named Sands

Of Pleasure is worth repeating: In the days before cameras were used, placing judges determined the order of finish. After losing the race by a nose (so the judges thought), Sands Of Pleasure was not, of course, taken to the winner's circle. The jockey instead tried to take it back to the barn whereupon the horse reared up, almost going out of control. Its trainer wondered if the horse thought it had won the race. The next time out, he placed Sands Of Pleasure in a race over its head—one it could not win. Being well beaten, Sands Of Pleasure calmly returned to its stall. For his next race, the trainer found a real soft spot. He instructed the jockey, in case of victory, not to take the horse to the winner's circle. Well, Sands Of Pleasure won by a length or two and the victory was not in doubt. Obeying his instructions, the jockey started back to the barn. At this point, as the tale goes (and "the jockey swears it to this day"), Sands Of Pleasure looked the rider in the eye, grabbed onto the bit, and proudly proceeded to the winner's circle!

Whether or not you believe this story (I do), horses know they are in a race. The good horses go all out to win. That is heart, and that is "class." For those who don't believe that horses know what's happening around them, try cooling one out too near the track after a race. As exhausted as it may be, once he hears the hoofbeats of his friends he will immediately pick up his head and get ready to run again. Once in a great while, you will see a frustrated horse actually trying to savage (i.e. bite) its competitor while running down the stretch. Although he's trying his best, this horse knows it will never catch the leader.

Sometimes during a race a jockey doesn't whip a tiring horse. The ignorant public thinks he's not trying to win. However, the knowledgeable handicapper understands that this horse has heart and is trying its best (e.g. Chief's Crown lost the 1985 Preakness by a head but was only lightly whipped because jockey Don MacBeth though it was all out trying to win anyway). Whipping will only make the horse believe he is being punished for doing his best. In the long run, it will only become discouraged. He will lose heart. Trainers that consistently enter horses in races where they are overmatched make a horse lose heart. A smart one will place a horse in a competitive class.

Anytime a horse is entered in a claimer (i.e. eligible to be bought by any licensed horseman that has entered a horse to run at the current meet) the trainer must think that there is a chance someone will claim it. Otherwise the horse is in too deep. To insure competitiveness in races, the racing secretary writes eligibility conditions for the race. For example, non-winners of two races, or non-winners of three races since August 1, etc. These are called the conditions of the race or class of the race. If the horse fits the conditions, he may be entered by the trainer. In claiming races, the trainer can usually race the animal where he wants. A $10,000 animal will beat a $5000 claimer but will be claimed and the owner will lose $5000. A $5000 claimer won't be bought for $10,000, but also won't win. Claimers, therefore, are a self-enforcing system.

The puzzle becomes especially interesting when a horse is dropped down the claiming ladder two or more classes. Handicappers must decide if the trainer is "cheating" (i.e. trying to win when the horse is obviously best without it being claimed) or if the animal is hurting and the trainer wishes to sell it to somebody else.

Sometimes a trainer drops a horse to give the animal courage (make him "brave"). He wants it to triumph easily over weaker competition. This helps the animal's attitude. After winning, the trainer may leave it in the same class to get him even more brave. Then a remarkable thing may happen. This horse, which had to be lowered down the claiming ladder, not only destroys the horses in the class before it was dropped, but steps up and beats even higher level competition. The trainer did nothing to improve the horse physically, but helped the horse's mental attitude. He made the horse brave. However, if the horse didn't have heart in the beginning (or became discouraged) the horse might never obtain it—and most don't once ruined.

Heart may sound like something mythical or magical. It is an intangible. No one knows for sure if a horse possesses it, until it is actually put to the test in a race. Leading breeders and trainers have written many articles about buying horses at sales.

They go into great detail concerning conformation, balance, bloodlines, bone structure, etc. Always, though, they mention the importance of how the horse carries itself around the walking ring. Is its head held high? Does it act like something royally bred? Does it appear to have an aura about it that spells champion? These experts rely more on their past experience than anything they can put their fingers on. In 1983, a Northern Dancer yearling was purchased for a record $10.2 million. If its new connections (i.e. owners and trainers) didn't believe it had heart, it would not have come close to setting any sales records.

The best horses at the track, the classy ones, retain their winning form longer than cheap animals do. Some cheap horses were once classy but have aged or succumbed to injury. Horses that win step up in class (face tougher competition). The higher the class, the greater the purse. At many small tracks a horse is unbeatable in $2500 claimers but can't win in $3200—the next class up. A lot of this probably has to do with the trainer's belief that while the horse may come close, he can't win. Therefore, the jockey doesn't go all out, but waits until the next time when the horse is dropped down to $2500 claimers again. Rulers Jester is a champ in $2500 claimers but doesn't look like much one class higher.

Rulers Jester — Ch. g. 4, by Court Ruling—Thumb Tack, by Poker
Own.—Roberts B D — **$2,500** Br.—Redson J H (Ark) — Tr.—Roberts B Dean — **116**
Lifetime 36 5 5 5 $25,070 — 1983 6 2 0 1 $3,593 — 1982 7 1 2 1 $8,510 — Turf 1 0 0 0 $110

19Aug83-	9Pen	fst	6f	:22⅗	:45⅗	1:11⅕	3↑ Clm 3200	1	5	5⁴	5³¼	5⁵	4⁷¼	O'Donnell E E		115	7.40	81-18	Copper Reign 110²¼ Lou's Craft 110⁴ Kasinoff 122¹	Rallied	7
3Aug83-	1Pen	fst	1	:47⅘	1:14	1:41⅖	Clm 2500	7	6	5⁴¾	2hd	1½	1¹¼	O'Donnell E E		119	*3.80	74-17	Rulers Jester 119¹¼ Victory Play 114nk Valedictorian 112²¼	Driving	10
22Jly83-	2Pen	fst	1⁷⁰	:47⅗	1:14	1:45⅕	Clm 3200	6	1	1½	1½	4⁴	6⁷	O'Donnell E E		116	3.50	67-22	Quathlamba 116³ DefiantKnight 119no SleepingBullet 116²	Used up	8
8Jly83-	4Pen	fst	6f	:22⅗	:45⅗	1:12⅕	Clm 2500	11	2	3⁵½	3⁶½	2²	1²	O'Donnell E E		116	2.30	83-19	Rulers Jester 116² Penowa Secret 109² Pet Gauge 116hd	Driving	12
29Jun83-	3Pen	fst	6f	:22⅗	:46⅕	1:12⅕	Clm 2500	8	1	3²	4²½	3²½	3nk	O'Donnell E E		113	6.90	83-21	Dr. Escar 109nk Quebec Dancer 116no Rulers Jester 113¹¼	Rallied	8
15Jun83-	8Pen	fst	6f	:22⅘	:46⅕	1:12⅕	Clm 3200	6	6	9⁵¼	11¹⁵	11¹⁷	11¹⁸	O'Donnell E E	b	115	7.70	65-23	Go on T. V. 119no QuebecDancer 115¹¾ DawnLanding 109½	Far back	11
5Apr82-	5GP	fst	1 1/16	:47⅕	1:12⅖	1:47	Clm 22500	1	2	2¹¹	5¹⁴	7¹⁸	7¹⁹	Saumell L	b	115	16.10	47-27	Mr. Alberto 117¹ Sol Brillante 117² Forlad 114⁵	Tired	8
1Apr82-	6GP	fm	*1 Ⓣ			1:39⅘	Clm 25000	3	4	7⁵¾	8⁹¾	6⁶¼	6⁶½	Saumell L	b	115	17.30	75-14	Joe Guss 113no De Chelly 117³ Spew 117²½	Brief foot	10

He used to be a $25,000 claimer. At the $2,500 level he shows two wins and a loss by only a neck. Dean Roberts dropped this horse into a $2,500 claimer on September 2 in the first race. It won and paid $7.20. Notice that this horse is a giant at this level, but nothing when raised in class.

Class—The word "class" has many meanings in this sport and oftentimes they are interrelated. "Roving Boy won that race on guts" said a horseman who had watched the colt from the beginning. "He knew where the wire was and made it just that far. That's what you call class." (From the *Thoroughbred Record Magazine* Nov. 9). The race was the Alibhai Handicap at Santa Anita on Nov. 2. Roving Boy, 1982's Eclipse Award winning 2 year old colt or gelding, had fractured his left tibia and then, shifting his weight to his right side, had completely shattered that tibia—yet held on to win by a nose!

The horseman who made this statement could have said Roving Boy had heart (which he obviously had) but class is an even more encompassing term. Cheap horses can have heart but classy horses run as fast as they can every time they face top competition. These horses don't specialize in one distance at one track, but can be raced at many distances away from home. Classy horses hold their form longer. A really cheap horse working out fast may use up its good race that morning. It will not race back to it. Higher priced animals can work out fast to sharpen up.

The *Racing Form* indicates the purse value of allowance races to make it easier to understand the level of competition. At the same track, a horse that races in "allowance 37000" has faced much tougher competition than one that races in "allowance 23000." Claiming races are obvious. But you must exercise judgment when dealing with horses from different tracks.

Most horses do not have "class." However, it is extremely important to recognize the concept of "class of the race." In other words, a horse may not have "class," as described, but can outclass its competition greatly even if it is a cheap claimer. For example:

Crown Debt — B. g. 3, by Crown Gift—Punch Line, by Hilarious — $5,000 — Br.—Knee C (NY) — Tr.—Townsend Stephen — 119
Own.—Spataro J M

Lifetime 10 2 0 2 $8,450 — 1983 4 2 0 0 $4,590 — 1982 6 M 0 2 $3,860

28Sep83- 7Pen	fst	6f		:22⅘	:46	1:12⅘		Clm 7500	6	7	$4^{1\frac34}$	$4^{4\frac12}$	$6^{4\frac12}$	$5^{9\frac34}$	Aguirre E C		115	5.50	71-25	Pure Red 113^{hd} Barrier Island $110^{4\frac12}$ NoCutClause$115^{1\frac12}$	Bothered	9
9Sep83- 1Pen	fst	6f		:23	:46⅘	1:13	3↑	Clm 5000	5	5	3½	3^{1}	1^{3}	$1^{3\frac14}$	Aguirre E C		118	2.30	79-19	CrownDebt$118^{3\frac14}$R!Jungl116^{nk}ThGoldnPlyboy$116^{1\frac12}$	Bore In, Clear	8
18Aug83- 9Atl	fst	6f		:22⅘	:46	1:12⅘	3↑	Md 5000	11	5	4^{4}	$2^{1\frac12}$	2½	1¾	Krone J A		117	*2.60	79-18	Crown Debt 117¾ Ziphawk 117^{4} Orazio Labate 117^{nk}	Driving	12
1Jan83- 4Aqu	fst	6f	⊡	:23⅘	:48	1:15		Md 18000	1	11	—	—	—	—	Miceli M		118	2.70	— —	ChrokIndigo$122^{1\frac14}$UltimtNtiv$115^{2\frac12}$DoublD122^{hd}	Refused to break	11
20Dec82- 3Aqu	fst	6f	⊡	:23⅕	:47⅕	1:13⅕		[S]Md Sp Wt	10	14	9^{10}	$8^{8\frac34}$	$8^{5\frac12}$	5^{8}	Miceli M	b	118	5.90	70-21	StiffUpperLip118^{1}MightyHuntr118¾Buck'sSpirit$118^{3\frac14}$	Slow Early	14
27Nov82- 9Aqu	fst	6f		:23⅗	:48⅖	1:13⅘		[S]Md Sp Wt	1	10	$7^{3\frac34}$	$7^{5\frac12}$	4^{8}	$4^{5\frac14}$	Miceli M		118	17.20	67-29	Tuffy's Love 118¾ Quadratic's Pride $118^{2\frac12}$ HangOut118^{2}	Late bid	12
27Oct82- 5Crc	fst	$1\frac{1}{16}$		:48⅘	1:15	1:49⅕		Md Sp Wt	1	8	8^{11}	$6^{6\frac12}$	$3^{7\frac12}$	$3^{9\frac14}$	Zuniga M		116	45.10	64-19	Judge My Budget$116^{7\frac12}$ErdTheThird$116^{1\frac34}$CrownDebt$116^{1\frac12}$	Rallied	8
13Oct82- 5Crc	fst	1		:48⅗	1:14⅘	1:43⅘		Md 35000	3	6	$3^{5\frac12}$	2^{4}	2^{2}	4¾	Zuniga M		117	8.20	68-24	Mr. T. Bowl 117^{hd} Addy Trio 117½ Hopeful Tiger 112^{nk}	Weakened	7

Crown Debt raced respectably in New York versus much tougher competition. At the $5,000 level it was unbeaten at smaller race tracks. On October 8, it dropped back down to $5,000 claimers. In addition, it dropped after being "bothered." Assuming it passes the paddock test (explained later), this horse looks unbeatable—and it was, paying $8.20!

Another obvious example was the sixth race at Louisiana Downs on June 22:

6th La. Downs

5 ½ FURLONGS. (1.04) TEXAS STALLION STAKES TRIALS. Purse $10,000. 2-year-olds eligible to the 1983 Texas Stallion Stakes. Weight, fillies, 117 lbs.; colts and geldings, 120 lbs.

Coupled—Triple Sec and Thibodaux.

Flax Mape
Ch. g. 2, by Outward Bound—Sky Breeze, by Sky High II
Br.—Haynes Preston F (Tex) 1983 0 M 0 0
Own.—Haynes P F 120 Tr.—Trosclair Gus
Lifetime 0 0 0 0
Jun 9 JnD 4f ft :49^{4} b Jun 4 JnD 5f ft 1:05 b May 31 JnD 4f ft :50 bg May 14 JnD 3f ft :37^{2} bg

Big Avenger
Dk. b. or br. c. 2, by Staunch Avenger—Sunshine Comtessa, by Native Orphan
Br.—Yancy Wayne C (La) 1983 5 1 0 0 $2,190
Own.—Franks J 120 Tr.—Brothers Frank L
Lifetime 5 1 0 0 $2,190
20May83-8LaD 4½f :23 :47^{4} :54^{3}m 8¾ 114^{5} 7 5^{5}¼ 4^{6} 4^{7} Faul J H^{8} Aw12000 80-14 WhrlngShttl,Mbry'sAx,PrIrshGold 10
16Apr83-6EvD 4½f :22^{4} :48 :54^{1}ft 7 116 6 4^{4} 5^{5}½ 6^{6}½ Barbazon D S^{3} Aw6000 83-14 SplshforGreen,NeverHunted,BigGol 9
4Apr83-4EvD 4½f :22^{4} :48 :54^{3}ft *2 115 5 2^{1}½ 2^{hd} 1^{hd} Barbazon D S^{9} Mdn 88-12 BigAvenger,PiecofPcific,Imn'sFinl 12
17Mar83-6DeD 4f :23^{1} :49^{2}ft 40 120 10 9^{7}½ 9^{7}½ 4^{3} Barbazon DS^{7} Fut Trls 83-13 BoldPlaymte,BritishNoble,Hesobd 10
6Feb83-3DeD 2½f :28^{4}ft 4½ 117 5 8^{5}¼ 8^{5}¼ Barbazon D S^{3} M50000 – – LittleRedLdy,HeroJuice,FoxySund 10
Jun 1 LaD Tr. 5f ft 1:02 hg

Good Buddy
Ch. c. 2, by Down the Cellar—Dan Queen, by College Hop
Br.—Roberts Robert F (La) 1983 3 1 0 0 $1,320
Own.—Roberts R F 115^{5} Tr.—Alleman Joseph
Lifetime 3 1 0 0 $1,320
10Jun83-5LaD 5f :22^{3} :47 1:00^{1}ft 25 117 8^{3}½ 7^{4}½ 6^{5}¼ 6^{5}¾ Perrodin E J^{7} Aw11000 84-17 ScrtMontn,FlshyBrdwy,PrnclyGrk 12
20May83-8LaD 4½f :23 :47^{4} :54^{3}m 4½ 119 8 4^{5} 8^{8}½ 10^{13} Perrodin E J^{5} Aw12000 74-14 WhrlngShttl,Mbry'sAx,PrIrshGold 10
7Apr83-4EvD 4½f :23 :49 :55^{2}sy 5¼ 115 2 1^{1} 1½ 1^{2} Sam J D^{4} Mdn 84-16 GoodBuddy,ChannelTwelve,RelGun 9
May 30 LaD 5f ft 1:02 b

Mr. Muffitt
B. c. 2, by Jay's Gig—All Temper, by Sea Tack
Br.—Fanning K (Tex) 1983 0 M 0 0
Own.—Fanning K 120 Tr.—Bean Ivan
Lifetime 0 0 0 0
Jun 11 LaD 5f ft 1:04^{2} bg Jun 1 LaD 5f ft 1:02^{3} hg May 24 LaD tr.t 4½f ft :56^{3} hg May 14 LaD 3f sl :38 bg

Bold Irish
Ch. c. 2, by Irish Ruler—First of Dawn, by Waking Dawn
Br.—King Joe & Betty (Fla) 1983 3 1 0 0 $1,650
Own.—Hanna B 120 Tr.—Robin Manuel
Lifetime 3 1 0 0 $1,650
27Mar83-10DeD 4f :22^{2} :47^{3}ft 11 120 8 10^{7} 7^{7} 8^{6}¾ SnyderL^{2} Jn Lafte Fut 88-05 ExprssivDoc,HopM.,ShtsNPillow 10
17Mar83-5DeD 4f :23^{2} :49 ft *9-5 120 3 1^{1}½ 1^{2} 1^{4}½ Barbazon DS^{4} Fut Trls 88-13 BoldIrish,FableRuler,DustAvenger 10
13Feb83-3DeD 2½f :28^{2}ft 15 118 10 8^{3} 4^{1}½ Bourque S J^{8} Mdn – – RomnJdgmnt,BrtshNobl,JllyNchls 10
Jun 14 EvD 5f ft 1:04 hg

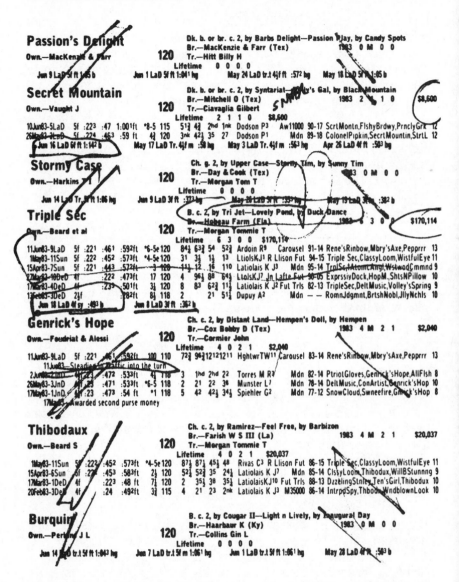

Passion's Delight — Dk. b. or br. c. 2, by Barbs Delight—Passion Play, by Candy Spots

Own.—MacKenzie & Farr — 120 — Br.—MacKenzie & Farr (Tex) — 1983 0 M 0 0

Tr.—Hitt Billy H

Lifetime 0 0 0 0

Jun 9 LaD 5f ft 1:05 b   Jun 1 LaD 5f ft 1:04^1 hg   May 24 LaD tr.t 4½f ft :57^2 hg   May 18 LaD 5f ft 1:05 b

Secret Mountain — Dk. b. or br. c. 2, by Syntariat—Polly's Gal, by Black Mountain

Own.—Vaught J — 120 — Br.—Mitchell O (Tex) — 1983 2 1 1 0 $8,600

Tr.—Ciavaglia Gilbert

Lifetime 2 1 1 0 $8,600

10Jun83-5LaD 5f :22^3 :47 1:00^{1}ft *8-5 115 5$^{1\frac{3}{4}}$ 4$^{\frac{3}{4}}$ 2^{hd} 1^{nk} Dodson P^3 Aw11000 90-17 ScrtMontn,FlshyBrdwy,PrnclyGrk 12

26May83-3LaD 5f :22^4 :46^3 :59 ft 4$\frac{3}{4}$ 120 3^{nk} 4$^{2\frac{1}{2}}$ 3^5 2^7 Dodson P^1 Mdn 89-18 ColonelPipkin,SecrtMountin,StrtL 12

Jun 16 LaD 6f ft 1:14^2 b   May 17 LaD Tr. 4½f m :58 hg   May 3 LaD Tr. 4½f m :56^3 hg   Apr 26 LaD 4f ft :50^3 hg

Stormy Case — Ch. g. 2, by Upper Case—Stormy Tim, by Sunny Tim

Own.—Harkins T I — 120 — Br.—Day & Cook (Tex) — 1983 0 M 0 0

Tr.—Morgan Tom T

Lifetime 0 0 0 0

Jun 14 LaD Tr. 5f ft 1:06 hg   Jun 9 LaD 3f ft :37^3 hg   May 26 LaD 3f ft :35^3 hg   May 19 LaD 3f ft :38^2 b

Triple Sec — B. c. 2, by Tri Jet—Lovely Pond, by Duck Dance

Own.—Beard et al — 120 — Br.—Hobeau Farm (Fla) — 1983 6 3 0 0 $170,114

Tr.—Morgan Tommie T

Lifetime 6 3 0 0 $170,114

11Jun83-9LaD 5f :22^1 :46^1 :59^{2}ft *6-5e 120 8$^{4\frac{1}{2}}$ 6$^{3\frac{3}{4}}$ 5^4 5$^{2\frac{3}{4}}$ Ardoin R^9 Carousel 91-14 Rene'sRinbow,Mbry'sAxe,Pepprrr 13

1May83-11Sun 5f :22^2 :45^2 :57^{3}ft *4-5e 120 3^1 3$^{\frac{1}{2}}$ 1$^{\frac{1}{2}}$ 1^3 LtiolsKJ^1 R Llison Fut 94-15 Triple Sec,ClassyLoom,WistfulEye 11

15Apr83-7Sun 5f :22^1 :44^3 :57^{2}ft 3 120 1$^{1\frac{1}{2}}$ 1^2 1^6 1^{10} Latiolais K J^3 Mdn 95-14 TrplSc,‡AtomcAngl,WstwodCmmnd 9

27Mar83-10DeD 4f :22^2 :47^{3}ft 17 120 4 9$^{6\frac{1}{2}}$ 8^8 6$^{4\frac{1}{2}}$ LtolsKJ^7 Jn Lafte Fut 90-05 ExprssiyDock,HopM.,ShtsNPillow 10

17Mar83-4DeD 4f :23^3 :50^{1}ft 3$\frac{1}{4}$ 120 8 8^3 6$^{2\frac{3}{4}}$ 1$^{1\frac{1}{4}}$ Latiolais K J^2 Fut Trls 82-13 TripleSec,DeltMusic,Volley'sSpring 9

13Feb83-3DeD 2½f :28^{2}ft 8$\frac{1}{2}$ 118 2 2^1 5$^{1\frac{1}{4}}$ Dupuy A^2 Mdn — — RomnJdgmnt,BrtshNobl,JllyNchls 10

Jun 18 LaD 4f sy :49^3 b   Jun 8 LaD 3f ft :36^2 b

Genrick's Hope — Ch. c. 2, by Distant Land—Hempen's Doll, by Hempen

Own.—Foudriat & Alessi — 120 — Br.—Cox Bobby D (Tex) — 1983 4 M 2 1 $2,040

Tr.—Cormier John

Lifetime 4 0 2 1 $2,040

11Jun83-9LaD 5f :22^1 :46^1 :59^{2}ft 100 110 7$^{2\frac{3}{4}}$ 9$^{6\frac{3}{4}}$12^{12}12^{11} HghtwrTW^{11} Carousel 83-14 Rene'sRinbow,Mbry'sAxe,Pepprrr 13

11Jun83—Steadied in traffic into the turn

2Jun83-2JnD 4f :23 :47^2 :53^{3}ft 4$\frac{1}{2}$ 118 3 1^{hd} 2^{hd} 2^2 Torres M R^3 Mdn 82-14 PtriotGloves,Genrick'sHope,AllFlsh 8

26May83-3JnD 4f :23 :47^1 :53^{3}ft *6-5 118 2 2^1 2^2 3^6 Munster L^7 Mdn 78-14 DeltMusic,ConArtist,Genrick'sHop 10

17May83-1JnD 4f :23 :47^3 :54 ft *1 118 5 4^2 4$^{2\frac{1}{2}}$ 3$^{4\frac{1}{2}}$ Spiehler G^2 Mdn 77-12 SnowCloud,Swneefire,Gnrick'sHop 8

17May83—Awarded second purse money

Thibodaux — Ch. c. 2, by Ramirez—Feel Free, by Barbizon

Own.—Beard S — 120 — Br.—Farish W S III (La) — 1983 4 M 2 1 $20,037

Tr.—Morgan Tommie T

Lifetime 4 0 2 1 $20,037

1May83-11Sun 5f :22^2 :45^2 :57^{3}ft *4-5e 120 8$^{7\frac{1}{2}}$ 8$^{7\frac{1}{4}}$ 4$^{5\frac{1}{2}}$ 4^8 Rivas C^3 R Llison Fut 86-15 Triple Sec,ClassyLoom,WistfulEye 11

15Apr83-6Sun 5f :22 :45^3 :58^{3}ft 2$\frac{1}{2}$ 120 5$^{2\frac{1}{4}}$ 5$^{2\frac{3}{4}}$ 3^5 2$^{4\frac{1}{4}}$ Latiolais K J^7 Mdn 85-14 ClssyLoom,Thibodux,WillBStunnng 9

17Mar83-1DeD 4f :22^3 :48 ft 7$\frac{1}{4}$ 120 2 3$^{5\frac{1}{2}}$ 3^8 3$^{5\frac{1}{4}}$ LatiolaisKJ^{10} Fut Trls 88-13 DzzelingStnley,Jen'sGirl,Thibodux 10

20Feb83-3DeD 4f :24 :49^{2}ft 3$\frac{3}{4}$ 115 4 2^1 2^3 2^{nk} Latiolais K J^3 M35000 86-14 IntrpdSpy,Thbodx,WndblownLook 10

Burquin — B. c. 2, by Cougar II—Light n Lively, by Inaugural Day

Own.—Perkins J L — 120 — Br.—Haarbaur K (Ky) — 1983 0 M 0 0

Tr.—Collins Gin L

Lifetime 0 0 0 0

Jun 14 LaD tr.t 5f ft 1:04^3 hg   Jun 7 LaD tr.t 5f m 1:06^1 hg   Jun 1 LaD tr.t 5f ft 1:06^1 hg   May 28 LaD 4f ft :50^3 b

Triple Sec, at this point in time, was the nation's top winning 2 year old with earnings of $170,144—almost 5 times the other horses' earnings combined! It romped by 7 lengths and still paid $3.60!

There are also classes within classes. One field of $2,500 claimers may race against each other most of the time and be tougher than the next bunch of $2,500 claimers. If a horse is racing in the same class, but on a different day of the week, it may be by design. Trainers love to look for soft spots.

Always read the conditions of the race to detect classes within classes. One $2,500 claiming race could have a purse of $2,700 and be for non-winners of two races that year. Another $2,500 race could be for $2,500 and non-winners of one race that year. In the *Form*, the next week, both are shown only as $2,500 races.

Another good bet at every track is the once-classy horse dropped way down because its form is off. Last time out it showed signs of regaining its form. Today, if he improves a little more he will be untouchable. In wide open races, it very often is the once-classy animal that comes out on top, and at a price.

Trainers

One handicapping rule is: KNOW YOUR TRAINERS. Know who wins and under what circumstances. It is the trainer who has entered this horse on this particular day for this particular race at this particular distance, with this particular jockey, etc. Take time to find out why. The good trainer has. He's mastered the condition book and, in many cases, has planned this spot for quite some time. The horse player must know the trainer's intentions and how much confidence the trainer has in his horse.

Being individuals, horses require individual attention. It isn't important here to give examples of horses that won after the trainer found some idiosyncrasy. But it is important that some trainers are more successful at finding the key than others. This shows up in conditioning. One horse needs lots of work, another may not. Some horses, like the late great Swale, need more time between races than others. Some trainers are good with young horses, others with fillies, colts, turf horses, going a distance for the first time (i.e. stretching out), and so on.

Because a trainer is a leader in the standings, for example, doesn't necessarily mean his horses do well on the turf or his first time starters win, etc.

The first thing a serious player should do when at a track that is unfamiliar is call the *Daily Racing Form* and get a month or two months of back issues. The cost is roughly $100. However, considering the amount of money bet each day, this is an excellent investment. This is necessary to calculate speed figures and adjusted speed figures, to check for track biases and chart reading (all of which are discussed later). Additionally, it is also extremely important to recognize trainer patterns. Trainer patterns are even more important at smaller tracks where cheaper horses (that don't hold their form) run. A winning trainer pattern is a solid indication (e.g. switch to a particular jockey) that this horse, who may have been hurting in prior races, is feeling good today. This doesn't show up in the past performances. Obviously this requires time and effort. If you are not an everyday player you still must try to understand the trainer's intentions while making your selections. This is not as good as knowing that a horse conforms to a winning pattern, but will be of significant benefit.

Kenny J. — Dk. b. or br. g. 5, by Droll Role—Jennie Murphy, by Royal Serenade — **$19,000** Br.—Carter Donald W (Ky) Tr.—Barrera Oscar S — **112**5
Own.—Barrera Oscar S

Lifetime					Year	Starts	1st	2nd	3rd	Earnings
65	8	12	6	$100,763	1983	5	2	1	0	$17,170
					1982	28	2	4	4	$20,103
					Turf	2	0	0	0	

Entered 16Apr83- 9 AQU

8Apr83- 2Aqu	my	7f	:22 3/5 :45 4/5 1:22 3/5	Clm 20000	10	1	2^{1}	1 1/2	1 2 1/2	1nk	Davis R G5	b	108	4.60	88-17	Kenny J. 108nk Need A Penny 112^{1} DealingDiplomat115hd	Driving	13
5Apr83- 2Aqu	fst	1	:46 3/5 1:11 3/5 1:37 1/5	Clm 11500	9	2	1hd	1^{6}	1^{6}	1^{3}	Davis R G5	b	110	*2.60	80-22	Kenny J. 110^{3} Atop It All 119 6 1/2 Two Too Many 115^{2}	Ridden out	10
29Mar83- 3Aqu	gd	1	:47 1/5 1:12 2/5 1:38 2/5	Clm c-7500	10	1	1 1/2	1 1/2	2^{2}	2 1 1/2	Miranda J	b	117	5.70	72-28	Delta Leader 112 1 1/2 Kenny J. 117^{9} Irish Poplar 112 1 1/2	Bumped	12
19Mar83- 1Aqu	my	1 1/4	:47 1/5 1:38 2/5 2:04 3/5	Hcp 10000s	2	1	2 1/2	7^{14}	8^{29}	8^{35}	Graell A	b	109	16.50	38-21	Count Advocate 113^{6} Imaromeo 124 3/4 Ardent Bid 111^{5}	Used early	9
26Feb83- 9Aqu	fst	6f	⊡:23 1/5 :47 4/5 1:13 1/5	Clm c-10000	2	5	2 1 1/2	3^{2}	5 6 1/2	6^{8}	Rogers K L	b	117	4.50	70-25	Foxmoor Flight 117 1/2 Rapido's Repeat 112 2 3/4 AManShort112^{4}	Tired	12
28Dec82- 9Haw	sly	6 1/2f	:22 3/5 :45 2/5 1:18 3/5	3↑Clm 15000	8	3	4 1 1/2	4^{2}	4 2 1/2	8^{11}	Strauss R	b	115	4.70	69-26	Mr. Cleve T. 117 1/2 Marty's First 114^{3} Thebian Ruler 117 1 1/2	Tired	9
[illegible]Dec82- 9Haw	fst	6 1/2f	[illegible] 18 1/5	3↑Clm 15000	12	1	7^{8}	4^{5}	3 2 1/2	3 1 3/4	Strauss R	b	116	7.60	80-26	Superstep 117 1 1/4 King Sid 115 1/2 Kenny J. 116nk	Rallied	12
14Dec82- 9Haw	fst	[illegible]	:22 1/5 :46[illegible]	3↑Clm 12500	5	5	7^{4}	7 5 1/2	3 1 1/2	2no	Louviere G P	b	116	5.60	80-25	Conestoga Eagle 116no Kenny J. 116nk Jims Lt. 113 1 1/2	Sharp	9
6Dec82- 5Haw	gd	6 1/2f	:22 4/5 :45 2/5 1:17	3↑Clm 10000	3	1	2hd	1 1/2	1^{1}	1 1 3/4	Strauss R	b	116	22.00	88-16	Kenny J. 116 1 3/4 Bold Plea 117 1 1/4 Rep's Streak 117nk	Driving	11
23Nov82- 9Haw	fst	6f	:22 1/5 :46 4/5 1:13	3↑Clm 12500	11	1	4 3/4	4 3 1/4	7 7 1/4	7 7 3/4	Medina N R	b	116	24.20	68-24	Dreamer Boy 109no William Bos 116 1 1/4 Bold Plea 118^{2}		11

LATEST WORKOUTS Apr 15 Bel tr.t [illegible] :[illegible]9 3/5 b Mar 9 Bel tr.t 3f sly :38 2/5 b

Kenny J. ran in the second race on April 17. He clearly shows the trainer's intentions. Ordinarily Kenny J. would be suspect for winning in 20 claimers and then being dropped. However, his trainer is the crafty Oscar Barrera. Oscar had entered this horse in an April 14th allowance race (it doesn't show here) and in a 25 claimer on April 16th ("Entered 16 APR83–9AQU"). A quick check shows that the ninth race at Aqueduct on April 16 was a $25,000 claimer. Oscar's original thought was that his horse might be good enough to beat much better ones than it faces today. Scratched both times, the reader may think this horse is hurting. *Look closer.* Oscar claims it for $7,500 and wins with it seven days later, and then again in a $20,000 claimer three days after that. Maybe Kenny J. was scratched because he needed rest or because Oscar wanted everyone to think it was hurt. Probably not, though. Kenny J. was probably scratched because Oscar was looking for the softest possible spot for Kenny J. It beat 20 claimers before and, if the horse is sound, it should be triumphant in 19's.

The key here is to realize that even if it is claimed for $19,000, Oscar makes a profit of $11,500 on the sale plus approximately $20,000 on purse money for the three victories—a total of $31,500 in 19 days. Not bad Oscar. Not bad at all. Kenny J. won by 2 lengths. At 9:5 he was a steal.

Another similar example, with the same trainer, was Roman Chef who ran in the first race of January 8. Roman Chef was entered in a $12,500 claimer the day before. (The 9th at Aqueduct on January 7th was a $12,500 claimer). Additionally, Roman Chef has romped in 10's (i.e. $10,000 claimers) before, and has never been beaten in this class. Oscar Barrera's first thought was that it could beat 12.5's. Therefore, entering it in 10's makes it even more attractive. At 3:1, Roman Chef was another bargain. Oscar Barrera's pattern and intentions were clear with both of these horses. The smart player recognizes a trainer's intentions and winning patterns.

Roman Chef
B. g. 8, by Roman Range—Sand Pail, by Beau Gar
Own.—Barrera O S — $10,000 — Br.—Lawrence J G (NY) — Tr.—Barrera Oscar S — 112⁵
Entered 7Jan83- 9 AQU

Lifetime						
92 11 14 15	1983	1	0	0	0	
$263,866	1982	24	2	2	5	$30,460
	Turf	2	0	1	0	$4,480

3Jan83- 3Aqu	fst	6f	⊡:23⅗	:47⅖	1:13⅖	Clm 15000	7	9	9^{11}	8^{12}	8^{11}	6^{7}	Davis R G5	b 110	8.40	70–25	BusyHilarious112hd RoguishMnner107½ Drk'NBold117nk	No speed	9
28Dec82- 2Aqu	fst	6f	⊡:23⅖	:47⅘	1:13⅗	3+Clm 10000	6	6	9^{11}	$5^{3\frac{3}{4}}$	$2^{1\frac{1}{2}}$	1^{7}	Davis R G5	b 112	3.40	76–24	Roman Chef 112⁷ Big Sport 112¾ Ironical 113 1¾	Drew out	11
22Dec82- 9Aqu	fst	6f	⊡:23⅕	:47⅗	1:13⅘	3+Clm 11500	6	11	$10^{8\frac{3}{4}}$	$8^{7\frac{1}{2}}$	$8^{7\frac{1}{2}}$	$4^{4\frac{1}{4}}$	Cordero A Jr	b 115	*4.20	71–22	Counselor George117hd Michael'sEdge117 2½ PokieJoe119 1¾	Rallied	11
15Dec82- 2Aqu	fst	6f	⊡:23	:46⅖	1:12⅖	3+Clm 16000	7	6	$7^{5\frac{1}{2}}$	$7^{8\frac{1}{2}}$	8^{7}	$8^{8\frac{1}{4}}$	Alvarado R Jr5	b 112	5.80	74–25	Need A Penny 117nk Moon Glider 117 3 OscarMyLove115 1¼	Outrun	8
4Dec82- 1Aqu	gd	1⅛	⊡:47⅘	1:12⅖	1:44⅗	3+Clm 18000	5	3	$3^{6\frac{1}{2}}$	$3^{3\frac{1}{2}}$	3^{5}	2^{6}	Alvarado R Jr5	b 108	*2.00	84–15	Our Celtic Heir 119 6 RomanChef108nk DaringBet117½	Gained place	7
24Nov82- 9Aqu	fst	1	:48	1:14	1:40⅘	3+Clm 18000	10	4	$4^{1\frac{1}{2}}$	2^{hd}	2^{1}	$2^{2\frac{3}{4}}$	Alvarado R Jr5	b 108	3.50	64–36	Mr. Nicefield 113¾ Roman Chef 108 1¼ Daring Bet 117 2¾	Gamely	10
19Nov82- 3Aqu	fst	7f	:23⅗	:47⅕	1:24⅘	3+Clm 20000	3	8	$8^{6\frac{1}{2}}$	$8^{6\frac{1}{4}}$	$6^{6\frac{1}{2}}$	$5^{2\frac{1}{4}}$	Cordero A Jr	b 117	5.50	75–23	Umaticca 117nk Abelardo 113 1¼ Desperate Journey 108¾	Rallied	9
13Nov82- 1Aqu	my	1	:47⅗	1:13	1:37⅘	3+Clm 20000	7	5	4^{3}	$2^{\frac{1}{2}}$	$3^{2\frac{1}{2}}$	$3^{2\frac{3}{4}}$	Cordero A Jr	b 117	4.80	75–25	Our Celtic Heir 113 1 Years Away117 1¾ RomanChef117 7	Weakened	7
4Nov82- 3Aqu	fst	6f	:22⅘	:46⅖	1:12⅕	3+Clm 16000	1	10	$10^{9\frac{1}{2}}$	9^{11}	$8^{7\frac{3}{4}}$	$3^{3\frac{1}{2}}$	Samyn J L	b 117	8.10	76–24	Rasselas 119 2 Ironical 112 1½ Roman Chef 117no	Rallied	10
28Oct82- 9Aqu	fst	1	:46⅖	1:11⅘	1:37	3+Clm 12500	5	7	1^{1}	1^{2}	1^{3}	$1^{2\frac{1}{2}}$	Davis R G5	b 112	3.90	81–14	Roman Chef 112 2½ Indigo Star 119nk Soudan 117½	Driving	10

LATEST WORKOUTS Dec 1 Bel tr.t 4f fst :49⅗ b

Although horses are individuals, trainers by their patterns, tip off the day when the horse is ready to do his best. Many trainers may not even be aware of their own routines. To understand a trainer's pattern, look at the past results and then turn back to the winner's past performances. Then note under what circumstances the horse won. What changes did the trainer make? Sometimes there is a switch to a particular jockey. Other trainers specialize in winning after dropping a horse in class, or switching to the turf, or with first-time starters, or two year olds. Still others win by stretching it out the first time, or winning the first time after a claim or layoff, or with shippers, etc. Sometimes, it is a combination of the above. If there are no changes, and the horse figures to win on form alone, write nothing. It is a good idea to also include second place finishers who ran close and lost due to poor racing luck, figuring that they might otherwise have won. With two months of data or approximately 500 races to examine, these patterns shape up rather quickly. It really isn't that much work and is well worth the effort.

My worksheet for Frank Brothers, a top trainer at Louisiana Downs and Oaklawn Park, looked like this (each line in the worksheet indicates a win and under what circumstances):

Frank Brothers

Big drop
Drop
Drop below claiming price
Switch to Snyder
Switch to Snyder
Switch to Snyder with fast workouts
Drop
Raise after win and fast workouts
Drop
Drop
Drop
Drop
Drop
First time after a claim

Drop
First time after a claim
Drop
Switch to Snyder
Drop
2 year old first time start with fast workouts

Drop means a drop in class. A big drop means dropping two or more classes. Larry Snyder is a top jockey at the track. At this point in time, Frank Brothers was obviously winning many races by running horses against softer competition than before. A drop plus a switch to Snyder makes the horse even more attractive and this means the size of my bet will increase. Trainers with large stables can afford to "cheat" with their horses. If caught once or twice, they don't suffer to the same extent as a trainer with a smaller stable. Also, other trainers may not claim from a top trainer fearing a claiming war that will leave them on the short end or simply reasoning that they may not be able to improve a horse trained by the top man at the track.

AT PENN NATIONAL:

Billy Henry

First time after a claim and switch to Aviles
Raise after big win
Drop and switch to Leasure
Raise after loss and switch to Leasure
Drop and switch to Rozelle
Switch to Fitzgerald
Switch to Aviles
Drop
Big drop and switch to Rozelle
Drop and switch to Rozelle
Switch to Rozelle
Ship from Keystone and switch to Rozelle
Drop and switch to Rozelle
Switch to Rozelle
Ship from Keystone and switch to Colton
First time after a claim

Henry obviously has great success by dropping horses down in class and putting Ron Rozelle aboard.

Below is a sample of some trainers and their winning patterns. Be careful. Patterns can change and many horses that win do not necessarily follow a pattern.

AT AQUEDUCT:

Oscar Barrera—claims a horse, shows a public workout, and races it—all within one week.

King Leatherbury—races mostly in Maryland but is tough with anything he ships into New York. He's also very good with horses that have at least a 30 day layoff, no public workouts and gets support at the windows. King Leatherbury likes to cash a bet, too.

Victor Nickerson—horses stretching out for the first time.

Angela Penna—excellent at training horses to go a distance.

Mack Miller—turf races, especially when the horse makes its turf debut.

Trainers who win with first time starters include: *Stanley Hough*, *Dick DeStasio*, *Howie Tesher*, *Jimmy Iselin* and *Billy Turner*. The late *Jim Maloney* was also excellent with first time starters. Now, I keep my eye on his son *Jim Maloney Jr.* to see if his success was passed on.

Johnny Parisella—everything owned by Ted Sabarese—especially fillies.

Jan Nerud and *T.J. Kelly*—two-year-olds.

T. J. Gullo—in 1983, won with horses first time after a claim at one point and then never won the first time after a claim at another.

AT LOUISIANA DOWNS:

George Hallock—raises a horse after losing!

J. Dorignac—first time after a claim and raise after a win.

Tommy Morgan—two-year-olds.

D. Andis—first time after a claim with a switch to Engle.

At Louisiana Downs, any time any trainer switches jockeys to Larry Snyder he must be respected. With Snyder in the irons, horses find the winner's circle.

AT PENN NATIONAL:

Bruce Kraveats—switch to Aviles (a top jockey).

Mario Beneito—shippers, especially from Keystone (now called Philadelphia Park) and Monmouth.

Dave Dumestre—first time after a claim.

Floyd Tolle—first time after a claim with a switch to Colton.

Michael Trivigno—dropping horses in class.

Pamela Arnold—switch to J. D. Prough.

It's very comforting to find a horse that figures to be best and also conforms to a winning pattern. A winning pattern is a strong indication of the trainer's intentions. If the trainer doesn't think the horse can win, he may be saving his horse for next week. He may instruct the jockey to race conservatively and go all out only if the race goes his way. Otherwise he may risk getting any share of the purse.

Trainer patterns are not the only indications of a trainer's intentions. Distance, weight, jockey, workouts, class, track condition, etc. can indicate whether or not the horse will make its top effort today. Reading between the lines is the only way to make this determination. A sprinter that has been tiring may be entered at a distance to build stamina. A router may be entered in a sprint to sharpen its speed. At large tracks all but stakes horses should show recent races and/or workouts. At smaller tracks, like Penn National, only a handful work out publicly, so this is not an indication of the horse's fitness. Most of the time, common sense is sufficient enough to estimate the trainer's intentions. For example, here is Danced All Night that raced at Aqueduct on February 19:

Danced All Night — Dk. b. or br. m. 5, by Best Turn—Bundle of Love, by Tudorka
Own.—Watters S Jr — Br.—Watters S Jr (Md) — Tr.—Watters Sidney Jr — **112**

Lifetime 35 2 7 4 $67,220	1983	3	1	1	0	$20,740
	1982	18	0	3	2	$20,780
	Turf	10	0	1	2	$7,820

Entered 18Feb83- 8 AQU

3Feb83- 8Aqu gd	2 1/16	⊡:50⅗	3:03⅘	3:38⅘		Handicap	4	6	67	58½	44½	2nk	Molina V H	109	5.70	— —	Rollix 105nk Danced All Night 1091 Irish Waters 1126½	Rallied	6
20Jan83- 5Aqu fst	1⅛	⊡:47⅕	1:14⅖	1:54⅘		ⒻAlw 21000	8	5	519	55	33	1hd	Molina V H	117	10.00	72-24	DancedAllNight117hdLdyNoble117nkBckstgeWhisper1171½	Driving	8
15Jan83- 7Aqu sly	1¼	⊡:48⅗	1:41	2:07⅗		Alw 22000	7	8	66	612	521	521	Molina V H	112	16.30	59-22	Masmak 1123½ The Mangler 1107½ Starhitch 1173	Tired	8
30Dec82- 7Aqu fst	1 1/16	⊡:49	1:14	1:47⅕	3↑	ⒻAlw 22000	8	6	56	811	813	712	Molina V H	117	3.70	65-24	Beside the Point 112½ Ranch Mink 110nk Simhala 115¾	No threat	8
19Dec82- 7Aqu fst	1 70	⊡:48⅘	1:14⅗	1:46	3↑	ⒻAlw 22000	1	4	47	44½	47	32½	Molina V H	117	2.20	78-23	Rim Recker 115no Simhala 1102½ Danced All Night 117hd	Rallied	6
8Dec82- 9Aqu fst	1 1/16	⊡:48⅗	1:14⅕	1:47⅖	3↑	ⒻAlw 22000	6	11	77½	21½	34	22¾	Molina V H	117	52.40	73-21	Jennifr'sJulp1152¾DncdAllNight117¾NtivNwYorkr1151½	Game try	11
25Nov82- 7Aqu sf	1⅛	Ⓣ:48⅕	1:13⅗	1:54⅕	3↑	ⒻAlw 20000	1	6	914	913	98½	911	Molina V H	117	30.90	62-28	PoliticsNTricks1202¾LovingHomeII1101½SlveNoMor115nk	Outrun	9
13Nov82- 5Aqu my	1⅛	:49	1:14⅘	1:53⅗	3↑	ⒻAlw 20000	5	5	64½	54½	414	416	Molina V H	117	16.80	51-25	Minor's Gift 11514 Bigger Enough 1101½ Bottome 115½	No factor	6
3Nov82- 8Lrl yl	1 1/16	Ⓣ:47⅗	1:13⅗	1:46⅕	3↑	Alw 10000	1	8	818	817	715	622	Grove P	113	53.60	50-33	Sun and Shine 1152½ Gray Dude 116nk Devoir 1139	Outrun	8
27Oct82- 7Lrl fst	1 1/16	:47⅘	1:14⅖	1:47⅘	3↑	ⒻAlw 10000	1	7	713	713	819	818	Passmore W J	116	6.80	51-27	Eager Miss 1132¾ Dynamo Dotty 1074 Bold La Gala 114nk	Outrun	10

LATEST WORKOUTS Feb 17 Bel tr.t 4f my :52 b Feb 11 Bel tr.t 3f fst :37⅘ b Jan 29 Bel tr.t 4f fst :52 b

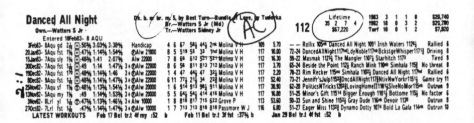

On this day, there was a major jockey switch from V. Molina to Angel Cordero, the Eclipse Award Winning Jockey for 1983 and later again in 1984. Before January 20, Danced All Night was 1 for 33 lifetime. On February 3rd she misses a neck. She is sharper now than ever and Sidney Watters must be more than anxious to get the top money while he can. He probably feels that had Cordero ridden last time, on February 3rd, Danced All Night could have had her picture taken. Today he's not taking any chances. Forget the odds, he wants the purse. The New York crowd saw the same thing and bet this winner down to 2:1. This is an obvious example, but nonetheless an important one and a good start at reading between the lines.

Another easy example is Rustic Love that won on March 21:

Rustic Love — Gr. f. 4, by Rustic Ruler—Artful Love, by Selectus

Own.—Reynolds Sue — $9,000 — Br.—Baille Michel (Mich) — Tr.—Iwinski Allan — 108[5]

Lifetime 36 4 10 2 $31,488 — 1983 3 1 0 0 $4,665 — 1982 23 3 6 2 $22,034

25Jan83- 4Key	my	$1\frac{1}{16}$	:48	1:13 4/5	1:49	ⓕClm 9000	1	2	2^{2}	$2^{2\frac{1}{2}}$	$2^{\frac{1}{2}}$	$4^{3\frac{1}{2}}$	Shurtz W R	b 111	3.40	56-28	No Key $115^{1\frac{1}{2}}$ Forever Native $116^{1\frac{1}{2}}$ Lady Tia $115^{\frac{1}{2}}$	Weakened	7
14Jan83- 6Key	fst	1^{70}	:47 4/5	1:12 4/5	1:44	ⓕClm 10000	5	6	6^{5}	5^{12}	$5^{8\frac{1}{2}}$	$5^{6\frac{1}{4}}$	Shurtz W R^{5}	b 108	8.20	74-22	Whitewalls $115^{\frac{1}{2}}$ Holly's Silver $119^{3\frac{1}{2}}$ SugarPockets110^{1}	No factor	12
5Jan83- 4Key	fst	1^{70}	:49	1:15 1/5	1:46 3/5	ⓕClm 7000	10	6	4^{7}	3^{1}	1^{hd}	1^{1}	Shurtz W R^{5}	b 108	4.80	67-29	Rustic Love 108^{1} To Much To Soon 113^{7} Mrs. Dulin109^{nk}	Driving	11
20Dec82- 2Key	my	6f	:22 4/5	:46 3/5	1:13 3/5	ⓕClm 6500	7	8	10^{11}	$7^{9\frac{3}{4}}$	4^{10}	2^{1}	Shurtz W R^{5}	b 107	6.90	73-29	O. D.'s Princess 117^{1} Rustic Love $107^{2\frac{3}{4}}$ Blue Eyes$116^{1\frac{3}{4}}$	Fin. Fast	12
10Dec82- 5Key	fst	6f	:22 3/5	:46 2/5	1:12 3/5	ⓕClm 9000	9	2	8^{5}	$7^{8\frac{1}{2}}$	9^{15}	9^{19}	Powers T M^{5}	b 108	8.80	59-21	Raspberry Brandy $111^{\frac{3}{4}}$ Whitewalls $120^{\frac{1}{2}}$ Iron Case $116^{1\frac{3}{4}}$	Outrun	9
27Nov82- 9Key	fst	6f	:23 2/5	:47 4/5	1:14 3/5	ⓕClm 7500	2	8	$6^{3\frac{3}{4}}$	4^{2}	1^{hd}	2^{hd}	Powers T M^{5}	b 111	4.60	68-29	O. D.'s Princess 115^{hd} Rustic Love$111^{2\frac{1}{4}}$TenorBetter116^{nk}	Gamely	9
17Nov82- 6Key	fst	6f	:23 1/5	:47	1:12 3/5	ⓕClm 7500	4	2	$6^{4\frac{1}{4}}$	$5^{2\frac{3}{4}}$	$3^{6\frac{1}{2}}$	$2^{2\frac{1}{4}}$	Powers T M^{5}	b 111	3.80	76-21	O. D.'sPrincess$115^{2\frac{1}{4}}$RusticLove$111^{\frac{3}{4}}$FritterAway116^{7}	Up for place	7
8Nov82- 7Key	fst	7f	:22 3/5	:45 3/5	1:26 3/5	ⓕClm 7500	6	9	8^{11}	6^{7}	$4^{4\frac{1}{2}}$	$2^{1\frac{1}{2}}$	Powers T M^{5}	b 111	4.70	73-27	O. D.'s Princess $113^{1\frac{1}{2}}$ Rustic Love$111^{3\frac{3}{4}}$Tammy'sDip118^{no}	Gaining	9
22Oct82- 6Key	fst	6f	:23 1/5	:47 4/5	1:14	ⓕClm 9000	3	6	$6^{4\frac{1}{2}}$	5^{3}	$4^{\frac{3}{4}}$	4^{4}	Shurtz W R^{7}	b 107	3.80	67-32	Miss Riddle 116^{2} Topless Brat $116^{\frac{3}{4}}$ Mean Marie $116^{1\frac{1}{2}}$	Hung	8
12Oct82- 5Key	fst	6½f	:22 4/5	:46 4/5	1:19 3/5	ⓕClm 9000	10	1	4^{4}	$5^{2\frac{1}{4}}$	$3^{1\frac{1}{2}}$	3^{3}	Shurtz W R^{7}	b 109	22.30	72-29	Amigo Tourista 114^{nk} Topless Brat $118^{2\frac{3}{4}}$ RusticLove$109^{\frac{3}{4}}$	Rallied	10

LATEST WORKOUTS Dec 30 Key 6f fst 1:19 3/5 b

Sue Sedlacek claimed this filly on February 9th after her debut in New York. After almost a month, and showing no public workouts, Rustic Love misses a length for all the marbles at almost 30:1. The trainer raised Rustic Love from $9,000 claimers to $14,000 claimers. Sue Sedlacek is sharp. If she claimed this horse shipping in from New Jersey, she probably knew something. Rustic Love's last effort is testimony to this. After a horse is claimed it is a new horse—its past is less important. Today Rustic Love will race in $12,500 claimers. Why? It just missed in higher company and should walk all over this bunch. IN ADDITION, even if Rustic Love is claimed today she was bought for only $9,000. This, plus the purse money, is a nice profit in less than two months. The trainer's philosophy could be that no one can complain selling a horse for a profit.

A trainer claims a horse believing that he can improve it or that it has potential. People who have been training for 40 years or more all say that no matter how long they're in the business they can't learn it all. This means that a horse may have a problem that its present trainer can't correct but someone else can. Once the problem is corrected, the horse might be able to step up greatly and win. The problem could be its diet, equipment, training schedule, the distance it's running, undiagnosed injury, or anything else for that matter. Again, horses are unique. Sharp trainers find the key—sometimes by accident. One of my horses evidently was abused at one time by a male groom or trainer. It now loves the girl groom who takes care of him. If she goes to the other end of the barn for water, he can be seen sticking his head over the stall door looking for her. This love and trust has undoubtedly helped improve his performance.

In most states, a claimed horse must move up 25% for a month. During this month horsemen say that it is "in jail." Owners pay a sales tax on claimed horses. Fundamentals indicate that a claimed horse is an extra plus because someone has spent a lot of money and sees a potential. In most cases this is correct—but *not* always. Go one step further. See who it was claimed from and by whom. As in any other business, there are experts and incompetents. Sometimes the *Form*, tells you that the horse has been privately purchased (e.g. Aqueduct's Fall Highweight stakes winner Chas Conerly). This should be treated the same as a claim. It is usually spotted by only remembering the old owner and it wasn't the same as the last time you looked in the *Form*.

Some trainers are particularly adept at winning with recent claims. One of the best is Oscar Barrera. In one two and a half month period he had 11 winners from horses he claimed. Nine won immediately and the other two won the second time out. Anytime Oscar claims a horse, works it out and brings it back to race all within a week—it's a worthwhile bet. The horses and their prices are listed below.

3/14	Dancer's Melody	$17.60
3/19	Count Advocate	$12.60
4/5	Ardent Bid	$10.40
4/7	Friendly Letters	$ 8.80
4/30	Exquisite Gal	$29.80
5/11	Gourmet	$ 9.60
5/23	Hot Words	$10.00
5/28	Colonel Law	$ 5.00
6/1	Joycapade	$ 4.80
6/1	Walking On Air	$ 7.60

An average payoff of more than $11.00! During this period, I couldn't wait for Oscar to claim the next horse. Incidently,

Exquisite Gal was ridden by the then virtually unknown Declan Murphy. Later Murphy won the 1983 Eclipse Award for the nation's leading apprentice. The moral of the story: bet Oscar Barrera's horses when they follow the pattern, but don't play poker with him. Oscar is one shrewd trainer. As a corollary, be careful of betting horses claimed from Oscar Barrera. Again, know the trainers!

Most people are shocked to discover the number of different types of equipment a trainer can choose from and the variety of decisions to be made. Sure, there are aluminum, bar and steel shoes. But did you know the blacksmith, per the trainer orders, will shave a hoof at a specific angle (i.e. relative to the ground)? By so doing, he will help the horse's stride or relieve pressure on an injured or weakened area. A blacksmith doesn't simply nail a shoe on. As a matter of fact, many races have been lost simply by a nail that was in too deep. The public may not always be privy to this information but is made aware of changes in shoes and blinkers. Handicappers must find out the reason for the change and then decide if it will hurt or help the horse's chances. Deputed Testimony was the only horse in the 1983 Preakness equipped with mud caulks (extra pieces of metal perpendicular to the ground to grab it more firmly). No doubt it helped him win. Other trainers probably expected the rain to hold off. Some have been accused of making equipment changes as an excuse for form reversal, meaning that the horse becomes a winner when he wasn't close previously. The equipment change neither helps nor hinders, but is offered as the reason for winning. In New York, a trainer can be suspended for form reversal and should be.

Never bet horses with steel or bar shoes unless they have won wearing them in the past. This is not common. It is a good idea to mention these animals in your notebook and wait for the day they switch to aluminum shoes.

Trainers will sometimes put blinkers on a horse when it bears in or out. Often they're used to help the horse relax. Other times, blinkers are removed if the horse is losing because it "loafs on the lead" and fails to see another horse passing until it's too late.

A trainer making an equipment change is probably trying to correct a problem. This is, therefore, a big plus.

Most trainers are in the business because they either love it or don't know how to do anything else. To make it in the racing world it is often necessary to start at the bottom. Hot walkers become grooms. Grooms can become exercise riders, jockeys and trainers. Some jockeys, when they get older or can't make the weight any longer, become trainers (e.g. Braulio Baeza).

For all but the top trainers and jockeys, earning a living can be a struggle. Owners may become displeased or impatient and give the horse to another trainer, or simply ship the horse elsewhere. And finding reliable help is a major problem to a trainer. Jockeys give horses bad rides. There is the frustration and anxiety of getting any horse fit and ready to race. A trainer may get a horse from birth or as a yearling. Sometimes, many times, the horse doesn't make it to the races as a two year old, or three or four year old or never for that matter. If the horse becomes injured the delay is even longer. If it dies, the owner gets the insurance (if he had a policy) but no one gets repaid for the time and effort already invested.

One of the toughest jobs for a trainer is dealing with owners. People buy race horses for a variety of reasons. Most enter the sport for tax reasons, for enjoyment, or because they are trying to win money (in purses or at the windows). But no matter what the reason, an owner wants the horse to win. No one wants to pay feed bills, vet bills, entry fees for stakes races, sales tax, etc. A man successful in his own business usually knows little or nothing about horses. He is forced to find someone he can trust in purchasing, training and racing a horse. He may be told it's a tough business, that 85% of the people who own horses lose money on paper, and that horses get injured. But, in most cases, it isn't until it actually happens that the realities sink in.

Owners are only human. They have daydreams of winning the Kentucky Derby. Like most people, they block out the bad and also want to blame someone else when things go wrong. That someone is the trainer.

Most trainers are hard-working people. Like the owners, they want to win. Nothing is more frustrating to a trainer than an animal that should win and doesn't. Unlike the owner, however, racing is the trainer's only business, usually not a hobby or a second business. The trainer doesn't want to lose customers. So he is, by necessity, an optimist. It can be incredible how inventive a trainer, any trainer, can be finding excuses why the horse lost and why he should be better next time out. And since a horse cannot speak, it is understandable why a problem may be hard to find. After months of injuries and bad racing luck, there is still the optimism.

Why doesn't the owner just give his horse to another trainer? Some do, but for the most part, this becomes a complicated answer. First, the owner wants to believe the trainer. The owner wants to win. He doesn't want to hear that his horse isn't good enough and should be dropped in class. Second, the trainer may have other horses by the same owner that are winning. Third, the race track is a microcosm. The owner fears that the new trainer won't put forth 100% effort because he knows or is a friend of the original trainer. Many owners don't know that much about horse racing. When the horse is winning the owner is happy. Bills only become a problem when things go wrong. When many owners pay vet bills or stable bills, they begin to question the trainer and his methods. They feel as if they're stuck. Trainers perceive this. Like the rest of us, they don't appreciate anyone doubting their skills. A trainer and owner, even while making money, may argue violently, just like business partners may do.

Frequently, many horses are owned by several people. The trainer must please all of them (and sometimes including their families), besides taking care of the horse.

Many racing fans don't realize that, frequently, big ownership groups (and there are many) have several trainers, besides the head trainer. These trainers race horses at several tracks, in different states sometimes, and can only monitor the horse's progress via a telephone conversation or an occasional visit. However, it is the head trainer's name that appears in the past performances. In some cases, it is really the second trainer who possesses the expertise about the horse, not the head trainer who is forced to become a bottom line man—much like the head of a big corporation who can't possibly be concerned with all the details.

Therefore, when travelling to a different track, be aware that the trainer listed may not be the one with whom you are familiar. His pattern may be different.

Trainers not only deal with jockeys, but also with the jockey's agent who is responsible for getting the jockey his mounts. With the pressure of dealing with owners upon them, it is not unusual for a trainer to publicly criticize a jockey for a bad ride in a big race. Such comments should be taken into consideration in your handicapping in the near future (before the differences are ironed out) when the jockey rides *against* that trainer. Some seek revenge and may try to cause a trainer's horse to lose a race at the expense of their own. Other trainers have favorite jockeys or "money men." In New York, Cordero rides for Frank Martin often, Velasquez for Johnny Campo, Venezia for Bob Dunham. At every track there are similar examples.

Some trainers switch to riders that they know they can count on—the money men. Often these are underrated jockeys and the trainer knows the horse will, therefore, go off at decent odds. Obviously, a switch to the money man is very significant. By reviewing the last month and a half or two month's results, as previously described, it is often possible to discover who these money men are. Again, this can change too, once the trainer thinks the public is catching on and the odds are being destroyed.

Trainers, even at large tracks, differ in expertise. If Frank Martin enters a horse in allowance company for non-winners of three races when it is eligible for non-winners of two, the horse must be conceded an excellent chance to win. Frank Martin's judgment merits respect. However, if a lesser trainer does the same thing, the trainer is probably overly optimistic and just looking for a price. Throw the horse out (i.e. he is not a contender). What a shame that this poor animal must race over its head.

Contrary to a popular belief, the race track is not one big family. There are trainers that openly feud with others (as do jockeys). Trainers may be jealous of another's success, saying how easily he got there or what breaks he got. Trainers compete with each other in the standings for recognition. Claiming wars are not uncommon. Handicappers must recognize this because it means that horses are being raced over their heads. Also grooms and second trainers are fired or leave due to work conditions.

Trainers, even the best ones, can make mistakes. Even the best can place too much value on a horse. Frequently, more than one trainer thinks he has a winner in the race. Sometimes a horse is raced or worked out when it shouldn't be. Injuries or ailments may go undetected. Even vets have to guess many times. It is true, however, that good trainers make better decisions more often and they make fewer mistakes.

To sum, the trainer not only trains a horse, but really runs a business. He deals with owners, jockeys, jockey agents, vets, accountants, pays bills, bills others and has frustrations, and anxieties. It helps to have this perspective before you walk to the window.

Jockeys

One quick look at the standings will show the top jockeys at the track. But a jockey is more than a statistic. He's an athlete and an integral part of handicapping and betting.

More than that, jockeys are people. They have weight problems, financial problems, marital problems and have hassles with trainers, owners and other jockeys. Just like other business people, many jockeys have succumbed to pressure and have been ruined by alcohol. Some can't handle instant fame. A few years ago, a hot young jockey who rode one of the nation's top horses was much publicized for his use of cocaine. His problems appear to be in the past now, however.

One popular misconception is the jockey's earnings. In New York, in 1983, jockeys got 6% of the purse for winning (i.e. 10% of the owners share of 60%), $55 for second, $45 for third and $35 otherwise. Not bad at all, IF the jockey rides regularly in New York and succeeds. Most don't and at smaller tracks they are paid even less. Also, others can take a share of their earnings—jockey agents (who get roughly 20% of their client's earnings), valets, Uncle Sam, lawyers, etc. The truth is that most jockeys struggle. On any given day an injury could end a career (e.g. Ron Turcotte).

Like everyone else, jockeys make mistakes. Even a top athlete makes mistakes. Baseball players err and football players fumble. But when a jockey makes an error, the trainer still has to answer to the owner. Often the answer is to replace the jockey. When a young jockey makes a mistake it can be even more costly. He must work extra hard for even a few mounts, and often not the better horses. When the word spreads that the new kid is no good it becomes even harder to get a mount, any mount. No one wants to take a chance on him.

Even top jockeys can fall from favor. Frank Lovoto won the Eclipse Award some years ago as the nation's leading apprentice. He suffered a serious leg injury from an accident and had to prove to trainers again that he didn't lose his ability or nerve. Jean Cruget, of Seattle Slew fame, also had to prove himself when he came back from retirement (it didn't take him long).

In New York, there is very little difference between most top jockeys and the other good journeymen. There are, though, some jockeys who are terrible by New York standards. The biggest difference between the best jockeys and the other riders is that top jockeys get live mounts and the better horses in big races. They can't make the horse run any faster but will keep it out of trouble and get the job done more often. Again, they make fewer mistakes. Winning big races is worth a lot more in breeding than purses. Flying Angel Cordero west or Laffit Pincay east for an important ride is looked on as a necessary expense and one that is cheap compared to the stakes involved. Chances are some local jockey could get the job done, but why chance it?

A switch from a top jockey to an average one is usually an indication that the horse isn't capable of winning, but be careful that the trainer isn't just looking for a better price.

Braulio Baeza was one of my favorites. Towards the end of his riding career he was having weight problems and his riding suffered. I didn't make the adjustment right away because I bet with my heart, not my head. Baeza, no doubt, was one of the finest jockeys ever.

At the race track, things change—even jockeys. Many hot apprentices become average riders when they lose their bugs. Many win because they got live mounts from trainers who want to take advantage of their weight allowances. Without the bug, some fall from favor. Horse players must make the adjustment. There are many examples of seemingly young talented men and women who were on the rise but later fell into relative obscurity almost overnight.

Many horsemen of the old school won't put an apprentice on a live mount until after he's learned from riding fifty or sixty losers. The betting implications are obvious. This isn't the case as often today because of the cost of racing. It can happen at small tracks where the pressures of big business aren't as great. Again, always know your trainers. What have they done in the past with apprentices? During the winter months, when many top New York jockeys head for the warm weather, new apprentices make their debuts. Some trainers are very adept at spotting new talent.

At Hazel Park in Michigan, it is rare to see an apprentice as a leading rider. This is due to the fact that Hazel Park is a 5/8 mile track. Races at six furlongs are, therefore, around two turns. There are too many pockets, switches and other traffic problems for most of these inexperienced riders to avoid.

Ever wake up and feel like not going to work? Jockeys can have off days, too. Maybe he doesn't feel well or one of his kids kept him awake all night. He still has to ride to honor a commitment or fear losing the mount. Take notice of who is hot and who isn't. The trainer does.

Some jockeys specialize in specific areas. Bob Ussery made a living by front running. Eddie Maple is particularly adept with two year olds, especially maidens. I'm not sure how, but Maple has a way of relaxing nervous or anxious young horses. The animal, once relaxed, doesn't waste his race in the paddock. Maple has a way of gaining the horse's confidence. On the turf look for Jean-Luc Samyn, Jean Cruget, Jorge Velasquez, Angel Cordero and Fernando Toro, among others. Riders that seem to do well in the slop include Jean-Luc Samyn, Greg McCarron and Anthony Graell.

Good turf riders work with the horse, in its rhythm. On a dirt track, a jockey gets subconscious feedback from the pounding of the horse's hooves. It is easier to work in harmony with the horse. The turf, however, absorbs this feedback and good turf riders, like those mentioned, don't waste the mount's energy. They ride more efficiently and effectively.

Some average jockeys move up on an off track. Others may be afraid to take chances. Some have poor eyesight and are hampered by the slop flying in all directions. On a really sloppy track, a jockey can go through six or seven pairs of goggles—flipping each pair away as they accumulate mud.

Jockeys also have fierce rivalries with each other on and off the track—whether it be the horses or a simple game of gin rummy, ping pong or basketball. Many times a leading rider feels he must put a new boy in his place. Unfortunately, this is often done on the track during a race. The young jockey can find himself crowded around a turn or buried in a speed duel. His mount is more important to him than that of the experienced rider. A good ride means other mounts, whereas a poor one may be a major setback. The old veterans try to keep the new kids in line.

Besides noticing who rides or who wins for whom, also note riding style because it may affect your selection. Some jockeys like Rolando Alvarado prefer to stay on the rail. This could hurt your chances of winning if the rail comes up dead and the jockey doesn't make the adjustment. Others ride on the outside and sometimes their mounts lose too much ground. Perhaps they had an accident coming up the rail sometime in the past. Some riders, like Cordero, have a sixth sense for track biases. They help your chances of success.

Owners can pressure trainers in their choice of rider selection. They want the hot young apprentice or top name jockey on their horse. It might be whoever is fashionable. Others may fit the horse better (e.g. like Maple on a 2 year old). Marfa, a 1983 Kentucky Derby favorite, needed strong handling. Velasquez provided this whereas others may not have been able to—even other top jockeys.

Jockeys are a major part of handicapping.

Whispering List
Own.—Everett-White **114**
Ch. f. 4, by List—Whisper Pam, by Whisper Jet
Br.—Kroop John (Ky) 1983 13 2 5 1 $16,440
Tr.—Dantin Lee $12,500 1982 0 M 0 0
Lifetime 13 2 5 1 $16,440

3Sep83-4LaD	170	:483	1:142	1:45 ft	*7-5	114	2½	1hd	12½	15	Ardoin R8	Ⓕ 10000	72-20	WhisperingList,Desbarats,TisaBaby	8
27Aug83-2LaD	6f	:224	:464	1:133ft	[illegible]	114	85¼	65½	62¾	22	Croker C R3	Ⓕ 12500	73-22	AskBby,WhispringList,GoingToFly	12
6Aug83-5LaD	170	:492	1:154	1:473sl	3	114	2hd	2hd	2hd	3¾	Croker C R2	Ⓕ 10000	58-33	Tmmy'sJyJy,Brth'sBby,WhsprngLst	8
23Jly83-5LaD	170	:473	1:13	1:444ft	4½	114	43½	32	22	21½	Croker C R8	Ⓕ 10000	71-24	SntRosBll,WhispringLst,Ruby'sDrm	9
2Jly83-1LaD	170	:464	1:13	1:462ft	8¾	114	31½	22½	33	22	Croker C R1	Ⓕ 10000	63-19	Tmmy'sJyJ,WhsprngLst,QnfthTrb	12
3Jun83-5LaD	6f	:23	:463	1:14ft	7½	114	1hd	31	23	26	Croker C R3	Ⓕ 8000	78-15	Von'sToy,WhispringLst,OWhtRlfts	12
28May83-4LaD	6f	:23	:474	1:153m	19	114	21½	21½	22	21½	Croker C R1	Ⓕ 8000	63-39	BonniBluJn,WhispringList,BssiBll	12
22Apr83-8LaD	6f	:221	:462	1:114ft	111	114	126¾	1114	1115	1213	Croker C R5	ⒻAw11000	71-16	Earl's Good Time,LtLite,PollyLee	12
23Mar83-2OP	6f	:221	:463	1:134ft	48	116	59	612	815	1111	Lively J9	7500	65-20	Glenwood Ace, Mr.Fondy,RareCap	12
9Mar83-5OP	6f	:232	:49	1:151ft	14	112	53¼	85½	1017	1020	Lively J8	Ⓕ 10000	49-29	Mid Morn, Snowbelle, Ritzy Rags	11

On September 10, a jockey switch seemed to make a big difference in this race at Louisiana Downs. Whispering List stepped up, but Ardoin wins easily by 7 lengths paying $7.20. After so many disappointments, the trainer switched riders and it paid off. Keep this in mind for the example on September 25:

Windsor Night — B. g. 5, by Will Hays—Spring Market, by Spring Double
Own.—Wilson B H — 114 — Br.—Clugston C & Smyth R (Fla) — Tr.—Suttle Elbert L — $12,500
Lifetime 52 4 6 8 $51,100 — 1983 9 0 0 1 $1,584 — 1982 15 0 1 4 $8,610 — Turf 2 0 0 0 $780

18Aug83-4LaD	6½f	$:22^3$	$:46^1$	$1:19^1$ft	11	114	$11^{8\frac14}$	$10^{6\frac12}$	$8^{4\frac12}$	4^1	Croker C R^8	8000	78-18	DyTimeTudor,PirteIslnd,JustGood	12
18Aug83—Rider lost his whip															
23Jun83-9LaD	170	$:47^3$	1:14	$1:45^4$gd	15	116	8^{11}	$7^{8\frac12}$	5^8	$3^{7\frac12}$	Croker C R^9	10000	60-44	RomnHills,Mgnetizr,WindsorNight	10
15Jun83-9LaD	170	$:47^3$	$1:13^3$	$1:45^3$ft	20	114	$6^{5\frac34}$	8^4	$7^{2\frac14}$	4^1	Croker C R^7	7500	68-23	DonB.Crtin,ScrminWilli,Hony'sStlt	12
24Apr83-1LaD	170			$1:45^1$gd	55	116	12^{19}	11^{14}	11^{22}	9^{24}	Croker C R^3	10000	47-23	BetOnBrd,WestIndRf,YourFirdBill	12
24Apr83—Fractional times unavailable															
13Apr83-5OP	$1\frac{1}{16}$	$:47^2$	$1:13^4$	$1:48^1$sy	26	114	10^{16}	10^{16}	10^{20}	8^{18}	Engle J^5	12500	49-28	Roman Hills, Dunster,HilariousCor	10
5Apr83-5OP	$1\frac{1}{16}$	:48	$1:13^4$	1:47 gd	24	116	8^{20}	8^{20}	8^{21}	8^{18}	Engle J^3	13500	55-26	JmestownTddy,Dunstr,YoungDrivr	10
22Mar83-5OP	$1\frac{1}{16}$	$:47^2$	$1:12^2$	$1:45^2$ft	21	116	9^{20}	9^{20}	9^{21}	9^{23}	Croker C R^3	16000	58-20	RoyalStearic,BobMacB.,Miel'sMgic	9
2Mar83-5OP	6f	$:22^2$	$:46^2$	$1:13^3$ft	56	116	12^{14}	12^{16}	10^{16}	10^7	Croker C R^8	16000	70-26	Time Call, Fitz's Night,Pocketless	12
23Feb83-5OP	6f	$:22^3$	$:47^4$	$1:14^1$gd	106	116	12^{20}	12^{16}	12^{14}	11^8	Croker C R^{12}	16000	66-26	Timmie'sDncer,Pick'm,Goldi'sSon	12
10Oct82-10LaD	170	$:47^1$	$1:13^2$	$1:45^1$m	9	114	7^{11}	6^8	5^7	4^6	Croker C R^5	18000	68-21	MisterRouge,Monty'sRole,Georglit	8

Sep 22 LaD 5f sl 1:07 b — Sep 17 LaD 5f ft $1:05^1$ b — Sep 8 LaD 5f ft $1:05^3$ b — Sep 1 LaD 3f ft :54 b

Lively 14:1

This is not to pick on Croker. If money can be made when the trainer switches from him, why not bet those horses? Maybe he's a good jockey that hadn't been feeling well? Who knows? But if the pattern works, don't ignore it. This horse was closing a lot of ground last time and might have won had Croker not lost his whip. Any jockey can lose his whip, but this helped to remind me of the jockey switch from Croker to Ardoin on Whispering List. Although I don't know much about Croker, what I do know is that Whispering List could only manage to come second with him, but won easily with Ardoin.

Today, Windsor Night is being raised and the trainer switches to Lively. At 14:1, why not? He won and paid $29.80.

The next time I see a switch from Croker, I might increase my bet. If I start losing these races I'll know that Whispering List and Windsor Night were flukes, but, in the meantime, I'm ahead of the game.

Sometimes it's preferable for an average rider to have the mount (e.g. the money man). Not every top jockey is a top turf rider or good with 2 year olds or good on an off track. The trainer has carefully selected the jockey. The handicapper must pay attention. Sometimes a rider is forced to accept a mount because he rides regularly for that owner or trainer, (e.g. in 1985, Angel Cordero missed a chance for his share of $2,600,000 in purse and bonus money with Spend A Buck, because he had previously committed to ride Track Barron). Other times the trainer picks a particular jockey because he knows the horse is ready and has complete confidence in that rider. Reading between the lines and remembering past occurrences will provide the answer. Betting the horse properly will provide the rewards.

Breeding

The intent of this section is not to make the reader an expert on breeding. Rather, it is to show the significance of breeding as it applies to betting. After a horse has gone a distance three or four times, breeding no longer matters. In its past races, the horse indicates whether or not it is suited for today's distance and track condition. A knowledge of breeding gives the player an edge in the area of first-time starters, turf debuts, mudders, and suitability to distance.

First-Time Starters—Breeders want their foals born as close to January 1 as possible. One born at the end of April or in May is considered a late foal. On January 1st every horse has a legal birthday. Only three year olds are eligible to compete in the Kentucky Derby, only two year olds in the Champagne Stakes, etc. Therefore, a February foal has more time to grow and mature and develop than a May foal. While it's not at all necessary to find out each horse's actual birthdate, this helps to explain why some horses make their debuts in February, some in March, some in August, etc.

What is important here, is that horses develop at different rates. Horses, like people, reach puberty at different times. Some sires consistently pass this trait on. *The Blood Horse Magazine* lists the leading sires of two year olds and also leading sires of broodmares. These lists may point out first-time starters with a good chance to win. Sires of first-time starters, that produce winners at first asking include Northern Dancer, Never Bend, Mr. Prospector, and Shecky Green.

Note: Another good way to select first time starters is to refer to *The Blood Horse Magazine* supplement which lists all horses sold at public auction and their price tags. Roughly 40% of horses that are registered are sold at these auctions. Horses are listed alphabetically by sires. To research ten or twenty horses takes only a few minutes. Timeless Native sold for $400,000 and appeared at Louisiana Downs for his first start against much weaker competition. He went off at only 4:5 but won easily. In this case, 4:5 was a terrific price. A word of caution—use this supplement as a guide only (i.e., don't make your entire decision based on it). Bargain horses can win the Kentucky Derby, too (e.g. Genuine Risk, a filly, won and previously sold for only $37,000 and Spend A Buck went for just $12,500). There are many such examples. However, there are also many expensive horses that never lived up to their potentials or the expectations of their owners (e.g., Chumming won races but was a disappointment to its connections. He was purchased for $1 million).

Turf Debuts—As mentioned previously, Nijinski II is well noted for passing down a turf ability. The *Daily Racing Form* refers to horses that stamp their offspring with a certain trait (and also have an impact on the industry) as chef-de-races. The general public is often fooled by horses that run poorly on dirt and then make their turf debuts. A trainer might test his "turf horse" on dirt to see if it can run on dirt too, or he might be getting the horse in peak condition on the dirt while building the odds. Other famous sires of grass horses include Prince John, Tom Rolfe, Roberto and Lyphard. There are many others. At your track, the best way to find out is to make a list of sires of winning turf races and see which ones turn up repeatedly.

In 1983, the *Daily Racing Form* published an article about Rose Crescent, by Nijinski II. In it, Mack Miller, who has an excellent reputation with turf performers, explained that Rose Crescent wasn't used to the turf its first time out. (Nijinski II's usually love the turf. The conformation of the hoof is such that these horses can grasp the turf better than other animals. Other horses improve on the turf because they don't like clumps of dirt hitting them in the face or eyes. When put on the turf they improve because there are no flying objects to dodge.) Months later in her last start she improved and ran second in allowance company. Mack Miller said that he expects her to improve and is entering her in a stakes race on the turf because he believes she has a shot for "black type." This is to be her last race. horses that win stakes races have their name printed in bold black letters in breeding-related publications. Winning stakes races makes mares more valuable as broodmares. The general public sees one poor turf performance and a second in cheaper company. Mack Miller says she's still improving and has an honest shot. Smart horse players trust his judgment. The turf came up soft and Rose Crescent won by a literal 20 lengths paying a handsome $17.00! Next time Mack Miller says something, smart horse players will become even smarter by listening and perhaps increasing their bets.

The reader should also note that horses that like one turf course may not like all turf courses. Grass may be cut lower on one course or be more dense. When the course changes from firm to yielding or soft, be careful. Most horses do not have equal success on all three types. Turf horses usually do well on off tracks but speed figures for turf and dirt courses are not interchangeable. Turf distances are only approximate and are hand timed. At some tracks hand time is not very credible. Betting must necessarily be more conservative.

Mudders—In regards to breeding, mudders are very similar to turf horses. Muddy and sloppy tracks occur frequently enough to demand an example. The following is rather obvious, but is used to illustrate a point.

Screen Trend — B. c. 3, by Silent Screen—Falling Evidence, by Prove It — Br.—Rolling Mill Farm (Md) — Tr.—Donato Robert A — 117 — Lifetime 2 1 1 0 $14,760 — 1983 2 1 1 0 $14,760 — 1982 0 M 0 0
Own.—Rafsky J K

3Mar83- 4Aqu fst 6f :23⅘ :47⅘ 1:11⅘ Md Sp Wt 11 1 2½ 1hd 1hd 1nk Beitia E 122 *1.20 88-21 Screen Trend122nk AllOfASudden122⁵⁄₄ ScarletHobeau122³ Driving 11
14Feb83- 4Aqu fst 6f :23 :46⅗ 1:11⅗ Md Sp Wt 12 9 3¹ 2hd 11 2½ Beitia E 122 14.10 85-13 Quati Gold 122½ Screen Trend122¾ AtomSmasher122½ Just failed 14

LATEST WORKOUTS ●Mar 10 Aqu 6f sly 1:11⅘ h (d) ●Feb 25 Aqu 5f fst 1:01⅕ h ●Feb 8 Aqu 4f fst :48⅘ h ●Feb 2 Aqu 5f fst 1:00 h

Screen Trend just broke his maiden and was moved up into an allowance race, the seventh race on March 21, for 3 year olds that have never won a race other than maiden or claiming. Fundamentals, as the reader will soon discover, dictate that horses moving up from maiden to allowance races are playable only if they have the highest speed and pace ratings. Screen Trend did. On a fast track he figured to be even money. But, can he run in the mud?

One quick look at the breeding says definitely, yes. He's by Silent Screen who sires speed horses that perform well in the mud. Additionally, Screen Trend is out of a Prove It mare. Further testimony to his mud running ability is Screen Trend's most recent workout on March 10. Any workout less than 12 seconds a furlong is a good indication of a horse's readiness to win. Longer workouts in superior times are even more positive. This workout of $1{:}11^{2}$ in the slop with the "dogs up" is truly awesome. (Note: "Dogs up"—abbreviated in the *Racing Form* as "(d)", means traffic cones are placed a few feet away from the wet rail forcing horses to go around a wider circumference and therefore, a longer distance.) Speed horses stretch out much better than closers (another fundamental) and front-runners move up on off tracks because the other horses are getting mud kicked in their faces. (The only track where I know this to be an exception is Penn National in Grantsville, Pa., where horses racing just off the pace often win in the slop. To date, no one has given me a satisfactory answer why. As a bettor, I just accept it.)

Screen Trend led all the way and drew off to win by 10. Even money was a terrific price for this horse. Handicapping knowledge—which also includes breeding knowledge—makes Screen Trend a good bet on a sloppy track.

The reader should also know that there are two kinds of sloppy tracks, although the race track and the *Form* do not differentiate. One is really "wet fast." Puddles of water can be seen. However, they really have not sunk deeply into the track surface. The footing underneath the water is firm. This track condition is listed as sloppy.

Once the water does sink in, mud, not muddy water, gets splashed around. This track condition is also called sloppy. Some horses, though, slip and slide on this type of sloppy track. They cannot really grasp it and do not extend themselves fully because they lose their confidence. Most mudders prefer both types of sloppy tracks, but some only one. This type of horse can be invincible on one but poor on the other. A knowledge of breeding will help predict how this minority will perform, but the effort required to gather this particular information is really too much for the casual race goer. At Aqueduct, some horses that have passed on the ability to perform well in the slop include Harvard Man and horses out of Dr. Fager mares and Bagdad mares. Interestingly, Riva Ridge was a terrible mud runner who produced above average mudders.

Distance—Shimatoree and Chinook Pass were bred to be sprinters. Their bloodlines show almost nothing but speed. Others, like Peat Moss are true distance horses and don't wake up in a sprint until after the wire. Sires of horses that do well in sprints include Northern Dancer, Raise a Native, Mr. Prospector, Never Bend and Shecky Green. There are many others and again, the intelligent horse player finds these out at his local track by keeping records of horses that sire successful sprinters. Note too, that this list is similar to those that sire first-time starters that win. This is because most horses make their debuts in sprint races. Good distance sires include Tom Rolfe, Vaguely Nobel, Hail the Pirates and Run The Gauntlet.

Early Speed vs. Closers—Breeding plays an important role in determining whether or not a horse will have blinding speed from the gate or stamina at the end, thus making him a closer. Of course, champions that win the classics may be able to do both. This knowledge is especially helpful in maiden races where most of the horses are first time starters running 5½ furlongs or less.

There are two types of speed horses—those that relax on the lead and those that do not. A relaxed horse can stretch out. The jockey is able to conserve the horse's energy without fighting it. On the other hand, it is easier to predict speed duels with horses that don't relax since the jockeys have no choice but to send their charges to the front. By using a pair of binoculars or watching the replay on track monitors it's fairly simple to determine whether or not the jockey is fighting his mount in order to rate it. This can be very useful knowledge the next time the horse runs. Serious players write this information down in a notebook.

In summary, do not overlook breeding. It can give the handicapper an edge at the betting window.

Horses are Living Creatures

Too many times, horse players forget that statistics in the *Racing Form* are just that—statistics. They forget that a living, dynamic, unique, wonderful athlete is behind all of those numbers. Reading between the lines, figuring out what those numbers on a piece of paper are really trying to say about this animal, is the key to successful handicapping. Always keep this in mind.

Like all athletes, horses are subject to injuries. Statistics indicating that a horse should be 10 lengths better than the field mean nothing if it is hurting. Injuries are discussed in depth in the section concerning the paddock and mentioned here only for the sake of completeness. Some trainers, like Oscar Barrera or Gilbert Puentes, specialize in nursing an injured animal back to the races. Others are very good at training a horse into shape so that it is ready to win at first asking after a long layoff due to an injury. Many longshots are found by knowing who these trainers are. The best way to find out is to list the trainer's name in your notebook each time it happens. Quickly, the pattern will form.

Loose on the Lead—This concept is strongly related to heart. Some horses gain their confidence during the race. They know that they have the track "all to themselves" and feel brave for the stretch run. These animals open up lengths on the field and keep the lead to the wire. However, once looked in the eye by a competitor, they become discouraged. Eileen's Lady is a good example.

Eileen's Lady

Own.—Parks A **118**

Dk. b. or br. f. 4, by Dr Jarrell—Carl's Lady, by Carl's Pro
Br.—Parks John (La) 1983 15 2 3 1 \$14,316
Tr.—Walker Charles W \$8,000 1982 15 4 2 1 \$13,555
Lifetime 30 6 5 2 \$27,871

25Aug83-6LaD	6f	$:22^4$	$:46^2$	$1:12^4$ft	9-5	118	$1^{1\frac{1}{2}}$	1^{hd}	2^{hd}	$2^{1\frac{3}{4}}$	Ardoin R^5	ⒻⓈ 8000	78-23	PcificSpice,Eilen'sLdy,Chngymind	10
10Aug83-2LaD	6f	$:22^4$	$:46^3$	1:14 ft	*$2\frac{3}{4}$	114	$1^{\frac{1}{2}}$	$1^{\frac{1}{2}}$	1^2	1^{hd}	Ardoin R^6	ⒻⓈ 8000	73-27	Eln'sLdy,SstrAnnYong,BrbrsDlght	10
5Aug83-5LaD	6f	:23	$:47^2$	1:14 ft	*8-5	115	$1^{\frac{1}{2}}$	1^1	$2^{1\frac{1}{2}}$	4^4	Ardoin R^2	Ⓕ 8000	69-27	SstrAnnYoung,Dbndy,BoldBobbB.	11
22Jly83-7LaD	6f	$:22^4$	$:47^1$	$1:14^1$sl	21	114	2^{hd}	1^2	1^4	1^5	Holland M A^{11}	Ⓕ 8000	72-33	Eileen'sLdy,Desbrts,BoldBobbieB.	12
13Jly83-2LaD	6f	$:22^3$	$:46^1$	$1:12^4$ft	$6\frac{3}{4}$	114	$4^{1\frac{3}{4}}$	6^8	8^{11}	$9^{9\frac{1}{4}}$	Ardoin R^6	ⒻⓈ 8000	70-23	KrtLdy,SistrAnnYoung,EysonHvn	11
1Jly83-6LaD	6f	:23	$:47^1$	$1:14^1$ft	$3\frac{1}{2}$	114	1^1	2^{hd}	2^{hd}	$2^{\frac{3}{4}}$	Ardoin R^7	Ⓕ 8000	71-25	Knockitout,Eileen'sLdy,SndyHook	12
30May83-2LaD	6f	$:22^3$	$:46^1$	1:12 ft	21	114	$5^{6\frac{1}{2}}$	$5^{7\frac{1}{2}}$	$5^{8\frac{3}{4}}$	$5^{9\frac{1}{2}}$	Frazier R L^5	ⒻⓈ 12500	73-17	Isn'tShePrtty,DibolicHroin,KrtLdy	12
19May83-4LaD	6f	$:23^1$	$:47^4$	1:16 m	11	109^5	$5^{1\frac{3}{4}}$	$4^{4\frac{1}{2}}$	$6^{9\frac{1}{4}}$	$6^{6\frac{3}{4}}$	Nicks R^{11}	ⒻⓈ 12500	56-34	Barme,DnDnRosn,CowboysnIndins	12
5May83-2LaD	6f	$:22^2$	:46	$1:12^3$ft	4	114	2^{hd}	$3^{3\frac{1}{2}}$	6^7	$8^{6\frac{3}{4}}$	Maple S^2	ⒻⓈ 12500	73-23	DbolcHron,Msctogoby,Chngymnd	12
25Apr83-8EvD	5f	$:22^4$	$:47^3$	$1:00^3$ft	24	106^5	2^{hd}	$4^{\frac{3}{4}}$	3^1	5^1	Borel C H^2	Aw6500	87-16	Tangi Girl, Hookin Bull, Wood Gun	8

Placed in a competitive class, \$8,000 claimers, Eileen's Lady wins races while loose on the lead on July 22nd and August 10th. However, on July 1 and August 25, she battles head and head with another horse and can only manage second. In races where she doesn't break well from the outset, Eileen's Lady is up the track. Interestingly, she is also an example of a horse that doesn't "fire" unless she competes for the lead from the gate. This is not uncommon. There are many horses that are never in a race unless they are used early. Eileen's Lady is an extreme example. Admittedly, these are hard to spot. The only way is to read between the lines or to own one like I did.

Understanding the differences between horses will improve your success at the windows. As a further explanation of loose on the lead, I offer this example:

Horse A	1^1	1^2	1^3	1^3	$1^{1/2}$	$:22^3$	$:45^3$	$1:10^4$
Horse B	$1^{1/2}$	1^{hd}	1^{hd}	$1^{1/2}$	1^2	$:22^3$	$:45^3$	$1:10^4$

Horse A was obviously loose on the lead, galloping along as he pleased with no one to pressure him. By the time he came to the top of the stretch Horse A got brave. When pressured he was able to hold the others at bay. On the other hand, Horse B had a much tougher race, although he set the same fractions. Horse B had to overcome energy wasted on anxiety. He could not set his own pace. All other things being equal, he would be a much better bet than Horse A today.

This raises a question often asked. How can a horse lose in a slower time than he won in the week before? Using the earlier example, Horse A went to the quarter in 22^3 and the half in 45^3. Obviously, the second quarter was 23 seconds. Remember that it galloped along as it pleased. That 23 seconds conceivably was split into two equal parts of 11.5 seconds each. Faced with competing against Horse B, this horse probably will be pressured. It may be forced to run the 23 seconds in 10.5 seconds and 12.5 seconds, as Horse B may have been forced to before. The difference in the first part may seem small, only one second, but this is equivalent to approximately 5 lengths! Horse A will have to expend more energy sooner. If he doesn't have the heart that Horse B displayed, he will become discouraged and quit or simply just tire from his early efforts. Remember, last time out, Horse A had a nice lead on the field making the half in 45^3. He may not understand or like another horse looking him in the eye even though he may reach the half in identical time today. Before, he was clearly superior to the field, but today is being forced to run harder just to keep up.

In any race, you must consider the possibility of any speedster, even a cheap one, getting loose on the lead. The sixth race at Penn National on Oct. 29, explains why it is always worth checking out.

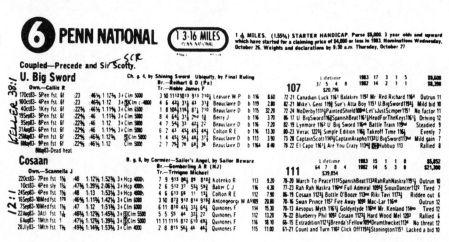

6 PENN NATIONAL — 1 3-16 MILES (PENN NATIONAL)

1 3/16 MILES. (1.55⅗) STARTER HANDICAP. Purse $5,000. 3 year olds and upward which have started for a claiming price of $4,000 or less in 1983. Nominations Wednesday, October 26. Weights and declarations by 9:30 a.m. Thursday, October 27

Coupled—Precede and Sir Scotty. SCR

U. Big Sword — 38:1 KELLER
Own.—Callie R
Ch. g. 4, by Shining Sword—Ubiquity, by Final Ruling
Br.—Reihart G D (Pa)
Tr.—Noble James F
107
Lifetime 37 5 4 8 $20,796 — 1983 17 3 1 5 $9,608 — 1982 14 2 1 1 $8,398

17Oct83- 5Pen	fst	6f	:23	:46⅕	1:12⅗	3↑ Clm 5000	3	10	11^{12}	10^{13}	9^{13}	$7^{10½}$	Leasure W P	b 116	8.60	72-21	Canadian Luck 116^1 Balakiev 119^2 Mr Red Richard 116^4	Outrun 11
10Oct83- 4Pen	fst	6f	:23	:46⅗	1:12	3↑ Ⓢ Clm c-4000	4	6	$4^{2½}$	$3^{1½}$	4^3	$3^{1¾}$	Beauclaire D	b 119	2.80	82-21	Mike's Gent 119¾ Sue's Atta Boy 115^1 U.BigSword$119^{1¾}$	Mild bid 10
4Oct83- 1Key	fst	6f	:22⅗	:46⅕	1:11⅘	3↑ Clm 6500	1	8	$10^{4½}$	$11^{6½}$	$8^{7¼}$	7^{10}	Beauclaire D	b 115	32.20	72-24	NoDerby$111^{5½}$PaintedShield109^{nk}Let'sJustScmper115^1	No factor 11
19Sep83- 9Pen	fst	6f	:22⅘	:46	1:11⅗	3↑ Clm 5000	8	4	$6^{4½}$	$3^{1½}$	2^{hd}	1¾	Berry J	b 116	3.70	86-17	U BigSword116¾SpanishBeat$116^{1½}$HeadForTheKeys$116^{1½}$	Driving 12
9Sep83- 8Pen	fst	6f	:22⅗	:46	1:12	3↑ Clm 5000	4	7	$5^{4½}$	3^3	$4^{2½}$	2^2	Beauclaire D	b 116	7.20	82-19	Lynmore 116^2 U Big Sword 116^{nk} Battle Train 119^{hd}	Steadied 9
31Aug83- 6Pen	fst	6f	:22⅘	:46	1:11⅘	3↑ Clm 5000	6	2	4^3	$4^{5½}$	$4^{5½}$	$4^{4½}$	Colton R E	b 116	13.30	80-23	Virrac $122^{3½}$ Simple Edition 116½ Takeoff Time 116½	Evenly 7
25May83- 4Pen	fst	6f	:22⅘	:46⅗	1:12⅗	Ⓢ Clm 5000	1	4	$4^{5½}$	$5^{6½}$	$4^{8½}$	$3^{7½}$	Beauclaire D	b 113	3.90	73-28	CaptainScott$114^{5½}$CaptainArapho113^2U.BigSword113^{hd}	Mild gain 7
8May83- 9Pen	fst	6f	:22⅘	:46⅕	1:12	Clm 5000	2	7	$7^{5½}$	7^8	$6^{8½}$	3^6	Beauclaire D	b 116^4	8.40	78-22	El Capo $116^{1½}$ Are You Crazy $113^{4½}$ DH Hubbup 113	Rallied 8

8May83-Dead heat

Cosaan — 12:1
Own.—Scannella J
B. g. 8, by Cormier—Sailer's Angel, by Sailor Beware
Br.—Gemberling A R (NJ)
Tr.—Trivigno Michael
111
Lifetime 64 7 8 4 $39,854 — 1983 15 1 1 0 $5,852 — 1982 14 5 3 0 $21,300

22Oct83- 7Pen	fst	1⅛	:48	1:12⅕	1:52⅗	3↑ Hcp 4000s	7	9	9^{13}	$8^{8½}$	8^9	$8^{10¾}$	Kotenko R	113	9.20	78-20	March To Peace111^3SpanishBeat113^3RahRahNaskra$119^{1½}$	Outrun 10
1Oct83- 4Pen	sly	1¼	:47⅗	1:39⅕	2:06⅕	3↑ Hcp 4000s	2	6	5^{12}	3^7	$5^{5½}$	$5^{9¾}$	Baker C J	116	4.30	77-23	Rah Rah Naskra 116^{hd} Full Admiral $109^{5½}$ SiouxDancer112^2	Tired 7
24Sep83- 4Pen	fst	1⅛	:48	1:13	1:53⅕	3↑ Hcp 4000s	4	6	6^{13}	6^8	1^1	$1^{3½}$	Colton R E	112	7.90	86-19	Cosaan $112^{3½}$ Bottle O'Booze 113no Riki Tavi $117^{3½}$	Ridden out 6
16Sep83-10Med	fst	170	:46⅘	1:11⅗	1:42⅕	3↑ Clm 6000	3	10	$8^{7¾}$	9^{10}	8^{14}	$9^{19¾}$	Antongeorgi W A5	109	20.80	70-16	Swan Prince 115^7 Fire Away 109^8 Mac-Lar 116^{nk}	Outrun 12
7Sep83-10Med	fst	1⅛	:47	1:12	1:51⅗	3↑ Clm 6000	6	11	8^{10}	$4^{3½}$	$3^{3½}$	$6^{4½}$	Quinones F	114	15.30	70-13	Aesopus Myth $116^{1½}$ Goldyntyde 116^{hd} Mr. Kenland 114no	Tired 12
22Aug83- 3Atl	fst	1 1/16	:48⅗	1:12⅗	1:45⅗	3↑ Ⓢ Clm 5500	5	5	5^5	4^4	$3^{2½}$	2^2	Quinones F	112	13.20	76-22	Blueberry Phil 109^2 Cosaan $112^{3½}$ Hard Wood Mel 120^3	Rallied 6
6Aug83- 1Mth	fst	1	:47⅕	1:12⅗	1:39⅗	3↑ Ⓢ Clm 5000	11	11	11^{15}	8^{12}	6^{10}	$4^{9½}$	Quinones F	116	18.10	66-15	Extradition$112^{1½}$Brenda'sFellow109^4Drumthwcket113^4	No threat 12
28Jly83- 1Mth	fst	1⅛	:49⅗	1:14⅗	1:53⅗	3↑ Clm 4000	2	8	8^{15}	$5^{6½}$	4^6	$4^{6½}$	Quinones F	115	11.00	61-21	Count and Turn 110^2 Click Off$119^{3½}$Stonington115^1	Lacked a bid 10

Precede * — Dk. b. or br. g. 9, by Limit To Reason—Persian Nell, by Persian Road II

Bury 9:2

Own.—Horn A Plenty Farm — Br.—Hickory Tree Farm (Va) — Tr.—Henry Billy J

107 — Lifetime 109 18 12 14 $102,758 — 1983 1 0 0 0 — 1981 24 6 4 2 $26,187 — Turf 12 0 0 3 $3,509

22Oct83- 9Key fst 1 1/16 :48 1:13⅗ 1:47⅘ 3↑Clm 3500	4 10 1111 1110 109¾ 87¼	Nied J Jr	112	4.70	58-21 ForAPurpose114hd ManAdvantage115hd Inthefstlne1072	No factor	12
31Oct81- 7Pen fst 1¼ :49 1:40 2:07⅘ 3↑Hcp 3500s	7 4 58 67½ 68 65¾	Pacheco D H Jr	121	*2.20	75-25 Fairways Image 112hd Sub Goal 1111½ Sky Speeder 1154	Outrun	7
17Oct81-10Pen fst 1 3/16 :48⅘ 1:13⅘ 1:59⅘ 3↑Hcp 3500s	5 7 66 78½ 78½ 710	Keller R L	123	*1.10	70-17 Nursery Tale 1124½ Promotional 120nk QurantaBay1094	No factor	9
10Oct81- 7Pen fst 1 3/16 :48⅘ 1:40⅗ 1:59⅗ 3↑Hcp 3500s	4 2 21 22 23 21½	Keller R L	124	*1.60	78-17 Promotional 1171½ Precede 1242 Bay View Towers 1131	2nd Best	8
26Sep81- 6Pen fst 1⅛ :47⅘ 1:12⅘ 1:52⅕ 3↑Hcp 3500s	1 5 45½ 44 43 2nk	Keller R L	124	*1.30	91-16 Nursery Tale 111nk Precede 1242 Promotional 1194	Rallied	6
30Aug81-11Del fst 1⅛ :48⅗ 1:12⅘ 1:51 3↑Alw 5000s	1 6 515 616 625 620½	Grove P	122	5.90	61-15 Auguroit 1227 Sub Goal 1175 Purgatory 1123½	Outrun	7
23Aug81- 3Del fst 1 1/16 :46⅗ 1:11 1:45 3↑Alw 5000s	5 5 513 512 521 515	Passmore W J	122	3.80	68-15 Auguroit 1222¾ Water Table 1171½ CounselorCalhoun1176	Outrun	5
15Aug81- 6Pen fst 1¼ :46⅘ 1:38⅗ 2:06⅗ 3↑Hcp 3500s	4 3 314 36 33½ 14	Keller R L	128	*.90	86-21 Precede 1284 Sky Speeder 1082 Granny's Beau 1144½	Drew clear	6

Quathlamba — Ch. g. 7, by His Majesty—Horn Quarter, by First Landing

7:2

Own.—Ruttenberg L — Br.—Smith & Yowell Mmes (Fla) — Tr.—DeMarie Charles A

120 — Lifetime 48 14 7 4 $71,993 — 1983 8 5 0 2 $14,382 — 1982 5 1 0 1 $5,680 — Turf 1 0 0 0

15Oct83- 7Pen fst 1 1/16 :48⅗ 1:14 1:47 3↑Hcp 4000s	7 8 916 913 611 38	Colton R E	b 120	*2.10	63-22 Top Figure 1072½ Spanish Beat 1135½ Quathlamba 120hd	Rallied	9
10Sep83- 6Pen fst 1 3/16 :48⅗ 1:13⅘ 1:59⅘ 3↑Hcp 4000s	7 8 810 815 59½ 36½	Colton R E	b 122	*.80	72-21 Dokimo 1122 Full Admiral 1134½ Quathlamba 1222½	Rallied	8
3Sep83- 7Pen fst 1⅛ :48 1:12⅘ 1:53⅕ 3↑Hcp 4000s	7 6 610 56 1½ 1nk	Colton R E	b 119	*1.20	86-17 Quathlamba 119nk RahRahNaskra1183 SkippingRaccon1141	Driving	7
13Aug83- 7Pen fst 1¼ :47⅗ 1:38⅗ 2:05 3↑Hcp 4000s	5 4 56 2½ 1½ 11½	Colton R E	b 113	*2.80	93-18 Quathlamba1131½ RahRahNskr1162½ He'sJustRight1141	Drew clear	8
30Jly83- 7Pen fst 1¼ :49⅗ 1:41 2:07⅕ 3↑Hcp 4000s	3 5 47 32 1½ 11	Montoya R	b 108	4.20	82-22 Quathlamba 1081 Rah Rah Naskra 1193 He'sJustRight1121	Driving	6
22Jly83- 2Pen fst 170 :47⅗ 1:14 1:45⅕ Clm 3200	4 6 67½ 31 12 13	Aviles R B	b 116	*2.10	74-22 Quathlamba 1163 Defiant Knight 119no SleepingBullet1162	Driving	8
9Jly83- 8Pen fst 170 :47⅗ 1:13⅗ 1:43⅘ Clm 2500	2 10 813 51½ 12 14	Aviles R B	b 116	2.00	81-14 Quathlamba 1164 Tyman 1162½ Kemasabe 111nk	Wide, clear	12
6Jun83- 4Pim fst 1 1/16 :48⅘ 1:14 1:47⅗ Clm c-5000	8 8 815 816 819 824¾	Brown G M7	b 110	6.70	42-20 Port Conway Lane 1152½ Bert F. B. 114½ Gay Bolero1142½	Trailed	8

***March To Peace** — B. g. 5, by Toujours Pret—Expertease, by Armistice

1:1

Own.—Kitsen Alta — Br.—Gelb L M (Ire) — Tr.—Kuhn Marvin H

117 — Lifetime 40 8 2 3 $31,711 — 1983 21 6 2 2 $25,846 — 1982 9 1 0 0 $3,000 — Turf 11 3 0 0 $7,480

22Oct83- 7Pen fst 1⅛ :48 1:12⅕ 1:52⅗ 3↑Hcp 4000s	6 7 78 53½ 1½ 13	Leasure W P	b 111	5.80	89-20 MarchToPeace1113 SpanishBeat1133 RahRahNskr1191½	Drew clear	10
14Oct83- 9Lrl fst 1⅛ :48 1:13⅘ 1:53⅕ 3↑Clm 4000	9 5 512 45 22 2¾	Kupfer T	b 115	3.90	79-28 Run Away Jack 115¾ March To Peace 1153 ShootOut119no	Rallied	11
5Oct83- 2Lrl fst 1 :47⅕ 1:13⅕ 1:39⅘ 3↑Clm 4000	8 4 54½ 22 22 32½	Kupfer T	b 115	4.10	70-19 Shoot Out 1151 Espionage 1081½ March To Peace1151	Weakened	9
22Sep83- 6Atl fst 1⅛ :48⅘ 1:13⅘ 1:53 3↑Clm 9000	6 5 65 54 55½ 59¾	Arroyave R D	b 116	8.60	63-25 Osage Chief 116hd BuddyHasher1162 ElephantBrew1167	No factor	6
13Aug83- 6Atl fst 1 1/16 :47⅗ 1:12⅗ 1:45⅕ 3↑Hcp 6500s	2 6 67½ 67 54 45¼	Arroyave R D	b 114	13.80	74-20 Last Hope 115hd Kiss Chris 1194½ Barefoot Boy 112¾	No mishap	7
30Jly83-10Atl fm 1 3/16 Ⓣ :49⅘ 1:13⅘ 1:58⅗ 3↑Clm 9000	8 8 73½ 63¼ 2hd 11½	Arroyave R D	b 114	13.60	72-18 March To Peace 1141½ Fast Flanker 1163 Fudgsickle122hd	Driving	12
23Jly83- 2Bow fst 1 1/16 :48⅕ 1:13⅗ 1:47 3↑Hcp 5000s	2 4 47½ 712 912 810½	Ruch L D	b 113	36.80	60-22 CallMeMaestro111nk Gambit'sDiscoDoc1201 NativeTour1172½	Tired	10
9Jly83-10Atl fm *1 3/16 Ⓣ 1:59 3↑Clm 6500	4 7 712 59 45 1no	Arroyave R D	b 116	3.70	88-13 March To Peace116no PointPleasant1041 TeepeeChief114½	Driving	10

LATEST WORKOUTS Sep 21 Atl 3f fst :38 b

Cloven — B. g. 4, by Hurok—Clova, by Gustav

Lucero 10:1

Own.—Daniela Stable — Br.—Randolph Theodora A (Va) — Tr.—Lebarron Keith

111 — Lifetime 14 3 3 2 $13,421 — 1983 8 3 1 0 $8,756 — 1982 6 M 2 2 $4,665 — Turf 1 0 1 0 $1,210

16Oct83- 9Pen fst 6f :22⅗ :46 1:11 3↑Clm 7500	2 10 1027 1014 1015 914	Burton J E	b 116	4.00	75-22 Tiaquin1141 MagnaMan1123½ WinnabowBridge1172	Unprepared st.	10
2Oct83- 5Pen gd 6f :23 :47 1:12⅗ 3↑Clm 7500	5 6 41½ 31½ 2½ 1nk	Burton J E	b 114	3.40	82-21 Cloven 114nk Virrac 1153¾ Winging Through 1151	Driving	9
24Sep83- 6Pen fst 6f :22 :45⅕ 1:11 3↑Clm 6250	6 9 44 2½ 3½ 22	Santos M H5	b 110	*2.40	87-19 Copper Reign 1102 Cloven 110½ Really Somebody 1191¼	Gamely	9
18Sep83- 3Pen fst 5f :22 :46 :58⅕ 3↑Clm 10000	1 5 32 42½ 42¼ 43¼	Santos M H5	b 108	6.40	90-17 Gridiron1131½ RoyalRythem1191½ GreatLdy'sMn109¼	Saved ground	6
31Aug83- 7Pen fst 6f :22⅕ :45⅘ 1:11⅗ 3↑Clm 5000	4 6 13 12 14½ 16½	Burton J E	b 116	*2.20	86-23 Cloven 1166½ TennesseePride116hd TheGoldenPlayboy1163	Driving	8
17Aug83- 7Pen fst 1 :48 1:13⅗ 1:41⅕ 3↑Clm 3500	6 1 12 2½ 54½ 67½	Baker C J	b 116	*1.70	68-22 AnotherTrder113¾ PunxsutwneyPhil1161 AlwysPreferred1111	Tired	10
17Jly83- 1Pen fst 6f :22⅗ :46 1:10⅘ Clm 10000	2 8 67 78½ 811 78	Montoya R	b 113	8.20	82-15 [D]HonoredOfficer113no SocillyAcceptd1142 Jd'sAc1132	Broke slow	8
1Jly83- 5Pen fst 6f :22⅗ :45⅗ 1:11⅘ 3↑Md 7000	11 2 13 13 16 14½	Colton R E	b 119	*2.20	85-17 Cloven 1194½ Rosie The Robber 1171½ Jim's First Girl1091½	Easily	12

Full Admiral — B. g. 7, by Full Pocket—Admiral's Dancer, by War Admiral

6:1

Own.—Beam Lisa — Br.—Kitchen E (Ky) — Tr.—Aldoff Marilyn

108 — Lifetime 110 9 13 12 $57,649 — 1983 20 4 4 1 $14,361 — 1982 19 0 1 5 $3,225

15Oct83- 7Pen fst 1 1/16 :48⅗ 1:14 1:47 3↑Hcp 4000s	4 4 22 44 814 813½	Rozell R M	109	4.40	57-22 Top Figure 1072½ Spanish Beat 1135½ Quathlamba 120hd	Tired	9
1Oct83- 4Pen sly 1¼ :47⅗ 1:39⅕ 2:06⅕ 3↑Hcp 4000s	3 1 13½ 12 1½ 2hd	Rozell R M	109	6.70	87-23 RahRahNaskra116hd FullAdmiral1095¾ SiouxDancer1122	Just failed	7
24Sep83- 4Pen fst 1⅛ :48 1:13 1:53⅕ 3↑Hcp 4000s	3 4 42 53½ 56½ 58¾	Lages J A	114	4.90	77-19 Cosaan 1123½ Bottle O'Booze 113no Riki Tavi 1173½	Outrun	6
10Sep83- 6Pen fst 1 3/16 :48⅗ 1:13⅘ 1:59⅘ 3↑Hcp 4000s	2 2 21 2½ 2½ 22	Lages J A	113	9.40	77-21 Dokimo 1122 Full Admiral 1134½ Quathlamba 1222½	Gamely	8
3Sep83- 7Pen fst 1⅛ :48 1:12⅘ 1:53⅕ 3↑Hcp 4000s	5 3 2hd 32½ 78½ 710¾	Rozell R M	b 112	5.50	75-17 Quathlamba 119nk Rah RahNaskra1183 SkippingRaccon1141	Tired	7
20Aug83- 7Pen fst 1½ :48 2:35⅗ 3↑Hcp 4000s	2 1 11 21½ 44½ 32½	Rozell R M	113	3.50	77-19 Evil Manevil 1132 WhatAVictory118½ FullAdmiral1132½	Weakened	8
6Aug83- 7Pen fst 1⅛ :47 1:11⅗ 1:52 3↑Hcp 4000s	1 1 16½ 15 13 13	Rozell R M	108	6.20	92-18 FullAdmiral1083 EvilManevil113¾ CommandPerfection1134	Driving	7
9Jly83- 7Pen fst 1 1/16 :46⅘ 1:11⅘ 1:44⅘ 3↑Hcp 4000s	5 3 35 36½ 59 410	Slaven M	113	5.20	72-14 WhipYourStern1176 MjesticLedr1133 WhtAVictory1201	Weakened	6

This race is a starter handicap. In these races, fundamentals dictate that horses that have won races of this type before do extremely well. Preference is given to the horse that has won most recently. The exception is the horse that qualifies for the conditions of the race (in this case, a horse that has started for a claiming tag of less than $4,000 as far back as January 1) but has recently been beating far better.

In the first case, March To Peace looks obvious. He won his last race in awesome fashion—and has raced twice at today's distance (1 3/16 miles) and won both times, although on the turf.

The horse that qualifies for the second case is Cloven. Throw out his last because he was unprepared for the start. The trainer switches jockeys indicating, most likely, his dissatisfaction with this. Cloven has beaten $7,500 claimers! He drops 3 pounds off that win, while March To Peace picks up 6 pounds off his win. At 1 3/16 miles weight is a definite factor. Most importantly, though, Cloven is the only speed. He could get loose on the lead. This may not be obvious at first, but look at August 31st and July 1st. No one will beat him to the half today. He will very likely be loose on the lead. Read between the lines a little further and throw out his mile race on August 17th, figuring he wasn't right that day. He was laid off for a month, dropped way down, and was nowhere.

Cloven is a question mark at the distance, but he's a speed horse stretching out and should get brave being loose on the lead. Also, he's the class of the race. At 10:1, why not?

Cloven was truly awesome. While loose on the lead he made the half in :47^1 and the three quarters in 1:12^3 and won by 6. He paid $22.80. March To Peace ran second and the exacta paid $77.20.

Maturing Horse—Two and three year old horses are still young, still learning. Some don't begin their careers until three or four. Many times the knees aren't knit together. An experienced trainer or groom can feel an indentation in the horse's knee. With a really valuable animal, no cost is spared and the knees are X-rayed. Patience is a virtue, especially for trainers. Horsemen swear that racing changes a horse. It matures him. Animals that are difficult to handle become more businesslike once at the races. Frequently, a young horse will start once or twice and then be laid off for six months or more. Based on its performance, the trainer decides that it needs more time to develop or that it has potential and should not be rushed. Maybe it needs to put more weight and muscle on. Horse racing history is full of ugly duckling stories. Just like children, horses learn at different rates. Some take to the turf the first time, others do not. Given this background, how can we relate it to betting?

Always look for horses on the improve. Stakes horses do not race as often as claimers and therefore can put in their best effort each race. Claimers race into and out of form. Maidens beginning their careers do not stay the same either. The third race at Aqueduct on March 3 is very typical.

20:1
Kiss Appeal B. f. 3, by Valid Appeal—Kiss of Fire, by Fire N Desire Lifetime 1982 1 M 0 0
Own.—Dawson Kathleen Br.—Dawson Kathleen G (NY) Tr.—Dawson Peter 121 1 0 0 0
15Oct82- 5Aqu fst 7f :23 :46⅗ 1:25⅗ ⓈAlw 24500 2 8 77½ 54 610 715 Fell J 116 30.30 59-26 Reine Prochaine 116 WimborneSky118no Scones116nk Off slowly 8
LATEST WORKOUTS Feb 26 Bel tr.t 4f fst :49⅗ h Feb 20 Bel tr.t 3f fst :37⅗ hg Feb 16 Bel tr.t 4f fst :50⅗ b Feb 10 Bel tr.t 4f fst :48 hg

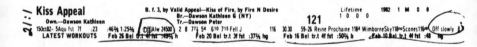

Kiss Appeal broke slowly in its only start Oct. 15. What makes this horse particularly interesting is that its debut was in allowance company—something rare for New York. Peter Dawson saw some potential in Kiss Appeal, but decided it needed some more time to mature. Today it drops down and is 20:1. Its previous potential, coupled with some time to mature and being dropped today, make it a bet. Kiss Appeal won and paid $45.

Fifth Moment
Own.—Benson Farm & Ranch 122
Ch. c. 3, by Fifth Marine—Proudest Moment, by Proudest Roman
Br.—Poirier Jean (Ky)
Tr.—Fox William I
1983 1 1 0 0 $2,160
1982 2 M 0 0 $850
Lifetime 3 1 0 0 $3,010

16Jun83-4JnD 6½f :23[3] :47[4] 1:21 ft *2 120 6[3]¾ 3nk 1[1]½ 1[10] DelahoussayeEP[8] Mdn 80-18 FfthMomnt,ThDvl'sRn,OnWySoth 10
16Jun83—Bumped soundly leaving the gate, and recovered
1Dec82-4FG 6f :22[4] :47[4] 1:14[2]m 22 114[5] 9[6] 8[6]¾ 7[7]½ 4[13] Fox T L[6] Mdn 60-30 StormWrrior,Bidbunch,RomnForc 12
7Oct82-5LaD 6½f :23[1] :47[2] 1:21[2]sy 2¾ 120 10[5]¾ 8[8]¾ 6[9] 5[6]½ Whited D E[4] Mdn 68-26 Alonely Fox,Mr.K.,Newassa'sMisty 12
● Jly 10 LaD 5f ft 1:00 b ● Jun 28 JnD 5f by 1:04 b Jun 3 JnD 5f ft 1:03 b

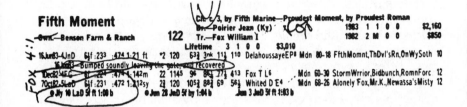

Fifth Moment is a clear example of a maturing horse. Its first start showed support at the windows indicating Fifth Moment had shown ability in training. Given six and a half months to mature, this horse came back on June 16 to win by 10, after being bumped soundly. Note, too, it was the favorite. While it may not be possible for anyone but an insider to know how well Fifth Moment matured this time, the smart horse player uses this knowledge in this horse's next race, July 14th. On July 10th it shows a much-improved workout, indicating its readiness for an even better effort today. Fifth Moment didn't disappoint, winning by 7 and paying an incredible $9.80.

Sour Horses—Put through rigorous training and racing, horses eventually need a vacation in much the same way people do. They need a break. Handicappers, reading between the lines, can see a sour horse tailing off. The trainer, if he's smart, will give the horse a layoff. When turned out in the paddock, the horse may not at first know the reason why. After a few days he understands he is on vacation and begins to enjoy himself by running and rolling in the paddock (a paddock is really any enclosed area) in the pastures. This helps the animal's attitude greatly. Horses that are turned out before they desperately need it will take less time to freshen. When betting an animal coming back from a layoff, those that had had success in the past after a layoff are usually a good risk. Bet them with confidence. They can go off at a price. The only other way to bet one of these horses is by using an expert eye. More on this in the paddock chapter. The vast majority of horses, though, usually need a race or two to get back into top shape.

There is no set time when to lay off a sour horse. The horse tells the trainer by changing its behavior and attitude. Maybe the horse doesn't stand facing the stall door or maybe he doesn't go all out in a race. Sometimes trainers squeeze one last race or two out of a sour horse because of the economics of racing. The horse may be able to manage a second or a third and thus pay some bills, or possibly the meet has only a couple of weeks left. Then the animal can get his vacation.

Horses are more than mere statistics. Trainers know this. Horse players that want to win money must also know it.

Handicapping Techniques

A Few Fundamentals

After exploring a little self-analysis and examining the pari-mutuel concept, looking the track from the inside, and the horse as a unique, individual and a living athlete, we are now ready for the next step: reviewing a few fundamentals. Many of the following are conventional in which most experts seem to concur. Others may be moot, but work for me. In any case, any and all fundamentals should be treated as *guidelines*, NOT rules. There are always exceptions in this business. Fundamentals simply seem to work in the majority of cases. They are listed, not necessarily in order of importance. And they are listed with the hopes that they will turn newcomers into more than novice handicappers, and give the educated fan an additional edge if he is not already familiar with all of them.

1. Each race and each horse is unique and must be treated as such.

2. Don't play horses with unfavorable jockey switches unless the trainer is using the lesser known jockey to get a better price (i.e., the money man).

3. At race tracks where horses regularly work out publicly, only play horses that have recent public workouts (unless the horse drops in class or switches to a top jockey or gives some other indication that the trainer's intentions are positive).

4. Most horses specialize at a particular distance. Speed horses have more success stretching out than do closers. Closers should not be bet when stretching out unless they have been closing exceptionally well in prior races.

5. Most horses, even expensive ones, don't win after a long layoff.

6. Horses stepping down in class, especially claimers, win more than their share of races (statistically speaking). In other words, if 20% of horses step down, but 30% of races won are won by horses that step down, they win more than their statistical share. Claimers that drop down do particularly well at smaller tracks. Those that drop two or more classes there, do even better.

7. Maidens do especially well after running second or third and do even better if they show improved workouts after a race.

8. Don't bet maiden claimers that have lost a maiden claimer before.

DAVIS 9:2

Brightest Hope Ch. c. 3, by Hold Your Peace—Sunny Day III, by Solazo Lifetime 1983 1 M 1 0 $1,870
Own.—Willcox Mrs A A $22,500 Br.—Willcox A (Fla) Tr.—Jackson Evan S 115⁵ 2 0 1 0 $1,870 1982 1 M 0 0
18Feb83- 4Aqu fst 6f ⊡:23⅘ :49 1:15 Md 15000 14 6 42¼ 31½ 1hd 2¾ Molina V H 122 6.60 68-27 Bishen 122¾ Brightest Hope 1221¾ Walkin' On Air 1171¾ Gamely 14
21Aug82- 6Sar fst 6f :23 46⅘ 1:11⅘ Md Sp Wt 2 2 1hd 68 715 710 Miranda J 118 30.20 71-14 Timely Hitter 118¾ Rising Raja 118nk HighHonors1182¾ Brief foot 7
LATEST WORKOUTS Mar 23 Bel tr.t 4f fst :50 b Mar 8 Bel tr.t 3f my :39 b Feb 25 Bel tr.t 3f fst :38⅘ b Feb 16 Bel tr.t 3f fst :37⅘ b

Brightest Hope ran in the fourth race on April Fool's Day. People may be superstitious, but good horse players bet with their heads and throw emotions aside. Brightest Hope is an exception to this guideline. He was beaten by a giant (Bishen won on February 18th and also won its next two). Brightest Hope missed only three quarters from the 14 post after a six month layoff. The jockey switch is also a big plus, signifying the trainer's intentions. Though this horse lost, he is being raised in class because he figures to improve off his tightener (i.e., the first race after the layoff). At 9:2 you can't pass it up. He won and returned $11.20.

9. Don't bet first time starters if any other horse, a previous starter, has shown any significant ability. Lack of experience and the trouble it causes can defeat horses that are green; even the best horses.

10. Trainers have a psychological barrier when their horses carry 120 pounds or more. Don't bet any horse carrying this weight unless the trainer gives some indication that he will go all out today, despite the weight (e.g., the horse has carried the weight successfully before, a good recent workout, etc.).

11. Picking up weight may be significant, but weight shifts are even more important. If a horse picks up 3 pounds it may not matter, but if his rival also drops 7 pounds, that is a 10 pound shift. In other words, weight is relative not only to your horse, but also to its competition.

12. Early speed is usually a tremendous advantage on a sloppy track. (One exception to this is Penn National where horses that race off the pace often do well.)

13. Come-from-behind horses usually win when the turf is soft. The soft turf is tiring and speed is at a disadvantage.

14. The rail may be "dead" after it rains or at any other time for that matter. Horses that have the #1 post may be at a tremendous disadvantage that day, but may come back running like champs the next time.

15. Always check the paddock area and post parade. At large tracks, don't play horses with front bandages. At smaller tracks, many animals run in lower classes because they are hurting. They win there with front bandages often enough to make them bettable, although the bet may be decreased.

16. Claimers don't usually win when moving up to allowance races.

17. Female horses usually don't beat male horses at big tracks. Most female jockeys don't win at big tracks but are playable at smaller ones.

18. Don't play underlays. (This is discussed later.)

19. Most shippers don't win the first time over the track unless shipping in from a nearby track.

20. Horses that don't race soon after they win or horses that drop down after they win are usually not playable. Trainers are anxious to make money when their horses are sharp. If a horse wins and doesn't race, or drops after a win, it is usually because the horse is hurting.

21. Three-year-olds don't beat older horses early in the year and seldom later in the year. At six or seven a horse is old at a large track but not at a small one.

22. Trainers may specialize with particular types of horses (e.g. claimers, turf horses, first time starters).

23. Jockeys may specialize with particular types of horses.

24. Sires pass traits to their offspring (e.g. turf horses, speed horses, etc.).

25. Horses, especially fillies, don't do well after two or three hard races, especially at big tracks.

26. Always read the conditions of the race. Know how to read and interpret the past performances.

27. Speed is favored in a small field. The speed horse, here, can control the pace and/or get loose on the lead.

28. Successful handicapping means putting *all* the pieces together and not letting any one facet alone determine your selection.

29. Winning means considering form, distance, weight, age, sex, speed, pace, class, jockeys, trainers, track conditions, track bias, trip handicapping, reading between the lines, etc., and putting it all together to make the *proper* bet. Betting is 50% of the game and often overlooked.

30. Winning consistently and over the long run is work.

31. Not everyone has the ability, discipline, make-up, etc., to win at the race track.

32. The casual bettor can have as much or more fun as the frequent race goer, but must lower his level of expectation of winning big money. Like anything else, the more hard work you put in, the greater your chances of success.

33. The race track and handicapping and betting should be exciting, challenging and fun. If it isn't, it may not be for you.

An example of putting some fundamentals together is Busy Hilarious who raced on January 3, in the third race.

Busy Hilarious B. h. 5, by Fast Hilarious—Get Busy, by Sadair
Own.—Sabarese T M **$16,000** Br.—Hecht Mary B (Fla) Tr.—Parisella John
1125 Lifetime 28 4 6 3 $56,065 | 1982 18 3 3 2 $38,300 | 1981 9 1 3 1 $17,765 | Turf 1 0 0 0

23Dec82- 1Aqu	fst	6f	⊡:23⅗	:47⅗	1:12⅗	3+ Clm 25000	5	4	4^{2}	$5^{2\frac12}$	$4^{1\frac12}$	$5^{4\frac34}$	Alvarado R Jr[5]	b 112	3.20	76-27	Happy Cannibal $117\frac12$ Psychosis $108\frac12$ SpaceMountain $112^{2\frac34}$	Steadied 6
13Dec82- 5Aqu	fst	6f	⊡:23⅕	:47⅕	1:12⅕	3+ Clm 22500	6	6	4^{7}	$5^{3\frac34}$	$4^{3\frac12}$	$3^{2\frac34}$	Vergara O	b 116	4.80	80-22	Riva's Magic $114^{2\frac34}$ CatchMatthew 110^{hd} BusyHilarious 116^{hd}	Rallied 8
15Oct82- 6Aqu	fst	6f	:22⅘	:46⅕	1:10⅗	3+ Clm 25000	7	5	6^{7}	$6^{7\frac12}$	$6^{5\frac34}$	$6^{4\frac34}$	Velasquez J	b 119	6.00	83-26	Amintore $112^{2\frac12}$ Desperate Journey 117no NoHeir $117^{1\frac12}$	Bumped st. 7
7Oct82- 3Bel	fst	6f	:22⅗	:46⅕	1:12⅕	3+ Clm 20000	8	7	$6^{4\frac34}$	$3^{4\frac12}$	2^{2}	$1^{\frac12}$	Velasquez J	b 117	1.80	81-20	Busy Hilarious $117\frac12$ Moon Glider $117^{4\frac34}$ Port On $117^{3\frac12}$	Driving 9
15Sep82- 2Bel	fst	7f	:23⅗	:46⅕	1:23	3+ Clm 20000	2	3	1^{hd}	1^{hd}	$2^{\frac12}$	$2^{3\frac34}$	Velasquez J	b 117	*2.00	83-14	HppyCnnibl $117^{3\frac34}$ BusyHilrious 117^{4} DesperteJourny 117^{3}	Weakened 8
5Sep82- 1Bel	fst	6f	:23⅕	:46⅗	1:11⅗	3+ Clm 20000	12	9	$4^{\frac34}$	$2^{1\frac12}$	$2^{2\frac12}$	$2^{2\frac34}$	Velasquez J	b 117	9.50	82-18	NonRecours $113^{2\frac34}$ BusyHilrious $117^{3\frac34}$ BigSport 108^{hd}	Best of others 12
11Aug82- 2Sar	fst	1⅛	:47⅕	1:11⅕	1:50⅕	3+ Clm 25000	4	1	$2^{\frac12}$	$3^{2\frac12}$	2^{4}	$5^{8\frac12}$	Fell J	b 117	12.60	75-16	MyFriendWillie $117^{1\frac34}$ Larking'sRun 117^{4} Laddy'sLuck $117^{2\frac34}$	Used up 8
4Aug82- 2Sar	fst	6f	:22⅗	:46	1:10⅘	3+ Clm 25000	2	9	5^{3}	7^{5}	$7^{5\frac12}$	8^{3}	Fell J	b 119	10.10	83-13	HappyCannibal $117\frac34$ Rapido'sRepeat $117\frac12$ CtchMtthew 119no	Outrun 14
10Jly82- 2Bel	fst	6f	:23	:47⅘	1:11⅘	Clm 25000	5	7	$6^{5\frac34}$	$3^{1\frac12}$	$2^{\frac12}$	1^{hd}	Fell J	b 117	8.80	83-20	BusyHilarious 117^{hd} CtchMtthew $117^{2\frac34}$ BigSport 114^{nk}	Wide, driving 8
30Jun82- 2Bel	my	6f	:22⅗	:45⅗	1:09⅘	Clm 35000	9	9	$6^{7\frac34}$	$8^{7\frac12}$	$9^{7\frac12}$	$9^{8\frac12}$	Beitia E	b 119	18.80	85-07	Thunder Bridge 117^{nk} Page Six 117^{1} Jim Balthrop $115^{4\frac12}$	Outrun 9

LATEST WORKOUTS Dec 5 Bel tr.t 4f fst :48 h Nov 26 Bel tr.t 4f fst :47 h

Busy Hilarious—Examples of some fundamentals that make this horse attractive include:

1. Drops

2. Drops to new low class

3. Drops after being steadied (i.e. drops after alibi or other favorable comment)

4. Ridden by hot apprentice

5. Parisella-Sabarese are a winning trainer-owner combination

6. Consistent horse.

7. Coming back into form after its November layoff.

Although only 4:5, Busy Hilarious was at fair odds and a decent bet. It won and paid $3.60. Form horses, those with fundamentals that can predicted, often return low prices because they are obvious to everyone. Reading between the lines can tell the smart bettor which horse is in form and which will go off at reasonable odds. This horse is obvious only to those that put in the extra handicapping effort.

Reading Between The Lines

Fundamentals are not enough. By this time, the reader should be well acquainted with the fact that each horse is unique and each race is a new ball game. Reading between the lines allows the bettor to put it all together, to delve beneath the surface, to look beyond the obvious and to realize larger profits. To some, this means more work. To others, like myself, this is the fun and the challenge of handicapping. Selecting a winner is a tremendous feeling. Picking winners, that your logic justifies, that almost no one else can see, is an even better feeling. Horse players do have egos. There is a certain satisfaction in answering correctly the questions, "Why did the trainer enter this horse in this race?" and "How will this horse perform today under these conditions?" Reading between the lines is the solution. Using it, the winner can be selected at any track, any day, and under any condition.

Here are two more examples to illustrate reading between the lines:

Mr. Tummy Tum — **B. g. 4, by Ruma Tum Tum—Mrs Board, by Ouija Board**

Own.—Cale R — **114** — **Br.—Green Vencil (Okla)** — **Tr.—Broomfield Gerald** — **$7,500**

1983	7	0	0	0	$724
1982	12	2	1	1	$4,171
Lifetime	19	2	1	1	$4,895

ENGLE 6:1

2Sep83-11LaD	1 1/16	:483 1:134 1:47 ft	29	1075	2½	2hd	22½	43¾	Fox W I Jr4	11500	73 —	TrustthTruth,Ywnwnn,DumpTruck	12
18Aug83-2LaD	6½f	:23 :461 1:183ft	70	1095	72	77¼	77¾	54¾	Touchet C7	8000	77-18	AtomicWin,ChecothKing,TierrVrd	10
23Jly83-1LaD	6f	:223 :461 1:13 ft	66	1095	105½	1113	1116	1114	Fox W I Jr1	8000	64-24	NorthTxAvngr,OnBoldScot,Fltmor	12
19Jun83-1LaD	1 1/16	:49 1:15 1:501sl	59	1095	63¾	79½	1116	1233	Fox W I Jr3	9500	28-35	FirstTriumph,Emntor,YoungDriver	12
5Jun83-1LaD	1 1/16	:474 1:131 1:464ft	63	114	103½	116½	1012	1021	DelahoussayeDJ6	9500	57-19	GroovyMovie,G.G.Dcision,SnowSd	12
29May83-1LaD	170	:463 1:122 1:422ft	57	114	1218	1211	1215	1217	Smith R A8	12500	68-14	ShdyCreer,WestIndRef,BucksGlor	12
19May83-7LaD	6½f	:231 :472 1:202sl	46	114	911	1012	813	813	Smith R A1	12500	60-34	HrComsSnt,NoblMomnt,KingOsis	10
11Sep82-8Cen	6f	:222 :462 1:132sl	7¾	120	715	616	620	614	Ford T L5	19000	59-25	Mr.DudlyDorit,PrfctLoom,ChrltAnn	7
14Aug82-7Cen	1	:483 1:154 1:444sl	7	119	513	815	99¾	75	Maxwell J P5	12500	50-32	HghStrkr,MssTudorJo,Mr.DdlyDort	9
31Jly82-8Cen	1	:474 1:134 1:411gd	11	115	610	79	59½	613	Kutz C M1	Aw2900	60-27	NghtHoc,SwngngDncr,Lvughn'sPrd	7

Mr. Tummy Tum is a once-classy horse that looks like he's been hurting. That is, until recently. For some reason, one that only his connections will ever know, on August 18 he woke up and gave notice. He was beaten by only 4 3/4 lengths, after losing by an average of 21 lengths for the four starts before that. The trainer, Gerald Broomfield, sees that Mr. Tummy Tum is feeling good for the first time in quite some time. He raised the horse all the way up to $11,500 claimers where it gets "bet down" to 29:1 and finishes a respectable fourth after showing some speed. Broomfield knows that he was a little too optimistic placing the horse in this race. He is still anxious to get this animal's picture taken (i.e. get him to the winner's circle). That is why he brings Mr. Tummy Tum back to the races on September 5, only three days later! Now he even drops Mr. Tummy Tum into a new low class of $7,500 claimers. Today Broomfield wants to take no chances. He also switches from an apprentice jockey to an experienced one.

Naturally, the bettor does not know for sure if all of the above is correct, but horse players can only form logical opinions from reasonable assumptions. And they are reasonable. They are also insightful. This is reasoning that most players, once they hear it, will agree. This is reading between the lines. It gives the bettor an edge over his competition because they do not do it.

Mr. Tummy Tum won and paid $14.60. Had the crowd reasoned likewise, the payoff would have been much lower.

Here's another:

LUCERO 7:2

Streyen Rythm — Ch. g. 4, by Native Rythm—Always Steyen, by Gay's Pal
Own.—Jenremovic Shetrin — $3,500 — Br.—Shetron Joann (Mass) — Tr.—Lebarron Keith — 122
Lifetime 2 0 0 0 $225 — 1983 1 M 0 0 — 1982 1 M 0 0 $225

27Jly83- 2Pen fst 6f :22 3/5 :46 3/5 1:12 3/5 3+ Md 7500 2 10 10^24 10^33 10^29 10^28 Profis W b 122 *2.90 53-21 Bens Best 115^2 Montrachet122^hd RosieTheRobber117^5 Broke slow 10
30Jly82- 4Suf fst 6f :22 4/5 :46 3/5 1:14 1/5 3+ Md Sp Wt 1 6 57 1/4 55 3/4 5^8 57 1/2 Boudrot D 115 6.30 62-26 DecisiveRulr122^2 1/2 Mr.Bric115^3 It'sFoggy115^1 1/2 Bobbled gate; wide 6

Streyen Rhythm is an interesting horse. He makes his debut in a Maiden Special Weight and is beaten 7 1/2 lengths after having two excuses—bobbling at the gate and being wide. His connections bring him back almost a year later and drop him into a $7,500 maiden claimer. Why did Keith Lebarron, a smart trainer, put him into a claimer and risk losing him? Simple. At small tracks $7,500 plus sales tax is a lot of money. Not many people there will risk this kind of money to buy a horse with only one lifetime start that hasn't raced in a year. Streyen Rhythm is sent off the *favorite* on July 27th and breaks slowly. This was the key. If he was beaten 28 lengths with no excuse, there's no way to bet him. However, after the poor start the jockey didn't push the horse. The good handicapper throws this race out completely. He saves Streyen Rhythm for next time.

Keith Lebarron takes great advantage of Streyen Rhythm's poor-looking performance. He now drops the horse into a $3,500 maiden claimer with not much chance of losing the horse (because it looks so bad). The only question today, September 24th, is the two month layoff. First, it is not unusual to race green horses with a month or so between races. Second, this horse has had trouble from the gate in both starts and the trainer probably needed the time to school it from gate. Betting the ranch on this horse isn't prudent, but Streyen Rhythm has alibis, a new jockey, a new low class, and was made the favorite after missing a year. (Horse players call these types of things "angles"). Additionally, he is 7:2 today—a good price. Streyen Rhythm did not disappoint. He returned $9.00.

Track Bias

"Of course, there are many factors that have a bearing on the outcome of a race, but nothing, repeat nothing, has more influence on a race than an existing track bias. When a track plays in favor of speed horses or for closers, for horses coming off inside posts or outside runners, everything—including class, recency and racing luck—becomes secondary to the bias." (Mike Watchmaker, the *Daily Racing Form*). Track biases demand respect. The stronger the bias the greater its effect on the outcome of the race.

Different race tracks have different biases and the same track can have different biases even on the same day. Winning means correctly evaluating them and estimating how they affect the outcome of the race.

At every track, for whatever reason, speed wins more than its share some days and less others. Most probably the explanation lies in the maintenance of the surface and the weather. The intelligent bettor notices whether front runners or closers are winning on the inside or outside. So many times the rail is dead. The horse looks poor on paper because of this, but comes back winning the next time, and at a price. So it was with Game Wil on Oct. 28:

Game Wil — Ch. g. 6, by Successful Game—Truwil, by John William — Lifetime 63 8 6 8 $26,866 — 1983 13 2 0 1 $3,385 — 1982 18 2 1 3 $5,534
Own.—Arenel Farms — $2,500 — Br.—Ludwig Esther H (Pa) — Tr.—Beneito Marie — 116

14Oct83- 9Pen	fst	6f	:23	:46⅘	1:12⅘	Clm 2500	4	6	2hd	22	35½	37	Fitzgerald R	b 119	10.20	74–22 Runic 1132½ Elmer's Tune 1194½ Game Wil 1191	Weakened	8
3Oct83- 2Pen	fst	5f	:23	:47⅗	1:00⅕	Clm 2500	1	4	52¾	52¼	2½	12	Beauclaire D	b 116	22.60	83–27 Game Wil 1162 Dream of Fire 1163 Joy Hills 116hd	Driving	10
10Sep83- 2Pen	fst	5½f	:22⅖	:46⅘	1:06⅘	Clm 2500	2	5	87¾	65¾	77¾	74¼	Kunitake E	b 114	29.30	80–21 Eagle's Duke 114no General Harper 1161 Tooit 116hd	No factor	8
3Sep83- 2Pen	fst	5½f	:22⅖	:46⅕	1:06	Clm 2500	7	7	98½	913	914	910¼	Bender P H	b 115	8.20	76–17 Made The Cut 116¾ Lucky Ruler 1191½ Sir VivianIvan114½	Outrun	9
10Aug83- 5Pen	fst	6f	:23	:46⅕	1:12⅖	Clm 2500	7	7	2½	2hd	31½	43	Bender P H5	b 109	29.40	79–19 DQBig Ben Bowie 116noPrinceDarlington1162Hotly1191	Weakened	11
1Aug83- 1Pen	gd	6f	:23⅗	:47⅖	1:13⅖	Clm 2500	6	4	43	45	811	711	Wagner B R	b 114	20.00	66–26 Back Poarch 1165 Luz De Oro 116½ Gun Dance 1161	Tired	8
16Jly83- 4Pen	fst	6f	:22⅖	:45⅘	1:11⅕	Clm 2500	6	6	77	69½	611	610	Wagner B R	b 114	47.30	78–13 Oat Duster 115no Quebec Dancer 1132 Lou's Craft 1123	No factor	9
2Jly83- 9Pen	fst	5½f	:22⅗	:46⅗	1:05⅘	Clm 2500	6	7	75¾	77½	87½	87¼	Wagner B R	b 113	23.80	80–16 Shays Dude 1162 Swaps Dawn 113½ Terry The Crow 114nk	Outrun	11

Mario Beneito got this horse going on Oct. 3. In its last race, Oct. 14, it faced a dead rail and "weakened." Throwing out the race with the dead rail, makes it a more than legitimate contender. Game Wil won and paid $33.00.

The most important and frequent biases are the *dead rail* and *inside/outside speed vs. closers*. They offer the big money-making opportunities.

If the rail is dead, it is easy to spot. Horses that win will have raced on the outside of the track. At Aqueduct, it's even easier to spot a dead rail. Just watch Angel Cordero. He's the master of this type of bias. If he's avoiding a certain spot or path on the course, there's a good reason for it.

The analysis of bias can be further divided into sprint and route races. Always look at sprint races only and route races only (and naturally, dirt races only and turf races only). Different parts of the track are not affected the same by the weather.

Some biases don't change. They are physically built in. It is a well known fact that Pimlico has sharp turns. Sharper than its sister track, Laurel. To recognize this is a good beginning, but what are the implications? A front runner from Laurel should improve at Pimlico while one at Pimlico should do worse at Laurel.

By its physical design, Aqueduct gives a horse an extra push past the top of the stretch when the wind is blowing in the right direction. A horse in the lead, at this point in the race, has an added advantage. Others, chasing it, may become discouraged when they see it gain two or three more lengths. Tiring horses may find added courage. If the horse is a pace-setter that tires near the wire, this built-in bias may make it a more solid bet.

When Bowie was open, in the winter months the track became frozen and was listed as such. For some reason, one part of the track by the 2 post was much better than the rest of the course. Horses that reached this point first, usually inside speed, won. Superior handicappers ask themselves, "What does this mean for the next time these horses race?" The winner's efforts must be discounted by some degree. This bias helped the horse look better than it actually was. More importantly, the pros looked for closers with outside post positions, and that ran well (maybe third or fourth), despite fighting the bias. Very often, the general public overlooks these mediocre-looking performances and the horse comes back a winner next time and at a price.

At Santa Anita the inside becomes deep when it rains. Outside horses have a tremendous edge. At Louisiana, when it rains, the track bias usually makes the first mudder out of the gate a winner.

At Aqueduct, during the winter, racing switches to the inner dirt track which has a smaller circumference than the main track. However, the stretch of the inner track is longer than that of the main track!

As mentioned previously, turf courses differ at every race track. The grass is cut differently or may be more dense or absorb moisture more efficiently. Horses may like some turf courses better than others. When in doubt, exercise caution.

Wind and temperature may not really be track biases but seem appropriate here. Wind may favor or hinder front runners. This depends on its direction and severity. If less than 10 or 15 miles per hour, ignore it. As far as temperature goes, suffice it to say that some horses prefer really hot or really cold weather. Get to know these animals.

Track biases are extremely important. They are added tools as you read between the lines. If not at the track, examine the result charts to see if inside or outside horses won and whether or not they were closers or front runners.

Trip Handicapping

When Little Current upset the field in the 1974 Preakness, all of a sudden the experts turned to the films isolating its trip in the Kentucky Derby two weeks before. It was obvious, even to a novice, that Little Current was all over the race track making two or even three moves after being steadied and checked due to traffic problems caused by the large field. Little Current also went on to win the Belmont Stakes, too. To a trip handicapper, Little Current was a stickout in the Preakness.

What is trip handicapping? Simply put, it is looking at each horse from start to finish and seeing how it ran a prior race and what factors affected its performance. How many lengths did bad racing luck cost it? Did the jockey hold the horse under tight restraint and not let it run? Was the pace too fast? Was there a speed duel? What about the effect of track bias? The final step is to attempt to forecast how the same animal will run next time out.

Viewing a race is an art in itself. The beginner watches only his horse. When it is nipped at the wire, only then does he watch the whole race in the re-run. Basketball fans know to watch everyone, not just the guy with the ball. It is the same to a trained bettor. Some watch the rear half of the field during the race with binoculars and then watch the replay on the television monitors at the track to view the half of the field in the lead. TV monitors are usually focussed only on the front half of the field. Others are capable of watching the entire field at once. It takes practice but it is simple enough. (In the press box, news-writers see different views of the race replayed on TV monitors. Included is the break from the gate and a head on view from the top of the stretch. Many races are won and lost at the gate. These are the films the stewards use to judge infractions during the race. Many tracks show these films to the public via TV monitors. They are well worth watching.)

Some happenings, like a slow-breaking animal, are obvious. On May 28th, Crozier's Tea stumbled badly at the break in a stakes race. Trip handicappers would throw out this race entirely. Delhoussaye didn't push Crozier's Tea after the terrible start. Its only other start was a victory (although disqualified from purse money). Note, too, that Crozier's Tea was well backed in her only two starts. Today's fifth race on June 16th, is an allowance race. Although dropping down, Crozier's Tea is still 3:1. Many times the public doesn't excuse a bad trip, although this one is obvious to an extreme. Crozier's Tea proved superior to her competition.

HiETT 3:1

Crozier's Tea — **B. f. 2, by Crozier—Teavoya, by Admirals Voyage**
Br.—Barber J E (Fla) — **1983 2 M 0 0**
Own.—Heubeck Harriett — **108^{5}** — **Tr.—Virgus Tina**
Lifetime 2 0 0 0

28May83-8LaD 5f $:22^{3}$ $:47^{1}$ $1{:}00^{1}$ft $2\frac{1}{2}$ 113 $12^{3\frac{3}{4}}$ $11^{5\frac{3}{4}}$ $8^{7\frac{1}{2}}$ $10^{6\frac{3}{4}}$ DlhssyDJ[1] (F)Swan Isle 83-15 St.Dmien'sStr,Nlet,Luren'sPrincss 14
~~28May83—Stumbled at the start~~
18May83-3LaD $4\frac{1}{2}$f $:22^{4}$ $:46^{4}$ $:53^{3}$ft 3 119 2 1^{hd} 1^{1} $1^{3\frac{1}{2}}$ DelhoussyeDJ[5] (F)Mdn 92-08 Crozr'sT,St.Dmn'sStr,TrplYorMny 12
18May83—Disqualified from purse money
Jun 11 LaD 3f ft $:37^{3}$ b **Jun 2 LaD 5f ft $1{:}05^{2}$ b** **May 18 LaD Tr. $4\frac{1}{2}$f ft :56 bg** **May 3 LaD 3f sy $:35^{3}$ bg**

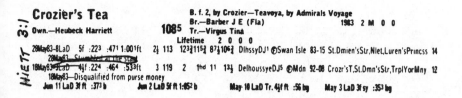

Other things to watch for may be more subtle. Chris McCarron makes reference to watching a jockey's stick (i.e. whip) to see if it is cocked or not. If the jockey takes out the whip to strike the animal and then decides not to, it is important to remember that he still considered hitting the horse. Therefore, the horse did not win as easily as it might have appeared to the untrained observer.

Keep a notebook listing horses in trouble and estimate how many lengths it cost him. The *Racing Form* may say checked, steadied, crowded, bumped, brushed, wide, or dwelt at the start, but it doesn't quantify the severity or impact of bad racing luck or a poorly judged ride.

Before the race goes off, determine how each horse is expected to run (i.e. front runner or closer) and then decide how it will run and watch the outcome.

If a front running horse breaks slow by four lengths and then rushes up to take the lead in 22^3, it actually ran in 21^4! (One length is equal to approximately a fifth of a second.) Any athlete running the first quarter mile too fast won't have anything left at the end. It is the same with a race horse. If this horse was beaten by 10 lengths by breaking slowly, it doesn't necessarily mean it would have been beaten by only 6 lengths normally. Breaking slowly cost it the race. It simply had nothing left at the end. Again, a good trip handicapper, therefore, would throw out this race entirely.

It is not enough to quantify bad racing luck. Here, too, you must read between the lines and analyze the effects of a poor trip on each animal. Getting bumped is one thing, but getting bumped while making a crucial move is another. Some animals have only one big move and getting bumped might cost all the marbles, not just some lengths. Other animals that are checked or steadied simply don't like being jerked around and being told to stop trying. Still others just don't like racing between rivals, regardless of the trip. Some horses are really particular, preferring the inside or outside of the track.

Not all front runners can be rated. They don't know how to relax on the lead. Others that do relax might be rank on a given day and refuse to be rated. The bettor must determine if the jockey is just sitting or pumping his arms, or fighting the horse to go slower. If an animal is one that must go to the lead, what kind of trip will it have today? Are there other such animals in the race? Take a look at the fractions. Did the jockey rate the horse properly?

Probably the easiest to quantify is the horse that races wide. A horse that loses lengths on the turn, can be assumed to have finished closer if it hadn't been wide. This assumption can be made for all horses. When two wide on a turn assume the horse loses two lengths. When three wide, three lengths, etc. In a two-turn race being wide on the first turn is a lot more costly. Turf courses are inside the main track and so the turns are sharper. Most turf races are around two turns and trip handicapping is that much more important. Also, be sure to differentiate between a horse that was forced wide and one that bore out. Horses that bear out are either tired, hurting, or require strong handling because of bad habits (e.g. Marfa). If such a horse shows up with a new rider, a change of equipment or after a layoff, it probably bore out in its last start.

The starting gate and the turns are the key places for the trip handicapper. Most of the problems occur there. Don't just watch for a bad trip, determine how much it cost the horse and be sure to write it all down.

The following are some examples of horses that won after they had bad trips, as indicated in the *Daily Racing Form* trouble line. This comment line is not as good as the *Form*'s charts which provide a more complete explanation, and the charts, in turn, do not compare with personal observation. However, for illustration purposes, examples of trip handicapping that anyone can spot (i.e. using the trouble line in the *Daily Racing Form* or by reading between the lines) are used here.

The first example occurred on April 22 at Aqueduct:

Maybe Morgen — B. f. 3, by Dewan—Pago Dancer, by Pago Pago
Own.—Fried A Jr — $30,000 — Br.—Kilroy & Rogers Jr (Ky) — Tr.—DeStasio Richard T — 119
Lifetime 10 0 0 3 $5,550 — 1983 4 M 0 2 $3,630 — 1982 6 M 0 1 $1,920

23Mar83- 2Aqu fst 7f :22 4/5 :47 1:26 3/5	ⒻMd 25000	2 14 [illegible] 54¾ 37	Velasquez J	b 121	2.60	61-28	BellCrmel121⁵ARreGift117²MybeMorgen121nk	Stumbled st, wide	14
3Mar83- 2Aqu fst 1 1/16 ⊡:48 1:14 1/5 1:48	ⒻMd 35000	6 5 47½ 46 47 59½	Asmussen S M5	b 116	6.10	63-21	CosmicSeaQueen119¾PourL'Oiseau116¾Pentecost1217¾	No threat	12
6Feb83- 4Aqu fst 1 1/16 ⊡:49 1/5 1:15 1:49	ⒻMd 45000	4 6 54½ 44 46½ 33½	Asmussen S M5	b 112	8.90	64-22	Bon Eglogue 121nk Pour L'Oiseau1123½MaybeMorgen1121	Rallied	8
29Jan83- 9Aqu fst 6f ⊡:22 4/5 :47 1:13 1/5	ⒻMd 45000	2 10 76½ 55¼ 53½ 44¾	Asmussen S M5	b 112	16.20	73-20	Real Jenny 1171 PourL'Oiseau1121½MinuteByMinute1172½	Evenly	12
31Dec82- 3Aqu fst 6f ⊡:23 4/5 :48 3/5 1:15 4/5	ⒻMd 35000	5 7 74¾ 79 84¾ 43	Asmussen S M7	b 110	7.30	62-25	ⒹLizzy'sGal1082½Marci'sBnquet117¾CrftySenorit113hd	Carried in	12
31Dec82-Placed third through disqualification									
10Dec82- 4Aqu fst 170 ⊡:49 1/5 1:15 2/5 1:47 3/5	ⒻMd 35000	10 8 56 43 53½ 55¼	Asmussen S M7	b 110	10.50	59-24	Epanoui 113½ First Excuse 1171 Bon Eglogue 113½	Lacked bid	10
28Nov82- 3Aqu fst 7f :23 :46 4/5 1:27 3/5	ⒻMd 35000	12 5 54¾ 31½ 33 43¼	Asmussen S M7	b 110	15.70	60-28	Knotty Blue 113nk Bravest Girl 1123 More Ciao 109hd	Weakened	13
24Sep82- 4Bel fst 6f :22 4/5 :47 3/5 1:13 1/5	ⒻMd 50000	6 9 76¼ 74½ 99 912	MacBeth D	b 117	16.40	64-22	GarrulousGal1173½FirstExcuse1141½GetOffMyCse1171¾	No factor	12
5Sep82- 4Bel fst 6f :23 1/5 :47 4/5 1:13	ⒻMd 65000	2 5 2hd 41 78 714	MacBeth D	117	20.90	63-18	No Limitations 1175¾ Hatch Rose 117hdGetOffMyCase1132½	Tired	11
15Aug82- 6Sar fst 6f :22 2/5 :45 4/5 1:11 3/5	ⒻMd Sp Wt	6 9 810 814 913 1012	Hernandez R	117	28.50	71-11	LadySauceBot117hdSwornSttement117½Melnie'sFlir1173¾	Outrun	14

LATEST WORKOUTS Apr 16 Bel tr.t 5f fst 1:03 2/5 b — Apr 9 Bel tr.t 4f my :47 4/5 h — Mar 20 Bel tr.t 3f my :37 b — Mar 13 Bel tr.t 4f my :49 3/5 b (d)

In its last start, March 23rd, Maybe Morgen shows a major jockey switch. DeStasio showed intentions of an all-out effort. However, as the *Racing Form* indicates, she had a terrible trip, breaking not just last, but 14th, after stumbling and then going wide trying to loop the field. Personal observation would show that it probably cost her more than 7 lengths (the margin at the wire). Lacking that, handicappers can easily notice that today DeStasio raises her in class (and kept Velasquez). This tells the bettor that DeStasio knows how terrible her last trip was. The combination of DeStasio, Velasquez, and her last effort makes Maybe Morgen a bet.

On October 14, Major Tell won paying $17.60 at Penn National:

Major Tell — B. c. 4, by Menocal—Majorette Ki, by Beau Gar
Own.—Ozanne Dorothy — $3,000 — Br.—Heubeck E Jr & Harriet (Fla) — Tr.—Roland Bonnie — 113
Lifetime 41 3 6 5 $28,870 — 1983 11 0 1 0 $2,333 — 1982 25 2 3 5 $20,407

5Oct83- 8Pen	fst $1\frac{1}{16}$	:48 1:13 1:47⅖	3↑Clm 3200	3 7	$6^{4\frac{3}{4}}$ $7^{5\frac{1}{2}}$ 5^{5} $4^{3\frac{1}{4}}$	Roland R R	b 118	17.40	66-24	Oyez $111^{1\frac{1}{2}}$ Roman Spear 116^{nk} Binc $116^{1\frac{3}{4}}$	Poor st.	10
28Sep83- 8Pen	fst 6f	:22⅘ :46⅖ 1:12⅕	3↑Clm 5000	12 2	$8^{6\frac{1}{2}}$ 9^{11} $8^{9\frac{1}{4}}$ $7^{6\frac{1}{4}}$	Roland R R	b 116	59.10	77-25	Takeoff Time 116^{2} Head For The Keys 116no Polaris 116^{3}	Outrun	12
3Sep83- 4Pen	fst 170	:47⅖ 1:13 1:45	Clm c-2500	6 5	4^{5} $5^{5\frac{1}{2}}$ $5^{7\frac{1}{2}}$ $5^{7\frac{1}{2}}$	D'Aleo K	b 116	3.70	67-17	Con Ga Doro 116^{2} Istria's Son $116^{1\frac{1}{2}}$ TheGoodLife$116^{3\frac{3}{4}}$	No factor	9
24Aug83- 9Pen	fst 6f	:22⅘ :46⅗ 1:12	Clm 2500	1 9	9^{13} $8^{9\frac{1}{2}}$ $7^{9\frac{3}{4}}$ $4^{8\frac{1}{2}}$	D'Aleo K	b 116	25.40	75-21	Dark Fate 116^{6} Mukilteo $111^{1\frac{1}{2}}$ It's Saturday Nite 116^{1}	Mild rally	10
16May83- 9Pen	sly 170	:48 1:13⅘ 1:46	Clm 5000	5 6	6^{7} 6^{9} 6^{12} 6^{13}	Burton J E	b 116	10.30	57-36	Sailor's Return $116^{4\frac{1}{2}}$ Whisper A Bit 116^{2} Ablaze $116^{\frac{1}{2}}$	No factor	9
26Mar83- 4Key	fst 7f	:22⅗ :46 1:25⅘	Clm 3500	6 7	$7^{7\frac{1}{2}}$ $10^{7\frac{1}{2}}$ 10^{10} $9^{8\frac{1}{2}}$	Vega A^{5}	b 110	9.90	69-23	Diamond Ace 117^{2} Cavalry Pal 112^{nk} Signal Keys117^{no}	No threat	12
18Mar83- 2Key	sly 1⅛	:48⅘ 1:14⅗ 1:56⅕	Clm 6000	10 7	9^{18} 10^{21} 10^{21} 10^{24}	Pagano S R	b 114	18.20	30-30	Agate Bay $111^{2\frac{1}{2}}$ RoyalTuffie120^{nk}Traveler'sStep$115^{\frac{1}{2}}$	Never close	10
21Feb83- 4Key	fst 170	:47 1:13⅗ 1:45⅘	Clm 8500	4 9	11^{18} 11^{18} 11^{21} 11^{15}	Pagano S R	b 116	7.30	56-30	Statee $116^{\frac{1}{2}}$ Freightliner 120^{2} Saint Paul $109^{1\frac{1}{2}}$	Outrun	11

LATEST WORKOUTS Sep 25 Pen 5f fst 1:01⅗ h

Major Tell is a recent claim. Although only 3 for 41 lifetime it raced against much tougher and seems to be a new horse after the claim. Today it is dropping down after running a respectable fourth last time out despite a poor start. That start probably cost it the race. If it was good enough to be right there with $3,200 claimers it should be even tougher with $3,000 claimers—and it was. Again, the daily race goer is at an advantage. It isn't necessary to guess how many lengths bad luck and poor trips costs. He knows.

On October 23, Cayuga's Water won paying a remarkable $33.00:

Cayuga's Water — Dk. b. or br. g. 6, by Authenticity—Cornell Miss, by [illegible]
Own.—Moran W — $2,500 — Br.—Graham S O (Va) — Tr.—Moran William — 109^{7}
Lifetime 56 9 6 12 $26,837 — 1983 12 4 0 1 $6,524 — 1982 19 2 0 5 $4,758 — Turf 2 0 0 0 $576

9Oct83- 3Pen	fst 6f	:23 :46⅕ 1:12⅕	3↑Clm 2500	5 8	$5^{1\frac{1}{4}}$ 9^{12} 8^{13} 8^{11}	FelicianoBMJr^{7}	b 112	4.70	72-21	Flyin' [illegible] Jupiter 122^{nk} Bridlewood Jim $116^{\frac{1}{2}}$	Hit rail	9
24Sep83- 1Pen	fst 5½f	:22⅕ :46⅘ 1:06	Clm 2500	1 6	3^{2} $3^{2\frac{1}{2}}$ $1^{2\frac{1}{2}}$ $1^{2\frac{1}{4}}$	FelicianoBMJr^{7}	b 109	11.90	86-19	Cayuga's Water $109^{2\frac{1}{4}}$ RedZipMan$119^{1\frac{1}{2}}$Tsh'sSoloTiger [illegible]	Driving	9
18Aug83- 6FL	fst 5½f	:22⅘ :47 1:07⅖	3↑Clm 2000	7 8	$4^{1\frac{3}{4}}$ 4^{3} $5^{6\frac{1}{2}}$ $7^{7\frac{1}{4}}$	Reynolds R L	b 119	6.90	72-24	U. S. Male $122^{\frac{1}{2}}$ Foolish Date 122^{hd} Good Friend Gene$113^{1\frac{1}{2}}$	Tired	11
22Jly83- 3FL	fst 6f	:23⅗ :47⅕ 1:14	3↑Clm 2500	10 4	$3^{\frac{1}{2}}$ 4^{3} 7^{8} 6^{13}	Dosher K	b 122	6.80	66-25	Senator Bill 119^{3} Kingofthefield 122^{4} Twin Fort $116^{1\frac{1}{2}}$	Wide	10
12Jly83- 3FL	fst 5½f	:22⅗ :46⅘ 1:07	3↑Clm 2500	2 4	1^{1} $1^{2\frac{1}{2}}$ 1^{3} 1^{2}	Dosher K	b 122	4.60	81-26	Cayuga's Water 122^{2} Foolish Date 116^{6} Pistol Rod 116^{nk}	Driving	9
11Mar83- 6Tam	fst 6f	:23⅕ :48⅕ 1:15⅕	Clm 3500	4 5	$2^{\frac{1}{2}}$ 2^{hd} $4^{3\frac{1}{2}}$ 5^{5}	Rincon R	b 122	3.40	64-33	MarsLanding$122^{\frac{1}{2}}$Kingofthefield109^{2}ValiantRomn$122^{2\frac{1}{2}}$	Gave way	10
28Feb83- 1Tam	fst 6f	:23 :47 1:14⅘	Clm 2500	4 5	2^{hd} 1^{1} $1^{\frac{1}{2}}$ $1^{2\frac{1}{2}}$	Rincon R	b 119	2.50	72-32	Cayuga's Water $119^{2\frac{1}{2}}$ Pagent Boy 116^{1} Ri Bolero 119^{2}	Driving	7
21Feb83- 10Tam	fst 6f	:22⅘ :47⅕ 1:13⅘	Clm 2500	1 7	$3^{1\frac{1}{2}}$ 2^{1} $1^{\frac{1}{2}}$ $1^{3\frac{1}{2}}$	Rincon R	b 122	4.50	76-27	Cayuga'sWater$122^{3\frac{1}{2}}$BrillintPlesure$122^{\frac{1}{2}}$CoupD'Essi$122^{3\frac{1}{2}}$	Drew off	9

Shipping in from Finger Lakes she wins at almost 12:1. Next time out she goes off approximately 9:2—and hits the rail! This race should be thrown out. William Moran switches riders, indicating he probably wasn't pleased with Cayuga Water's last trip. Throwing out the last race should make the horse 5:1 or so. However, the general public did not read between the lines, although it seems rather obvious here, and sent him off at better than 15:1!

Trip handicapping is yet another piece to the puzzle. It is important to quantify bad luck and poor trips whenever possible. The best way is by viewing the race. The next best thing is checking the results charts, the trouble line in the paper, and reading between the lines.

Adjusted Speed Figures

Adjusted speed figures are probably the most sophisticated and time-consuming technique used to handicap horses. They are recommended to only the very serious bettors. It is entirely possible to win big money without them. Having been weaned on harness racing, I personally think trip handicapping is more important. Adjusted speed figures, though, provide serious players with yet another edge.

Speed figures in the *Daily Racing Form* only indicate how many fifths of a second a horse raced from the track record at the distance. The track's record is assigned "100." For each fifth slower, one point is subtracted from the 100. A horse that runs one second slower is therefore assigned a "speed rating" of 95. The "track variant" indicates how many fifths of a second the average winning horse on that particular day raced slower than the track record. The quality of racing from day to day may vary greatly and therefore, this figure is not as accurate as it might be. It is a relative figure, not an absolute one.

If two horses run six furlongs in 1:12 on the same track on two different days will they run the same time today? Adjusted speed figures may indicate that the track was two-fifths fast on day #1 and three fifths slow on day #2. The times must be adjusted. If the track was two-fifths fast the first day, assume that horse would have run $1{:}12^2$ on a track that was neither fast nor slow. The second horse, likewise, would have run $1{:}11^2$ on a track that was neither fast nor slow. After adjusting these times note that these two horses were really one full second apart—or approximately 5 lengths! Now, how does the horse player know if the track was slow or fast and by how much? Once the meet is open for several weeks there is enough data to calculate these figures (use last year's data, if available, to calculate figures for the first six to eight weeks and then update it after the first two months of racing this year. If last year's figures are not available, adjusted speed figures cannot be used for the first 1 1/2–2 months). To get figures initially is work, but to update these figures daily only takes two or three minutes.

First, find the average time that horses at your track run a particular distance in a particular class. This must be done for *each* class and for *each* distance. Turn to the results of each day and write down the winner's time for each class and each distance on *fast* tracks only, for dirt races only. If horses are close to the winner, it is a good figure. If the winner got loose on the lead or was much superior than its competition (e.g. maybe the trainer was cheating) this figure must be discounted or thrown out entirely. This is subjective, but necessary. This is also the reason why one person's figures can be better than those of another.

If you separate the female and male races you may not have enough data to get a good average. Therefore, in sprints for fillies and mares subtract two-fifths from the winner's time. In routes for only fillies and mares subtract three-fifths from the winner's time. These new figures can then be averaged with the male figures for that class and distance (i.e. $25,000 claimers and $25,000 filly claimers at six furlongs can then be averaged). The same is true for state-breds (i.e. subtract two-fifths for sprints and three-fifths for routes). In sprints for maiden claimers subtract five-fifths of a second from the winner's time, and in routes for maiden claimers subtract seven-fifths from the winner's time. (If a sprint for only female state-breds subtract two-fifths for being a female *and* another two-fifths for being a state-bred.) In this manner you can average a six furlong race for maidens and a six furlong race for state-bred maidens.

After you have written down a couple of months' figures for each class and each distance you can add them together and divide by the total number of figures to get the average time (or expected time) that each winner should run each race at each distance in each class.

Now you are ready to adjust the speed figures for each day (i.e. in the past two months and each day in the future). Compare each sprint race on a given day to the average time and compare each route on the same day to the average time. My little chart looks like this:

Sprint	Route

If the first race is a sprint that went two fifths faster than expected I fill in the chart like this:

Sprint	Route
−2	

If slower than expected a plus sign appears. After nine races let's assume my chart looks like this (I actually abbreviate sprint and route:

S	R
+2	+4
+1	+5
−1	+0
0	
+1	
+1	

The figures are seldom perfect. In this example for sprints, the average variant is a little greater than zero (+2 +1 −1 +0 +1 +1 divided by 6 = +4/6) and so the track was 4/6 fifths slow. Rounding to the nearest fifth means it was one fifth slow or +1. For route races there is one figure out of whack – the +0, so throw it out (but not completely as you will soon see). Average +4 and +5 and get +4 1/2 fifths. This is rounded down to +4 fifths because of the zero. Thus, you have one variant for sprints and another for routes (i.e. +1 and +4, respectively, or +1/+4) which is then written down under the S/R column in the chart on page 95.

Next, we must apply these variants. It's sloppy to write $1{:}11^2$, 1:12, $1{:}13^4$, etc. Therefore, I might arbitrarily assign 1:13 an *adjusted speed figure* of "95". This makes 1:12 (which is 5 fifths faster than 1:13) a "100" and 1:14 a "90" and so on. If the winner goes in $1{:}12^1$ and the track is +1 (i.e. one-fifth slow) give that race a "100" adjusted speed figure (i.e. $1{:}12^1$ = 99 + 1 = 100).

The last problem is to compare figures when horses run different distances. For this I use Andy Beyer's theoretical speed charts. Theoretically, a horse that runs six furlongs around one turn in 1:13 (a "95" rating) should run a mile and a sixteenth in $1{:}47^2$ around two turns. Therefore, a $1{:}47^2$ becomes a "95", a $1{:}47^4$ becomes a "93" and so on.

My average times for each distance and class (and the assigned ratings for winner's times) might look like this for sprint races at Penn National:

Class	**5 f**	**S/F**	**5½F**	**S/F**	**6 f**	**S/F**	**1 Mi**	**S/F**
2,500 (claimers)					1.13	95		
3,125					1.12^4	96		
3,500					$1:12^3$	97		
4,000					$1:12^2$	98		
5,000					$1:12^1$	99		
6,250					1:12	100		
7,500					$1:11^4$	101		
8,000					$1:11^3$	102		
10,000					$1:11^1$	104		
12,500								
15,000					1:11	105		
20,000					$1:10^4$	106		
NW2 (non-winners 2 races)					$1:11^2$	103		
Maiden					$1:12^4$	96		
Maiden Claimers								

Fillies, Mares and State-breds
Subtract from winner's time:
Sprint 2-fifths Route 3-fifths

Maiden Claimers
Subtract from winner's time:
Sprint 5-fifths Route 7-fifths

This tells us that any horse running 6 furlongs in 1:11 is assigned a "105."

Adjusted speed figures for each race are then calculated by taking the winner's time, looking at the previous table for its assigned speed figure, and then adding or subtracting the track variant as applicable.

This all fits into a neat chart as shown on the next page. The numbers on the left side are days of the month and the numbers on top represent race numbers.

For each day and each race you have the winner's figure. Also, include the sprint and route variants (+1/+4), the track bias and any miscellaneous comments that may be important.

When handicapping, notice what day and in what race each horse ran. Turn to your adjusted speed chart and see the figure for the winner. If this horse lost by 4 lengths subtract 4 from the winner's figure. Write this final number in the *Racing Form* next to the horse. Do this for each horse for each race in the past performances that you have figures for.

The next step is to eyeball each horse's speed figures to see if any horse is much superior to its competition (i.e. has a much higher rating —4 or 5 points higher is a good ballpark figure). If so, adjusted speed figures are weighted more heavily in the selection process. Sometimes speed figures will give one contender an edge. They are really useful in understanding how good a horse's race was on an off-track and how many fifths the track was really off. It's difficult to calculate adjusted speed figures for turf races. There just aren't enough of them. Distances are approximated and usually hand timed. Adjusted speed figures really are an edge in handicapping shippers. Many people "make figures" for their local track only. They are at a real loss in quantifying a shipper's performance. This is one reason why some shippers go off at bigger odds than they should.

Race Date	1	2	3	4	5	6	7	8	9	10		S/R	Track Cond.	Track Bias	Misc.
1															
2															
3															
4															
5															
6															
7															
8															
9															
10															
11															
12															
13															
14															
15															
16															
17															
18															
19															
20															
21															
22															
23															
24															
25															
26															
27															
28															
29															
30															
31															

D \ R	1	2	3	4	5	6	7	8	9	10		S/R	Track Cond.	Track Bias	Misc.
1	100	94	105	109	X	91	93	107	105			-2/5	FAST	—	
2	96	95	88	93	88	94	94	104	X			-7/-10	SLOPPY	SPEED	
3	89	92	97	92	95	97	100	97	97			-7/-10	MUDDY	SPEED	
4	102	91	90	86	99	96	103	99	100			-6/-6	WET FAST	SPEED	
5	93	95	X	91	100	97	103	102	91			-2/-5	GOOD	SPEED	
6	88	90	96	91	96	96	99	103	95			-7/-7	MUDDY	SPEED	
7	X	X	X	X	X	X	X	X	X						
8	88	95	94	98	90	96	97	99	93			-2/-2	FAST	SPEED	
9	95	79	93	91	94	95	95	107	X			+9/+4	FAST	—	
10	99	91	90	83	76	100	101	101	87			-2/+1	FAST	—	
11	97	95	93	93	93	92	103	X	95			-2/-1	FAST	—	
12	92	94	89	90	97	95	90	102	91			-1/0	FAST	—	
13	95	87	95	90	101	97	107	98	97			+2/+3	GOOD	—	
14	X	X	X	X	X	X	X	X	X						
15	97	96	86	93	97	79	93	94	88			-2/+3	FAST	—	
16	86	80	94	95	98	95	94	106	94			-2/-2	MUDDY	—	
17	93	82	94	85	93	96	97	100	87			+2/+5	GOOD	—	
18	99	97	96	93	90	101	103	X	91			0/0	GOOD	INSIDE SPEED	
19	101	86	90	89	96	93	88	104	92			0/-2	FAST	INSIDE SPEED	
20	103	87	94	90	94	95	99	103	95			0/0	FAST	—	
21	X	X	X	X	X	X	X	X	X						
22	96	98	93	100	105	90	98	101	92			+1/+3	FAST	—	
23	97	87	85	93	75	96	94	99	85			0/0	FAST	—	
24	86	X	96	76	100	93	95	95	84			0/0	FAST	—	
25	X	X	X	X	X	X	X	X	X						
26	85	95	98	95	104	96	97	111	92			+3/+5	FAST	INSIDE SPEED	
27	98	97	91	90	94	91	96	102	90			0/0	FAST	—	
28	96	103	100	87	91	95	88	100	X			0/0	FAST	—	
29	93	X	92	84	92	91	104	102	92			0/0	FAST	—	
30	96	86	X	97	93	89	96	102	88			0/0	FAST	—	
31	92	95	82	91	88	91	99	X	99			+1/-1	FAST	—	

Adjusted Speed Figures for AQUEDUCT—December, 1982

D \ R	1	2	3	4	5	6	7	8	9	10		S/R	Track Cond.	Track Bias	Misc.
1	X	77	87	87	100	92	97	105	96			+2/+2	FAST	—	
2	95	92	93	X	80	88	95	98	88			0/0	FAST	—	
3	92	92	89	88	92	96	99	101	84			+1/0	FAST	—	
4	X	X	X	X	X	X	X	X	X						
5	87	82	99	84	99	92	96	96	99			-2/0	FAST	—	
6	87	84	95	92	88	90	94	99	X			-6/-4	SLOPPY	SPEED	
7	98	90	92	94	82	86	88	102	99			-9/-5	WET FAST	MOSTLY SPEED	
8	90	84	X	91	100	96	101	102	91			-7/-9	WET FAST	SPEED	
9	103	94	X	90	93	83	94	95	103			-4/-7	FAST	—	
10	93	89	91	86	99	84	98	100	80			-5/-3	FAST	—	
11	X	X	X	X	X	X	X	X	X						
12	104	95	96	86	X	96	108	104	98			0/0	FAST	—	
13	X	96	93	88	100	85	92	97	89			+3/+3	FAST		
14	91	89	92	90	99	94	100	107	X			-4/+2	FAST	OFF PACE	
15		94	100	100	96	91	X	97	93			+2/+2	WET FAST		
16	–	–	X	X	X	X	X	X	X				SLOPPY	CANCELLED CARD	AFTER RACE 2
17	X	X	X	X	X	X	X	X	X					NO RACING	
18	X	X	X	X	X	X	X	X	X					NO RACING	
19	100	83	88	87	92	92	102	91	94			0/0	FAST	CLOSERS	
20	88	84	87	86	87	87	100	99	96			-3/-1	FAST	CLOSERS	
21	X	84	76	88	91	94	105	92	102			-5/-16	FAST	CLOSERS	
22	100	98	101	101	96	106	104	111	93			-9/-9	FROZEN	CLOSERS	TRACK LIGHTENING FAST
23	82	91	92	88	95	95	98	103	96			-8/-6	FROZEN	MOSTLY CLOSERS	
24	91	93	92	89	91	97	97	100	99			-8/-6	SLOPPY	OFF PACE	
25	X	X	X	X	X	X	X	X	X						
26	94	94	90	100	97	91	100	99	90			-5/-5	FAST	—	
27	X	94	88	95	96	91	103	98	91			-5/-6	FAST	CLOSERS	
28	82	94	96	88	92	91	101	82	91			+2/-3	FAST	OFF PACE	
29	X	102	99	95	88	89	106	100	89			-5/-2	FAST	SPEED + OFF PACE	
30	80	90	90	86	96	95	97	105	97			-5/-5	FAST	—	
31	X	97	91	87	101	83	104	94	92			-8/-8	FAST	OFF PACE	

Adjusted Speed Figures for AQUEDUCT—January, 1983

D \ R	1	2	3	4	5	6	7	8	9	10		S/R	Track Cond.	Track Bias	Misc.
1	X	X	X	X	X	X	X	X	X						
2	X	92	96	86	98	102	101	93	96			-2/-1	FAST	CLOSERS	
3	93	82	97	93	104	91	91	X	85			-8/-8	WET FAST	OFF PACE	
4	91	87	94	92	93	98	92	101	89			-4/-2?	FAST	—	
5	105	X	97	97	103	94	91	105	95			0/-2	FAST	—	
6	X	81	92	87	107	96	93	107	X			0/0	FAST	SPEED & OFF PACE	
7	82	94	89	90	94	X	99	106	95			-5/-7	MUDDY	SPEED & OFF PACE	
8	X	X	X	X	X	X	X	X	X						
9	102	89	/	89	91	97	105	102	84			-2/-2	FAST	SPEED	
10	93	81	99	91	95	91	101	98	102			-5/-5	FAST	—	
11	82	88	95	89	—	—	—	—	—			-4/-4?	FAST	SNOW—NO RACING AFTER RACE 4	
12	X	X	X	X	X	X	X	X	X					NO RACING	
13	X	X	X	X	X	X	X	X	X					NO RACING	
14	X	96	99	96	96	101	100	105	93			-6/-6	FAST	MOSTLY CLOSERS	SATURDAY'S CARD
15	X	X	X	X	X	X	X	X	X						
16	92	84	87	91	96	85	99	107	88			-3/-1	FAST	OFF PACE & CLOSERS	
17	93	94	94	89	102	98	107	99	97			-4/0	FAST	MOSTLY CLOSERS	
18	X	X	81	88	91	88	101	107	92			+3/+3	FAST	OFF PACE	
19	96	95	91	94	91	95	X	108	98			0/-6	FAST	—	
20	X	83	92	87	101	94	92	100	X			+1/-1	FAST	CLOSERS	
21	88	93	82	94	94	93	107	111	83			-5/0	FAST	CLOSERS	
22	X	X	X	X	X	X	X	X	X						
23	94	92	98	92	90	79	98	95	87			-4/-1	FAST	OFF PACE	
24	84	92	99	89	103	92	97	101	92			+2/0	FAST	—	
25	X	98	89	89	97	92	94	94	X			0/+3	FAST	—	
26	105	95	92	91	93	98	99	103	98			+4/+2	FAST	MOSTLY CLOSERS	
27	X	82	93	88	104	95	92	104	X			+3/+5	FAST	—	
28	87	79		90	97	92	96	102	96			-3/+3	FAST	SPEED & OFF PACE	

Adjusted Speed Figures for AQUEDUCT—February, 1983

D \ R	1	2	3	4	5	6	7	8	9	10		S/R	Track Cond.	Track Bias	Misc.
1	X	X	X	X	X	X	X	X	X	X					
2	94	88	105	88	96	93	100	101	101	96		+1/+1	FAST	—	
3	X	97	100	98	92	102	X	100	99	100		0/+2	FAST	—	
4	98	96	103	X	99	104	X	101	104	X		-2/-2	FAST	SPEED + OFF PACE	MOSTLY INSIDE POSTS
5	X	95	101	98	X	98	X	97	92	92		+1/0	FAST	—	
6	X	X	X	X	X	X	X	X	X	X					
7	93	93	93	96	96	100	95	94	95	—		+1/-1	FAST	SPEED	
8	X	X	X	X	X	X	X	X	X	X					
9	96	98	97	90	87	98	99	101	95	106		+1/0	FAST	SPEED	
10	97	95	94	102	86	X	102	100	87	87		0/-3	FAST	SPEED + OFF PACE	MOSTLY INSIDE POSTS
11	90	X	94	95	X	105	104	101	96	X		-2/0	FAST	SPEED + OFF PACE	
12	89	96	104	96	98	105	100	103	93	—		+2/0	FAST	SPEED + OFF PACE	MOSTLY INSIDE POSTS
13	X	X	X	X	X	X	X	X	X	X					
14	93	96	94	94	87	87	94	90	101	—		0/+4	FAST	—	
15	X	X	X	X	X	X	X	X	X	X					
16	93	85	97	99	88	99	99	95	95	97		0/+1	FAST	—	
17	99	98	88	98	96	96	X	93	95	96		-2/-2	FAST	—	
18	101	101	103	101	X	X	X	104	98	X		0/0	FAST	—	
19	97	94	100	93	97	105	98	97	102	—		0/+3	FAST	MOSTLY CLOSERS	
20	X	X	X	X	X	X	X	X	X	X					
21	99	86	93	93	95	94	89	99	98	—		0/-6	SLOPPY	OFF PACE SOME SPEED	
22	X	X	X	X	X	X	X	X	X	X					
23	94	88	93	97	99	93	97	91	89	103		+3/+4 1-6th 0/0 7→	FAST	—	
24	97	89	91	X	102	105	X	97	102	89		0/0	FAST	MOSTLY CLOSERS	
25	94	93	103	109	X	106	X	105	101	X		0/0	FAST	CLOSERS	
26	92	94	89	97	94	99	98	94	97	—		-3/-3	FAST	—	
27	X	X	X	X	X	X	X	X	X	X					
28	91	97	84	95	87	90	99	101	96	—		+2/-1	FAST	CLOSERS	MOSTLY INSIDE 6 POST
29	X	X	X	X	X	X	X	X	X	X					
30	87	99	86	99	98	101	104	98	102	94		+3/+2	SLOPPY	CLOSERS	

Adjusted Speed Figures for
PENN NATIONAL—September, 1983

D \ R	1	2	3	4	5	6	7	8	9	10		S/R	Track Cond.	Track Bias	Misc.
1	90	87	103	X	89	97	103	97	94	94		0/+4	SLOPPY	SPEED + OFF PACE	6 POST + IN
2	102	89	97	105	102	100	X	107	97	X		+4/+3	GOOD	MOSTLY CLOSER	
3	94	94	90	97	88	104	96	88	93	—		+4/+3	FAST	—	
4	X	X	X	X	X	X	X	X	X	X					
5	92	88	97	103	93	97	100	98	101	—		+4/+3	FAST	—	
6	X	X	X	X	X	X	X	X	X	X					
7	93	94	100	99	93	94	99	96	97	94		+1/0	FAST	CLOSERS	
8	97	84	84	98	95	94	X	101	97	97		0/0	FAST	CLOSERS	
9	96	90	100	93	X	101	X	97	104	X		+1/-1	FAST	CLOSERS	
10	83	95	90	100	97	100	X	90	97	X		0/0	FAST	CLOSERS	
11	X	X	X	X	X	X	X	X	X	X					
12	94	95	92	82	95	96	96	97	95	—		+5/+6	SLOPPY	CLOSERS	
13	X	X	X	X	X	X	X	X	X	X					
14	96	94	102	101	86	94	98	94	98	91		+1/0	FAST	MOSTLY SPEED	
15	89	93	104	96	84	95	X	105	100	91		+2/+2	FAST	CLOSERS + SPEED, NO OFF PACE	
16	94	98	90	103	95	99	X	100	102	X		-3/-1	FAST	—	
17	92	97	88	99	101	97	103	93	100	—		+3/+6	FAST	SOME CLOSERS	
18	X	X	X	X	X	X	X	X	X	X					
19	91	94	89	87	97	96	96	93	97	—		+3/+3	GOOD	—	
20	X	X	X	X	X	X	X	X	X	X					
21	92	95	100	98	103	92	100	99	98	98		+3/+3	FAST	—	
22	95	87	97	91	89	102	X	101	94	97		-3/0 1-5th +2/0 after	FAST	—	
23	93	91	102	91	94	105	99	99	95	95		0/0	SLOPPY	MOSTLY INSIDE CLOSERS	
24	94	79	95	102	99	100	95	104	95	—		+5/+8	GOOD	SPEED + OFF PACE	
25	X	X	X	X	X	X	X	X	X	X					
26															
27															
28															
29															
30															
31															

Adjusted Speed Figures for PENN NATIONAL—October, 1983

At the Betting Window

Bravo Angus was all over the race track. What terrible luck. Rich and I saw the same thing. We just counted the days until he would race again. When that day came, we decided to make the biggest win bet of our lives. **Bravo Angus** was going off at 9:2—a real overlay. But at the track, our confidence weakened. It was a lot of money for two kids to lose. So we decided to be more conservative and bet to win and place. On this particular Saturday there was a big crowd and Rich and I found ourselves six or eight seats apart. **Bravo Angus** had a perfect trip and won going away! We won! Hundreds. But I wasn't happy. Horse players can sometimes be greedy and this was one of those times. Only a bettor can really understand winning and still being miserable. After all, we waited and waited for this moment. Our original bet was win only. I turned to Rich. Sure enough, there he was, sitting down, his head almost to his knees, shaking. He, also, was upset because we blew the bet. He knew it and so did I, even though we won big!

The most difficult part of winning is betting. The only way to measure success at the race track is by counting the money won. It does us no good to go to the track, pick three, four or even five winners and come home even or a loser. Your wins must at least cover your losses. No one can win every race. The idea is to come out ahead over the long run.

If betting is 50% of the game and so important, why is so little time spent on betting strategy? Most people aren't aware of its importance. Otherwise, they would give it more attention. Others are aware, but don't have the necessary discipline or objectivity to carry out their strategy. While reaching into their wallets, a funny thing happens. Emotion starts to take over. Most horse players really don't decide what to bet or how much to bet until the very last minute. At the windows, they finally decide which horse, how much, and what combinations to play. People can do hours of homework before coming to the track, but once there, want reassurance. They want to know how their friends bet or where the "smart money" is going.

Winning at the races is not an overnight process. It takes time and effort to succeed at anything. Betting is no exception. The examples that follow will help a great deal to improve the reader's betting. Remember, though, once you pass through those gates, things change. Beware! It takes a great deal of discipline and objectivity. Unfortunately, experience becomes the best teacher. With very few exceptions, most successful bettors today, were once terrible bettors. Through losing and hair-pulling they began to recognize the importance of successful wagering. Make a conscious effort to build your gambling skills. Every horse player should strive to become an intelligent bettor.

Probably the most significant change in betting in recent years can be attributed to the exotics—exactas, triples, the pick four, the pick six, etc. The old school of betting suggested win bets only, and that place and show betting was only the inferior handicapper's way to minimize his losses. Now that the bettor has other opportunities (i.e. the exotics), this philosophy is no longer correct. To grind it out, day after day, is very difficult—especially at some smaller tracks where horses don't race to form as often. Many readers have undoubtedly been weaned on the win-only philosophy. The following may seem a bit radical, but it is not. In fact, it is state-of-the-art. *Every* successful professional gambler I know bets with the following attitude:

—Profits and losses are measured over the long run.
—Money won is the measurement of success, not the percentage of winning selections.
—Exotics offer the biggest money making opportunities.

Winning means accepting your losses. People who play the stock market successfully know they can't always purchase only stocks that move up. At some point, they accept their losses and sell. Of course, there are many stock players who can't do this either and end up losers. Still, gambling on horses must be treated like any other investment. You must look at the "risk vs reward" and know you can't win every time.

Measure winning and losing over a longer period of time. Success over a month or an entire meet is more practical (a meet is the length of time the track is open during that season). In this manner, it is easier to accept losing for the day. The bettor is thus able to maintain an objectivity and discipline. A confidence in himself and his abilities, with the knowledge that the breaks will even out, allow him to approach the next visit to the races with a level head and an open mind. This is more than just a statement. It is an overall philosophy. Successful bettors *need* confidence.

Knowing that one big win can more than make up for many losses is vital. It allows bettors to bet more intelligently. They look for the one or two big races that will make them a winner for the month. Most players don't go as often as once a week. However, they can adjust this attitude for their own goals by looking for the race or two that will make them big winners for the day and then bet aggressively. Formerly, the good horse player's goals would be to select 30% to 40% winners—to grind it out. Smart bettors, now, don't care what the percentage is as long as they are making money. Again, be more concerned about your profits than your percentage of winners.

Exotics, bet properly and at the proper times, offer the race goer an opportunity to make big money for a relatively small investment.

An exotic is a type of wagering where the bettor must correctly select more than one horse's order of finish in the same race or in different races. Payoffs in exotics are determined in a similar manner to all other types of wagering. Separate pools are created for each type of exotic and the pari-mutuel concept is applied. For example, the daily double:

> The daily double is picking the winner of two consecutive races—usually races #1 and #2. For instance, let's say horse A wins race #1 and horse G wins race #2.

Total daily double pool	$1000
Total on winning combination (A/G)	$100

Therefore, $1000 – $170 ($1000 × 17% takeout) = $830 – $100 on winning combination = $730; and $730 ÷ 100 = 7.3:1. Therefore, a $2 daily double ticket returns 2 × $7.30 plus the original $2 or $16.60. This is the same calculation for win, place and show. For some exotics (e.g. triples), the takeout is greater (e.g. 25% rather than 17%) than for win, place and show.

Making substantial money playing 2:1 and 3:1 shots to win each day means gambling a lot of money and being right often. The smart player uses that same 3:1 shot as the key horse (i.e., the one used almost always) in exotic wagering. Admittedly, this is frustrating when the 3:1 horse wins, but the exotic bet loses. The bettor sacrifices a few visits to the cashier's window in exchange for larger long-term profits.

Now is the time to learn when to bet, how to bet, and how much to bet.

After finishing handicapping, but before betting, you must decide if you are getting your money's worth—if the return justifies the risk. This means successfully forecasting the odds at which each horse will go off and also determining the odds that are acceptable. This is called "fair odds." With a little experience, it is an easy method to apply. This is, again, judgment, but can be remarkably accurate.

Anything less than fair odds is an *underlay*. Anything more is called an *overlay*. We never, never (almost never) bet underlays—and we love overlays. Again, even though a horse seems best, we incur risk in every race, no matter how slim. The *return* must justify the *risk*. In any race the horse could lose its rider, get hurt, already be hurt and no one knows it, or simply be the victim of a terrible start or poor racing luck. Using judgment, we must estimate its chances relative to its competition. If similar horses in similar situations go off at 2:1 then this horse is a good bet if it is 2:1 or better (maybe even 9:5). Each race is unique and adjustments must be made.

The next skill that must be developed is predicting closing odds at the track. You can wait until the last minute but you never know what the final odds are until you cannot bet any more (a small disadvantage to the pari-mutuel system of wagering). With experience, this, too, comes easily.

Estimates of fair odds change once arriving at the track due to late scratches, jockey switches, over-weights, etc. At small tracks in particular, a jockey switch to the top jockey can really hurt the odds. On the other hand, the top jockey might be so much better than the other rider that he more than makes up for the lower odds. He reduces the risk. Then, the return doesn't have to be as great to justify the bet. Very often, though, the switch results in an underlay. The smart bettor is careful and, again, judges each situation on its own merits.

There is nothing wrong with betting a chalk horse (i.e., a favorite). Countless bettors are never satisfied when the best bet of the day is only 2:1 or 7:5. They have the false impression that no one wins betting chalk. Some other horse has a chance for second, so they couple it with the favorite in the exacta. Naturally, the chalk wins by lengths while the other horse finishes well out of the money, or worse yet, runs third. Instead of making a 200% return on the investment (at 2:1), 100% of the investment is lost.

For the same reason, many times the favorite in the last race of the day goes off at longer odds than normal. Those who are losing for the day want to play catch up. Although they really like the favorite, betting it still means returning home a loser. Well, no one wants to go home a loser, right? Therefore, they force a bet on a longshot or play an otherwise unplayable exacta or triple.

Once the horse is selected and its fair odds are determined, the amount to wager still must be decided. First the individual player must decide on the level of confidence in his selection. if you are 100% confident (which is rare) than bet your *maximum bet* (m.b.).

The maximum bet is a key concept in successful betting. It is an amount each individual must determine for himself based on what he can afford and on his style of play. *Every* bet is based on it. A 100% confidence level means that after considering all of the factors, only the worst racing luck will prevent this horse from winning. Otherwise, it can fall down and still win by 5 lengths. More than one of these a month is rare. If you are 90% sure of winning, bet 90% of your maximum bet. At an 80% level, bet 80% of the maximum bet. Now that you have decided which horse to play and how much to play, you must decide how to divide that money on win, place, show, and/or exotics.

All factors come into play—not only the horse's past performances, the jockey, track condition, and so on. Also, how much sleep you had the night before, how well you are currently doing, and distractions and pressures can play a role too. You should carefully monitor the classes of races, the distances, and the types (i.e. dirt or turf) you do well. At some tracks I do unusually well with maiden races but fail terribly with cheap claimers. Maintenance crews at different tracks vary in adeptness. They can cause variations in the turf course. I stay away from grass races at these tracks. At Louisiana Downs, I do not bet when it rains, unless there is a good mudder who is sure to be first out of the gate. That oval can be three, even four seconds off when it pours. It gets that deep. Adjusted speed figures become meaningless under such circumstances. State-breds are easy for me in some states, but next to impossible in others. You must determine this for yourself and bet accordingly. This is not a quantitative decision. It is more of a calculated gut decision, one that is not difficult with practice. If it is an exacta race, spread your money on the combinations that maximize your chances of winning and maximize your profit. The examples that follow will make this procedure clear.

The odds should be used to assist you in playing "savers"—small secondary bets to break even for the race in case your primary bets lose. This may mean a place bet, reversing exactas, betting second and third choices in an exacta or daily double, etc. Why miss a $14.00 place price because you bet win only and the horse runs second? Sure he could be the best horse, but he may encounter traffic problems. If this animal is not a consistent sort—wins when he is right but is up the track otherwise—a win-only bet may be appropriate. However, if this longshot is fairly consistent and other factors point to its making an all out effort today, a place bet may also be appropriate. Betting a greater percentage of the maximum bet to place is indicated when you believe the favorite won't do better than third. The return will, therefore, be bigger and the risk will be justified. Again, it's risk vs. reward.

In another race, you may like your horse's chances if it doesn't hook up in a speed duel. If you figure there's a 70% chance of this, bet no more than 70% of your maximum bet. To make matters more complicated—if you think two closers are sure to finish first and second, you should also bet 30% of your maximum bet on these two in the exacta (if betting both types of bets will yield a profit that justifies the risk). Furthermore, that 30% must be split according to which closer you prefer. Betting is an art.

Another common situation is playing longshots. If the horse is 7:1 or more and you do not really like anything for second, play the horse straight (i.e. to win). Nobody wants to miss a nice win price only to blow it in the exactas. Sometimes, you may bet 60% or 70% to win, get greedy, and put the other 40% or 30% in exacta combinations. Making this determination before going to the track helps you be more objective.

How does the horse player know when to bet exotics? The casual race goer may be content collecting $2.60 on a show bet, but the serious player wants to make big money. Exotics are usually played whenever they are offered. However different situations require splitting exotic bets differently.

How can you tell if this race is wide open? If the horses haven't run the distance before or haven't run on the turf before, or are shipping in from three or four different tracks, the race is almost always wide open. At the beginning of a meet most races are wide open because horses are coming back after long layoffs, or are first-time starters, or perhaps they are racing over a new track surface. There may be a lot of baby races, (i.e., races for 2 year olds), for horses who have never started before. Cheap claimers at small tracks also make for wide open races (and it may not be certain if these horses are hurting until they race). Races of this type are easy to spot. Finding the winner becomes simply a matter of handicapping expertise, experience and discipline.

(Wide open races also make mechanical and computerized systems less reliable. They rate horses relative to one another. They don't look at the race as a whole. The best horse will not always win. For example, cheap speed might hurt your front runner's chances. But it might not. You must make this determination. That cheap speed might make you decrease your bet, but it doesn't necessarily make the race unplayable.)

Betting the Exotics

Daily Double—If the horse you really like is in the double, play it with the combination you really like in the second part of the double. This is the simplest double to play, because you have a definite opinion in both races. However, if the other half of the double is wide open, it may pay to play the first horse with everything in the other race (i.e., wheel it). In either case, don't play the double if a straight bet on the horse in the first race has a far greater chance of yielding a decent profit. Also, betting the daily double doesn't mean betting the same amount on each double combination. Sometimes splitting the bet between win (and place) and double combinations is more desirable. This may sound vague but will become more concrete in the later examples.

The total amount invested always relates to the maximum bet. If you win the first half of the double, at a price, you must consider backing yourself up by betting those contenders you are concerned about in the second race that are not included in your double combinations. If your original double wins, you lose some money this way. However, bet correctly, you can lock in an almost certain profit by backing yourself up. This depends on your style of play and the specific situation.

Quinellas—This is the best place bet at the track! What does this mean? As mentioned previously, betting a quinella means picking the first and second place finishers but not in the exact order as in the exacta (e.g. if you bet 1–2 and they finish 2–1 you still win). In certain situations, particularly when you think only the favorite can beat you, quinellas become very, very attractive. For example, let's say your horse is 6:1 and the favorite 7:5. If you put 50% of your bet on the 6:1 shot to win and 50% on the quinella combination with both of these horses you are much better off than betting 50% to win and 50% place on the 6:1 horse. Why? The 6:1 shot figures to pay, let's say $4 or $5 to place if the favorite comes in second. But the quinella should pay much more than $5 and maybe even $10 or $12 for the same thing (i.e. the same thing to you). Remember, before the race you considered a place bet because you were worried about the favorite beating you. Thus, in this case, the quinella pays more than place and is a much more attractive bet.

A quinella also becomes attractive when two horses can't be separated in your handicapping, providing they don't kill each other off (e.g., a speed duel) or one doesn't win at the other's expense.

Exactas—At 8:1 or 10:1 it is usually a good idea to play the horse to win only. Why risk a good price horse in the exactas? However, smart bettors who like two or three or even four horses for second, get greedy (and properly so) and bet their longshots in exactas. Suppose this horse is 60% of the M.B., one possible betting scenario is:

30% to win
10% with horse A in exactas
15% with horse B in exactas
5% with horse C in exactas
60% of M.B.

(Note: 10% with horse A in exactas can mean 8% with the long shot first and horse A second in addition to 2% with horse A on top and the longshot for second). Exactas must always be reversed. *Always.* To what extent is the only question. The above is only one possible scenario. It must be determined by the bettor, his selection, and the race.

When betting exactas it is almost always desirable to play some combinations more than others. You may lose the exactas, even though your top choice wins. But in the long run, you will make a much greater amount of money. And yet, exactas may not be for you. Stay with whatever works best for you.

Triples—Sometimes the solid 3:1 shot is in the triple and the race seems wide open for place and show. Basically, there are two intelligent choices here depending on how much you are willing to risk. Personally, I prefer to wheel the 3:1 horse on top of everything else (play all the combinations so that if my horse wins I win the triple). In a ten horse field this costs $144 (nine horses can run second, eight can run third—$9 \times 8 = 72$ combinations at $2 each). Huge payoffs are won in this manner. If a bettor cannot afford to lose that amount of money or simply just doesn't want to risk it, he should bet the 3:1 horse to win.

Sometimes two horses stick out in the triple and can be wheeled with everything for third. In a ten horse field there are eight such combinations ($16) per wheel. If one horse is much better than the other, you can wheel it on top of your second choice and play everything for third. Or you can do that twice and then wheel your second choice on top of your first with everything for third once (as a saver).

Another possible combination is to take your first two choices and play them with two or three other horses for third. One of my favorite bets is to key one horse on top of three others for second and third.

Just like exactas, the total amount bet on the race is a percentage of the maximum bet. This, then, is broken down into appropriate types of wagering and combinations. In triples, there are more possible combinations. These require even more thought than exactas. Each situation is unique.

Pick Six—The only way to hit a pick six is to be very lucky or to have a lot of money and accept a good possibility of losing it. It is usually necessary to find a key horse in each of two or three races and play them with all the horses in the other races. The superior handicapper and money manager with a bankroll may have a fighting chance to win here and win big, but this is a rough game. I don't recommend it as a way to bet for most people. The casual bettor can invest a few bucks to take a shot at winning big money, of course. But the expectations must be realistic.

Betting at small tracks—At these tracks, where pools are small, it is possible to get good prices in the place and show pools—overlays. The amount bet in each pool is publicly displayed on the tote board. With some quick mental calculations or even a calculator, it is possible to find such overlays. In these cases a place or show bet may be justified. They occur at large tracks but not as often and not as big. Be careful when betting exactas and quinellas to be sure you are getting a fair price. The correlation between the odds on the horse in the win pool and that same animal in the exotic pools isn't always as direct. Many times, though, it works to the bettor's advantage. Pick six returns at small tracks can be small (maybe $5000 or $6000 as opposed to possibly $100,000 at large tracks) and, therefore, may not be justified. Again, each situation is unique.

Reading the odds board and stable betting—Some stables, owners and trainers, bet. Others do not. The intelligent player is aware of this and knows the players. They can be found by recognizing patterns. At small tracks, because the pools are small, it is more obvious. If the place price is high compared to the win price it may be an indication that the stable or owner bet the horse big to win. Remember, though, the stable that bets doesn't always win. They lose like everyone else. Some owners bet to pay their bills and most probably lose. Some, however, are successful at betting. Get to know which get the job done at your track. A word of caution here: horsemen, by nature, are an optimistic bunch. They have to be to survive. So much time, effort, and money is spent preparing a horse for a race only to be lost through injury, illness, or poor racing luck. Therefore, in each race more than one, maybe even four or five, trainers think they have a winner.

A horse that is 2:1 when it should be 10:1 can be an excellent bet, if it follows a successful pattern. Maybe a trainer is really sharp at knowing when a hurting animal is right and bets it or tells the owner to bet it. The trainer has done nothing wrong. He's just cashing in on an opportunity after months of losing. The good horse player recognizes this by reading the tote board. Why is this horse 2:1? Betting 100% of the M.B. is not recommended, but using this horse in exactas and triples might be.

When a 2:1 shot is on the board at 4:1, it is usually because the horse is hurting. But the situation that arises most often is the horse that goes off a little less than you thought it might. Maybe it's 9:5 instead of 5:2 or 4:1 instead of 6:1. I especially like cases where I've read between the lines and was convinced the general public didn't catch what I did, but thought it was his connections who bet the horse down. In this case, 4:1 is not an underlay. A situation such as this can change my original estimation of risk and my estimation of fair odds and improve my success at the window.

Putting It All Together

The examples here are used to illustrate betting in the most realistic way, with actual races. The percentage of the maximum bet played in these examples is much higher than is typical because these races were chosen to show the reader how to handicap and bet. Therefore, the winners were especially clear. The more obvious the choice, of course, the greater the percentage of the maximum bet.

Aqueduct is one of the biggest tracks in the country. The quality of racing in New York and California is the best in the country, particularly during the summer months. The Aqueduct races that follow were run mostly during the winter meet. The lowest class run at this time of year is $7,500 claimers. It is a time when many jockeys migrate to the warm weather and many apprentices make their debuts. New Yorkers are sharp handicappers and bettors.

"Form" horses (those that figure to win on paper) don't pay big prices. Many New Yorkers don't like to play shippers believing that other tracks are cheaper and therefore, shippers are not as good. Often, though, they overlook animals that are destroying competition elsewhere. Some shrewd trainers find soft spots and send their horses to New York and trip handicappers often catch longshots here (like every other track). Even if your track is small, it is still a good idea to go through all the Aqueduct examples. The jockeys and trainers may be different but the fundamentals, reading between the lines, and the methods of the money management never change.

9 AQUEDUCT — 6 FURLONGS INNER DIRT TRACK AQUEDUCT (START / FINISH)

6 FURLONGS. (INNER-DIRT). (1.08⅘) CLAIMING. Purse $8,000. 4-year-olds and upward. Weight, 122 lbs. Non-winners of two races since December 1 allowed 3 lbs. Of a race since then, 5 lbs. Claiming price $7,500. (Races when entered to be claimed for $6,500 or less not considered.)

Try Within — Ch. g. 5, by Within Hail—We Try Harder, by Blue Prince — $7,500 — Br.—Bwamazon Farm (Ky) — Tr.—Arnold George R II — 117
Own.—Bwamazon Farm
Lifetime 17 2 2 3 $23,465 | 1982 6 0 1 0 $3,812 | 1981 11 2 1 3 $19,653 | Turf 2 0 0 1 $1,599

McCARRON 6:1

3Nov82- 9CD	gd	1 1/16	:49⅕ 1:14⅖ 1:48⅖	3+ Clm 18000	7 7 811 810 813 65¾	Brumfield D	b 118	15.60	60-26	Magnetizer 1181½ Exraled Spade 114nk On The Charles 116no		8
13Oct82- 8Kee	fst	1⅛	:47⅘ 1:12 1:50⅕	3+ Clm 25000	5 7 79½ 59 713 923	Brumfield D	b 117	6.60	63-16	Buffalo Hart 117½ Sorroto 1175½ Western Buffalo 11710		11
8Sep82- 6AP	fst	1	:45⅗ 1:10⅘ 1:35⅗	3+ Alw 10000	1 6 618 59½ 49½ 28	Romero R P	b 117	9.20	76-22	Hold All Calls 1148 Try Within 1171½ Saabra Chief 112no		6
4Aug82- 6AP	sly	1	:47⅕ 1:12⅗ 1:39⅕	3+ Alw 10000	2 5 54½ 54 55½ 410	Fires E	119	5.60	55-31	Navajo Trail 115no Saabra Chief 1124 Hold All Calls 1126		5
26Jly82- 6AP	fst	1	:46⅗ 1:12⅕ 1:38	3+ Alw 10000	1 6 612 66½ 56 44	Clark K L	119	7.50	67-25	Crown The King 112hd Saabra Chief 1131¾ Navajo Trail 1142½		6
5Jly82- 6AP	fst	1	:46 1:00⅖ 1:35⅗	3+ Alw 10200	4 6 67½ 54½ 45 46¾	Clark K D	119	20.20	76-14	Shambari 1141½ Worldly Wisdom 111½ Navajo Trail 1145		6
3Nov81- 4CD	fst	1 1/16	:48⅘ 1:13⅘ 1:45⅘	Alw 16000	5 8 816 816 89 824	Lively J	115	5.00	55-20	Exactly E. 1124 Clearly Proud 1183 War Marcher 1121½		8
5Sep81- 5AP	gd	7f	:22⅖ :45⅘ 1:25	3+ Alw 10900	8 8 812 810 87 78	Lively J	118	3.90	69-24	Super Ridge 117hd Piasa 118nk Defection 1133		8
25Aug81- 7AP	sly	1	:46⅗ 1:13⅕ 1:40⅖	3+ Alw 11800	3 7 714 712 59 38	Lively J	117	3.80	51-39	Rage's King 1175 Granfalloon 1173 Try Within 1171		7
4Aug81- 8AP	gd	1	:45⅘ 1:11⅗ 1:39⅕	3+ Alw 11100	6 5 56¾ 33 1hd 12	Lively J	114	*1.20	65-27	Try Within 1142 Davey Dandy 1143 Cunning Cregan 112no		6

LATEST WORKOUTS Dec 31 Bel tr.t 4f fst :53 b

Grappa — Ch. g. 5, by Farewell Party—Go Cap, by Groton — $7,500 — Br.—Shosberg Jane M (NY) — Tr.—Daggett Michael H — 117
Own.—Kelley Mrs W A
Lifetime 15 2 1 3 $32,170 | 1982 9 1 1 3 $16,270 | 1981 1 0 0 0 $660

5:1

27Dec82- 2Aqu	fst	6f ⊡	:23⅗ :47⅕ 1:12⅖	3+ Clm 18000	8 9 87½ 912 927 927	Beitia E	b 113	24.00	55-22	Abelardo 117nk Moon Glider 1174½ Psychosis 113no	Outrun	9
3Apr82- 6FL	fst	5f	:23⅖ :48 1:01⅕	3+ Alw 5000	5 7 52¾ 52¾ 52¾ 42	Hanks M	b 119	*2.80	83-20	Satans Legend 117½ Herbobed 110hd Stormy LaCima1101½	Evenly	9
28Mar82- 6FL	gd	4½f	:22⅗ :46⅖ :52⅘	3+ Alw 5000	10 8 75½ 44½ 34	Hanks M	b 119	3.80	92-08	Bum's Rush 1101 Itsabore 1073 Grappa 1192½	Wide,rallied	10
19Mar82- 1Aqu	fst	7f	:23⅕ :47 1:26⅗	3+ Ⓢ Clm 18000	2 5 22 24 45 66	Cordero A Jr	b 117	4.70	62-35	Royal Manner 117½ Zoom Googus 1114 Hudson Ruler 1121	Tired	12
3Mar82- 3Aqu	fst	1 1/16 ⊡	:48⅕ 1:13⅘ 1:47	3+ Ⓢ Clm 19000	1 5 42½ 33 32½ 33¾	Cordero A Jr	119	*2.30	74-16	Hudson Ruler 1122¾ Vin Ce Vin 1171 Grappa 119¾	Bore in turn	11
24Feb82- 5Aqu	fst	6f ⊡	:23⅕ :46⅘ 1:12⅖	Ⓢ Clm 30000	10 3 22 2hd 21½ 31	Cordero A Jr	115	4.00	81-19	All Guns 110nk Vin Ce Vin 115¾ Grappa 115nk	Weakened	14
27Jan82- 3Aqu	fst	6f ⊡	:23⅕ :46⅘ 1:11⅗	Ⓢ Clm 20000	11 6 41½ 22 2hd 11½	Montoya D	118	4.50	87-10	Grappa 1181½ Lady Christina 1071 Smug 1083	Driving	14
20Jan82- 5Aqu	fst	6f ⊡	:23 :46⅗ 1:11	Ⓢ Alw 19000	5 3 22 21½ 25 210	Cordero A Jr	117	3.20	79-15	Onesuch 11710 Grappa 1171¾ Steel Shot 112hd	Best of others	12
3Jan82- 1Aqu	fst	6f ⊡	:23⅗ :47⅗ 1:13⅕	Ⓢ Clm 30000	1 8 52½ 64 62¾ 43¾	Montoya D	113	14.00	74-19	Quiche 119¾ Hudson Ruler 1142¾ Naughty Morty 117nk	Evenly	9
9Feb81- 9Aqu	gd	6f ⊡	:22⅘ :46⅗ 1:11⅗	Clm 16000	11 10 55½ 55½ 46½ 410	McKnight R E	119	7.40	76-17	R. Zweily 1197½ Victory Row 1141 Heljer 1191¾	Wide	11

LATEST WORKOUTS Dec 23 Bel tr.t 5f fst 1:03 b Dec 10 Bel tr.t 6f fst 1:17 b Dec 5 Bel tr.t 6f fst 1:15⅕ h Nov 28 Bel tr.t 6f fst 1:16⅘ b

Handball Kid — Dk. b. or br. c. 4, by Turn and Count—Lost for Words, by Verbatim — $7,500 — Br.—Hancock & Lancaster & Smith (Ky) — Tr.—Sech Steve — 1107
Own.—Jakubovitz J
Lifetime 16 3 1 0 $11,650 | 1982 14 3 1 0 $10,930 | 1981 2 M 0 0 $720

Entered 1Jan83-10 MED

LEASURE 56:1

18Nov82-10Med	fst	170	:47⅗ 1:13⅕ 1:44⅖	Clm 6000	7 11 1116 1020 1119 1023	McKnight R E	b 113	14.70	56-19	Mud 1144 Wheat Grain 1134 Restless Typhoon 115½	Outrun	11
2Nov82-10Med	fst	6f	:22⅖ :46⅕ 1:13	Clm 6000	4 12 1213 1016 1014 87½	McKnight R E	b 113	21.10	71-18	Levitread 115no Blondie Duck 113¾ Wheat Grain 118¾	Outrun	12
19Oct82-10Med	fst	6f	:22⅗ :45⅘ 1:12	Clm 6250	11 8 1112 1017 1119 1017	Alvarado R Jr	b 110	4.40	66-16	Wheat Grain 1102 Levitread 1156 Duke's Imp 115nk	Outrun	12
11Oct82-10Med	fst	6f	:22⅗ :46⅖ 1:12⅗	Clm 8000	8 10 1011 813 69½ 66¾	Melendez J D5	b 110	3.80	73-18	Whisk Away 116¾ Mr.RedRichard1152½LivelyArts1181	Broke in air	10
2Oct82- 2Med	fst	6f	:22⅘ :46⅘ 1:12⅘	Clm 8000	2 9 42 42½ 55 77¾	Pagano S R	b 115	4.50	71-18	Road To Battle 118nk Jet Tex 118¾ Mr. Red Richard 1153¾	Tired	9
23Sep82- 4Med	fst	6f	:22⅘ :46⅘ 1:13⅕	Clm 9000	4 10 76½ 67¾ 25 22½	Alvarado R Jr7	b 106	9.00	74-24	Centumvirate 1182½ Handball Kid 1065 Front 1101	Best of others	12
4Aug82- 2Mth	fst	6f	:22⅖ :45⅕ 1:11⅕	Clm c-14000	2 6 77½ 813 910 710	LizarzburuPM5	b 110	5.30	74-19	Roman Spray 1165 Double Declining 119¾DaddyFrank1073	Outrun	9
23Jly82- 2Mth	fst	6f	:23⅕ :46⅘ 1:12⅘	Clm 12500	8 3 54 52¾ 42 1¾	LizarzburuPM5	b 111	17.50	76-22	Handball Kid 111¾ George The Ruler 119¾BuckDance116½	Driving	8
25Jun82- 1Mth	fst	6f	:22⅗ :46⅕ 1:13	Clm c-6500	4 5 77½ 77 54½ 1¾	Thornburg B	b 119	5.60	75-16	Handball Kid 119¾ Dancers Wine 1111½ Extradition 115½	Driving	7
18Jun82- 3Mth	fst	6f	:22⅘ :46⅘ 1:12⅖	3+ Md 6500	5 3 32 11½ 13 13½	Thornburg B	b 115	9.40	78-16	HandballKid1153½RocklandRascal1221½GlintHenry1154	Drew clear	7

LATEST WORKOUTS Dec 31 Med 3f fst :36 b

Southern Prince — Ch. g. 4, by Prince Dantan—High Beaugard, by Beau Gar — $7,500 — Br.—Iandoli L E (Fla) — Tr.—Krohn Nat — 117
Own.—Krohn Deborah
Lifetime 14 1 1 1 $7,410 | 1982 13 1 1 1 $7,410 | 1981 1 M 0 0

4:1

20Dec82- 9Aqu	fst	6f ⊡	:23 :46⅘ 1:13	Clm 10500	11 2 53½ 65½ 53 52¾	Migliore R	b 113	49.70	76-21	ElevatorShoes105nkComeUpPence1171½Blue'sChoice108nk	Evenly	12
6Dec82- 2Med	fst	6f	:22⅘ :47 1:12⅘	Clm 8000	5 1 21½ 55½ 611 618	Alvarado R Jr5	b 110	9.80	63-23	Barrikated 110½ Blondie Duck 1101½ T. V. Emperor 11510	Tired	7
10Nov82- 9Aqu	fst	7f	:23⅕ :46⅘ 1:25⅕	3+ Clm 10000	8 6 1hd 21½ 1117 1115	McCarron G	b 115	23.40	60-24	Desperate Journey 1124¾ Singing Soldier 117no Sones 113¾	Tired	12
1Nov82- 9Aqu	fst	6f	:22⅘ :46⅕ 1:11⅗	3+ Clm 10000	8 7 73¾ 64 64½ 53½	McCarron G	b 115	26.70	81-23	Untamed 1131 Silver Screen 112hd Judger Verdict 1172	Wide	9
7Oct82- 9Bel	fst	6f	:22⅘ :46⅘ 1:12⅗	Clm 20000	6 10 76¾ 89 89 1011	McCarron G	b 113	44.80	68-20	ChristopherStr1144DoubleAtom117¾RighteousAnger1171½	Outrun	11
19Sep82- 2Bel	fst	6½f	:23⅕ :46⅘ 1:18⅘	Clm 20000	2 7 1hd 32½ 1017 1019	Santagata J10	b 109	32.70	63-20	Castle Gem 1173½ Christopher Star 1073½Blue'sChoice1081½	Tired	11
7Sep82- 4Med	fst	6f	:22⅕ :45⅗ 1:12⅖	Clm 16000	3 5 11½ 2hd 31 87½	LizarzburuPM5	b 110	11.80	74-13	Irish Spots 1151 Tayac 1101½ I'm Pure Gold 115no	Tired	9
26Jly82- 4Del	fst	6f	:21⅘ :45⅖ 1:12	Clm 23500	3 5 21½ 21 54½ 57½	Walford J	b 114	*1.70	73-21	Rahaly 109no Frisky Rigorous 1193½ Trail Talk 1131	No excuse	6
11Jly82- 7Del	fst	6f	:22⅕ :45⅗ 1:10⅘	3+ Alw 8000	3 3 11½ 1½ 22 35	Walford J	b 110	7.30	82-17	GlintSheen1174½LinD.Chrger114½SouthernPrince110no	Weakened	7
3Jly82- 6Del	fst	6f	:22⅖ :46 1:13	Clm 18500	7 2 11 2hd 23 21	Adams J K	116	6.80	75-21	Choptank 1191 Southern Prince 1161½FriskyRigorous1093	Gamely	7

Milliard * — Dk. b. or br. h. 5, by Key To The Mint—Courting Days, by Bold Lad — $7,500 — Br.—Taylor E P (Md) — Tr.—Brice Harold B Jr — 117
Own.—Chem-Dance Stable
Lifetime 17 2 2 1 $15,960 | 1982 12 2 1 0 $13,360 | 1981 4 M 1 1 $2,600 | Turf 1 0 0 0

SANTAGATA 6:1

24Jly82- 3Bel	fst	1	:46⅗ 1:11⅗ 1:36⅗	Clm 12500	2 6 611 712 723 829	Rogers K L	117	44.00	54-16	Motor Cop 1175¾ Marlago 117¾ Roman Chef 1174¾	Outrun	8
17Jly82- 3Bel	fst	1 1/16	:47⅗ 1:12⅘ 1:45⅗	Clm 12500	6 4 73¾ 65½ 610 616	Rogers K L	117	37.80	58-21	OurBoldIntention1107FunnyR.J.1191½Jeff'sChmp117hd	Early foot	8
7Jly82- 3Bel	fst	1⅛	:46⅖ 1:11⅗ 1:50⅘	Clm 12500	1 4 56 69 520 526	Miranda J	117	12.00	47-18	Funny R. J. 1173¾ Sound Decision 1133½ Cerro Indio 1172	Evenly	7
18Jun82- 2Bel	fst	1⅜	:48 1:37⅘ 2:16⅖	3+ Hcp 12500s	7 6 69½ 88½ 717 722	Miranda J	112	17.30	76-15	Two Too Many1175½SpartanMonk1074½UltraSuede1174	No factor	9
23May82- 2Bel	gd	1¼ Ⓣ	:49 1:39⅕ 2:05⅕	3+ Hcp 10000s	9 2 23 811 819 820	Miranda J	112	7.40	48-32	Elito 1082½ Philanthropic 122½ Flying Straight 1112¾	Tired	9
29Apr82- 7Aqu	fst	1⅛	:48⅖ 1:13⅗ 1:52⅕	3+ Alw 20000	8 2 42 53½ 75¾ 76¾	Miranda J	121	38.50	67-22	Khatango 1141½ Desperado 116hd Atop It All 121hd	Tired	8
22Mar82- 8Aqu	fst	1⅛	:49⅕ 1:13⅗ 1:52⅕	Alw 17000	7 3 45 58 614 616	Avalon W A III5	112	37.40	58-33	Lueders 1175½ Lake Carnegie 1175¾ Bid The Limit 1171	Tired	7
4Mar82- 1Aqu	fst	1⅞ ⊡	:49 2:34⅖ 3:00⅕	Hcp 10000s	9 1 1½ 41½ 68½ 616	MacBeth D	112	8.60	85-15	Census 112nk Wimpfybell 1234 Two Too Many 1135½	Tired	9
11Feb82- 6Aqu	fst	1⅝ ⊡	:50⅖ 2:07⅗ 2:47	Hcp 10000s	6 1 2hd 1hd 21½ 26¾	Puckett H	107	16.40	70-17	Wimpfybell 1186¾ Milliard 107¾ L'Arabique 105no	Evenly	8
3Feb82- 2Aqu	sly	1⅛ ⊡	:49⅘ 1:16⅕ 1:58⅘	Clm 10000	9 2 2hd 11½ 13 15¾	Puckett H5	112	18.10	52-37	Milliard 1125¾ Prince Quince 1151½ Worthy of Praise108½	Driving	10

LATEST WORKOUTS Dec 31 Bel tr.t 3f fst :38⅘ b Dec 26 Bel tr.t 6f fst 1:19 b Dec 22 Bel tr.t 7f fst 1:35 b ●Dec 17 Bel tr.t 6f gd 1:15 h

35:1

Pink Monk

Own.—Ginsberg J

Ch. g. 5, by Double Edge Sword—Flamingo Girl, by Red Monk
$7,500 Br.—Alsquith Stable (Md)
Tr.—Bolton Amos E

117 Lifetime 41 5 3 5 $41,946 | 1982 8 0 0 0 $900 | 1981 24 4 3 4 $34,284 | Turf 1 0 0 0

Date-Race	Trk	Cond	Dist	Fractions	Class	PP St 1C 2C Str Fin	Jockey	Wt	Odds	Sp-Var	Top three	Comment
26Dec82- 2Aqu		fst	6f	⊡:23⅖ :47⅘ 1:13⅘	3↑Clm 9000	8 7 42½ 42½ 710 1021	Kaenel J L	b 114	49.40	55-24	Roman Chef 1127 Big Sport 112¾ Ironical 1131¾	Tired 11
17Dec82- 1Aqu		my	6f	⊡:23⅗ :48⅖ 1:13⅘	3↑Clm 9000	1 7 52½ 76¾ 1019 1019	Thibeau R J7	b 106	40.40	56-31	Joan's Poker 1173½ YutzieBoy1172RedRang110no	Showed nothing 11
8Dec82- 3Aqu		fst	6f	⊡:23⅕ :46⅘ 1:12⅘	3↑Clm 9000	12 3 67¼ 811 1216 1316	Thibeau R J7	b 106	8.60f	64-21	Roguish Manner 1131¾ Michael's Edge1174¼YutzieBoy1172¼	Tired 14
20Nov82- 2Aqu		fst	6f	:23 :46⅗ 1:12⅖	3↑Clm 9000	1 13 118½ 1113 1216 1213	Velez R I	b 113	53.00	66-21	Singing Soldier 1171 Yutzie Boy 1172 Omas Josh 1121¾	Far Back 13
25Feb82- 9Aqu		fst	6f	⊡:23⅗ :47⅘ 1:13⅖	Clm 7500	8 5 43½ 32 3nk 42¾	Avalon W AIII5	b 112	3.60	74-20	Saltseller 1172½ Billy Boy D. 112hd Power Master 117nk	Faltered 10
18Feb82- 1Aqu		fst	6f	⊡:23 :47⅕ 1:13	Clm 8000	7 11 1118 1112 76 43½	Avalon W AIII5	b 108	8.10	75-22	Out There 1141¾ Saltseller 108hd Lock The Vault 1081¾	Rallied 12
29Jan82- 2Aqu		fst	1⅟16	⊡:47⅘ 1:13⅖ 1:45⅕	Clm 12500	10 2 2hd 32½ — —	Avalon W AIII5	b 112	9.40	— —	Elegant Disguise 1078½ Plethora 1172 L'Arabique 114½	Eased 12
16Jan82- 3Aqu		fst	6f	⊡:22⅕ :45 1:10⅕	Clm 15000	3 10 96½ 77¼ 86¼ 86¼	Gomez E R5	b 110	17.70	86-10	Jeffery C. 1122½ Greville 117nk Key Measurements 117no	Outrun 11
9Dec81- 3Aqu		gd	6f	⊡:23 :47 1:13	Clm c-16000	4 4 1½ 2½ 2½ 32¾	Cordero A Jr	b 117	*2.40	76-17	Cordial Welcome 1172 Residuary 115¾ Pink Monk1171	Weakened 7
23Nov81- 7Lrl		fst	6f	:22⅗ :47 1:12	Clm 20000	5 10 76½ 56 36½ 312	Kaenel J L	b 114	4.20e	71-28	Rowdy Rudy 1139 Hard Hit 1163 Pink Monk 1141½	Bid, tired 12

LATEST WORKOUTS Dec 5 Bel tr.t 4f fst :49 h Nov 17 Bel tr.t 4f fst :50⅗ b

14:1

Upper Tier

Own.—Pulvino T

B. h. 5, by High Echelon—Song Of Tara, by Menetrier
$7,500 Br.—Farnsworth Farm (Fla)
Tr.—Wright Floyd

117 Lifetime 15 4 1 1 $11,084 | 1982 15 4 1 1 $11,084 | 1981 0 M 0 0

Date-Race	Trk	Cond	Dist	Fractions	Class	PP St 1C 2C Str Fin	Jockey	Wt	Odds	Sp-Var	Top three	Comment
26Dec82- 2Aqu		fst	6f	⊡:23⅖ :47⅘ 1:13⅘	3↑Clm 9000	3 9 64¾ 64½ 45½ 49½	Faine C	b 11?	13.50	66-24	Roman Chef 1127 Big Sport 112¾ Ironical 1131¾	No threat 11
17Dec82- 1Aqu		my	6f	⊡:23⅗ :48⅖ 1:13⅘	3↑Clm 10000	8 9 63 63¾ 65½ 66	Faine C	b 117	25.20	69-31	Joan's Poker 1173½ Yutzie Boy 1172 Red Rang 110no	Lckd ltrally 11
28Nov82- 6Pen		fst	6f	:22⅖ :45 1:09⅗	3↑Clm 10000	3 5 52¾ 59 611 69½	Markgraf R A7	b 108	24.40	86-14	Native Cup 1154½ Inkolater 1103 Precious Pacha 1151	No threat 7
14Nov82- 4Pen		fst	5f	:21⅘ :45 :58⅖	3↑Clm 10000	1 7 711 713 714 715	Faine C	b 113	27.30	77-16	Musical Mickey 1163½AttaBoyPres1131½HarveyKeck1141¾	Trailed 7
25Jly82- 8FL		fst	1	:47⅘ 1:12⅖ 1:40⅖	3↑Alw 6000	9 5 45½ 35 36½ 712	Faine C	b 119	6.30	71-22	Cross His Heart1167Michael'sMoment113hdJohn'sSlash108½	Tired 9
16Jly82- 8FL		fst	6f	:22⅘ :46⅗ 1:12⅕	3↑Alw 5700	1 9 64½ 42 21½ 1½	Faine C	b 113	21.10	88-26	Upper Tier 113½ Native Flanker 1132 Mighty Peter 1121½	Driving 9
30Jun82- 7FL		fst	6f	:22⅘ :46⅘ 1:13⅕	3↑Alw 5400	1 7 42½ 42½ 3½ 2½	Faine C	b 113	17.80	82-26	Mighty Peter 112½ Upper Tier 1131Michael'sMoment1131	Bore in 8
16Jun82- 8FL		fst	6f	:22⅕ :45⅖ 1:11⅗	3↑Clm 8000	6 6 45 43 31½ 54	Faine C	b 111	25.40	87-17	Native Flanker 1132Pogo'sSong1101MontanaEagle118½	Gave way 7
19May82- 8FL		gd	1	:47⅘ 1:13⅘ 1:41⅘	3↑Clm c-6250	3 6 55½ 34½ 713 724	Kisielewski S	b 122	5.60	52-21	Ha'Penny Moon1131½KingdomKirk1193Lloyd'sCall1192½	Bore out 7
9May82- 5FL		gd	5½f	:23⅘ :48⅗ 1:08⅕	3↑Clm 5000	4 3 52¾ 31 1hd 1¾	Kisielewski S	119	2.60	81-28	Upper Tier 119¾ Karen's Prince 1094 Gallant Joy 1221½	Driving 6

LATEST WORKOUTS ●Nov 22 Pen 4f sly :49⅘ h

MELENDEZ 15:1

Russell Sprout

Own.—Shapiro T

Dk. b. or br. g. 4, by Illustrious—Navy Band, by Sailor's Guide
$7,500 Br.—Russell C (Va)
Tr.—DeBonis Robert

112⁵ Lifetime 15 1 3 2 $4,900 | 1982 13 1 3 2 $4,900 | 1981 2 M 0 0

Date-Race	Trk	Cond	Dist	Fractions	Class	PP St 1C 2C Str Fin	Jockey	Wt	Odds	Sp-Var	Top three	Comment
14Dec82-10Med		fst	6f	:22⅗ :45⅘ 1:12	Clm 9000	8 7 74¾ 76½ 67 86¾	Miceli M	116	36.10	77-17	Barrikated 108nk Blondie Duck 110½ No Buts 115¾	No factor 10
27Nov82- 3CT		fst	6½f	:23⅖ :47⅖ 1:22⅘	3↑Alw 4500	9 6 22 24 37 913	Dupuis T J	118	*1.00e	58-26	Tampa Bay 1201 Lucky Pageant 118no Pity My Pat 114¾	Tired 9
14Nov82- 1CT		fst	4½f	:22⅖ :47⅖ :53⅘	3↑Md Sp Wt	7 2 23 2½ 14	Dupuis T J7	112	*.60	85-10	Russell Sprout 1124 Full of Hell 119½ Rough Takeoff114¾	Driving 10
31Oct82- 1CT		fst	4½f	:22⅘ :47⅖ :53⅘	3↑Md Sp Wt	5 3 3nk 2hd 3½	Dupuis T J7	111	*.90	84-13	NtivePukk118½CollosIBlundr118noRussllSprout111¾	Lacked A Bid 10
17Oct82- 1CT		fst	4½f	:22⅖ :46⅖ :52⅘	3↑Md Sp Wt	2 4 2½ 21½ 22	Shaw N W	118	*1.30	88-11	Windpipe 1202 Russell Sprout1183WhiteMonk1154	Best of others 9
13Oct82- 3Bow		fst	6f	:23⅕ :47⅕ 1:12⅕	3↑Md 13500	10 2 31½ 3½ 59 612	Shaw N W	117	23.90	67-28	Brave Consort 1192½ Roaring Jet 119½ My Guardsman 1143	Tired 11
16Sep82- 1Bow		fst	6f	:22⅘ :46 1:11⅘	3↑Md 13500	10 2 53¾ 54½ 56¾ 59½	Shaw N W	116	10.50	71-22	Chief Manelski 1131¾ Doctor Flag 1153 RoyalDundee1211¾	Evenly 12
22Aug82- 5CT		fst	4½f	:22⅗ :46⅕ :52⅗	3↑Md Sp Wt	3 2 21½ 21½ 23	Shaw N W	118	*1.90	88-10	Big Image 1183 Russell Sprout 1186 Full of Hell 1181½	Evenly 9
18Jly82- 4CT		fst	4½f	:22⅖ :46⅖ :52⅘	3↑Md Sp Wt	3 6 32½ 32 2no	Shaw N W	117	8.20	90-10	Buddy'sG.W.117noRussllSprout1174½PssionistGl1171½	Just missed 10
11Jly82- 4CT		fst	4½f	:22⅖ :45⅘ :52	3↑Md Sp Wt	2 8 55 47 816	Shaw N W	117	7.80	78-09	Shau Kar 1177PukkaPower1174DeterminedDaddy117nk	No factor 10

DAVIS 6:5

Yutzie Boy

Own.—Triple Fox Stable

B. h. 5, by Delta Oil—Snow Buddy, by Kauai King
$7,500 Br.—Fox Breeding & Bloodstock (Ky)
Tr.—Ramos Faustino F

112⁵ Lifetime 10 2 2 1 $22,850 | 1982 3 0 2 1 $6,050 | 1981 7 2 0 0 $16,800

Date-Race	Trk	Cond	Dist	Fractions	Class	PP St 1C 2C Str Fin	Jockey	Wt	Odds	Sp-Var	Top three	Comment
17Dec82- 1Aqu		my	6f	⊡:23⅗ :48⅖ 1:13⅘	3↑Clm 10000	9 6 41 31½ 2½ 23½	Caraballo R	117	4.90	71-31	Joan's Poker 1173½ Yutzie Boy 1172 Red Rang 110no	Bid,wknd 11
8Dec82- 3Aqu		fst	6f	⊡:23⅕ :46⅘ 1:12⅘	3↑Clm 10000	6 6 54½ 66½ 36½ 36	Caraballo R	117	*2.60	74-21	RoguishMnner1131¾Michel'sEdge1174¼YutziBoy1172¼	Evenly late 14
20Nov82- 2Aqu		fst	6f	:23 :46⅗ 1:12⅖	3↑Clm 10000	10 5 43 4¾ 22 21	Caraballo R	117	29.20	78-21	Singing Soldier 1171 Yutzie Boy 1172 Omas Josh 1121¾	Rallied 13
5Nov81- 4Aqu		fst	6f	:22⅗ :46⅕ 1:11⅗	Clm 15000	2 6 56 65½ 68½ 611	Samyn J L	115	4.00	72-22	Satans Legend 1192½ Jill Believes1151½SwiftWonder1172½	Outrun 6
22Oct81- 9Med		fst	6f	:22⅕ :45⅗ 1:11⅗	Clm 16000	3 8 54 58 913 915	Molina V H5	113	*2.70	70-17	ⒹSlady Baby 1154 PerfectShot1181¾FortunateWeather1153	Tired 10
14Oct81- 2Aqu		fst	6f	:22⅘ :46 1:11⅕	Clm 25000	11 8 98½ 1011 108½ 97¼	Samyn J L	115	3.60	78-16	Carob Star 117½ Swift Wonder 114hd ⒹBay Diplomat117¾	Outrun 11
20Sep81- 5Bel		fst	6f	:23⅖ :47 1:12⅕	Clm 30000	4 7 42 3½ 1½ 11½	Samyn J L	119	8.10	81-27	Yutzie Boy1191½GeneralElection110nkCopperSoldier115hd	Driving 7
12Sep81- 3Med		fst	6f	:22⅗ :46⅕ 1:10⅘	3↑Alw 12000	3 4 2hd 44½ 513 615	Miranda J	112	3.20	74-20	Roman Castle 1153 Key To Riches 1147 Moon Glider 1124	Tired 7
2Sep81- 1Bel		fst	6f	:22⅖ :45⅘ 1:10⅗	3↑Md 45000	6 3 1hd 1½ 1½ 1nk	Cordero A Jr	114	6.30	89-14	Yutzie Boy 114nk Native Tour 109no Bright Planet 114½	Driving 9
16Aug81- 1Sar		sly	6f	:22 :45⅖ 1:12⅘	3↑Md 45000	3 4 31½ 59 47½ 63½	Cordero A Jr	115	9.10	73-23	Raja The Great 1171½ Swift And Proud 117¾NativeTour1141	Tired 10

LATEST WORKOUTS Dec 29 Bel tr.t 3f fst :36⅕ h Nov 10 Bel tr.t 5f fst 1:04⅕ b

CLAYTON 32:1

Regal Naskra

Own.—Merscot Stable

B. h. 5, by Naskra—Just Our Jill, by Mr Randy
$7,500 Br.—Hemphill H H (NY)
Tr.—Desantis R

110⁷ Lifetime 22 1 1 3 $12,148 | 1982 14 1 1 2 $9,388 | 1981 7 M 0 1 $2,760 | Turf 3 0 0 1 $2,760

Date-Race	Trk	Cond	Dist	Fractions	Class	PP St 1C 2C Str Fin	Jockey	Wt	Odds	Sp-Var	Top three	Comment
24Nov82-10Med		fst	6f	:22⅗ :46⅘ 1:14⅕	3↑Clm 9000	11 3 54 1114 1117 1122	Santagata N	b 114	80.10	50-23	Perfect Motion 1161½NeverRome116noSpecialFlair107¾	Early foot 11
17Nov82- 4Med		fst	6f	:22⅘ :46 1:11	3↑Clm 10500	4 5 32 912 919 924	Smith D D	b 114	32.10	54-19	Jesterson'sQuest1164½MikeMihlik1113PhiBetKey1192	Early speed 9
27Oct82- 7Med		yl	1⅟16	Ⓣ:48⅖ 1:14⅖ 1:48⅗	3↑Alw 11000	2 11 1213 1122 1131 1142	Diaz J R	b 117	117.10	— —	Commodus 118no Castelets 118hd Settimino 1172	Outrun 12
13Oct82- 5Aqu		fst	7f	:22⅘ :45⅘ 1:24⅖	3↑ⓈAlw 24500	6 7 89 916 922 925	McCarron G	b 117	62.60	54-20	Key Count 114½ Major Leader 1146¾ Face The Music 1142	Outrun 9
3Sep82- 8FL		fst	170	:47⅗ 1:13⅗ 1:46⅘	3↑ⓈAlw 9100	5 8 1121 1120 1022 1013	Diaz J R	b 122	37.60	54-21	Lists Lullaby 113¾ Malendrino 112¾ Baltic 1162½	Outrun 11
22Aug82- 8FL		fst	6f	:23 :46⅖ 1:13⅗	3↑ⓈAlw 8800	4 6 76 76¾ 710 76	Diaz J R	b 122	5.50	76-21	Phoenix Bird 1141 Big Izzy 1151 Sea Holly 1161	Outrun 7
8Aug82- 4FL		fst	5½f	:22⅗ :46⅘ 1:06⅗	3↑ⓈMd Sp Wt	1 4 32 32 3½ 12	Diaz J R	b 122	1.80e	89-13	RegalNaskra1222VicariousVicson114nkAnEsternNtive1101	Driving 9
20Jly82- 2FL		sly	6f	:23⅖ :47⅗ 1:15	3↑ⓈMd Sp Wt	8 4 45½ 57½ 43½ 43½	Diaz J R	b 122	3.50	70-30	Tarahumara 1151½ Cap Chap 115¾ Perfect Rocket1151½	No factor 8
4Jly82- 1FL		fst	5½f	:22⅘ :47⅖ 1:07⅗	3↑ⓈMd Sp Wt	5 3 41½ 43½ 51¾ 2¾	Diaz J R	b 122	5.90	83-23	Ardie's Suretry 115¾ RegalNaskra1221½CraftyRogue115no	Gamely 8
27Jun82- 3FL		fst	6f	:22⅗ :46⅘ 1:12⅘	3↑ⓈMd Sp Wt	7 5 75¼ 66 56½ 311	Diaz J R	122	8.60	74-23	Mr. Tatt 11410 Doctor Tad 114½ Regal Naskra 122nk	Mild bid 10

LATEST WORKOUTS Dec 24 Bel tr.t 5f fst 1:06⅗ b Dec 20 Bel tr.t 4f fst :53⅕ b Nov 13 Bel tr.t 4f sly :52⅗ b (d)

JANUARY 2—RACE 9 (Triple Wagering)

Try Within—A once classy animal. Hasn't raced in two months, drops way down to Aqueduct's cheapest level and only had six starts last year. Running the wrong distance today. A tightener. Not a contender.

Grappa—Dropping down but last race was nowhere with no excuse after an eight month layoff. **Grappa** is 5:1 and I don't know why. I would consider betting him off the board, but his last race is poor. I just can't see him winning. The board, though, makes him the one to worry about. Concern about horses that are bet for no apparent reason is not uncommon. However, the smart bettor knows that solid handicapping and money management will win out. If not today, in the long run. Not a contender.

Handball Kid—Being raised after being nowhere at the Meadowlands. 56:1 might actually be an underlay! Not a contender.

Southern Prince—Raised last week after being nowhere the race before. A decent effort last time with a 92 speed figure—the highest in the race. Drops today. Last time out he was almost 50:1. The paddock really helps with a horse like this. Without it, all we know is that **Southern Prince** is inconsistent. He may feel good today, he may not. After a decent effort on Nov. 1st, this horse was beaten 15 lengths and 18 lengths. Seems like **Southern Prince** held together last time, but isn't likely to repeat. Also, at 4:1 he is a huge underlay.

Milliard—Beaten a total of 113 lengths in his last five races! Wrong distance today. Drops, but his last races were so poor it probably won't help. Not a contender.

Pink Monk—Nowhere last four races. Drops, but Not a contender.

Upper Tier—Drops, but well beaten before while losing ground in the stretch. Originally from Finger Lakes and Penn National–has never been a classy horse. Not a contender.

Russell Sprout—Recently broke maiden at Charles Town (a small track). Cheap, nowhere last two, and nowhere at today's distance. Not a contender.

Yutzee Boy—Laid off a year, then two seconds and a third in $10,000 claimers. Consistent. Second highest adjusted speed figure in race —90. Drops. Picks up Robbie Davis (a hot apprentice) and loses five pounds. This is a huge jockey switch. The one to beat.

Regal Naskra—Beaten 126 lengths last five races! Not a contender.

THE BET: The obvious choice here is **Yutzee Boy**. The next step is to bet properly. This horse is such a stick out that it is a 95% of the maximum bet. This determination is never absolute. It is based on past experience. Some horse players might argue that it really should be an 85% or 90% bet. However, most knowledgeable bettors would agree with the selection and that it is a strong play. With time and experience, the reader will be able to make his own determination. After **Yutzee Boy**, the race is so wide open that anything can run second. Therefore, **Yutzee Boy** should be played with everything in the triple. With any luck at all, the triple can pay a price. As a saver, play **Yutzee Boy** and **Southern Prince** with everything twice and **Southern Prince** and **Yutzee Boy** with everything once. That way, if these two favorites come in there is still a profit.

RESULTS: **Yutzee Boy** ($4.40), **Pink Monk, Russell Sprout**. Triple paid $1,541.00.

TOTAL BET:	**Yutzee Boy** with everything	$144
	Savers	$ 48
		$192

PROFIT: $1349.00

If your maximum bet is more than $202 (95% of $202 = $192), your profit is even higher. Otherwise, **Yutzee Boy** must be played by himself to win. The ten dollar player makes $12 for the race and should be happy. Remember, each horse player has different goals and must have different levels of expectations. The smaller bettor makes only $12 but risks only $10, not $192.

FEBRUARY 2—RACE 6 (No exotic waging)

6 AQUEDUCT — 6 FURLONGS, INNER DIRT TRACK, AQUEDUCT (START / FINISH)

6 FURLONGS. (INNER-DIRT). (1.08⅘) ALLOWANCE. Purse $22,000. Fillies and Mares. 4-year-olds and upward, which have never won two races other than Maiden, Claiming or Starter. Weight, 122 lbs. Non-winners of a race other than maiden or claiming since January 15, allowed 3 lbs. Of such a race since January 1, 5 lbs.

Jeannine's Suite — Own.—Griffo V W — Dk. b. or br. f. 4, by Tersion—Garden Music, by Western Sky II — Br.—Sullivan A H (Ky) — Tr.—Alpers Sue — **117**

Lifetime 12 2 4 3 $47,960 — 1983 2 0 1 1 $7,700 — 1982 10 2 3 2 $40,260

5:1

Date/Race	Cond	Dist	Fractions	Race	PP St	Calls	Jockey	Wt	Odds	Speed	Top finishers	Comment	Field
22Jan83- 5Aqu	fst	6f	⊡:23⅕ :46⅘ 1:11	ⒻAlw 22000	5 5	52½ 53 32½ 33¾	Migliore R	119	3.50	85-07	Minor's Gift 1172¾ Ring On Doc 1101 Jeannine'sSuite1191	Rallied	8
2Jan83- 7Aqu	fst	6f	⊡:23 :47 1:13	ⒻAlw 23000	2 8	76½ 65½ 46½ 23½	Alvarado R Jr5	117	6.30	75-28	Ebullient 1123½ Jeannine's Suite 117noLadyLothario112nk	Gamely	9
16Dec82- 7Aqu	sly	6f	⊡:23 :47 1:12⅘	3↑ⒻAlw 21000	3 5	53¾ 42½ 41¾ 1½	Migliore R	115	8.70	80-23	Jeannine's Suite115½Je'DaQua1152IncredibleMoment1103	Driving	6
27Nov82- 6Aqu	fst	6f	:23⅗ :47⅗ 1:12⅗	3↑ⒻAlw 19000	4 6	41¾ 44 47½ 411	Skinner K	117	4.00	68-29	Chime 1152¾ Je'Da Qua 1208 Backstage Whisper 108nk	Weakened	6
13Oct82- 7Aqu	fst	6f	:23 :46⅗ 1:11⅘	3↑ⒻMd Sp Wt	4 4	32 31½ 14 16½	Bailey J D	119	*.40	82-20	Jeannine's Suite 1196½InYourLIfe119nkGail'sWish1195	Ridden out	6
26Sep82- 6Bel	fst	6f	:23⅖ :46⅗ 1:11⅗	3↑ⒻMd Sp Wt	3 5	52 41 2hd 2nk	Bailey J D	118	3.40	85-19	Cerlvo118nkJennine'sSuite1186½TopCommndrss1222¾	Just missed	9
9Sep82- 6Bel	fst	6f	:23 :47 1:12⅘	3↑ⒻMd Sp Wt	4 10	97½ 63½ 2hd 2hd	Bailey J D	118	6.30	78-21	RoseCrescent118hdJeannine'sSuite1181¾Je'DaQu118nk	Just failed	12
31Jly82- 3Bel	fst	6f	:23 :46⅘ 1:11⅘	3↑ⒻMd Sp Wt	1 1	3½ 31½ 33 34½	McCarron G	116	9.90	78-15	Ranch Mink 1163 Je'Da Qua1161½Jeannine'sSuite1162¾	Weakened	7
30Jun82- 9Bel	fst	7f	:23⅕ :46⅕ 1:23⅕	3↑ⒻMd Sp Wt	5 7	41½ 2hd 35 48	Samyn J L	114	9.20	78-11	CarefullyHidden1141¾LeapoftheHeart114nkJe'DQu1146	Weakened	9
7Jun82- 3Bel	my	6f	:22⅘ :46⅕ 1:10⅘	3↑ⒻMd Sp Wt	1 4	11 1½ 34 311	McCarron G	114	6.30	79-13	Lady Noble 114½ Ceralvo 11410 Jeannine's Suite 1141	Tired	9

LATEST WORKOUTS Jan 18 Bel tr.t 4f fst :47⅗ h — Jan 12 Bel tr.t 5f fst 1:04 b — Dec 28 Bel tr.t 4f fst :49⅘ h — Dec 14 Bel tr.t 4f fst :49 b

Metbychance * — Own.—Bresnan M L — B. f. 4, by Our Native—Q Up, by Distinctive — Br.—Carl W A (Ky) — Tr.—Scanlon Robert N — **117**

Lifetime 10 2 4 0 $29,100 — 1983 1 0 0 0 $1,500 — 1982 6 1 3 0 $20,260

6:1

Date/Race	Cond	Dist	Fractions	Race	PP St	Calls	Jockey	Wt	Odds	Speed	Top finishers	Comment	Field
1Jan83- 8Med	fst	1 1/16	:47⅗ 1:12 1:45	ⒻHandicap	4 2	2hd 1hd 3½ 44¼	Gonzalez M A	110	4.90e	80-18	Martie's Double 112½ Luminaire 1141 Snub 1152¾	Weakened	9
18Dec82- 8Lrl	fst	1	:46⅗ 1:12⅕ 1:37⅖	ⒻA Arundel H	10 5	63¾ 911 1016 1025	Gomez E R	108	21.20	60-19	Kattegat's Pride 1191 Wedding Party 1177DelicateIce115no	Tired	10
27Nov82- 7Med	fst	6f	:22⅖ :46⅕ 1:12	ⒻDenville	5 7	99¾ 47 34½ 22¼	Gonzalez M A	112	6.30	81-21	Syrian Sands 1142¼ Metbychance 112½ VisualEmotion1124	Rallied	9
27Nov82-Run in Two Divisions 7th & 9th Races													
12Nov82- 6Aqu	fst	7f	:23⅕ :45⅘ 1:24⅕	3↑ⒻAlw 20000	8 2	51½ 31 32 23½	Gonzalez M A	117	8.30	77-21	Flag Waver 1173½ Metbychance 117¾LadyHatchet1101½	No match	8
2Nov82- 9Aqu	fst	1	:47⅖ 1:12⅖ 1:37⅗	3↑ⒻAlw 21000	7 4	3nk 11½ 11½ 2nk	Cordero A Jr	115	2.90	78-16	Lizzie's Light 108nk Metbychance 1152 Tis A Kitten 1171¾	Failed	8
11Oct82- 7Med	fst	6f	:21⅘ :45⅗ 1:12	3↑ⒻAlw 10000	3 7	711 510 3½ 12¼	Gonzalez M A	113	27.60	83-18	Metbychance 1132¼ GreekAxe113½MontchaninGirl1163	Drew clear	8
1Aug82- 8WO	fst	6f	:22⅕ :45⅗ 1:11⅕	3↑ⒻAlw 12800	4 9	75¾ 76¾ 812 814	Duffy L	118	7.15	73-16	Wyndurgal 110no Fighting Spirit 1195¾ Hearts N' Spades 121nk		9
19Nov81- 5Grd	sly	1	:48 1:14 1:41⅘	ⒻMd Sp Wt	1 5	52½ 11 16 15¾	Leblanc J B	117	*1.80	71-30	Metbychance 1175¾ Rumbatan 110nk Chocolate Pet 115½		11
1Nov81- 5WO	fst	6½f	:23 :46⅗ 1:18⅘	ⒻMd Sp Wt	12 3	52½ 31½ 23 22½	Stahlbaum G	119	*2.75	77-21	Artic Caster 1152½ Metbychance 119nk Chaleur 1174		12
22Oct81- 3WO	sly	5f	:23⅗ :48⅕ 1:01⅖	ⒻMd Sp Wt	8 9	108½ 1114 1015 811	Stahlbaum G	119	*2.10	68-40	Captive Queen 1192½ Victorian Grata 1162½ Miss Hyperion 1142½		13

LATEST WORKOUTS Dec 28 Med 5f fst 1:01⅗ h — Dec 8 Med 1 fst 1:42 b

Visual Emotion — Own.—Jones B C — Ch. f. 4, by King Emperor—Join The Waves, by Sailor — Br.—Jones Brereton C (Ky) — Tr.—Campo John P — **117**

Lifetime 9 2 0 3 $28,582 — 1982 9 2 0 3 $28,582 — 1981 0 M 0 0

8:5

Date/Race	Cond	Dist	Fractions	Race	PP St	Calls	Jockey	Wt	Odds	Speed	Top finishers	Comment	Field
16Dec82- 6Med	gd	6f	:22⅕ :45 1:10⅖	3↑ⒻMiss Prspy H	4 8	4¾ 31½ 99¼ 914	Miranda J	112	5.00	77-17	Meringue Pie 114¾ Stellarette1121MoonStarMiss1121	Sp'd for 1/2	9
6Dec82- 8Aqu	my	6f	⊡:22 :45⅕ 1:10	3↑ⒻAlw 21000	7 1	15 15 16 16¾	Miranda J	115	2.60	94-15	VisulEmotion1156¾Je'DQu1154IncredibleMomnt110no	Ridden out	7
27Nov82- 7Med	fst	6f	:22⅖ :46⅕ 1:12	ⒻDenville	9 1	14 11½ 2½ 32¾	Miranda J	112	11.30	80-21	SyrianSands1142¼Metbychance112½VisualEmotion1124	Weakened	9
27Nov82-Run in Two Divisions 7th & 9th Races													
6Nov82- 5Lrl	fst	6f	:22⅕ :46 1:11⅖	3↑ⒻAlma North	2 4	12 11 2hd 52½	Miranda J	113	16.80	84-11	Kattegat's Pride 1161½ Count OnSadye110hdErnestine122nk	Tired	10
27Oct82- 4Kee	fst	7f	:22⅗ :46⅕ 1:25⅗	3↑ⒻAlw 13500	1 12	11½ 1½ 2hd 35½	Brumfield D	116	3.10	73-18	OldMotherHubbrd1154½ProperChoice1131VisulEmotion1161	Tired	12
31Jly82- 3Dmr	fst	6f	:21⅘ :45 1:10⅖	3↑ⒻAlw 16000	6 7	41¾ 85 1214 1215	Olivares F	115	6.30	71-15	My Native Princess 115¾ Entereza 1171 Tony's Darling 1152	Tired	12
27Jun82- 2Hol	fst	7f	:21⅗ :44⅖ 1:22⅗	3↑ⒻMd Sp Wt	4 2	1hd 1½ 12½ 11½	Olivares F	115	8.40	84-12	Visual Emotion 1151½ RunAmberRun1152PastPleasures115¾	Tired	12
5Jun82- 6Hol	fst	6f	:22 :44⅘ 1:10	3↑ⒻMd Sp Wt	2 5	32 23½ 23½ 34½	Olivares F	115	52.60	82-18	C'EstMoChr1154½Kss'EmGoodby116hdVsulEmoton1154½	Good try	8
29May82- 6Hol	fst	6f	:21⅘ :45 1:10⅖	3↑ⒻMd Sp Wt	10 10	89¼ 916 910 1012	Shoemaker W	114	25.80	73-18	Rise De Pie 1152½ Foxy Tammie114nkBelleParleuse114¾	No speed	10

LATEST WORKOUTS Jan 29 Bel tr.t 4f fst :52 b — ●Jan 26 Bel tr.t 4f fst :46⅘ hg — Jan 22 Bel tr.t 6f fst 1:13⅗ h — Jan 9 Bel tr.t 5f fst 1:01⅗ hg

These are the three main contenders. **Visual Emotion** was overmatched in the last, but was a giant on December 6th. The 103 adjusted speed figure is clearly superior to the rest of the field. Also superior are her workouts on January 26th. **Visual Emotion's** progress is evident after returning from her summer layoff. She is the only speed in the race and figures to get loose on the lead.

Metbychance finished ahead of **Visual Emotion** at the Meadowlands on November 27th which could fool the "paper" handicappers. Since then, **Visual Emotion** has improved greatly and has shown a liking to Aqueduct's inner dirt course. **Jeannine's Suite** is a contender with a first, a second, and a third in her last three starts, but **Visual Emotion** appears to be the better of the two.

THE BET: **Visual Emotion's** workouts indicate that she is ready to repeat the December 6th performance. Remembering that her workouts before the December 6th race were similar to those shown here, I raise my preliminary 85% of M.B. to 95%.

RESULT: **Visual Emotion** left the gate and never looked back. She won by 7 and paid $5.20.

5 AQUEDUCT 6 FURLONGS INNER DIRT TRACK AQUEDUCT START FINISH

6 FURLONGS. (INNER-DIRT). (1.08⅘) CLAIMING. Purse $15,500. 4-year-olds and upward. Weight, 122 lbs. Non-winners of two races since January 15 allowed 3 lbs. Of a race since then, 5 lbs. Claiming price $30,000; for each $2,500 to $25,000, 2 lbs. (Races when entered to be claimed for $20,000 or less not considered.)

Sun Dial — B. g. 4, by Time Tested—Reta N, by Turn to Reason
Own.—Davis A S — $27,500 Br.—Small D R (Md) Tr.—Moschera Gasper S — 110⁵

Lifetime						
30 6 1 6	1983	3	1	1	1	$9,430
$46,930	1982	16	2	0	5	$15,540
	Turf	1	0	0	0	$1,080

14Feb83- 5Aqu	fst	6f	⊡:23⅕	:46⅘	1:11⅗	Clm 25000	6	4	2hd	2hd	2½	2¾	Davis R G5	b 112	7.30	85-13 Bright Search 117¾ Sun Dial 112hd Bit of Coral 117½	Gamely	10
31Jan83- 2Aqu	fst	6f	⊡:22⅗	:46	1:11	Clm c-20000	4	2	2½	2hd	41	36	Alvarado R Jr5	b 114	5.20	83-15 Need A Penny 1191¾ Firstee 1224½ Sun Dial 114nk	Weakened	8
12Jan83- 6Bow	gd	7f	:22⅘	:45⅘	1:25⅗	Clm 16500	3	1	14	15	11½	1½	Passmore W J	b 117	4.90	77-33 Sun Dial 117½ Once Twice 119¾ Fire On Three 1144½	Driving	8
31Dec82- 5Lrl	fst	6f	:22⅘	:46⅘	1:12⅗ 3↑	Clm 16000	7	2	2hd	2hd	33½	42	Passmore W J	b 117	3.50	78-24 BoldandLucky1151½FireOnThree115nkAzureSpring117½	Weakened	7
15Dec82- 7Lrl	my	1	:47⅗	1:14	1:41⅗	Clm 16000	10	1	12½	21	88¾	911	Passmore W J	b 117	*1.50	54-29 DBalongo 108¾ Nor Bay 115nk Knight Traffic 1131	Faltered	11
4Dec82- 3Lrl	sly	6f	:22⅗	:46⅕	1:11⅖	Clm 16000	9	3	2hd	16	16	17	Passmore W J	b 115	3.40	86-19 Sun Dial 1157 Sailing Light 1155 Cut The Mark 115½	Handily	10
23Nov82- 8Med	fst	6f	:22	:45	1:11⅗	Clm 16000	9	4	31½	36½	510	612	Thornburg B	b 115	4.20	73-23 Beguine 1106 Professor Vis 1092½ Special Pocket 115½	Tired	10
8Nov82- 7Lrl	fst	6f	:22⅖	:46	1:11⅖	Clm 20000	8	2	12	1hd	22½	35	Wright D R	b 115	4.20	81-26 Kaye's Prince 115hd Azure Spring 1145 Sun Dial 1153¼	Weakened	9
27Oct82- 6Lrl	fst	6f	:22⅘	:46⅘	1:12⅖	Clm 25000	7	4	21	31	52¼	61½	Delgado A5	111	4.20	79-27 On Watch 1131 Pass The Leader 113nk Cupo'Sunshine116no	Tired	10
24Sep82- 5Bow	fst	7f	:23⅕	:46⅖	1:24⅘	Clm c-23500	2	5	31	32½	35	38½	Smith G P	119	3.70	72-26 On Watch 114½ Dean's Big Dude 1158 Sun Dial 119¾	Weakened	6

Need A Penny — Gr. h. 5, by Sir Wimborne—Surf Queen, by Native Rythm
Own.—Rafsky J K — $30,000 Br.—Cogswell Mrs C C (NY) Tr.—Donato Robert A — 117

Lifetime						
37 5 3 4	1983	5	2	0	0	$26,400
$92,440	1982	15	1	0	2	$14,520
	Turf	5	0	0	0	

16Feb83- 8Aqu	fst	6f	⊡:23⅕	:46⅖	1:10⅘ 3↑	SH Hughes H	1	9	1112	1114	811	710	Beitia E	b 110	12.80	82-23 Master Digby 1237 Jan's Kinsman 120¾ Big Izzy 117hd	Outrun	11
31Jan83- 2Aqu	fst	6f	⊡:22⅗	:46	1:11	Clm 20000	5	8	89	66½	1½	11¾	Beitia E	b 119	4.90	89-15 Need A Penny 1191¾ Firstee 1224½ Sun Dial 114nk	Driving	8
22Jan83- 2Aqu	fst	6f	⊡:23	:45⅘	1:10⅘	Clm 25000	13	7	137½	1314	99	75¾	Beitia E	b 119¼	11.50	85-07 Tolerable 1171¾ Duck Call 117nk T. V. Repairman 1172½	Outrun	13
22Jan83-Dead heat																		
9Jan83- 2Aqu	fst	6f	⊡:23⅕	:46⅘	1:12⅖	SAlw 28000	9	9	87¾	77	22½	1½	Beitia E	b 117	27.70	82-17 Need A Penny 117½ Turn Bold 119¾ Actor's Aroma 1171½	Driving	12
1Jan83- 9Aqu	fst	6f	⊡:23⅗	:47⅕	1:12⅘	Clm 22500	8	3	117	108¾	75¾	44½	Velez R I	b 115	20.90	76-25 Happy Cannibal 1194 Page Six 117nk Psychosis 113hd	Rallied	12
26Dec82- 5Aqu	fst	1 1/16	⊡:48	1:13⅘	1:46⅗ 3↑	SAlw 29500	8	6	41¾	52	68½	619	Beitia E	b 117	16.80	61-24 Key Count 1107 Key to Success 1152 Senate Seat 1202½	Tired	8
15Dec82- 2Aqu	fst	6f	⊡:23	:46⅖	1:12⅖ 3↑	Clm 16000	4	8	87	88¾	33½	1nk	Beitia E	b 117	16.30	82-25 Need A Penny 117nk Moon Glider 1173OscarMyLove1151½	Driving	8
6Dec82- 9Aqu	my	6f	⊡:22⅖	:46	1:11⅗ 3↑	Clm 16000	1	9	911	912	89½	65½	Beitia E	b 117	11.50	81-15 RoylMnner119hdCounterEspionge1172½CounterAttck1171½	Outrun	10
19Nov82- 3Aqu	fst	7f	:23⅗	:47⅕	1:24⅘ 3↑	Clm 20000	8	1	32½	53¼	43½	42	Beitia E	b 117	15.70	75-23 Umticc117nkAbelrdo1131½DesperteJourny108½	Lacked a response	9
8Nov82- 7Aqu	fst	7f	:22⅘	:45⅘	1:24⅖ 3↑	SAlw 26000	7	10	1216	1112	97¼	74½	Beitia E	b 117	32.30	74-26 Rajab'sSon1151½SaratogaSunrise1151½PeacefulTune110hd	Outrun	12

VENEZIA 7:1

The Bloody Best — Dk. b. or br. g. 4, by Blood Royal—Call Me Queen, by Lt Stevens
$25,000 Br.—Perkins J L (Ky) Tr.—Nadler Herbert — 1085 — Lifetime 35 6 6 2 $37,145 — 1983 3 0 0 0 $870 — 1982 23 4 6 2 $30,146 — Turf 2 0 0 0 $797
Own.—Best Friends Stable
20Feb83- 2Aqu fst 6f ⊡:23⅗ :47⅕ 1:12⅕ Clm 20000 1 12 127¾118¼ 73¼ 41¼ Smith A Jr b 117 4.50 82-20 Inner Circuit 117no Dark 'N Bold 1121¼ Rexexplode 114hd Rallied 12
24Jan83- 8Aqu sly 170 ⊡:46⅘ 1:12 1:42⅘ Alw 23000 2 2 21½ 33 617 632 Venezia M b 117 15.20 56-15 Milieu 119nk Brae Axe 1104 Chapter One 1228¾ Tired 6
13Jan83- 5Aqu fst 6f ⊡:23 :47 1:12⅗ Clm c-30000 11 12 1210121311151012 Graell A b 117 5.90 69-26 Beguine 1151½ Self Pressured 1175½ Ted Brown 108hd Outrun 12
31Dec82- 7Haw fst 6f :21⅘ :45⅕ 1:11⅕ 3↑ Alw 17500 3 8 67½ 67½ 2hd 2nk Lopez R D b 112 7.40 85-25 First Transworld 113nk The Bloody Best1123½Redford1151½ Sharp 10
11Dec82- 5Haw fst 6½f :23⅕ :46⅗ 1:18⅘ Clm c-20000 5 9 83½ 63½ 12½ 12½ Hightower T W b 115 3.40 81-24 The Bloody Best 1152½UnitedPrize115noCraftyRibot115nk Driving 10
7Dec82- 9Haw fst 6½f :23 :46 1:16⅘ 3↑ Clm 15000 6 6 63 75½ 43 12½ Hightower T W b 113 20.30 89-19 The Bloody Best 1132½ Cat Whistle 117noMissy'sLast1153 Driving 9
15Nov82- 9CD fst 6½f :23⅕ :46⅘ 1:18⅘ 3↑ Clm 17500 6 8 85¾ 74½ 45½ 46 Brumfield D b 116 18.30 82-22 Last Farewell 1083½ Great Balance 1172¾ Operable 117no No rally 12
17Sep82- 6AP my 7f :23 :45⅘ 1:24⅕ Clm 25000 2 6 43 58 520 624 Evans R D b 119 9.80 57-27 Chandy Turn 1179 First Transworld 115hd Will Riley 1173½ Tired 7
24Aug82- 8EIP my 6f :23 :46⅘ 1:13⅘ 3↑ Alw 9500 1 6 67 54½ 54½ 33½ Barrow T b 115 3.60 76-30 NoisyBryn115hdPluie'sSylvester1153½TheBloodyBest115½ Mild bid 6
17Aug82- 6EIP fst 6f :23⅕ :46⅘ 1:11⅗ Clm 20000 3 6 42 41½ 32 1½ Barrow T b 115 5.30 90-12 TheBloodyBest115½SinisterSun1123HardHededHenry1102 Driving 8
LATEST WORKOUTS ●Feb 11 Aqu ⊡ 4f fst :48 h Jan 31 Aqu ⊡ 4f gd :48⅘ h Jan 21 Aqu ⊡ 4f fst :48⅘ h Jan 8 Bel tr.t 4f fst :48 h

6:1

Self Pressured — Dk. b. or br. g. 6, by The Pruner—Self Made, by Gun Bow
$30,000 Br.—Peters L J (Fla) Tr.—Kurtz Gus R — 117 — Lifetime 63 6 11 9 $122,700 — 1983 3 0 1 0 $3,520 — 1982 13 0 2 3 $12,160 — Turf 4 0 0 0 $1,020
Own.—Schwartz B K
26Jan83- 4Aqu fst 6f ⊡:23 :46⅗ 1:11 Clm 35000 2 8 86½ 95¾ 86 75½ McCarron G 117 8.70 83-17 Space Mountain 108½MincedWords1171¾TempestStar117¾ Outrun 10
13Jan83- 5Aqu fst 6f ⊡:23 :47 1:12⅗ Clm 30000 4 9 65½ 75½ 23 21½ McCarron G 117 *3.00f 79-26 Beguine 1151½ Self Pressured 1175½ Ted Brown 108hd Rallied 12
3Jan83- 4Aqu fst 6f ⊡:23⅘ :47⅕ 1:12⅘ Clm 35000 3 7 74½ 65½ 66 58 McCarron G 117 14.90 74-25 Rasselas 1172½ Pleasure Bid 117hd Rigid 1121 Outrun 8
11Dec82- 1Aqu fst 6f ⊡:23 :46⅘ 1:12⅕ 3↑ Clm 45000 2 7 710 78¾ 77½ 77½ Beitia E 113 26.50 76-20 CrockfordLad1141¾NorthernRegent1131½HerefordMn108½ Outrun 7
1Dec82- 9Aqu my 6f ⊡:22⅘ :45⅗ 1:10⅗ 3↑ Clm 45000 5 9 10201019 917 916 Beitia E 113 28.30 75-09 Was He Fuzzy 1082 Really Smart 1171½HerefordMan1152½ Outrun 10
9Jun82- 1Bel fst 1⅟₁₆ :46 1:10 1:42⅕ Clm 45000 7 5 55½ 69½ 613 713 Martens G 115 6.00 78-11 Escambia Bay 117nk Assension 1134 Palace 1145¾ Raced wide 7
16May82- 2Aqu fst 6f :22⅘ :45 1:10 Clm 45000 8 9 914 913 711 65½ Velasquez J b 117 6.30 85-19 CourtWise117nkWestgateBrunswick108nkSubordinte1171½ Outrun 9
7May82- 5Aqu fst 6f :22⅗ :45 1:10⅕ Clm 45000 9 1 54 710 511 55 Velasquez J b 113 6.10 85-21 Caphal 1144 Happy Cannibal 117nk Court Wise 114½ Mild rally 9
16Apr82- 1Aqu fst 6f :22⅘ :45⅗ 1:10⅗ Clm 45000 4 6 613 612 68 37 Velasquez J 113 2.70 81-27 Happy Cannibal 1131 Caphal117⁶SelfPressured1132½ Rallied wide 6
26Mar82- 5Aqu fst 6f :23 :46⅘ 1:11⅘ Clm 45000 4 8 88¼ 87¾ 66¼ 43 Velasquez J 113 4.20 79-35 DPriority 1132 Piece of Ice 1171 Silver Screen 117no Wide 8
26Mar82-Placed third through disqualification
LATEST WORKOUTS Feb 20 Aqu ⊡ 4f fst :49 h Feb 9 Aqu ⊡ 4f fst :49⅘ h ●Dec 30 Aqu ⊡ 4f fst :48 hg

10:1

Thunder Bridge — Ro. g. 5, by High Echelon—Successfully Yours, by Successor
$27,500 Br.—Lake Donald (Ky) Tr.—Pascuma Warren J — 115 — Lifetime 39 5 4 5 $66,305 — 1983 3 0 1 0 $3,190 — 1982 23 3 3 3 $50,040 — Turf 1 0 0 0
Own.—Denmark Muriel
10Feb83- 1Aqu fst 6f ⊡:23⅕ :47 1:12⅘ Clm 25000 4 14 148½109¼ 52½ 2¾ Graell A 117 9.40 81-18 Colonel Law 117¾ThunderBridge117½ReverseDecision113½ Rallied 14
29Jan83- 2Aqu fst 1⅟₁₆ ⊡:47⅘ 1:12⅘ 1:45⅗ Clm 30000 5 11 99½ 66 67¾ 67½ Santagata N 113 15.30 77-20 Solid Credit 117hd Clarinet King 112no Startop'sAce1124½ Outrun 12
13Jan83- 5Aqu fst 6f ⊡:23 :47 1:12⅗ Clm 30000 8 7 97½ 98½ 810 67½ Santagata N 117 5.10 73-26 Beguine 1151½ Self Pressured 1175½ Ted Brown 108hd No factor 12
27Dec82- 5Aqu fst 1⅛ ⊡:48⅘ 1:13⅘ 1:53⅗ 3↑ Clm 35000 1 6 68 44½ 46½ 38 Santagata N 113 5.60 70-22 WasHeFuzzy1173ClrinetKing1125ThunderBridge1131½ No menace 7
16Dec82- 5Aqu sly 6f ⊡:22⅗ :46⅕ 1:12 3↑ Clm 35000 3 7 816 713 79½ 74½ Maple E 117 11.00 79-23 Big Izzy1103HappyCannibal115hdBrightSearch1171 Showed Little 9
11Nov82- 9Aqu fst 6f :22⅘ :46 1:10⅗ 3↑ Clm 35000 9 9 83¾ 64¾ 99¾ 99¼ MacBeth D 117 22.60 79-19 Was He Fuzzy 1193¾ Term Paper 117½ Tony Mack 117no Outrun 10
13Oct82- 2Aqu fst 6f :23 :46⅕ 1:10⅘ 3↑ Clm 35000 2 8 109½1012 910 98¼ MacBeth D 117 4.80 79-20 Was He Fuzzy 117nk Hereford Man 115¾ Court Wise1151¾ Outrun 10
29Sep82- 5Bel fst 7f :23⅗ :46⅕ 1:22⅘ 3↑ Clm 45000 3 4 31½ 32 44½ 48½ MacBeth D 113 11.60 80-18 CrockfordLd113noPrivteSun1025½NorthernRegent1153 Weakened 8
6Sep82- 2Bel fst 7f :23 :46 1:23⅕ 3↑ Clm 45000 2 9 85 86½ 53½ 53 Migliore R 113 8.30 83-17 Solid Credit 113½ Crockford Lad 117½Philanthropic1151½ Mild bid 9
26Aug82- 6Sar gd 6f :22 :45⅕ 1:09⅘ 3↑ Clm 45000 1 5 55½ 53 54 34 Maple E 113 4.10 87-12 Subordint1192¾CrockfordLd1171½ThundrBrdg113hd Wide into str. 5
LATEST WORKOUTS Feb 19 Bel tr.t 4f fst :49 h ●Feb 6 Bel tr.t 3f fst :36⅘ h Jan 26 Bel tr.t 5f fst 1:01⅘ b Jan 21 Bel tr.t 3f fst :36⅘ h

ALVARADO 9:1

Dark 'N Bold — Dk. b. or br. g. 4, by What Luck—Irish Party, by Irish Lancer
$27,500 Br.—Warner M L (Ohio) Tr.—McCoy Donald — 1105 — Lifetime 8 2 1 1 $17,410 — 1983 3 1 1 1 $11,530 — 1982 5 1 0 0 $5,880
Own.—Magid S E
20Feb83- 2Aqu fst 6f ⊡:23⅗ :47⅕ 1:12⅕ Clm c-20000 9 4 3½ 31½ 1hd 2no Davis R G5 b 112 8.10 83-20 Inner Circuit 117no Dark 'N Bold 1121½ Rexexplode 114hd Gamely 12
2Feb83- 9Aqu fst 6f ⊡:22⅘ :46⅘ 1:12⅘ Clm 15000 6 11 97¾ 79¼ 43½ 12½ Davis R G5 b 110 8.50 82-24 Dark 'N Bold 1102½ Infinite Saga 117¾MisterChris1172 Drew clear 12
3Jan83- 3Aqu fst 6f ⊡:23⅗ :47⅘ 1:13⅘ Clm 16000 6 4 22 21½ 33½ 34½ Beitia E b 117 27.50 72-25 BusyHilrious112hdRoguishMnner1074½Drk'NBold117nk Weakened 9
29Nov82- 1Aqu my 1⅛ :47⅘ 1:13 1:53 Clm 25000 3 1 2hd 21 613 622 Bailey J D b 117 15.40 48-24 Milieu 1172¾ Tribal Prince 1101½ Fire Away 1104 Tired after 6 fur. 7
19Nov82- 9Aqu fst 1 :47⅘ 1:13 1:39⅗ 3↑ Md 15000 9 2 11 1½ 13 11½ Beitia E b 120 *2.40 68-23 Dark 'N Bold 1201½ Nitro Express 111½ Pink Party 1135 Driving 12
8Nov82- 2Aqu fst 7f :23⅘ :47 1:26⅘ 3↑ Md 15000 2 14 94½ 96¾ 65 44½ Beitia E b 120 3.70 63-26 Alturas 1202 Pink Party 1112½ Spirited Song 120no Rallied 14
28Oct82- 6Aqu fst 6f :22⅘ :45⅕ 1:10⅗ 3↑ Md Sp Wt 1 6 64 712 713 711 Beitia E 119 44.70 77-14 I'm Peppy 1192 Fleet Receiver 119no Primary Care 119no Outrun 7
18Oct82- 4Aqu fst 6f :22⅕ :46⅘ 1:13 3↑ Md 25000 1 7 67 8111412 1412 Beitia E 119 20.80 64-23 Oscar MyLove1222½AndrewScott119noFireman114hd Lacked room 14
LATEST WORKOUTS Feb 17 Bel tr.t 4f my :50 b Jan 31 Bel tr.t 4f gd :50⅘ b Jan 26 Bel tr.t 5f fst 1:04⅘ b Jan 21 Bel tr.t 4f fst :50⅕ b

GOMEZ 58:1

J. C.'s Double — Gr. c. 4, by J C's Shadow—Carolyns Serenade, by Royal Serenade
$30,000 Br.—Cataldo J H (Fla) Tr.—Minassian Harry Jr — 117 — Lifetime 8 1 0 2 $8,810 — 1983 2 0 0 0 — 1982 4 1 0 1 $7,820
Own.—Cataldo J
6Feb83- 5Aqu fst 6f ⊡:22⅘ :46⅕ 1:10⅗ Alw 20000 3 6 42½ 78 816 918 Alvarado R Jr5 b 112 38.00 73-22 Northern Magus1177½I'mSoMerry1102½BoldTrumpeter117no Tired 9
26Jan83- 4Aqu fst 6f ⊡:23 :46⅗ 1:11 Clm 35000 9 4 41¾ 51¾ 99 1011 Davis R G5 b 112 27.30 78-17 Space Mountain 108½ Minced Words1171¾TempestStar117¾ Tired 10
31Dec82-10Med fst 6f :22⅘ :46 1:12⅕ 3↑ Md Sp Wt 10 1 2hd 13 12½ 1no Cole A K5 b 114 *2.50 82-15 J. C.'s Double 114no Smart Talk 1193 Jump Shot 1191¾ Driving 10
26Feb82- 4Hia fst 6f :22⅘ :45⅘ 1:12⅘ Md 40000 1 2 1½ 1½ 1hd 32¼ Brumfield D b 116 6.10 79-18 Valiant Fashion 1202½ Fine Risk 118hdJ.C.'sDouble1161 Weakened 12
10Feb82- 7Hia fst 6f :22⅘ :45⅘ 1:12⅗ Md 50000 2 2 1hd 2hd 33 75 Riera R Jr 120 9.70 75-23 Anne's Darling 116no Strictly Straight 120½ Pin Puller 1181 Tired 12
16Jan82- 6Hia fst 6f :22⅘ :46⅕ 1:11⅗ Md Sp Wt 5 9 54 66½ 46 710 Riera R Jr 120 21.60 75-15 GallantWind1205TenciousLeder1202½NewDiscovery1202 No factor 12
12Dec81- 5Med fst 6f :23⅗ :47⅘ 1:12⅕ Md Sp Wt 1 7 713 715 718 725 Thornburg B 118 6.50 57-21 Shay's Rebellion 1182½ Peter Owen1182½Flippydoo1139 Lost irons 7
5Dec81- 4Med fst 6f :23⅗ :47⅗ 1:12⅘ Md Sp Wt 1 5 11½ 12 22 37¾ Thornburg B 118 8.20 71-21 Cyane's Best 1186¾ A Real Leader 1131 J. C.'s Double 1182 Tired 9
LATEST WORKOUTS Jan 22 Bel tr.t 5f fst 1:02⅕ b ●Dec 29 Med 4f fst :48⅕ hg

3:1

Bright Search — B. g. 5, by Search For Gold—Bright Design, by Truxton King
$30,000 Br.—Braugh Ranches & McGill (Tex) Tr.—DeBonis Robert — 119 — Lifetime 40 9 3 5 $82,625 — 1983 5 1 0 0 $10,980 — 1982 13 4 1 3 $47,205 — Turf 1 1 0 0 $9,600
Own.—Chasrigg Stable
14Feb83- 5Aqu fst 6f ⊡:23⅕ :46⅘ 1:11⅗ Clm 25000 2 3 1hd 1hd 1½ 1¾ Miranda J b 117 2.50 86-13 Bright Search 117¾ Sun Dial 112hd Bit of Coral 117½ Driving 10
3Feb83- 5Aqu gd 6f ⊡:22⅕ :44⅘ 1:10⅕ Clm 45000 6 2 1½ 12 2hd 57 Migliore R b 113 *1.80e 86-18 Beguine 1082¼ Minced Words 1131¼ Really Smart 1131 Weakened 8
22Jan83- 3Aqu fst 6f ⊡:23 :45⅗ 1:10 Clm 40000 2 4 1½ 11½ 2hd 52¾ Migliore R b 117 8.50 91-07 NorweginPocket117noKentuckyEdd1122½RllySmrt117nk Gave way 10
14Jan83- 5Aqu fst 6f ⊡:23⅕ :46⅘ 1:11⅘ Clm 45000 6 5 11 11½ 2hd 46¾ Davis R G5 b 108 11.00 80-19 Happy Hooligan 1192¼ Fanny's Fox 117½ JefferyC.1174 Weakened 10
1Jan83- 5Aqu fst 6f ⊡:22⅘ :46 1:12⅗ Clm 45000 11 2 12 11½ 11½ 42 Davis R G5 b 109 9.90 79-25 Happy Hooligan 117no Surf Club 113nk Jeffery C.1171¾ Weakened 11
22Dec82- 4Aqu fst 6f ⊡:23⅘ :47⅕ 1:12⅕ 3↑ Clm 45000 1 1 1hd 1hd 3½ 54½ Miranda J 113 9.70 79-22 Crockford Lad 1192 Palimony 112hd Cut High 1192 Weakened 12
16Dec82- 5Aqu sly 6f ⊡:22⅗ :46⅕ 1:12 3↑ Clm c-35000 9 1 13 13 12 33 McCauley W H b 117 3.20 81-23 Big Izzy 1103 Happy Cannibal 115hd Bright Search1171 Gave Way 9
10Dec82- 8Aqu fst 6f ⊡:22⅗ :46⅕ 1:11⅘ 3↑ Alw 37000 1 3 1½ 1hd 43½ 417 MacBeth D b 117 9.50 70-24 In From Dixie1153½MightyNasty1125¼King'sFashion1158 Stopped 5
2Dec82- 6Med gd 6f :22 :45⅕ 1:10⅘ 3↑ Alw 25000 1 2 12½ 1½ 21½ 312 MacBeth D b 119 1.40 79-18 Obgyn 1136½ Peter Owen 1155 Bright Search 1191½ Tired 6
13Nov82- 7Med gd 6f :22 :45⅘ 1:10⅗ 3↑ Alw 25000 3 2 13 14 14 14 MacBeth D b 115 3.80 90-15 Bright Search 1154AlhambraJoe119nkGreyBucket1131 Drew clear 6
LATEST WORKOUTS Feb 22 Bel tr.t 4f fst :49⅘ b Jan 30 Bel tr.t 4f fst :49⅕ b

Colonel Law B. c. 4, by Wardlaw—Happy Pearl, by Hard Work Lifetime 1983 3 1 0 0 $8,700
$30,000 Br.—Lasater Farm (Fla) 119 17 6 2 1 1982 14 5 2 1 $29,455
Own.—Spiegel R Tr.—Schaeffer Stephen $38,155
10Feb83- 1Aqu fst 6f ⊡:23⅕ :47 1:12⅖ Clm 25000 7 7 43 33 1½ 1¾ Santagata N 117 5.40f 82-18 Colonel Law 117¾ThunderBridge117½ReverseDecision113½ Driving 14
22Jan83- 2Aqu fst 6f ⊡:23 :45⅘ 1:10⅗ Clm 25000 1 8 105½ 87½ 76 54¾ Clayton M D7 110 17.00 86-07 Tolerable 1171¾ Duck Call 117nk T. V. Repairman 1172½ No factor 13
5Jan83- 9Aqu fst 170 ⊡:48⅖ 1:14 1:44⅕ Clm c-20000 8 7 96¾ 911 919 817 Clayton M D7 110 3.90 64-24 CounslorGorg112noSoldGoldSoul1174Intrfrnc1123½ Unruly pre. st. 9
28Dec82- 8Med fst 170 :47⅕ 1:11⅗ 1:42⅘ Clm 20000 3 1 1½ 12½ 11½ 2½ Clayton M D7 111 *2.50 86-18 HoldYourSnapper114½ColonelLw1117IronLegcy1153½ Weakenedd 9
18Dec82- 7Med fr 6f :22⅖ :45⅖ 1:10⅖ Clm 18000 4 4 31 1hd 1½ 12½ Clayton M D7 106 7.20 91-07 Colonel Law 1062½ Professor Vis 1085 Mento 1151 Drew clear 7
9Dec82- 2Med fst 6f :23 :46⅗ 1:12⅘ Clm c-14000 2 9 810 79¾ 59½ 54½ Jenkins W E 113 *2.20 75-23 NightlyBttle118noCutTheMrk1102½HoldYourSnpper1101½ Late bid 9
2Dec82- 8Med gd 6f :23 :46⅕ 1:11⅗ Clm 10500 6 3 2hd 1hd 12 13 Jenkins W E 113 6.40 85-18 Colonel Law 1133 In the Process 1132 Low Echelon 1102 Driving 7
26Nov82-10Med fst 1 1/16 :48 1:12⅗ 1:46⅘ Clm c-8000 4 2 1hd 13 15 14½ Nemeti W 115 *2.30 75-21 Colonel Law 1154½ Jollysum's Boy 1151 Dr. Porcaro 1136 Driving 10
11Nov82-10Med fst 1 1/16 :47⅗ 1:12⅖ 1:45⅖ Clm 8000 2 1 11½ 11½ 1hd 23½ Nemeti W 115 *1.30 78-18 Triple Risk 1153½ Colonel Law 1154 Jollysum's Boy 1157 Gamely 12
2Nov82- 2Med fst 170 :46⅘ 1:12⅕ 1:43⅗ Clm 6250 6 2 1½ 12 15 110 Nemeti W 116 2.60 83-18 Colonel Law 11610 Alive at Five 1165 C. M.'sStar116½ Ridden out 10
LATEST WORKOUTS Feb 21 Bel tr.t 4f fst :49⅘ b Feb 8 Bel tr.t 3f fst :36⅘ h Feb 2 Bel tr.t 3f fst :35⅗ h Jan 17 Bel tr.t 4f fst :47 h

16:1

Richness Dk. b. or br. g. 4, by Cornish Prince—Rough Mood, by Dedimoud Lifetime 1983 1 0 0 0
$30,000 Br.—Spendthrift Farm (Ky) 117 12 2 0 1 1982 7 1 0 0 $7,930
Own.—Harbor View Farm Tr.—Schulhofer Flint S $19,210 Turf 1 0 0 0
4Feb83- 6Aqu fst 6f ⊡:22⅘ :46⅕ 1:13⅗ Clm 30000 8 7 117 1312 98¼ 99¾ Miranda J b 117 35.00 67-20 Term Paper1122¾CatchMatthew113¾T.V.Repairman117¾ No factor 14
5Dec82- 5Aqu gd 1 1/16 ⊡:47⅕ 1:12 1:45⅗ Clm 50000 5 4 45 712 814 814 Alvarado R Jr5 b 112 18.20 71-16 Brae Axe 117¾ Asticou 1133½ David K. 1133½ Tired 10
31Oct82- 9Aqu yl 1⅛ Ⓣ:48⅖ 1:14 1:53 3↑Clm 40000 3 3 32½1213123112 41 Fell J b 114 11.60 38-29 Freon 1195½ Campus Capers 117¾ Haste to Finish 113hd Tired 12
20Oct82- 3Aqu fst 6f :22⅗ :45⅘ 1:10⅗ Clm 50000 8 5 65 64 65½ 65½ Fell J b 117 8.40 82-21 Flippydoo 117¾ Moro 117nk Coolest 117¾ Raced wide 9
1Oct82- 7Bel fst 6f :23 :46⅕ 1:10⅗ 3↑Alw 20000 5 3 53 513 620 625 Fell J b 114 7.20e 63-28 King Naskra 112½ Citius 11611 Double Burner 1143¾ Tired 6
11Sep82- 5Bel fst 6f :22⅘ :45⅗ 1:10⅗ 3↑Alw 20000 7 5 43 47 713 713 Fell J b 113 9.50 77-12 Roughcast 1221½ Citius 1181¾ Faces Up 1132½ Tired 7
13Feb82- 6Hia fst 6f :22⅖ :45⅗ 1:11 Alw 13000 12 2 31½ 21½ 22 1¾ Migliore R b 116 14.30 88-14 Richness 116¾ Pathline 120hd Chan Balum 1203 Driving 12
30Jan82- 5Hia fst 6f :22 :45 1:10⅗ Alw 13000 5 5 43 55½ 59½ 811 Fell J b 116 *2.40 79-12 Thru A Straw 1181½Compo'sTempo1161½GuilfordRoad1161½ Tired 10
26Nov81- 5Aqu fst 7f :23⅖ :46⅗ 1:24 Alw 16000 9 2 1½ 1hd 2hd 31¾ MacBeth D b 119 28.60 79-21 Fit to Fight 122nk Cut Away 1171½ Richness 119¾ Weakened 10
14Nov81- 3Aqu fst 6f :23 :46⅘ 1:11⅕ Alw 16000 1 6 63½ 55½ 54½ 46 Fell J b 122 4.60 79-22 Lost Creek 1225 Cut Away 112½ Guilford Road 117½ Even try 7
LATEST WORKOUTS Feb 19 Bel tr.t 4f fst :49⅗ h Feb 11 Bel tr.t 4f fst :49⅗ b Feb 1 Bel tr.t 4f fst :49 b Jan 26 Bel tr.t 4f fst :50⅕ b

LOVATO 30:1

T. V. Repairman Dk. b. or br. c. 4, by T V Commercial—Athlete's Foot, by Prince Tenderfoot Lifetime 1983 2 0 0 2 $3,600
$30,000 Br.—Bwamazon Farm (Ky) 117 14 3 1 3 1982 7 2 0 1 $16,260
Own.—Bwamazon Farm Tr.—Arnold George R II $27,260
4Feb83- 6Aqu fst 6f ⊡:22⅘ :46⅕ 1:13⅗ Clm 30000 4 4 1hd 1½ 11½ 33½ McKnight J b 117 4.70 72-20 TermPaper1122¾CatchMatthew113¾T.V.Repairman117¾ Weakened 14
22Jan83- 2Aqu fst 6f ⊡:23 :45⅘ 1:10⅗ Clm 25000 10 2 1hd 11½ 1hd 32 McKnight J b 117 42.90 89-07 Tolerable 1171¾ Duck Call 117nk T. V. Repairman1172½ Weakened 13
17Aug82- 8AP fst 7f :23⅕ :46⅖ 1:24⅖ 3↑Alw 10000 2 5 11½ 1hd 41½ 58 Clark K D b 113 9.70 72-27 Crown TheKing1121LBCommander1194FrederickTown1192½ Tired 6
7Aug82- 7AP sly 7f :23 :46⅖ 1:26⅖ 3↑Alw 10000 6 1 2½ 2hd 22 48½ Clark K D b 115 *2.30 61-37 Home Game 122nk L B Commander 1227 Rackit Back 1121½ Tired 6
10Jly82- 6AP sly 7f :22⅗ :45⅘ 1:24⅖ 3↑Alw 9500 1 4 2½ 11½ 14 16 Clark K D b 113 4.70 80-28 T.V.Repairman1136LBCommander119hdSbrChief1112¾ Ridden out 8
22Jun82- 9AP fst 6f :22⅗ :46⅖ 1:12 3↑Alw 9800 6 3 2½ 42 66 611 Fires E b 113 6.60 71-24 True Wish 1121½ Sorroto 119¾ Double Accord 122hd Tired 6
12Jun82- 6AP fst 6f :22⅕ :45⅕ 1:10⅗ 3↑Alw 11000 7 3 41½ 32 22½ 45¾ Fires E b 113 2.00 83-17 Double Accord 1195 Nearctic Sand 110no Diabolo Lobo113¾ Tired 8
20Apr82- 4Kee fst 6f :22 :45⅖ 1:11⅗ Alw 14500 1 7 1½ 11½ 14 13¾ Brumfield D b 116 *1.50 85-15 T. V. Repairman 1163¾Dreamtide1101SmartNative1192 Ridden out 8
7Apr82- 3Kee fst 6½f :22⅖ :45⅗ 1:16⅘ Alw 14500 2 4 12 12 2hd 36½ Brumfield D b 115 3.80 87-13 Unswerving 1185½ Diamond Kas 112¾ T. V. Repairman 1151 Tired 9
23Oct81- 4Kee sly 6f :22⅕ :45⅗ 1:11⅘ Alw 14500 6 5 3½ 42 42 45¾ Lively J 117 5.40 77-22 Raging Colors 117½ Boston Zip 1173 Double Burner 1172½ Tired 11
LATEST WORKOUTS Feb 1 Bel tr.t 4f fst :50 b Jan 20 Bel tr.t 3f fst :39 b Jan 15 Bel tr.t 4f fst :51⅗ b Jan 10 Bel tr.t 5f fst 1:01⅗ h

12:1

Quiet Old Friend Dk. b. or br. c. 4, by My Old Friend—Quiet Purpose, by Intentionally Lifetime 1982 10 2 0 0 $26,340
$25,000 Br.—Star L D (NY) 113 21 2 4 4 1981 11 M 4 4 $27,780
Own.—Star L D Tr.—Hubley Mark $54,120 Turf 1 0 0 0
19Sep82- 1Bel fst 6f :22⅘ :46⅗ 1:12 3↑Clm 10500 7 12 1011 87½ 88 55 Santagata N 112 18.10 77-20 Navy Chaplain 1192½Abelardo1171¾SirSizzlingNehoc113½ Mild bid 12
27Aug82- 9Sar fst 6f :22⅗ :46⅕ 1:10⅘ Clm 18000 4 11 1010 88 45 47½ Montoya D 113 30.30 78-14 Duck Call 1196½ Blue's Choice 106½ Heres Anthony 113½ Hung 12
30Jly82- 2Bel fst 1 1/16 :46⅗ 1:11⅕ 1:44⅕ Clm 25000 9 7 77 86 1113 1113 Samyn J L 117 15.10 68-16 Mirildo 1171½ Ardent Bid 1151½ Tribal Prince 1131½ Fell back 12
23Jly82- 9Bel fst 6f :22⅘ :46 1:11⅗ Clm 45000 3 7 86½ 89 98½ 96½ Samyn J L 113 20.30 78-21 Old King Cole 117nk Private Sun 117¾ Flippydoo 117¾ Outrun 11
10Jly82- 4Bel fst 1 :46⅘ 1:11⅘ 1:37⅗ 3↑ⓈAlw 27500 4 9 88 811 1018 1022 Bailey J D 113 18.80 56-20 ShyGroom1136PovrtyHollowKd1171SrtogSnrs1132½ Broke poorly 11
30Jun82- 5Bel gd 1 1/16 Ⓣ:48⅕ 1:12 1:43⅗ Clm 75000 1 7 77½ 76½ 710 59¾ Molina V H 112 27.20 73-26 RedBrigde1164¾UncleJeff1222½TheYoungSquire1182½ Raced wide 7
12Jun82- 4Bel fst 6f :23⅕ :46⅕ 1:11 3↑ⓈAlw 26000 2 4 64 56 58½ 511 Molina V H 114 12.60 76-14 Redline 112nk Zoom Googus 1174½ Ample Native 1121¾ No threat 7
7Jun82- 7Bel gd 7f :22⅗ :45⅖ 1:23⅘ 3↑ⓈAlw 24500 2 3 33½ 22 22 11½ Molina V H 109 27.30 83-13 QuietOldFriend1091½Rajb'sSon1124LottHolcomb1121½ Drew clear 8
8May82- 6Aqu fst 7f :22⅘ :45⅘ 1:23⅘ 3↑ⓈAlw 24500 8 3 64½ 67 815 916 Molina V H 108 17.00 66-19 Master Digby 1147½ Major Leader 115¾ All Eternity 113½ Outrun 11
3Jan82- 9Aqu fst 6f ⊡:23⅗ :47⅘ 1:13⅕ ⓈMd Sp Wt 7 2 1hd 12 13 1½ Molina V H5 117 3.30 78-19 Quiet Old Friend 117½ Catch Me 1221½ PeacefulTune1225 Driving 12
LATEST WORKOUTS Feb 20 Bel tr.t 5f fst 1:04⅘ b Feb 16 Bel tr.t 4f fst :48⅗ h Feb 11 Bel tr.t 5f fst 1:05 b Jan 27 Bel tr.t 3f fst :39 b

MOLINA 30:1

FEBRUARY 24—RACE 5 (Exacta Wagering)

Sun Dial—Raise after a loss. This horse wins on January 12th and December 4th after getting loose on the lead. Today it doesn't figure to shake loose and is too cheap to fight it out with these.

Need A Penny—Greatly overmatched in last. The race on January 31st was a superior effort with adjusted speed rating of 96. Before that, the 13 post and a good effort closing 8 1/4 lengths the last quarter and doing it in :23[1] (the last quarter of the race was :24^{4} and **Need A Penny** gained 8 1/4 lengths)! Before that race, a win. This horse should be tough today, especially with all the speed in this field.

The Bloody Best—Another horse raised after a loss. Not a contender.

Self-Pressured—Doesn't look like much, but it didn't look like much until the last time it raced in 30 claimers and had a 98 adjusted speed rating—the highest in the race. Although seventh last time out, its adjusted speed rating was still 95. The trainer has been reluctant to drop this horse in the past. Stepping down is a sure sign of an all out effort today.

Thunder Bridge—Yet another raise after a loss.

Dark 'N Bold—Decent effort last time and a victory in 15 claimers the time before. Ordinarily, I'd throw this horse right out because it was raised after a loss. However, **Dark 'N Bold** was just claimed, so we must look further. Today is February 24th. It's not likely that Donald McLoy can improve this horse much in just four days. Therefore, not a contender.

J.C.'s Double—Nothing last two and an unfavorable rider change. Not a contender.

Bright Search—Recently **Bright Search** was quitting in the stretch. It won last time after a speed duel. However, it didn't win big in a cheaper class, steps up today, picks up weight and there is even more speed in the field today. An underlay at 3:1. Throw it out. This is a false favorite.

Colonel Law—Coming off a nice win. However, he is stepping up today and picks up more weight than it has ever carried. I can't see **Colonel Law** winning, but at 16:1 probably should be included in exactas.

Richness—Stepped down last time and was sent off at even bigger odds! Ninth by 9 1/4 with no excuse. Not a contender.

T.V. Repairman—Cheap speed in field full of speed.

Quiet Old Friend—Big raise after running fifth in 10 claimers five months ago. No way.

THE BET: With all the speed in the field **Need A Penny** looks even better. Although overmatched in last, his connections thought that his race on January 31st was impressive enough to run him in a state-bred handicap. The nice thing about that race is that Beitia didn't push him after realizing he was overmatched. The New York crowd is letting this horse go off as an overlay because they didn't throw out the race on February 16th. The bet for the race is 75% of the M.B., all on exactas because there are only two horses that figure to run second and the favorite is definitely beatable. I split my exacta bets this way:

Need a Penny—Self-Pressured	25%
Self-Pressured—Need A Penny	20%
Need A Penny—Colonel Law	12%
Colonel Law—Need a Penny	8%
Need A Penny—Bright Search (a saver)	5%
Bright Search—Need A Penny (a saver)	5%
	75% of the M.B.

RESULTS: **Need a Penny** closed to win after the speed gave way. He paid $13.20. **Self Pressured** ran second to complete a $2 exacta with $92.00. This exacta paid a terrific price because the favorite didn't come first or second. Just like we figured. Putting the money on **Need a Penny** to win would have returned less in this case. It's great to win. It's even greater when the race was bet correctly.

7 AQUEDUCT

1⅛ MILES
INNER DIRT TRACK
AQUEDUCT
START FINISH

1⅛ MILES. (INNER-DIRT). (1.49⅕) ALLOWANCE. Purse $37,000. 4-year-olds and upward which have not won two races of $12,500 at a mile or over since October-1. Weight, 122 lbs. Non-winners of three races of $15,000 at a mile or over in 1982-83 allowed 3 lbs. Of two such races in 1982-83, 5 lbs. Of such a race since January 1, 7 lbs. (Maiden, Claiming, Starter and State-bred races not considered.)

Her Pal

GONZALEZ 10:1

Ch. g. 6, by Don's Pal—Her Likeness, by Amarullah
Br.—Streaker Mary Ann (MD)
Tr.—Streaker Mary Ann
Own.—Streaker Mary Ann

115 — Lifetime 102 12 10 14 $170,101 — 1983 3 0 0 0 $1,867 — 1982 33 3 3 7 $60,670 — Turf 13 1 1 0 $15,750

Entered 26Feb83- 8 BOW, finished 11

29Jan83- 8Bow fst 1 1/16 :48⅕ 1:13⅕ 1:45⅘ 3↑ⓈGl Stryker H 5 3 21½ 32½ 46½ 45¾ Delgado A 109 7.10 71-22 Tim Tamber 113nk A Magic Spray 118½ Boston Tea 108⁵ Tired. 6
15Jan83- 8Bow fst 7f :22⅕ :45 1:23⅘ 3↑ⓈStr De Nsk H 5 1 45½ 79½ 77½ 54¾ Delgado A 110 10.20 83-23 Lord Duck 1161½ A MagicSpray115²WhatAMichael120¹ No factor 10
3Jan83- 8Bow fst 1 1/16 :48 1:13⅕ 1:45⅘ 3↑Resolution H 1 2 55½ 86½ 813 617 Hutton G W 111 11.40 68-29 AppealApproved115²AMagicSpray1114½HushHushFlash114¹ Tired 8
23Dec82- 8Lrl fst 6f :22⅘ :46 1:11⅘ 3↑Alw 16000 5 1 57¾ 65 52¾ 3hd Adams J K 117 10.70 86-23 Lord Duck 117no What A Michael 122hd Her Pal 117¹ Rallied 7
11Dec82- 8Lrl fst 1⅛ :11⅘ 1:37⅗ 1:50⅘ 3↑W. Haight H 4 3 38 33 33½ 32¾ Hutton G W 112 36.30f 90-10 Hush Hush Flash 1091½ Blackie Daw 118¹ Her Pal 112nk Fin. well 13
26Nov82- 8Lrl yl 1⅛ Ⓣ:47⅘ 1:12⅘ 1:52 3↑ⓈConstlat'n H 5 4 49 612 718 716 Miller D A Jr 113 19.10 61-30 Tim Tamber 1133¾ Clarinet King 113¾ Count Disco 113⁴ Tired 9
13Nov82- 8Med gd 1 1/16 :47⅘ 1:11⅘ 1:43⅘ 3↑Alw 25000 1 1 1hd 21 45 45 Kaenel J L 117 16.20 86-15 Double Leader 122¹ Aye's Turn 115no Con Diego 110⁴ Tired 8
6Nov82- 4Lrl fst 1 1/16 :47⅘ 1:12⅕ 1:43⅘ 3↑Handicap 6 3 41¾ 41½ 43 55 Kaenel J L 113 12.00 92-11 Blackie Daw 1192¼ Castle Knight 1182¼ SunnyWinters118no Tired 7
30Oct82- 6Lrl fst 7f :23 :46⅗ 1:24⅕ 3↑Alw 16000 8 3 73¾ 42 1hd 1¾ Kaenel J L 119 14.30 90-15 Her Pal 119¾ Bronze Hill 114nk Sunny Winters 122no Driving 8
25Oct82- 8Lrl sly 1 :47⅘ 1:13⅕ 1:39 3↑Alw 20000 5 2 3½ 55 57½ 49¾ Hutton G W 115 16.60 67-32 Mile High Club 1151½ Peace ForPeace117⁸IssueJoined119nk Tired 8

LATEST WORKOUTS Feb 22 Lrl 6f fst 1:17 b — Feb 19 Lrl 4f gd :49⅘ b — Feb 9 Lrl 5f fst 1:06 b — Jan 27 Lrl 4f fst :51⅘ b

Rainbow Connection *

DAVIS 10:1

B. m. 5, by Halo—Hangin Round, by Stage Door Johnny
Br.—Coker Mrs G T (Ont-C)
Tr.—Carroll Del W II
Own.—Farish W S III

105⁵ — Lifetime 29 7 7 0 $382,126 — 1983 1 0 0 0 — 1982 11 0 3 0 $78,752 — Turf 14 2 2 0 $143,335

17Feb83- 8Aqu fst 6f ⊡:22⅘ :46⅕ 1:11⅘ Alw 35000 2 2 68½ 79 78½ 68¾ Melendez J D⁵ 107 11.90 80-17 Space Mountain 1121¾ I'm SoMerry1081½TenBore1171½ No factor 7
5Sep82- 8Bel fm 1¼ Ⓣ:48⅘ 1:37 2:01⅘ 3↑ⒻFlwr Bowl H 4 12 1223 1225 1217 1229 Maple E 116 14.40 50-13 Trevita 117no Hunston 108½ Hush Dear 112¾ Trailed 12
22Aug82- 9FE fm 1½ Ⓣ:47⅘ 2:03⅘ 2:28⅘ 3↑Niagara H 6 4 516 78 610 712 Stahlbaum G 118 2.20 87-03 Lord Elgin 1142½ Fiddle Dancer Boy1152½JadosaToker1161½ Tired 8
17Jly82- 9WO yl 1¼ Ⓣ:48⅘ 1:40⅘ 2:07⅘ ⓈCan Maturity 5 8 78½ 42½ 2hd 2½ Stahlbaum G 121 3.80 67-32 FrostKing126½RinbowConnection121¾LeGrndSeignur1265½ Rallied 9
19Jun82- 8Hol fm 1⅛ Ⓣ:47⅘ 1:11⅘ 1:47⅘ 3↑ⒻBev Hills H 1 6 612 611 55½ 43¾ McHargue D G 116 23.60 89-07 Sangue 119² Ack's Secret 123¹ Miss Huntington 117¾ Outrun 6
30May82- 8GG fm 1⅜ Ⓣ:46⅘ 1:38⅘ 2:16⅘ 3↑ⒻYrbaBuenaH 10 10 1019 54 55 46½ Toro F 117 7.40 79-23 Sangue 1172½ Berry Bush 119¹ Mademoiselle Ivor 112³ Rallied 10
16May82- 7Hol fm 1⅛ Ⓣ:47 1:11⅘ 1:47⅘ ⒻConvenience 8 9 811 86½ 73½ 63½ Toro F 118 *1.70 88-07 Viendra 1141½ Coax Me Home 114hd Mademoiselle Ivor 114¹ 10
21Apr82- 9SA fm 1¼ Ⓣ:44⅘ 1:34⅘ 1:59⅘ S. Jacinto H 4 10 919 84½ 73½ 63 Hawley S 115 4.20 86-10 Durban Deep 115¾ Monarch 115nk Kilty 113hd Outrun 10
21Apr82-Run in Two Divisions: 8th & 9th Races
3Apr82- 8SA fst 1¼ :46⅕ 1:35⅘ 2:00⅘ ⒻS Barbara H 1 8 810 69½ 610 58¾ Toro F 117 3.00 77-16 Ack's Secret 1224½ Landresse 116no Plenty O'Toole 114⁴ Outrun 8
7Feb82- 8SA fst 1¼ :45⅕ 1:34⅘ 2:00⅘ C. H. Strub 2 6 68½ 87¾ 718 719 McHargue D G 114 8.20 68-13 It's The One 118⁴ Dorcaro 115³ Rock Softly 115nk Outrun 8

LATEST WORKOUTS Feb 24 Bel tr.t 5f fst 1:01⅘ h — Feb 11 Bel tr.t 3f fst :36⅘ b — ●Feb 7 Bel tr.t 5f gd 1:01⅘ h — Jan 31 Bel tr.t 1 gd 1:43⅘ b

Deedee's Deal

3:1

Dk. b. or br. g. 6, by Hickery—Me Carla, by Gallant Romeo
Br.—Amlung R (Fla)
Tr.—Ribaudo Robert
Own.—Martini N A

117 — Lifetime 68 15 13 13 $282,832 — 1983 5 2 0 2 $45,840 — 1982 14 4 4 3 $95,242 — Turf 18 4 3 3 $72,240

18Feb83- 8Aqu fst 1 1/16 ⊡:48 1:13⅕ 1:45⅘ Alw 37000 1 6 41¾ 21½ 1hd 1¾ Cordero A Jr b 115 *1.20 85-27 Deedee's Deal 115¾ Rain Prince 110⁴ Daring Bet 115² driving 7
9Feb83- 8Aqu fst 1 70 ⊡:49 1:14 1:43⅕ Alw 37000 3 5 42½ 42 33 33 Miranda J b 115 3.80 83-20 Kentucky Edd 1152½CampusCapers115½Deedee'sDeal1151½ Rallied 6
28Jan83- 7Aqu fst 1 1/16 ⊡:49⅘ 1:14⅘ 1:45⅘ Clm 75000 2 3 3½ 32 2hd 1no Cordero A Jr b 117 *1.60 85-25 Deedee's Deal 117no Evasive John 1121¾ Tarberry 115¹ Just up 6
14Jan83- 8Aqu fst 1 70 ⊡:48⅘ 1:13 1:43 Alw 40000 3 8 85½ 45 33 31¾ Cordero A Jr b 115 3.90 85-19 Mouse Corps 112¹ Master Digby 115¾ Deedee's Deal 115² Rallied 8
2Jan83- 8Aqu fst 1⅛ ⊡:49 1:13⅘ 1:52 Assault H 3 4 53½ 54½ 512 516 Hernandez R b 114 6.60 70-28 ThirtyEightPaces1175½FbulousFind116⁶SkinDncer1112½ Fell back 5
22Dec82- 5Aqu fst 1 1/16 ⊡:48⅘ 1:13 1:46 3↑Handicap 3 6 610 57½ 25 25½ Cordero A Jr b 112 6.80 77-22 GoodbyeStrter1165½Deedee'sDel112½StiffSentence122¹¹ Game try 6
27Nov82- 8Med fst 1 1/16 :47 1:12 1:45⅘ 3↑Alw 25000 4 6 711 63½ 2½ 2hd Cordero A Jr b 115 5.50 82-21 Boogie Woogy117hdDeedee'sDeal115²Aye'sTurn1152½ Just missed 8
16Sep82- 1Bel fm 1¼ Ⓣ:48⅘ 1:36⅘ 2:01⅕ 3↑Clm 75000 2 3 42½ 33 36 38½ Cordero A Jr b 117 *.70 82-13 NicePirate117⁵Philnthropic1161½Deedee'sDel1172½ Bid, weakened 5
30Aug82- 3Sar fm 1 Ⓣ:47⅕ 1:10⅘ 1:35⅕ 3↑Clm 75000 2 4 53½ 33½ 24 22 Cordero A Jr b 119 *2.00 98-09 Harmonizer 115² Deedee's Deal 1191¾ BoogieWoogy1171½ Rallied 8
16Aug82- 2Sar fm 1 1/16 Ⓣ:46 1:10 1:41⅘ 3↑Clm 72500 9 8 89¾ 45 31½ 1no Cordero A Jr b 115 5.80 88-13 Deedee's Deal 115no King Neptune 119¾ DiscoCount1131½ Driving 9

Mouse Corps *

3:2

Ch. h. 5, by Within Hail—Scarlet My Dear, by Grey Dawn II
Br.—DuPont Mrs W III (Ky)
Tr.—Sedlacek Michael C
Own.—Lane G

112⁵ — Lifetime 29 12 6 2 $163,061 — 1983 3 1 1 0 $35,968 — 1982 6 5 0 1 $69,000

19Feb83- 8Aqu fst 6f ⊡:23⅕ :46⅕ 1:10⅘ 3↑Sprtng Plt H 5 5 54½ 31½ 21 31½ Alvarado R Jr 112 6.10 91-20 Top Avenger 120hd ⒹLet Burn 1171½ Mouse Corps 112² Steadied 5
19Feb83-Placed second through disqualification
14Jan83- 8Aqu fst 1 70 ⊡:48⅘ 1:13 1:43 Alw 40000 8 7 21½ 2hd 1hd 11 Alvarado R Jr⁵ 112 *2.30 87-19 Mouse Corps 112¹ Master Digby 115¾ Deedee's Deal 115² Driving 8
1Jan83- 8Aqu fst 6f ⊡:23 :46⅘ 1:11⅘ 3↑Paumonok H 6 1 64½ 75½ 63½ 55 Migliore R 119 4.10 82-25 InFromDixie126nkMortgageMan1164½FortMonroe110nk No factor 8
19Nov82- 5Aqu fst 6f :22⅘ :46⅕ 1:10⅘ 3↑Clm 100000 6 5 87¾ 74¾ 41 3nk Alvarado R Jr⁵ 117 *1.10 89-23 Cut High 116hd Fanny's Fox 112nk Mouse Corps 117nk Hung 9
4Nov82- 3Med fst 6f :22⅕ :45⅕ 1:09⅕ 3↑Alw 28000 2 5 22½ 21½ 2½ 11½ Alvarado R Jr⁵ 114 1.80 97-14 Mouse Corps 1141½ Triocala 117⁴ Royal Hierarchy 115½ Driving 6
19Oct82- 6Med fst 6f :22⅘ :45⅕ 1:10 3↑Handicap 4 7 52½ 41¾ 21 1½ McCauley W H 114 3.20 93-16 Mouse Corps 114½ Main Stem 113¹ Havagreatdate 1132½ Driving 8
3Oct82- 5Bel fst 7f :23⅘ :47⅕ 1:24⅕ 3↑Alw 32000 4 6 63½ 43 2½ 1¾ Alvarado R Jr⁷ 108 5.60 81-20 Mouse Corps 108¾ Samba Boy 1152½ Aye's Turn 1151¾ Driving 8
25Sep82- 2Bel fst 7f :23⅘ :47⅕ 1:24⅕ 3↑Clm 70000 8 7 72¾ 62½ 3½ 1no Alvarado R Jr⁷ 106 5.00 81-15 Mouse Corps 106no Fanny's Fox 117½ Alshurouk 1173¾ Up in time 9
11Sep82- 7Med fst 6f :23 :46⅕ 1:10⅘ 3↑Clm 40000 1 5 2½ 12½ 12 13¾ Lizarzaburu P M⁵ 111 3.90 90-16 Mouse Corps 1113¾ In The Bucks 1141½ Manny T. 116⁴ Driving 7
4Dec81- 6Med gd 1 1/16 :46⅕ 1:10⅘ 1:42⅘ Wintr Qtr H 3 5 46½ 31 78½ 89½ Santagata N 111 13.10 87-15 ClassicGoGo118³WellDecorated117nkThirtyEightPaces1201¾ Tired 9

LATEST WORKOUTS Feb 14 Aqu ⊡ 5f fst 1:00⅘ h

Grand Felice

19:1

Ch. h. 5, by Full Pocket—Julie Tim, by Blade
Br.—Nuckols Bros (Ky)
Tr.—Wright Floyd
Own.—O'Connor R F

117 — Lifetime 34 5 13 1 $78,453 — 1983 4 1 1 0 $23,780 — 1982 16 2 3 1 $39,140 — Turf 13 1 9 0 $5,933

21Feb83- 8Aqu fst 1⅛ ⊡:46⅘ 1:11 1:50⅕ 3↑Grey Lag H 6 3 31 32 89¾ 913 Faine C 112 41.20 82-22 Sing Sing 122½ Fabulous Find 115¾ Lark Oscillation 113¹ Tired 9
14Feb83- 7Aqu fst 6f ⊡:22⅘ :46⅕ 1:10⅘ Alw 35000 8 6 74½ 72½ 65½ 64 Faine C 117 18.30 86-13 Main Stem 110no With Caution 1192½ MortgageMan117hd Outrun 8
19Jan83- 1Aqu fst 1⅛ ⊡:48⅕ 1:13 1:52⅘ Alw 29000 1 1 2hd 1hd 1hd 22 Faine C 117 7.40 82-24 ⒹEvasive John 112² Grand Felice 117¾ John's Gold 117⁴ Tired 6
19Jan83-Placed first through disqualification
9Jan83- 9Aqu fst 1 70 ⊡:48⅕ 1:12⅘ 1:42 Alw 29000 1 2 2hd 1hd 1hd 2hd Faine C 117 16.60 92-17 Tarberry 112hd Grand Felice 1171½ ClimbingHigh1191½ Just failed 10
30Dec82- 8Aqu fst 6f ⊡:23 :46⅘ 1:11⅘ 3↑Alw 27000 7 2 43 55 58½ 54 Faine C 117 16.10 82-24 Lost Creek 115no Mr. Howard 1141¾ King Naskra 1151¾ Tired 7
19Dec82- 1Aqu fst 1 1/16 ⊡:49 1:13⅘ 1:45⅘ 3↑Clm c-47500 2 3 31½ 34½ 26 23½ Miceli M 117 *2.50 80-23 Subordinte1083½GrndFelic1172¾NorthrnRgnt1133¾ Best of others 6
10Dec82- 1Aqu fst 1⅛ ⊡:48⅕ 1:13⅘ 1:52⅘ 3↑Clm 45000 5 5 53½ 53¾ 11½ 12¾ Miceli M³ 113 6.80 82-24 GrndFelice1132¾CmpusCpers117nkCremeDeLFete113¾ Drew clear 7
26Nov82- 8Med fst 1 1/16 :47⅘ 1:12⅕ 1:45⅕ 3↑Alw 16000 3 2 21½ 22 44½ 44½ Miceli M b 116 7.20 78-21 Class Hero 1131½ Wind Jet 116³ Big Greg 116nk Tired 7
12Nov82- 5Aqu fst 7f :22⅘ :45⅕ 1:23⅘ 3↑Clm 50000 6 3 53 43 77¾ 85½ Miceli M b 117 10.70 79-21 Surf Club 113no Crockford Lad 117¾ Northern Regent113nk Tired 8
28Oct82- 7Aqu fst 1 :45⅘ 1:09⅕ 1:34⅘ 3↑Alw 25000 4 4 33½ 47 58½ 59 Miceli M 117 14.10 85-14 Citius 1141½ King Neptune 117³ Hominy Hill 1143½ Tired 7

LATEST WORKOUTS Feb 2 Bel tr.t 4f fst :49 b

9:5

Accipiter's Hope — B. h. 5, by Accipiter—Miss Switch, by Royal Levee
Own.—Snyder H I — Br.—Dimauro S A (NY) — Tr.—DiMauro Stephen L
115 — Lifetime 46 9 9 9 $405,212 — 1983 2 0 1 0 $11,078 — 1982 15 3 4 4 $176,544 — Turf 1 0 0 0

16Feb83- 8Aqu	fst	6f	⊡:23⅕	:46⅗	1:10⅘	3↑ ⓈH Hughes H	6	10	108	78½	54½	47¾	Lovato F Jr	126	2.30	84-23	Master Digby 1237 Jan'sKinsman120¾BigIzzy117hd	Circled horses	11
29Jan83- 7Aqu	fst	6f	⊡:22⅗	:45⅕	1:09⅘	Alw 35000	3	8	77½	56½	69½	24¾	Lovato F Jr	117	9.30	90-20	Let Burn 1224¾ Accipiter's Hope 117½ Main Stem 110hd	Gamely	8
6Oct82- 8Bel	fst	1⅛	:46⅕	1:11⅗	1:50	3↑ ⓈBongard H	3	7	79	53½	47	39	Cordero A Jr	119	*.70	68-28	FerlessLeder112½DedictedRullh1179½Accipiter'sHope1194¾	Rallied	8
22Sep82- 8Bel	gd	1	:47	1:10⅘	1:35⅗	3↑ ⓈHudson H	5	6	43½	32	2½	21	Cordero A Jr	120	*1.10e	87-16	ShyGroom1171Accipiter'sHope1204DedictedRullh1191½	Mate won	6
22Aug82- 9FL	fst	1 1/16	:47⅘	1:12⅗	1:44⅕	3↑ Rochester Cp	2	4	32	21	13	13	Whitley K	109	*1.20	97-21	Acciptr'sHop1093DynmcMov1122½KngOfMrdGrs1091½	Ridden out	9
10Aug82- 9Mth	fst	1	:46⅕	1:10	1:35⅗	3↑ Sal Mile H	5	10	910	67½	55½	34¾	Santagata N	116	7.50	91-16	CountHisFleet116¾ExplosiveBid1174Accipiter'sHope116no	Rallied	12
28Jly82- 8Bel	my	1	:47⅗	1:11⅘	1:37⅕	3↑ ⓈEvanShipman	5	7	31	31	32½	33½	Samyn J L	126	6.50	76-21	Prosper 1173½ Jan's Kinsman 119nk Accipiter'sHope1264	Even try	7
4Jly82- 8Bel	fst	1¼	:47⅗	1:35⅗	1:59⅗	3↑ Suburban H	6	6	68½	55½	69½	616	Samyn J L	111	59.20	86-14	Silver Buck 1113 It's The One 1243¾ Aloma'sRuler112½	No Factor	8
12Jun82- 8Bel	fst	1⅛	:46⅗	1:10⅗	1:47⅗	Nassau Cty H	1	4	44½	31½	1hd	21½	McCarron G	114	5.80	88-14	Princelet 1131½ Accipiter's Hope 1144¾ Indian Toast1104	2nd best	7
29May82- 7Bel	gd	1	:46	1:10⅗	1:35⅗	3↑ ⓈAlw 37000	6	3	31½	55½	612	617	Cordero A Jr	121	*2.00	71-13	Naskra's Breeze 1193 Sheer Survival 1195¾ Sir Frank 119½	Tired	6

LATEST WORKOUTS Feb 23 Bel tr.t 5f fst 1:02⅕ b — Feb 9 Bel tr.t 4f fst :50⅘ b — ●Jan 23 Bel tr.t 5f fst 1:00⅘ h — ●Jan 13 Bel tr.t 3f fst :35⅘ h

THIBEAU 33:1

First Class Act — B. g. 4, by An Act—Sneeze, by Cyane
Own.—Lorel Stable — Br.—Raab S (NY) — Tr.—Nocella Vincent
108⁷ — Lifetime 17 4 3 2 $98,796 — 1983 2 0 0 0 — 1982 15 4 3 2 $98,796 — Turf 3 1 0 0 $17,250

5Feb83- 5Aqu	fst	1 1/16	⊡:49	1:14⅕	1:46	ⓈAlw 41000	5	5	42½	43½	57	55¾	Migliore R	b 119	6.00	77-20	Gatlinburg 1101 Shy Groom 1151½ Big Izzy 1101	No rally	6
8Jan83- 7Aqu	fst	170	⊡:47	1:12	1:42	Alw 40000	1	7	86½	67½	611	58¾	Migliore R	b 115	5.30	83-16	Waj. Jr. 1102 Lark Oscillation 1158 RainPrince110¾	No Contender	9
29Dec82- 8Aqu	fst	1 1/16	⊡:48	1:12⅗	1:46	3↑ ⓈAlex M Robb	5	6	63½	52½	33½	21½	Migliore R	b 116	7.50	81-24	Master Digby 1161½ First ClassAct116½Jan'sKinsman1194¾	Rallied	6
16Dec82- 8Aqu	sly	170	⊡:47⅗	1:12⅗	1:42⅗	3↑ ⓈHandicap	3	6	45½	43½	57½	513	Migliore R	b 109	8.30	77-23	Master Digby 109¾ Naskra's Breeze 1287¾ Tiempo105nk	No factor	6
18Oct82- 1Aqu	fst	1⅛	:49⅕	1:14	1:52⅗	3↑ ⓈHandicap	1	4	46½	34½	31½	1no	Samyn J L	b 112	3.70	73-23	FirstClassAct112noFearlessLeader1241½SoftMorning1101½	Driving	6
14Oct82- 5Aqu	fst	1⅛	:47	1:11⅗	1:50⅗	3↑ ⓈAlw 27500	4	5	56½	44½	2hd	1no	Samyn J L	b 116	5.90	81-20	First Class Act 116no SaratogaSunrise1141½Danderoo114¾	Driving	6
6Oct82- 8Bel	fst	1⅛	:46⅕	1:11⅗	1:50	3↑ ⓈBongard H	8	5	57	75½	612	515	Samyn J L	b 109	21.50	62-28	FerlessLeder112½DdictdRullh1179½Accipitr'sHop1194¾	Raced wide	8
30Sep82- 7Bel	fm	1 1/16	ⓣ:47	1:12	1:45⅗	3↑ ⓈAlw 26000	6	7	614	58½	2½	13¾	Samyn J L	b 113	3.50	74-15	First Class Act 1133¾ Bluff 1131½ Major Leader 113nk	Ridden out	[illegible]
19Sep82- 9Bel	fst	7f	:22⅗	:46⅕	1:24⅗	3↑ ⓈAlw 24500	11	10	107½	77¾	54½	43½	Pincay L Jr	b 117	5.60	75-20	Calcutta Sweep 1132 Semaj 1101½ Key Count 113nk	Wide	11
5Sep82- 9Bel	fst	1 1/16	:46⅗	1:11⅘	1:45⅕	3↑ ⓈAlw 26000	9	6	63½	42	31½	3hd	Samyn J L	b 113	5.60	76-18	Danderoo 113no Mc Michael 106no First Class Act 1131½	Bumped	[illegible]

LATEST WORKOUTS Feb 25 Bel tr.t 4f fst :51⅕ b — ●Feb 3 Bel tr.t 4f sly :48 h — Jan 29 Bel tr.t 6f fst 1:15⅗ h — Jan 23 Bel tr.t 5f fst 1:01⅘ h

MARCH 2—RACE 7 (Exacta Wagering)

This is not an obvious race, but a fun one because the winner paid a price and broke the track record. It is one that most people picked wrong, but the correct reasoning is solid. These types of races are particularly gratifying.

Her Pal—Can't see the line on February 26th but **Her Pal** came in 11th. Additionally, he is a shipper and just raced four days ago. Unfavorable jockey change. Throw him out.

Rainbow Connection—Second start after a layoff—a decent tightener. Ran against some of the nation's top grass horses (e.g. **Sangue**, **Treita**). This horse is the class of the field. However, this horse's best effort on the dirt is being beaten by 7 lengths. More importantly, its workouts are mediocre. **Rainbow Connection** looks like she needs another race. This is why it's not a contender. It's simply not ready after being laid off.

Deedee's Deal—Good at a mile and a sixteenth but flattens out a mile and an eighth.

Mouse Corps—An obvious closer who prefers a sprint but was versatile enough to win at a mile and seventy yards. At a mile and a sixteenth though, he tired. However, he raced with impressive company—**Classic Go Go, Well Decorated** and **Thirty Eight Paces**. The pace of the race on January 14th was slow, so I'm still not convinced he can go a respectable mile and an eighth. A contender, but a lukewarm one.

Grand Felice—After being claimed on December 19th, a tightener and then a giant effort on January 9th going head and head all the way. Next another all out race and a victory. After that came an easy race at the wrong distance. Then on February 21st Floyd Wright got overly optimistic placing **Grand Felice** in the Grey Lag Handicap (either that or he was building the odds for today). The horse was 9th beaten 13, but look at the race a little closer. Its adjusted speed rating was still 98, although well beaten! On Dec. 1, 1982, the only other time he ran today's distance, his adjusted speed figure was 99! More importantly, and the key, is the pace in its last race—the half in :46^4 and six panels in 1:11, **Grand Felice** is right there. He is the only speed today and ready to run. He's 19:1 only because many people didn't take a close look and only saw a ninth beaten 13 lengths. Also, Faine doesn't ride on the Aqueduct circuit regularly.

Accipiters Hope—Two nice tighteners after a layoff and a classy horse. The logical favorite and a contender.

First Class Act—Only one workout in 25 days. Also, at 33:1 is dead on the board (i.e., the odds board) probably hurting. Throw him out.

THE BET: 70% of the M.B. The bet would be more with a top jockey. 15% to place (because of the jockey) and 55% on exactas, including 20% on exactas wheeling **Grand Felice** on top.

Exactas:	**Grand Felice—Accipiters Hope**	15%
	Accipiters Hope—Grand Felice	10%
	Grand Felice—Mouse Corps (saver)	5%
	Mouse Corps—Grand Felice (saver)	5%
		35%

Note: The exactas I like most with **Grand Felice** include the two favorites. Wheeling **Grand Felice** on top, therefore, is better than playing her to win. If the favorite or second choice doesn't run second, the exacta payoff will be huge with a 19:1 shot on top.

RESULTS: **Grand Felice** broke the track record after being loose on the lead! He paid $40.20. **Accipiter's Hope** completed a $184.40 exacta. **Mouse Corps** was third and interestingly enough, lacked a closing response (according to the chart comments in the *Form*). Too bad this wasn't a triple race.

5 AQUEDUCT (7 FURLONGS — AQUEDUCT)

7 FURLONGS. (1.20⅕) ALLOWANCE. Purse $20,000. 3-year-old fillies which have never won a race other than Maiden or Claiming. Weights, 121 lbs. Non-winners of a race other than Claiming since April 1 allowed 3 lbs. Of such a race since March 15, 5 lbs.

6:1

Ida Lewis
Dk. b. or br. f. 3, by Restivo—Big Mad, by Hail To Reason
Br.—Martin T B (Fla)
Own.—Martin M T — Tr.—DeStasio Richard T
118 — Lifetime 1 1 0 0 $10,800 — 1983 1 1 0 0 $10,800 — 1982 0 M 0 0
26Mar83- 6Aqu fst 6f :23 :46⅘ 1:12 ⒻMd Sp Wt 2 10 3³½ 3²½ 1½ 1⁴ Lovato F Jr 121 10.40 81-19 Ida Lewis 121⁴ Sauce Of Life121½Killthepianoplayer121no Driving 10
LATEST WORKOUTS Apr 12 Bel tr.t 5f fst 1:03 b Apr 5 Bel tr.t 4f fst :49⅖ b Mar 12 Bel tr.t 6f sly 1:16 b (d) Mar 5 Bel tr.t 5f fst 1:03⅕ hg

~~T. V. Snow~~ SCR
Ch. f. 3, by It's Freezing—Elda's First, by Pago Pago
Br.—Polk A F Jr (Ky)
Own.—Lippman R — Tr.—Dunham Bob G
116 — Lifetime 5 1 2 0 $15,840 — 1983 2 0 1 0 $5,660 — 1982 3 1 1 0 $10,180
17Mar83- 7Aqu fst 6f :23⅖ :47⅕ 1:12 ⒻAlw 20000 6 5 3½ 3nk 21 2¾ Venezia M 116 5.10 80-27 Rosie's Way 113¾ T. V. Snow 1161½ Fissure 118½ Wide 8
5Jan83- 7Aqu fst 6f ⊡:23 :46⅘ 1:12⅘ ⒻAlw 21000 1 6 7⅞ 67½ 511 410 Venezia M 116 13.00 72-24 Ahsoloud 113noPleasureCay1161CaptivatingGrace119¾ No factor 8
13Dec82- 6Aqu fst 6f ⊡:23 :47⅘ [illegible] ⒻAlw 21000 7 8 [illegible] 52½ 57½ 512 Venezia M 116 4.60 [illegible] Lady Norcliffe 1165¾ Prize Amber 1111HeraicF[illegible]hd No factor 9
26Nov82- 7Aqu fst 6f :22⅘ :46⅘ 1:12⅘ ⒻAlw 19000 8 [illegible] 3nk 31½ 1hd 2nk Shelton K L10 106 23.50 80-20 Saucy Lindy 116nk T. V. Snow 1065¾ Rare Lady 118hd Gamely 10
15Nov82- 4Aqu gd 6f :23⅕ :4[illegible] 1:12⅘ ⒻMd 30000 [illegible] 6 31 1hd 1hd 1½ Rogers K L 117 4.60 73-24 T. V. Snow 117½ High Schemes 1105 Hello Julie 117½ Driving 14
LATEST WORKOUTS Apr 12 Aqu 5f my 1:00 h Apr 5 Aqu 4f fst :50⅘ b Mar 30 Aqu 5f fst 1:04 b Mar 14 Aqu 5f fst 1:02 h

8:5

Far Flying
B. f. 3, by Far North—Nalees FLying Flag, by Hoist The Flag
Br.—Humphrey Pamela S (Ky)
Own.—Humphrey G W Jr — Tr.—Kay Michael
118 — Lifetime 2 1 1 0 $14,540 — 1983 1 1 0 0 $10,800 — 1982 1 M 1 0 $3,740
31Mar83- 6Aqu fst 6f :22⅕ :45⅘ 1:11⅖ ⒻMd Sp Wt 8 3 2hd 1½ 13 13¾ Cordero A Jr 121 *.90 84-21 Far Flying 1213¾ Teriyaki Stake 1211AngelicImp1211½ Ridden out 9
25Sep82- 6Bel fst 7f :23 :46⅖ 1:24⅘ ⒻMd Sp Wt 2 10 11 1½ 21½ 24 Miranda J 117 7.40 74-15 Seton'sEncounter1174FrFlying1172½StrtARumor117hd Weakened 11
LATEST WORKOUTS Apr 13 Bel tr.t 5f fst 1:00 h ●Mar 29 Bel tr.t 3f gd :34⅘ hg ●Mar 21 Bel tr.t 4f fst :46⅘ h Mar 16 Bel tr.t 3f fst :36⅘ b

SAMYN 23:1

Lucas Lou
B. f. 3, by Cojak—Park Top, by Victoria Park
Br.—Fox Breeding & Bloodstock (Ky)
Own.—Triple Fox Stable — Tr.—Ramos Faustino F
116 — Lifetime 12 1 2 2 $18,300 — 1982 12 1 2 2 $18,300 — Turf 1 0 0 0
28Dec82- 7Aqu fst 1⅛ ⊡:48⅖ 1:14 1:54⅘ ⒻAlw 22000 5 6 612 612 615 514 Santiago A 116 13.60 58-22 Longwinner1166BlazonSara1214MarvelousMontuk1162½ No factor 7
18Dec82- 5Aqu fst 170 ⊡:48⅗ 1:14⅗ 1:46 ⒻAlw 22000 2 6 52½ 67 64¾ 63 Samyn J L 116 2.20 69-20 Talk About Home 116hd Blazon Sara 121nk OurTrisha111¾ Outrun 6
28Nov82- 1Aqu fst 1 :47⅗ 1:13 1:39 ⒻAlw 20000 5 4 42 32 22½ 22½ Samyn J L 116 4.00 69-28 Pretty Sensible 1162½ LucasLou1167BestOfMyLove1212 Lugged n 6
4Nov82- 7Aqu fst 1 :47⅕ 1:12⅗ 1:38⅗ ⒻAlw 20000 5 6 65 75¾ 76½ 78 Samyn J L 116 10.30 65-24 GrrulousGl116¾LuluMonAmour1111Seton'sEncounter1164 Outrun 8
23Oct82- 5Aqu fst 7f :23⅗ :48 1:26 ⒻAlw 19000 4 8 61¾ 83¾ 43½ 35½ Samyn J L 116 16.60 65-21 Regal Ties 1162½ Seton's Encounter 1183 Lucas Lou1161½ Rallied 9
11Oct82- 1Bel fm 1⅛ Ⓣ:48⅘ 1:12⅘ 1:43⅗ ⒻAlw 20000 2 6 66½ 715 723 731 Samyn J L 116 11.90 52-11 National Banner 118½LegalBreeze1183HoldMeCloser1161½ Outrun 7
30Sep82- 8Bel fst 7f :22⅗ :46⅖ 1:25⅕ ⒻAlw 19000 10 9 1010 75 45½ 34½ Samyn J L 116 72.40 71-24 Am Capable 1162½ Future Fun 1162 Lucas Lou 116hd Rallied 12
20Sep82- 7Bel fst 6f :22⅗ :46⅖ 1:11⅘ ⒻAlw 19000 4 5 76½ 65 57 48½ Cordero A Jr 116 15.70 75-23 No Limitations116½SaucyLindy1167¾ComeBackCindy116hd Rallied 7
15Aug82- 7Key fst 5½f :22⅖ :46⅖ 1:06⅕ ⒻAlw 9500 3 6 69 611 614 610 Jewell J J5 115 9.90 79-20 Mercury Miss 1176 Erin's Bosun 114½ Ceylon Burgoo1123 Trailed 6
23Jly82- 4Bel fst 6f :23 :47⅖ 1:13⅗ ⒻMd 35000 7 3 43½ 42½ 2½ 1¾ Cordero A Jr 117 2.50 74-21 Lucas Lou 117¾ Mack's Renee 1173½ First Excuse 106¾ Driving 10
LATEST WORKOUTS Apr 11 Bel tr.t 6f my 1:15 hg Apr 6 Bel tr.t 6f fst 1:13⅘ h Apr 2 Bel tr.t 5f fst 1:02⅖ h Mar 29 Bel tr.t 4f gd :50 b

8:5

Able Money
Dk. b. or br. f. 3, by Distinctive—Able Maid, by Good Behaving
Br.—Miranda & Sierra (Fla)
Own.—Donnelly Faith — Tr.—Russo Anthony J
116 — Lifetime 1 1 0 0 $10,800 — 1983 1 1 0 0 $10,800 — 1982 0 M 0 0
20Feb83- 6Aqu fst 6f ⊡:22⅘ :46⅘ 1:11⅘ ⒻMd Sp Wt 11 6 22 1½ 15 16¾ Smith A Jr 121 17.60 85-20 AbleMoney12163ShwneeCreek1211¾HighSchemes114¾ Ridden out 14
LATEST WORKOUTS Apr 14 Bel tr.t 4f fst :50 b Apr 6 Bel tr.t 6f fst 1:20 b Mar 31 Bel tr.t 6f fst 1:20 b Mar 26 Bel tr.t 6f fst 1:16⅖ b

JD BAILEY 5:1

Future Fun
Gr. f. 3, by What a Pleasure—Imminence, by Native Charger
Br.—Tartan Farms (Fla)
Own.—Tartan Stable — Tr.—Nerud Jan H
116 — Lifetime 10 1 2 1 $37,592 — 1982 10 1 2 1 $37,592 — Turf 1 0 0 0
Entered 14Apr83- 8 AQU
14Nov82- 8Aqu fst 1⅛ :49⅕ 1:14 1:52 ⒻDemoiselle 7 5 67¼ 66½ 69 610 Cordero A Jr 112 4.90 65-23 OnlyQueens1161¾GoldSpruce1132½NationalBnner1132 No menace 7
1Nov82- 8Aqu fst 1 :46⅘ 1:11⅕ 1:37 ⒻTempted 5 3 32 47 35 22½ Bailey J D 113 10.50 79-23 Only Queens 1142½ Future Fun 113nk Blue Garter 1147½ Wide 6
23Oct82- 5Aqu fst 7f :23⅗ :48 1:26 ⒻAlw 19000 7 4 94½ 99¾ 98½ 57½ Venezia M 116 2.90 64-21 Regal Ties 1162½ Seton's Encounter 1183 Lucas Lou 1161½ Wide 9
30Sep82- 8Bel fst 7f :22⅗ :46⅖ 1:25⅕ ⒻAlw 19000 11 2 53 42 23 22½ Cordero A Jr 116 3.70 73-24 Am Capable 1162½ Future Fun 1162LucasLou116hd Best of others 12
18Sep82- 3Bel fm 1 Ⓣ:46⅕ 1:10⅗ 1:35⅕ ⒻAlw 20000 6 2 21½ 56½ 59 511 Cordero A Jr 116 5.10 78-08 Lituya Bay 1172½ Singadon 1164¾ National Banner 118½ Tired 7
1Sep82- 5Bel fst 6f :22⅗ :46⅕ 1:10⅘ ⒻAlw 19000 6 7 44 53 33 43¾ Bernhardt E JJr10 106 7.20 84-13 OnTheBench1162¾BelleOLetti116nkLadySuceBot118¾ Raced wide 7
4Aug82- 8Sar fst 6f :22⅕ :45⅖ 1:11 ⒻSchuylervile 4 6 67 712 713 714 Venezia M 114 24.80 71-13 WkndSurpris1141ShrThFntsy1161FlyingLssi1144¾ Stumbled early 7
12Jly82- 8Bel fst 5½f :23⅕ :46⅖ 1:05⅕ ⒻAstoria 1 3 45½ 44½ 38 38 Venezia M 112 7.20 81-16 Gala Jubilee 119no Blue Garter 1128 Future Fun 1125¾ Rallied 4
2Jun82- 8Bel fst 5½f :22⅗ :45⅘ 1:04⅕ ⒻRosedale 2 3 31½ 31½ 32½ 44½ Cordero A Jr 116 5.70 89-11 GlJubilee1162WeekendSurpris116¾SubvrsivChick1161¾ Weakened 7
9May82- 4Aqu fst 4½f :23⅗ :47⅖ :54 ⒻMd Sp Wt 3 6 43 31½ 1nk Cordero A Jr 117 4.20 92-08 Future Fun 117nk Front Landing 117¾ Regal Ties 1178½ Driving 7
LATEST WORKOUTS Apr 11 Bel tr.t 4f my :51 b Apr 1 Bel tr.t 4f fst :50⅖ b Mar 27 Bel tr.t 4f fst :51 b

5:1

Fissure
Dk. b. or br. f. 3, by Tentam—Cracking, by Never Bend
Br.—Live Oak Stud (Fla)
Own.—Live Oak Plantation — Tr.—Kelly Patrick J
116 — Lifetime 3 1 0 2 $15,600 — 1983 3 1 0 2 $15,600 — 1982 0 M 0 0
26Mar83- 5Aqu fst 7f :23⅕ :46⅗ 1:23⅘ ⒻAlw 20000 4 6 53½ 53 38 39¾ Gonzalez M A 118 3.60 72-19 I'm A Southpaw 1168 Poppa's BigLil1091¾Fissure1181¾ Lk'd rally 6
17Mar83- 7Aqu fst 6f :23⅖ :47⅕ 1:12 ⒻAlw 20000 4 7 52½ 41¾ 41½ 32½ Gonzalez M A 118 *2.10 79-27 Rosie's Way 113¾ T. V. Snow 1161½ Fissure 118½ Rallied 8
24Feb83- 6Aqu fst 6f ⊡:23⅗ :48⅕ 1:14 ⒻMd Sp Wt 2 13 107½ 74½ 2½ 12½ Gonzalez M A 121 31.10 74-24 Fissure1212½BambooFan1162¾PensiveDame1212½ Greenly, driving 14
LATEST WORKOUTS Apr 12 Bel tr.t 4f fst :48⅗ h Apr 7 Bel tr.t 4f fst :50 b Apr 2 Bel tr.t 4f fst :49⅖ h Mar 14 Bel tr.t 4f fst :49⅘ b

APRIL 16—RACE 5 (Exacta Wagering)
Track Sloppy

Right away you can see there are only three contenders: **Ida Lewis, Far Flying** and **Able Money**. (Note **Ida Lewis** won her first start at 10:1— a Dick DeStasio maiden!) These horses are separated quite easily because **Far Flying** will make the half a full second or more faster than the other two. Combine this with a sloppy track plus Cordero and we're in business.

THE BET: 90% of the M.B. all in exactas. Why? Time to get aggressive. **Far Flying** figures to win all by herself. Therefore,

Far Flying—Able Money	55%
Able Money—Far Flying (saver)	5%
Far Flying—Ida Lewis	25%
Ida Lewis—Far Flying	5%
	90%

If **Able Money** was 6:1 and **Ida Lewis** 8:5, I would have bet 25% on **Far Flying—Able Money** and 55% on **Far Flying—Ida Lewis. Able Money** and **Ida Lewis** are separated only by the odds. Adjusted speed figures might have helped but weren't available.

THE RESULTS: **Far Flying** won by an incredible 14 lengths and returned $5.40. **Able Money** was second, **Ida Lewis** third. The exacta paid $14.40—a real overlay.

6 **AQUEDUCT** 7 FURLONGS AQUEDUCT START FINISH

7 FURLONGS. (1.20⅘) THE TEMPEST QUEEN STAKES. $30,000 Added. Fillies and Mares, 3-years-old and Upward which have not won a race of $25,000. By subscription of $50 each, $50 to enter; $100 to start. Weights, 3-year-olds 112 lbs., Older 124 lbs. Non-winners of a Sweepstakes allowed 3 lbs., Of three races of $15,000 in 1982-83, 5 lbs.

Coupled—Miss Actress and Maggie Gold.

Chime — B. f. 4, by Bold Forbes—Watch Fob, by Tompion
Own.—Peters L J — Br.—Gaines & Hart (Tenn) — Tr.—Tesher Howard M
119 — Lifetime 18 4 3 3 $77,129 — 1983 3 1 1 0 $23,229 — 1982 15 3 2 3 $53,900

HERNANDEZ 3:1

10Apr83- 6Aqu	sly	6f	:22⅘	:45⅘	1:11⅘	3↑Ⓕ Miss Disco	5	7	78	67½	48	2½	Samyn J L	b 119	10.50	81-23 Rosa D'Argent 119½ Chime 1191 Liz Matizz 119no	Wide,	8
14Jan83- 7Aqu	fst	6f	⊡:22⅘	:45⅘	1:11⅘	ⒻAlw 30000	1	4	63	64½	48½	67½	Beitia E	b 122	4.00	81-19 Pert 1141½ Hopeful Contract 117hd Mt. Helen 1194½	No factor	8
1Jan83- 7Aqu	fst	6f	⊡:23⅕	:47⅘	1:13	ⒻAlw 27000	4	6	52½	31	1hd	12	Beitia E	b 122	*.90	79-25 Chime 1222 Master Switch 112no Miss Actress 1171½	Driving	6
13Dec82- 1Aqu	fst	6f	⊡:23⅘	:47⅘	1:13⅘	3↑ⒻAlw 23000	1	1	12½	11½	12½	13½	Samyn J L	b 120	*.80	77-22 Chime 1203½ Fire in the Sky 115hd Lady Lothario 110nk	Driving	6
27Nov82- 6Aqu	fst	6f	:23⅘	:47⅘	1:12⅘	3↑ⒻAlw 19000	6	5	2hd	11½	12½	12½	Cordero A Jr	b 115	*1.10	79-29 Chime 1152½ Je'Da Qua 1208 Backstage Whisper 108nk	Driving	6
29Oct82- 5Aqu	fst	6f	:22⅘	:46	1:09⅘	3↑ⒻAlw 19000	8	7	43	42	44	45½	Cordero A Jr	b 114	*.70	87-14 I'm For Fun1143½Versailles1081½LadyNoble114½	Lacked response	8
18Oct82- 7Aqu	fst	7f	:23⅘	:46⅕	1:23⅘	3↑ⒻAlw 19000	4	3	2hd	12	11	2hd	Cordero A Jr	b 114	*.80	82-23 Lizzie's Light 108hd Chime 1143 Rose Crescent 1143	Gamely	7
20Sep82- 5Bel	fst	6f	:22⅘	:45⅘	1:11	3↑ⒻAlw 19000	6	6	77	44½	43½	3nk	Cordero A Jr	b 113	3.10	87-23 Leap of the Heart 115hd Flag Waver 113nk Chime 1133½	Bumped	7
4Sep82- 7Bel	fst	6f	:22⅘	:46	1:10⅘	3↑ⒻAlw 17000	2	4	56	45½	31½	42½	Velasquez J	113	10.00	85-13 LadyHatchet1062½RanchMink113nkLeapoftheHert1151½	Weakened	8
16Aug82- 5Sar	fst	6f	:22⅕	:45⅘	1:10⅘	3↑ⒻAlw 19000	4	7	74½	54	53½	32½	Velasquez J	113	7.90	85-13 Annulus 112½ Ranch Mink 1141½ Chime 1131½	Wide	8

LATEST WORKOUTS ●Apr 2 Aqu 6f fst 1:16 b ●Mar 27 Aqu 5f fst 1:00⅘ h ●Mar 21 Aqu 6f fst 1:14⅘ h Mar 15 Aqu 5f fst 1:02⅘ h

Intentional Move — B. f. 4, by Tentam—Lunar Dancer, by Northern Dancer
Own.—Evans E P — Br.—Evans E P (Va) — Tr.—Kelly Thomas J
119 — Lifetime 11 2 3 2 $41,500 — 1983 4 1 3 0 $26,020 — 1982 7 1 0 2 $15,480

13:1

5Apr83- 7Aqu	fst	1	:48	1:14	1:39	ⒻAlw 21000	4	2	2hd	1½	12	1½	Santiago A	b 117	*.70	71-22 Intentional Move 117½ExactlyTricky1178FoolishLuck1171	Driving	7
24Mar83- 7Aqu	fst	7f	:23⅘	:47⅘	1:25⅕	ⒻAlw 20000	5	2	2½	2hd	11½	2nk	Santiago A	b 117	2.80	75-26 VenusStr117nkIntentionlMove117[illegible]KinlochLke110nk	Just failed	8
19Feb83- 1Aqu	fst	6f	⊡:23⅘	:47⅘	1:12⅘	ⒻAlw 20000	6	3	21½	21½	2hd	2hd	Santiago A	b 117	*1.50	80-20 Moody Day117hdIntentionalMove1177½ALittlePrincess122hd	Wide	7
19Jan83- 6Aqu	fst	6f	⊡:23⅕	:47⅘	1:13⅘	ⒻAlw 21000	6	4	31	42½	41½	21½	Santiago A	b 117	17.60	75-24 Versailles 1171½ IntentionalMove1171½MajesticMama112½	Rallied	11
27Dec82- 7Aqu	fst	6f	⊡:23⅘	:47⅘	1:12⅘	3↑ⒻAlw 21000	3	7	—	—	—	—	Hernandez R	b 120	6.30	— — Svarga 1208½ Versailles 1151½ Real Notion 1151½	Pulled up	7
9Dec82- 6Aqu	fst	6f	⊡:23⅘	:48⅘	1:14⅘	3↑ⒻMd Sp Wt	7	3	2hd	2hd	1hd	11½	Hernandez R	b 120	8.30	70-30 IntentionalMove1201½LoyalDiplomt1203FlmouthBy120½	Drew out	8
29Aug82- 2Sar	fst	7f	:22⅘	:45⅘	1:25	3↑ⒻMd Sp Wt	8	7	1014	1016	1014	1014	Velasquez J	b 117	*1.50	63-15 StrokeofTwelve117½BroadwayStrlet117½SlveNoMore1172½	Outrun	10
19Aug82- 3Sar	fst	6½f	:22	:45⅘	1:18⅘	3↑ⒻMd Sp Wt	4	11	1011	1114	76	3hd	Hernandez R	b 117	11.00	78-17 IncredibleMoment117noAstorStret117noIntntionlMov117½	Rallied	14
9Aug82- 6Sar	my	6f	:22⅕	:45⅘	1:10⅘	3↑ⒻMd Sp Wt	9	6	911	1013	917	822	Hernandez R	117	5.90	65-16 LeapoftheHeart117½IncredibleMoment1177Gil'sWish117½	Outrun	13
24Jun82- 6Bel	fst	6f	:22⅘	:46	1:10⅘	3↑ⒻMd Sp Wt	7	6	63½	43½	46	38½	Hernandez R	114	5.80	81-12 Via Appia 114½ AllMyMemories1148IntentionalMove1141½	Rallied	13

LATEST WORKOUTS Apr 18 Bel tr.t 6f fst 1:16⅘ b Apr 13 Bel tr.t 3f fst :36⅘ b Apr 1 Bel tr.t 6f fst 1:17⅕ b Mar 14 Bel tr.t 5f fst 1:05 b

Distinctive Moon Gr. f. 4, by Distinctive—Eloquent Es, by Palestinian
Br.—Elias Bros Farm (Fla)
Own.—Brennan R Tr.—Nobles Reynaldo H
119 Lifetime 25 4 4 7 $90,576 | 1983 3 0 0 1 $2,750 | 1982 16 2 3 5 $48,404 | Turf 5 0 1 2 $19,445
2Apr83- 8Hia fm 1⅛ Ⓣ 1:42 3↑ⒻBal Harbour 11 8 810 610 64¾ 74½ MacBeth D 113 11.60 83-12 Great Nation 1181½ Syrianna 128¾ Florida Jig 120nk No factor 12
2Apr83-Run in Two Divisions, 6th & 8th Races
14Mar83- 9Hia fst 6f :22⅘ :45⅕ 1:10 3↑ⒻⓈOrngeBlmH 2 3 86 89 88¼ 77¾ MacBeth D 115 *2.80 85-18 Florida Jig 1162½ Made Glorious 114¾ ATearInHerEye1131 Outrun 8
2Mar83- 8GP fst 7f :23⅕ :47 1:24⅘ ⒻAlw 25000 4 1 22 21½ 21½ 31¾ MacBeth D 117 2.50 80-24 Vany 1171 Point to Victory 112¾ Distinctive Moon 1171 Lckd bid 10
8Nov82- 6Med fst 170 :45⅘ 1:11⅕ 1:42⅕ ⒻLakewood 1 3 30 31½ 42½ 31¼ MacBeth D 114 *1.50 88-18 BrightChoic115nkNightHrss1141½DstnctvMoon1144 Lacked Room 8
25Oct82- 6Med sly 6f :22⅕ :46⅘ 1:11⅕ ⒻColonia 2 6 511 47½ 36½ 34½ MacBeth D 112 6.40 80-29 Bravest Miss 1142 SyrianSands1144½DistinctiveMoon1124½ Evenly 6
25Sep82- 8Med fm 170 Ⓣ:46⅘ 1:10⅘ 1:39⅘ ⒻStar Bright 5 9 108 68½ 611 511 Beitia E 112 3.60 81-08 Dearly Too 1148 Luminaire 112nk Hat Tab Girl 1121½ Lacked bid 12
25Sep82-Evening Program
11Sep82- 8Med fm 1⅛ Ⓣ:47 1:10⅘ 1:41⅘ ⒻBoil Sprg H 3 7 73½ 42 43 34½ MacBeth D 114 7.50 90-09 Larida 1194 Doodle 115½ Distinctive Moon 114¾ Rallied 11
11Sep82-Evening Program; Run in two Divisions 6 & 8 Races
29Aug82-10Del fst 1⅛ :47⅘ 1:11⅘ 1:50⅕ ⒻDel Oaks 10 8 88½ 87½ 68¾ 47 Lopez C C 112 11.60 79-19 Lady Eleanor 1155 Sailing Hour 112¾ Milingo 1151½ Rallied 10
17Aug82- 9Mth yl 1⅛ Ⓣ:49⅗ 1:13⅘ 1:46⅘ ⒻLi'l Slvr H 5 1 1½ 1hd 2hd 2no Lopez C C 114 6.00 69-34 Immense 115no Distinctive Moon 1144½HailBabe1161½ Drifted out 11
7Aug82- 7Mth fst 1 :46⅘ 1:11⅕ 1:38⅘ ⒻDesert Vxn 2 5 62½ 45½ 42 2no Lopez C C 113 *1.80 81-15 Linda North119noDistinctiveMoon113¾RoyalAnthem1132 Steadied 7
LATEST WORKOUTS ●Apr 15 Aqu 3f fst :36 h Mar 26 Hia 5f fst 1:01 b ●Feb 25 Hia 6f fst 1:14 b

13:1

Miss Actress Dk. b. or br. f. 4, by Mr Cockatoo—T V Actress, by T V Lark
Br.—Lasater Farm (Fla)
Own.—Spiegel R Tr.—Schaeffer Stephen
119 Lifetime 29 4 2 4 $96,500 | 1983 5 1 1 1 $24,100 | 1982 10 1 0 1 $10,000 | Turf 3 0 0 0 $1,500
30Mar83- 7Aqu fst 6f :22⅘ :46⅕ 1:10⅘ ⒻAlw 35000 2 2 33½ 68 68½ 611 Smith A Jr 117 14.80 76-24 VisualEmotion1221½Annulus1172½HopefulContract115½ Early foot 6
19Feb83- 8Key fst 6f :22⅘ :46⅕ 1:12 3↑ⒻMilady H 7 10 117½118½ 810 89¾ Tejeira J 115 *1.70e 71-27 SenoritaQuerida1151½Coprincess1152½FrenchLocket1111½ Dull try 12
24Jan83- 7Aqu sly 6f ⊡:22⅘ :46 1:11 ⒻAlw 25000 6 1 11½ 11½ 13 16 Cordero A Jr 117 *1.30e 89-15 Miss Actress 1176 Swift And Sudden 1191SingingOak1172 Driving 8
14Jan83- 6Aqu fst 6f ⊡:23 :46⅘ 1:12⅘ ⒻAlw 27000 3 3 1hd 2½ 21 2nk Santagata N 117 —— 82-19 Rosa D'Argent 110nk Miss Actress 117no Ebullient1121½ Game try 6
14Jan83-Raced for purse money only
1Jan83- 7Aqu fst 6f ⊡:23⅕ :47⅘ 1:13 ⒻAlw 27000 5 1 2½ 41½ 31½ 32 Migliore R 117 12.00 77-25 Chime 1222 Master Switch 112no Miss Actress 1171½ Weakened 6
27Nov82- 7Med fst 6f :22⅘ :46⅕ 1:12 ⒻDenville 4 5 78¾ 914 815 714 Migliore R b 112 13.40 69-21 Syrian Sands 1142½ Metbychance 112½VisualEmotion1124 Outrun 9
27Nov82-Run in Two Divisions 7th & 9th Races
30Sep82- 9Bel fm 7f Ⓣ:22⅘ :45⅘ 1:23 3↑ⒻAlw 23000 3 8 64½ 76½1013 1014 MacBeth D b 113 27.20 75-15 Bedside 1132¾ Waving 115nk Hopeful Contract 113½ Tired 10
11Sep82- 6Med fm 1⅛ Ⓣ:46 1:10 1:41⅘ ⒻBoil Sprg H 4 3 32 84½ 98 97½ MacBeth D b 112 40.50 87-09 Sunny Sparkler 113¾ Fact Finder 113¾ Milingo 117nk Tired 10
11Sep82-Evening Program; Run in two Division 6 & 8 Races
28Aug82- 7Sar fst 7f :21⅘ :44⅘ 1:22⅘ 3↑ⒻAlw 23000 3 3 2hd 21½ 32 32¾ MacBeth D b 112 24.70 87-13 Number 1121½ Vestris 1121½ Miss Actress 1125¾ Weakened 6
LATEST WORKOUTS Apr 18 Bel tr.t 4f fst :47⅗ h Mar 26 Bel tr.t 6f fst 1:15⅕ b Mar 16 Bel tr.t 4f fst :48⅕ h

CLAYTON 15:1

Visual Emotion Ch. f. 4, by King Emperor—Join The Waves, by Sailor
Br.—Jones Brereton C (Ky)
Own.—Jones B C Tr.—Campo John P
119 Lifetime 13 5 0 3 $81,082 | 1983 4 3 0 0 $52,500 | 1982 9 2 0 3 $28,582
30Mar83- 7Aqu fst 6f :22⅘ :46⅕ 1:10⅘ ⒻAlw 35000 3 4 12 11½ 13 11¾ Cordero A Jr 122 *1.10 87-24 VisualEmotion1221½Annulus1172½HopefulContrct115½ Ridden out 6
6Mar83- 8Aqu fst 6f ⊡:22⅘ :45⅗ 1:10⅘ 3↑ⒻCorrection H 3 5 2½ 21½ 33 45¾ Santagata N 111 6.20 86-19 JonesTimeMachine1212FancyNaskra1121RosD'Argent1072¾ Tired 8
18Feb83- 7Aqu fst 6f ⊡:23⅕ :47 1:12⅘ ⒻAlw 25000 5 2 11½ 13 12 11½ Miranda J 119 *.70 82-27 Visual Emotion 1191½ Annulus 1172 Quiet Poppa 117no Driving 8
2Feb83- 6Aqu fst 6f ⊡:22⅘ :45⅗ 1:11⅕ ⒻAlw 22000 8 2 14 15 16 17 Miranda J 117 *1.60 88-24 Visual Emotion 1177 Versailles 117nk Lady Hatchet 112no Easily 8
16Dec82- 6Med gd 6f :22⅕ :45 1:10⅘ 3↑ⒻMiss Prspy H 4 8 4¾ 31½ 98½ 914 Miranda J 112 5.00 77-17 Meringue Pie 114¾ Stellarette1121MoonStarMiss1121 Sp'd for 1/2 9
6Dec82- 8Aqu my 6f ⊡:22 :45⅕ 1:10 3↑ⒻAlw 21000 7 1 15 15 16 16¾ Miranda J 115 2.60 94-15 VisulEmotion1156¾Je'DQu1154IncredibleMomnt110no Ridden out 7
27Nov82- 7Med fst 6f :22⅘ :46⅕ 1:12 ⒻDenville 9 1 14 11½ 2½ 32¾ Miranda J 112 11.30 80-21 SyrianSands1142½Metbychance112½VisualEmotion1124 Weakened 9
27Nov82-Run in Two Divisions 7th & 9th Races
6Nov82- 5Lrl fst 6f :22⅕ :46 1:11⅘ 3↑ⒻAlma North 2 4 12 11 2hd 52½ Miranda J 113 16.80 84-11 Kattegat's Pride 1161½ Count OnSadye110hdErnestine122nk Tired 10
27Oct82- 4Kee fst 7f :22⅘ :46⅕ 1:25⅘ 3↑ⒻAlw 13500 1 12 11½ 1½ 2hd 35½ Brumfield D 116 3.10 73-18 OldMotherHubbrd1154½ProperChoice1131VisulEmotion1161 Tired 12
31Jly82- 3Dmr fst 6f :21⅘ :45 1:10⅘ 3↑ⒻAlw 16000 6 7 41¾ 85 1214 1215 Olivares F 115 6.30 71-15 My Native Princess 115¾ Entereza 1171 Tony's Darling 1152 Tired 12
LATEST WORKOUTS Apr 12 Bel tr.t 4f fst :47⅕ h Mar 26 Bel tr.t 5f fst 1:01⅕ h Mar 23 Bel tr.t 4f fst :48⅕ h ●Mar 2 Bel tr.t 4f sly :47 h

VELASQUEZ 4:5

Maggie Gold Ch. m. 5, by Rebellious—Jackaleem, by Loom
Br.—Murray Mr-Mrs E A Jr (Md)
Own.—Spiegel R Tr.—Schaeffer Stephen
119 Lifetime 35 10 7 2 $118,110 | 1983 4 1 0 0 $16,500 | 1982 20 7 4 0 $83,420
6Mar83- 8Aqu fst 6f ⊡:22⅘ :45⅗ 1:10⅘ 3↑ⒻCorrection H 1 7 66 69 58½ 611 Graell A 108 24.50 81-19 JonesTimeMchine1212FncyNskr1121RosD'Argent1072¾ No factor 8
19Feb83- 8Key fst 6f :22⅘ :46⅕ 1:12 3↑ⒻMilady H 4 7 95½107¾1011 109¾ Migliore R 114 *1.70e 71-27 SenoritaQuerid1151½Coprincess1152½FrenchLocket1111½ Far back 12
5Feb83- 9Aqu fst 6f ⊡:23 :47⅕ 1:13 ⒻAlw 25000 8 3 22 2hd 1hd 1½ Migliore R 117 3.50 79-20 Maggie Gold 117½ Irish Toy 112¾ Princess Ebony 117nk Driving 10
24Jan83- 7Aqu sly 6f ⊡:22⅘ :46 1:11 ⒻAlw 25000 1 4 51¾ 21½ 33 49 Migliore R 117 *1.30e 80-15 Miss Actress 1176 Swift And Sudden 1191 Singing Oak1172 Tired 8
1Dec82- 1Aqu fst 6f ⊡:23⅘ :46⅘ 1:11⅘ 3↑ⒻAlw 27000 5 1 11 2hd 4¾ 41½ Migliore R 119 3.20 84-17 I'm InTime117noRosaD'Argent110nkLaNinouchka1121½ Weakened 5
22Nov82- 7Aqu fst 6f :23⅘ :47⅘ 1:12 3↑ⒻAlw 28000 3 5 42 3nk 12½ 11½ Migliore R 117 8.80 81-23 Maggie Gold 1171½ I'm For Fun1201½LeapoftheHeart115½ Driving 9
7Nov82- 2Aqu fst 6f :22⅘ :46⅘ 1:11⅘ 3↑ⒻClm 45000 10 1 1hd 1½ 13 1nk Migliore R 113 4.10 83-19 Maggie Gold 113nk Harlem Queen 1172¾ Frezil 1172½ Driving 10
17Oct82- 2Aqu fst 6f :23⅘ :47⅘ 1:12⅘ 3↑ⒻClm 35000 4 6 62¾ 1½ 12½ 1nk Migliore R 115 4.10 79-27 Maggie Gold 115nk Sharonna 110½GoodHeaven'sGirl117no Driving 7
7Oct82- 5Med fst 6f :22 :45⅘ 1:11⅘ 3↑ⒻClm 32000 3 5 21½ 2hd 13 14½ Migliore R 116 *1.70 84-19 Maggie Gold 1164½ April Prom 1162 Paula's Priority1102¾ Driving 6
21Sep82- 8Med fst 6f :22⅘ :46⅕ 1:12⅘ 3↑ⒻClm 32000 5 2 21 2½ 21½ 22 Cordero A Jr 116 *.80 77-27 Paula's Priority 1062 Maggie Gold1162AprilProm1163 Carried out 6
LATEST WORKOUTS Apr 18 Bel tr.t 4f fst :47⅕ h Apr 7 Bel tr.t 4f fst :47⅘ h Mar 27 Bel tr.t 4f fst :48⅘ h Mar 21 Bel tr.t 4f fst :49⅘ h

~~MIGLIORE~~ 15:1

Bestowed B. f. 4, by Steward—Envisioned, by Bold Native
Br.—Harbor View Farm (Fla)
Own.—Harbor View Farm Tr.—Schulhofer Flint S
119 Lifetime 23 5 2 6 $93,144 | 1983 4 1 0 0 $24,288 | 1982 12 2 1 3 $41,236 | Turf 2 0 0 1 $2,520
30Mar83- 7Aqu fst 6f :22⅘ :46⅕ 1:10⅘ ⒻAlw 35000 6 1 54 43 45½ 55¾ Miranda J b 119 11.20 81-24 VisualEmotion1221½Annulus1172½HopefulContrct115½ No menace 6
19Mar83- 8Aqu my 7f :22⅘ :45⅗ 1:23⅕ 3↑ⒻDistaff H 4 4 46 55 57½ 48 Miranda J b 111 21.90 77-21 Jones Time Machine1221½FancyNaskra1134¾Adept1112 No factor 6
20Feb83- 7Aqu fst 6f ⊡:22⅘ :46 1:12 ⒻAlw 35000 2 7 63¾ 86½ 42 11 Miranda J b 115 19.70 84-20 Bestowed 1151 Aironlass 115¾ Ebullient 110½ Going away 12
14Jan83- 7Aqu fst 6f ⊡:22⅘ :45⅗ 1:11⅕ ⒻAlw 30000 3 5 78½ 79¾ 79 57 Miranda J b 117 18.20 81-19 Pert 1141½ Hopeful Contract 117hd Mt. Helen 1194¾ No factor 8
27Dec82- 8Aqu fst 6f ⊡:23⅕ :46⅘ 1:11⅘ 3↑ⒻAlw 30000 3 3 31½ 68 69 410 Miranda J b 115 5.80 76-22 I'm In Time 117½ Pert 1179 Esplanade 110½ Weakened 6
17Dec82- 8Aqu gd 6f ⊡:23⅘ :47⅘ 1:12⅘ 3↑ⒻAlw 37000 4 7 74½ 68 811 412 Samyn J L b 113 21.40 70-25 Hoist Emy'sFlag1138Ebullient108noPenny'sChelly1153½ No factor 8
2Aug82- 7Bel fm 6f Ⓣ:23 :45⅘ 1:09⅘ 3↑ⒻAlw 32000 1 3 3½ 65 75½ 65½ Velasquez J b 112 15.20 89-17 Poz 1152 A Status Symbol 1111½ Patella 115no Brief speed 8
18Jly82- 7Bel fst 6f :22⅘ :46 1:11⅘ 3↑ⒻAlw 32000 6 5 3½ 33½ 48½ 49¾ Maple E b 112 14.60 74-20 Wendy's Ten 1044¾Andy'sAction1191½AutumnGlory1173½ Bumped 7
8May82- 8Mth fst 6f :22⅘ :45⅕ 1:10⅕ ⒻHerecom'sbrd 8 2 51¾ 46½ 412 313 Fann B b 120 5.90 76-22 Platinum Belle 1165 Smooch 1157½ Bestowed 120¾ No menace 9
28Apr82- 8Aqu sly 6f :22⅘ :45⅘ 1:10 ⒻPrioress 6 1 84¾ 76½ 67½ 57 MacBeth D b 112 20.90 84-21 Trove 118nk Larida 1142¾ Dearly Too 112¾ No factor 8
LATEST WORKOUTS Apr 21 Bel tr.t 4f gd :49 h Mar 27 Bel tr.t 4f fst :48 h Mar 14 Bel tr.t 5f fst 1:00 h Mar 8 Bel tr.t 4f my :49 b

25:1

Swift And Sudden Dk. b. or br. f. 4, by Shecky Greene—You Cant Tell, by Run for Nurse
Own.—Glorieso Patricia Ann
Br.—Glorieso Patricia & R (Ky)
Tr.—Glorieso Patricia A
119
Lifetime 13 4 3 3 $47,552
1983 8 1 3 2 $29,257
1982 5 3 0 1 $18,295

13Apr83- 8Key	fst	6½f	:22⅖	:44⅖	1:16⅖	ⒻAlw 12500	8	1	52	31½	2½	1½	Lovato F	112	*.90	91-22	SwiftAndSudden112½SunshineNSvn1123½BowwMidn1171½	Driving	8
31Mar83- 7Aqu	fst	1	:45	1:09⅘	1:36⅖	3+ⒻAlw 27000	4	3	2½	1½	11½	3¾	Lovato F	121	15.30	83-21	Regal Taheka110¾PetitBall121hdSwiftAndSudden1213¾	Weakened	8
19Mar83- 6Key	my	170	:46⅗	1:11⅗	1:41⅘	3+ⒻPoqussingH	10	3	22	21½	55	58	Lovato F	111	4.90	83-19	Princess Roberta 1141½ Faisana 114½ Halo Again 113nk	Slow start	11
19Mar83-Run in Two Divisions: 6th & 8th Races																			
26Feb83- 7Aqu	fst	1⅛	⊡:48⅖	1:13⅕	1:54	ⒻAlw 27000	7	3	21	2½	2½	22	Lovato F	117	18.10	74-25	DncdAllNght1222SwftAndSuddn117¾BrngMFlowrsII1127¾	Gamely	9
19Feb83- 8Key	fst	6f	:22⅗	:46⅕	1:12	3+ⒻMilady H	1	8	52½	75	77	56½	Lovato F	111	9.20	74-27	Senorita Querida1151¾Coprincess1152½FrenchLocket1111½	Evenly	12
24Jan83- 7Aqu	sly	6f	⊡:22⅘	:46	1:11	ⒻAlw 25000	2	3	21½	31½	23	26	Lovato F	119	5.20	83-15	Miss Actress 1176 Swift And Sudden1191SingingOak1172	Gamely	8
12Jan83- 8Key	fst	6f	:22⅘	:46⅖	1:11⅘	ⒻAlw 11500	2	4	2hd	1hd	1hd	2nk	Lovato F	118	*1.70	82-27	No Joke Lady 115nk SwiftAndSudden1185Dejeuner1151½	Brushed	6
1Jan83- 8Key	fst	7f	:22⅗	:45⅗	1:25	ⒻMy Juliet H	2	6	4nk	52½	33½	36	Lovato F	111	11.30	76-28	SnoritQurd1126NoJokLdy112hdSwftAndSuddn111no	Bid, wekened	11
21Dec82- 8Key	fst	6f	:22⅗	:46⅖	1:13⅗	3+ⒻAlw 10500	8	3	2½	2½	11	12¾	Lovato F	116	*1.60	74-27	SwiftAndSudden1162¾Ronnlee117nkRosendBetty1161½	Ridden out	8
23Nov82- 7Key	fst	6f	:22⅗	:46	1:12	3+ⒻAlw 10000	3	5	24	22	1hd	12½	Lee R F	114	1.90	81-23	SwiftAndSudden1142½HxOnYou1133DoublDcquiri1184	Drew clear	8

LATEST WORKOUTS ●Apr 7 Key 4f fst :47⅘ h Mar 26 Key 5f fst 1:00 h Mar 14 Key 4f gd :48 h

Chime—Nice race last time closing tons of ground while racing wide. However, Tesher has tried **Chime** at seven furlongs before and, despite a good second, decided her best distance is six panels. Also **Chime** races five pounds heavier today than in that race. She is a question mark at seven and has an unfavorable jockey switch.

Intentional Move—Picks up weight after losing ground at seven furlongs on March 24th. Although winning at a mile, the speed rating is poor. Furthermore, **Intentional Move** is suspect after winning and not racing for 18 days.

Distinctive Moon—Shipper. One workout or race in 21 days. Hasn't raced with this much weight before. Throw her out.

Miss Actress—Nothing at the distance. Picks up weight. Bad jockey switch. Not a contender.

Visual Emotion—Stretching out, should be right there, but only has one workout or race in 24 days. This is not her pattern (see previous example, too). She looks like a false favorite at 4:5.

Maggie Gold—Wrong distance, picks up weight and hasn't raced in 48 days after two poor efforts. Not a contender.

Bestowed—Wrong distance and only one recent workout.

Swift and Sudden—Giant race on March 31st against **Regal Taheka**, being on top at the half and three quarters (in :45 and 109^4 respectively on a track that was not lightening fast—track variant was 21) and under 121 pounds. April 13th is another superior race at Keystone. Although this horse is shipping in, it has raced and done well in New York and is not travelling far, coming from New Jersey.

THE BET: I *know* **Swift And Sudden** can go the distance, but I *assume* **Visual Emotion**, who is suspect anyway, can. With **Swift And Sudden's** speed, she can look **Visual Emotion** in the eye and may cause her to get discouraged. **Visual Emotion** is 4:5 and an underlay, the other 9:2 and an overlay. Therefore 65% on **Swift And Sudden**. The bet would be greater here, except for concern that **Visual Emotion** will hurt **Swift And Sudden** in a speed duel.

RESULTS: **Swift And Sudden** and **Visual Emotion** fought it out the entire way before the latter gave way finishing second. **Swift And Sudden** paid $11.40.

Louisiana Downs

Louisiana Downs is a relatively new track. It opened in 1974. It is currently among the top fifteen in the country in average daily handle. Almost half of its customers come from nearby Texas where there is no thoroughbred racing. Many people also come from Oklahoma. The meet usually begins in late April after Oaklawn Park's meet ends (in Hot Springs, Arkansas). Oaklawn is open for only two months and in 1982 was fifth in North America in average daily handle. Because the Oaklawn meet is so early in the year there is no two-year-old racing there. This means that Louisiana Downs has more two-year-old racing than you might expect, especially with its program for Louisiana state-breds. Here, there is even a Futurity restricted to Arkansas breds only.

The top trainer is Frank Brothers. Larry Snyder is the top jockey. There are also many weekend players. From my experience it seems that there are many casual players who go to the race track just to have a good time. Of course, there's nothing wrong with that. However, these players, like many casual players, are not satisfied with chalk horses (i.e. favorites). This means that more horses go off as overlays.

At this track I do exceptionally well with maiden races and with the more expensive claimers. I know, too, to stay away from cheap claimers for the most part. At each track, it is necessary to identify your strengths and weaknesses and adjust your betting accordingly.

At Louisiana Downs, when the track is off it is really off—maybe even three or four seconds off! Adjusted speed figures for this off-track mean nothing. The mud gets so deep and either a horse likes it or he does not. The first mudder out of the gate usually wins. Prior to and during the period in which the following races were run, there was a lot of rain. So much so that adjusted speed figures became meaningless.

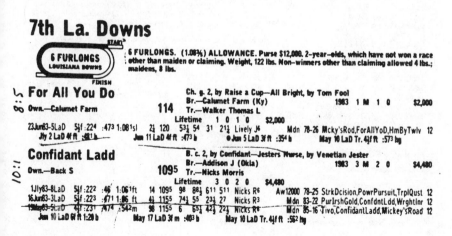

7th La. Downs

6 FURLONGS. (1.08⅗) ALLOWANCE. Purse $12,000. 2-year-olds, which have not won a race other than maiden or claiming. Weight, 122 lbs. Non-winners other than claiming allowed 4 lbs.; maidens, 8 lbs.

8:5
For All You Do — Ch. g. 2, by Raise a Cup—All Bright, by Tom Fool
Own.—Calumet Farm — 114 — Br.—Calumet Farm (Ky) — 1983 1 M 1 0 $2,000
Tr.—Walker Thomas L
Lifetime 1 0 1 0 $2,000

23Jun83-5LaD 5½f :22⁴ :47³ 1:08¹sl 2¼ 120 5³¼ 5⁴ 3¹ 2¹¼ Lively J⁶ Mdn 78-26 Mcky'sRod,ForAllYoD,HmByTwlv 12
Jly 2 LaD 4f ft :48¹ b Jun 11 LaD 4f ft :47³ b ●Jun 5 LaD 3f ft :35⁴ b May 10 LaD Tr. 4½f ft :57³ hg

10:1
Confidant Ladd — B. c. 2, by Confidant—Jesters Nurse, by Venetian Jester
Own.—Back S — 109⁵ — Br.—Addison J (Okla) — 1983 3 M 2 0 $4,480
Tr.—Nicks Morris
Lifetime 3 0 2 0 $4,480

1Jly83-8LaD 5½f :22² :46 1:06¹ft 14 109⁵ 9⁸ 8⁸½ 6¹¹ 5¹¹ Nicks R⁶ Aw12000 78-25 StrkDcision,PowrPursuit,TrplQust 12
16Jun83-3LaD 5½f :22³ :47¹ 1:06 ft 4½ 115⁵ 7⁴½ 5⁵ 2³½ 2⁷ Nicks R³ Mdn 83-22 PurIrshGold,ConfdntLdd,WrghtInr 12
19May83-5LaD 4½f :23¹ :47⁴ :54²m 98 115⁵ 6 6⁵¼ 4²½ 2²½ Nicks R⁶ Mdn 85-16 Tivo,ConfidantLadd,Mickey'sRoad 12
Jun 10 LaD 6f ft 1:20 b May 17 LaD 3f m :40³ b May 10 LaD Tr. 4½f ft :56² hg

Jai Cellar B. c. 2, by Down the Cellar—Jaipurette, by Jaipur
Br.—Jorgensen James H (Tex) 1983 4 1 0 1 $1,775
Own.—Barcelona D 117^5 Tr.—Roberts Herb
Lifetime 4 1 0 1 $1,775

20:1

1Jly83-8LaD 5½f :22^2 :46 1:06^{1}ft 17 117^5 3nk 3^3 5^{10} 6^{13} Faul J H^4 Aw12000 76-25 StrkDcision,PowrPursuit,TrplQust 12
20Jun83-1EvD 4f :23 :47^{3}ft 5¾ 118 2 1hd 1^4 1^6 Cahanin J T^3 Mdn 95-08 JaiCellr,BenGreen,TributeToChrloi 9
17Mar83-7DeD 4f :23^1 :49^{2}ft 15 120 1 4¾ 6^{5}¼ 7^{7}¾ Patin B C^9 Fut Trls 78-13 Beatemheadon,StrateMast,I'mPul 10
10Mar83-3DeD 4f :23^4 :50^{3}ft 5 118 2 1^1 2hd 3^{1}¼ Patin B C^5 Mdn 79-18 SplshforGreen,NothingIsEsy,JiCllr 10
Jun 28 LaD Tr. 5f gd 1:02^4 hg

Darby's Raider Ch. c. 2, by Native John—Darby Joan, by Big Joker
Br.—Beller J (Tex) 1983 1 M 0 0 $720
Own.—Beller J 114 Tr.—Pederson Phillip
Lifetime 1 0 0 0 $720

MAPLE 7:1

1Jly83-8LaD 5½f :22^2 :46 1:06^{1}ft 32 114 12^{13}12^{12} 9^{14} 4^{11} Young S A^2 Aw12000 78-25 StrkDcision,PowrPursuit,TrplQust 12
Jun 28 LaD 3f gd :37^4 b Jun 21 LaD 4f ft :48^2 b Jun 7 LaD Tr. 5f m 1:02^3 hg May 27 LaD 5f ft 1:01^4 b

Leonora's Guy Dk. b. or br. c. 2, by El Rastro—Leonora's Gal, by Approbation
Br.—McDermott M (Fla) 1983 2 1 0 0 $6,600
9:5 Own.—Clark R 122 Tr.—Herndon H W
Lifetime 2 1 0 0 $6,600

30Jun83-5LaD 5½f :22^4 :47^3 1:07^{3}gd 4¾ 120 3nk 1½ 1^2 1^{3}½ Herrera C^4 Mdn 82-27 Leonora'sGuy,FearlessNtive,LUno 11
9Jun83-5LaD 5f :22^3 :47 1:00^{3}ft 14 120 8^{4}¼ 8^{7}¼ 7^8 4^5 Herrera C^{12} Mdn 83-20 Stark Decision, Pitchit,SatinBoots 12
9Jun83—Was forced wide on the turn
Jun 21 LaD 3f ft :36 b Jun 4 LaD 4f ft :47^4 b May 29 LaD 4f ft :47^4 b May 24 LaD 4f ft :58^2 b

Big Daddys Dilemma Ch. c. 2, by Honey Jay—Firey Note, by Royal Note
Br.—McKinney F W (Ky) 1983 0 M 0 0
Own.—Stevens G 109^5 Tr.—Fox Patsy
Lifetime 0 0 0 0

FOX 22:1

Jly 1 LaD 5f ft 1:03 b Jun 16 LaD 5f ft 1:03 b Jun 10 LaD 3f ft :38^3 bg

What A Whistle Ch. c. 2, by Harry's Secret Joy—Miss Cher Lo, by Whistling Kettle
Br.—Shuffield V (Ark) 1983 4 1 0 0 $7,000
Own.—Shuffield V 122 Tr.—Shuffield Vern
Lifetime 4 1 0 0 $7,000

10:1

1Jly83-8LaD 5½f :22^2 :46 1:06^{1}ft 7½ 122 4^{1}¼ 4^5 7^{12} 8^{15} Fletcher R^3 Aw12000 74-25 StrkDcision,PowrPursuit,TrplQust 12
18Jun83-3LaD 5f :22^2 :46^4 :59^{4}ft 4 120 1^2 1^{1}½ 1^2 1½ Fletcher R^6 Mdn 92-17 WhtAWhistle,LUno,AbsoluteTrsur 10
19May83-5LaD 4½f :23^1 :47^4 :54^{2}m 15 120 2 1hd 1^1 4^{5}½ Romero G^3 Mdn 82-16 Tivo,ConfidantLadd,Mickey'sRoad 12
5May83-5LaD 4½f :22^3 :47^3 :54^{2}ft 52 115^5 7 7^{6}½ 7^7 5^2 Valovich C J^8 Mdn 86-13 Nitap, Macho Devil, Mickey'sRoad 12

Latonka Warrior Dk. b. or br. c. 2, by Lanyon—Tonkawa Winds, by Winds at War
Br.—Burress Kathryn & B B (Okla) 1983 5 M 1 0 $2,600
Own.—Burress Kathryn & B B 109^5 Tr.—Burress B B Sr
Lifetime 5 0 1 0 $2,600

COURT 24:1

1Jly83-8LaD 5½f :22^2 :46 1:06^{1}ft 70 109^5 1hd 2^{1}½ 4^{8}½ 7^{14} Fortner J L^1 Aw12000 75-25 StrkDcision,PowrPursuit,TrplQust 12
23Jun83-5LaD 5½f :22^4 :47^3 1:08^{1}sl 10 115 2^2 4^{3}½ 5^3 6^{7}½ Nicks R^8 Mdn 72-26 Mcky'sRod,ForAllYoD,HmByTwlv 12
26May83-3LaD 5f :22^4 :46^3 :59 ft 12 120 1hd 3^{1}½ 4^8 4^{13} Berry M C^{12} Mdn 83-18 ColonelPipkin,SecrtMountin,StrtL 12
26May83—Was six wide and tired
12May83-3LaD 4½f :23^1 :48^2 :55^{2}m 20 120 3 1hd 1hd 2hd Berry M C^{11} Mdn 83-17 Mbry'sAx,LtonkWrrior,HyPrtyChif 12
5May83-5LaD 4½f :22^2 :47^3 :54^{2}ft 12 120 3 3^3 5^{4}½ 7^{3}½ Herrera C^9 Mdn 84-13 Nitap, Macho Devil, Mickey'sRoad 12
Jun 28 LaD 4f gd :49^2 bg Jun 10 LaD 5f ft 1:07^3 b May 10 LaD 4f ft :52^2 b

VALOVICH 26:1

Naval Tribute B. c. 2, by High Tribute—Flotilla, by Naval Escort
Br.—De'Agano Sharon (La) 1983 0 M 0 0
Own.—De'Agano Sharon 111 Tr.—De'Agano P J
Lifetime 0 0 0 0
Jly 4 LaD 6f ft 1:16^4 b Jun 28 LaD tr.t 5f gd 1:03^2 hg Jun 23 LaD 5f m 1:06^2 bg(d) Jun 22 LaD 3f ft :39 hg

FORTNER 66:1

Behr Song Dk. b. or br. f. 2, by Pollinize—Wahine, by What Luck
Br.—Stansberry R (Okla) 1983 0 M 0 0
Own.—Okla HorseshoeingSchoolInc 111 Tr.—Roth Jack B
Lifetime 0 0 0 0
Jun 28 LaD tr.t 5f gd 1:03^2 hg

JULY 8 — RACE 7

For All You Do—Maiden in allowance company. Closer stretching out. Throw it out. Another false favorite.

Confident Ladd—Another maiden. Throw it out.

Jai Celler—Tired at 5 1/2 furlongs and going longer today. Not a contender.

Darby's Raider—Another maiden. . .

Leonora's Guy—Alibi as a first time starter and then a real nice win, front running on a good track. Being a speed horse and winning impressively, **Leonora's Guy** should have no problem stretching out a bit.

Bid Daddy's Dilemma—First time starter and in allowance company. Not a contender.

What A Whistle—Poor race last time with no excuse. Extra distance will hurt. Not a contender.

Latonka Warrior—Another maiden. . .

Naval Tribute and **Behr Song**—First time starters in allowance company. Throw them out.

THE BET: 100% of the M.B. on **Leonora's Guy** to win. There's nothing, absolutely nothing, in this field that looks like a threat to him and only three first time starters (and in allowance company, too).

RESULTS: **Leonora's Guy** won going away and paid $5.80. The favorite, **For All You Do**, ran sixth.

1st La. Downs

6 FURLONGS. (1.08⅗) MAIDEN. SPECIAL WEIGHT. Purse $11,500 (includes $1,500 supplement). 2-year-olds, accredited Louisiana-bred. Weight, 120 lbs.

Tickle Tun'g
B. c. 2, by Pachuto—Zenith's Pride, by Zenith
Br.—Adcock J (La) 1983 1 M 0 0
Own.—Poland Bernice 120 Tr.—Richey Tony
Lifetime 1 0 0 0
8Jly83-10LaD 6f :22 :45^{1} 1:12^{1}ft 11 113 10^{12}10^{15} 7^{13} 6^{8} Ardoin R^{3} [S]Stardust 74-[illegible] DzzelingStnley,TripleQuest,Hsobd 11
Jly 4 LaD 3f ft :36^{3} b Jun 27 LaD 5f m 1:05 b Jun 20 LaD 6f sl 1:03^{3} b (d) Jun 14 LaD tr.t 5f ft 1:02^{1} hg

Hail to Empire
B. c. 2, by Winds of Thought—Sassy Me, by Star Envoy
Br.—Carter H (La) 1983 0 M 0 0
Own.—Carter H Z 120 Tr.—Bean Ivan
Lifetime 0 0 0 0
Entered 13Jly83- 4 LAD
Jly 6 LaD 5f m 1:03^{3} hg Jun 25 LaD 5f m 1:03^{3} b Jun 1 LaD 5f ft 1:05^{3} hg May 24 LaD Tr. 4½f ft :58^{3} hg

Bold Imp
Dk. b. or br. c. 2, by Above Board—Spacette, by Condiment
Br.—Hullett L R (La) 1983 1 M 0 0
Own.—Hullett L 120 Tr.—Ferrester Kevin
Lifetime 1 0 0 0
6May83-3LaD 4½f :22^{4} :47^{3} :54^{1}ft 56 120 6 8$^{8\frac{1}{4}}$ 8$^{9\frac{3}{4}}$ 8^{10} White J R^{11} [S]Mdn 79-11 FrnchJim,CrimsonLwMn,BgMnKn 12
Jun 22 LaD 4f ft :53^{2} b

Crimson Law Man
B. c. 2, by Nalees Man—Crimson Express, by Crimson Satan
Br.—Cagle Mr & Mrs H W (La) 1983 2 M 2 0 $4,400
Own.—Dot Ragg Stable 115^{5} Tr.—Arceneaux George
Lifetime 2 0 2 0 $4,400
3Jun83-4LaD 5f :22^{3} :46^{3} :59^{2}ft 2¼ 120 10^{7} 9$^{6\frac{3}{4}}$ 4$^{4\frac{1}{2}}$ 2^{2} Smith R A^{4} [S]Mdn 92-15 Hsobd,CrimsonLwMn,PowrPursut 11
6May83-3LaD 4½f :22^{4} :47^{3} :54^{1}ft 4¼ 115^{5} 4 3$^{1\frac{1}{2}}$ 3^{1} 2$^{\frac{3}{4}}$ Faul J H^{9} [S]Mdn 88-11 FrnchJim,CrimsonLwMn,BgMnKn 12
Jun 1 LaD 5f ft 1:02 b May 24 LaD 3f ft :38^{2} b May 18 LaD 3f ft :38 b May 14 LaD 5f sl 1:04 b

M. J.'s Best
Ch. g. 2, by Better Bee Best—Sun Baked Cake, by Old Ky Ham
Br.—Oglesby M (La) 1983 0 M 0 0
Own.—Oglesby M & Mary 115^{5} Tr.—Wiles Millford
Lifetime 0 0 0 0
Jly 10 LaD 5f ft 1:05^{3} b May 24 LaD Tr. 4½f ft 1:00 hg

Supracrop
Ch. g. 2, by Honey Mark—Barbizelle, by Barbizon
Br.—Roberts R F (La) 1983 0 M 0 0
Own.—Roberts R F 115^{5} Tr.—Alleman Joseph
Lifetime 0 0 0 0
Jly 5 LaD 4f ft :52^{3} b Jun 28 LaD Tr. 5f gd 1:03^{3} b Jun 8 LaD 5f ft 1:04 b May 19 LaD 3f m :39^{2} b

Shecky Jay
Ch. c. 2, by Shecky Greene—Commercialette, by T. V. Commercial
Br.—McCogden Farm (La) 1983 2 M 0 0
Own.—Jerome F 120 Tr.—Brothers Frank L
Lifetime 2 0 0 0
17Jun83-7LaD 5½f :21^{4} :46 1:06 ft 22f 110 7^{8} 7^{11} 7^{15} 8^{17} Sorrows AGJr^{3} [S]Flare 73-21 DzzelingStnley,TripleQuest,BrbdNl 13
20May83-3LaD 4½f :23^{2} :48^{1} :55 m 7¼ 120 9 7$^{7\frac{3}{4}}$ 5^{7} 8^{9} White J R^{4} [S]Mdn 76-14 FbleRuler,EsopsProblem,Subrogte 12
Jun 10 LaD 4f ft :49^{3} b

Zip Native
B. f. 2, by Pacific Native—Miss Francie, by Francis S.
Br.—Swaw J F Jr (La) 1983 0 M 0 0
Own.—Bearden J 120 Tr.—Norman Gene
Lifetime 0 0 0 0
Jun 28 LaD Tr. 5f ft 1:02^{4} hg ●Jun 24 LaD 3f sl :36 hg Jun 22 LaD 3f ft :36^{1} b Jun 11 LaD 4f ft :48^{2} b

JULY 14—RACE 1

Throwing out first time starters leaves **Tickle Tun'g, Bold Imp,** and **Crimson Law Man** and **Shecky Jay**. First time starters are green and still learning. They win, but statistics are on our side if a previous starter shows anything. Immediately, the field narrows.

Tickle Tun'g—Made his debut in a state-bred handicap! He closed a ton of ground running the distance and had some support at the windows. This is a nice first race for this horse. Today this 2 year old drops all the way down to state-bred maidens after only six days off—a sure positive sign of the trainer's intentions.

Bold Imp—Nowhere last time with no support at the windows.

Crimson Law Man—Even money because he picks up Larry Snyder after running second in both his starts. However, this horse is a huge underlay. It hasn't run past five furlongs. At Louisiana Downs there is a big difference to the horses running this extra furlong. Its last start was 41 days ago. throw it out (but worry a little because of the switch to Larry Snyder).

Shecky Jay—Drops from state-bred handicap to state-bred maidens, BUT was nowhere AND already was well beaten in a state-bred maiden race.

THE BET: At this track maidens run especially well dropping down after making their debuts in allowance company and higher. **Crimson Law Man** had two cracks at the winner's circle in maiden company and failed. Although concerned about Larry Snyder, the smart bettor must stick with his bet. I really respect a jockey switch to Larry Snyder at this track. If he beats me this time, he beats me. Smart bettors play for the long run. No saver bet here because he is even money. Therefore, the correct bet is 75% of the M.B. to win on **Tickle Tun'g**. With anyone else besides Snyder on **Crimson Law Man** the correct play is 95% on **Tickle Tun'g**—that's how much I respect Larry Snyder riding a horse for the first time at this track.

RESULTS: They ran one, two with **Tickle Tun'g** winning going away and paying $9.60.

5th La. Downs

1 MILE 70 YDS
LOUISIANA DOWNS
START FINISH

1 MILE 70 YARDS. (1.39⅗) CLAIMING. Purse $7,800. Fillies and mares. 3-year-olds and upward. Weight, 3-year-olds, 113 lbs.; older, 121 lbs. Non-winners of two races since June 23 allowed 3 lbs.; a race at a mile or over since then, 7 lbs. Claiming price $10,000. (Races where entered for $8,000 or less not considered.)

Queen of the Tribe

Own.—Bailey B **114**

Ch. m. 5, by Vertee—No Court'n, by Noholme II
Br.—Irish Acres Farm (Fla)
Tr.—Gaston Jim **$10,000**
Lifetime 50 2 5 8 $22,081

1983	10	0	1	1	$2,168
1982	22	1	2	7	$10,559
Turf	4	0	1	0	$2,233

2Jly83-1LaD	1^{70}	$:46^4$	1:13	$1:46^2$ft	64	114	$9^{9\frac{3}{4}}$	6^6	4^6	3^2	Frazier R L^8	Ⓕ 10000	63-19	Tmmy'sJyJ,WhsprngLst,QnfthTrb	12
15Jun83-5JnD	1^{40}	$:48^2$	1:14	1:43 ft	$6\frac{3}{4}$	115	$7^{6\frac{1}{2}}$	$6^{7\frac{1}{2}}$	$6^{5\frac{1}{2}}$	6^{17}	Walker B J Jr^9	Ⓕ 7500	66-21	Summerline,AskMeTht,MystryDust	9
4Jun83-1LaD	1^{70}	$:47^4$	$1:14^1$	$1:45^3$ft	27	114	$11^{6\frac{3}{4}}$	10^4	$7^{7\frac{1}{4}}$	$7^{9\frac{3}{4}}$	Poyadou B E^1	Ⓕ 10000	59-18	Tmmy'sJyJy,PlyforBev,MissWrdlw	12
13May83-9LaD	1^{70}	$:48^1$	$1:15^2$	$1:48^2$m	26	109^5	11^{15}	10^{17}	10^{21}	10^{30}	Jacobs J J^9	Ⓕ 8000	25-37	Tammy'sJyJy,Dibundy,MissWrdlw	12
6May83-7LaD	6f	$:22^3$	$:46^4$	1:13 ft	28	109^5	10^5	$9^{7\frac{3}{4}}$	7^7	$6^{8\frac{1}{4}}$	Jacobs J J^2	Ⓕ 8000	70-19	CrystalNtive,EerieLight,NeverLow	11
6Mar83-1FG	6f	$:22^1$	$:45^3$	$1:12^3$ft	15	115	10^{11}	$10^{8\frac{3}{4}}$	$7^{6\frac{1}{4}}$	$7^{7\frac{1}{2}}$	Martino M^4	8500	74-20	FuelPirate,LaVerdad,TimelyMagic	11
27Feb83-5FG	6f	:22	:46	$1:13^1$ft	34	113	12^{12}	$9^{8\frac{3}{4}}$	$7^{4\frac{1}{4}}$	$4^{3\frac{3}{4}}$	Poyadou B E^1	Ⓕ 9000	75-26	Tally May, Lady Jack, Miss Ethel	12
11Feb83-8DeD	$6\frac{1}{2}$f	:24	:49	$1:24^1$ft	$6\frac{1}{2}$	117	$5^{5\frac{1}{4}}$	4^4	3^2	2^1	Martino M^5	Ⓕ 7500	76-22	FilAdvnce,QueenoftheTrib,AlyssJn	10
14Jan83-9DeD	$6\frac{1}{2}$f	$:24^3$	$:49^2$	$1:23^3$ft	4	117	$9^{9\frac{1}{4}}$	$9^{9\frac{1}{4}}$	8^{11}	$6^{9\frac{1}{2}}$	Martino M^9	Ⓕ 8500	70-24	Jiggy Bride,CrazyFanny,SteppingH.	9
5Jan83-10FG	$1\frac{1}{16}$	$:48^1$	$1:14^2$	$1:48^4$ft	12	116	8^6	4^5	4^3	$4^{2\frac{1}{2}}$	Martino M^1	Ⓕ 8500	65-20	WillsheWin,HiddenChrms,AquRule	12

Jly 17 LaD 5f ft $1:04^3$ b

Too Much Work

Own.—Schultz Alamae **114**

Ro. f. 4, by Famed Comedian—Royal Roan, by Royal Levee
Br.—Jolt Stables Inc (La)
Tr.—Schultz R D **$10,000**
Lifetime 25 2 3 4 $18,252

1983	14	2	3	0	$12,560
1982	10	M	0	4	$5,692

15Jly83-3LaD	$1\frac{1}{16}$	$:48^3$	1:14	$1:49^4$m	3	114	2^1	2^{hd}	$1^{2\frac{1}{2}}$	1^1	Snyder L^3	Ⓕ c8000	63-32	TooMuchWork,Brth'sBby,TrcysGrl	11
9Jly83-2LaD	1^{70}	$:47^2$	1:13	$1:43^4$ft	4	114	2^{hd}	2^{hd}	3^2	$4^{6\frac{1}{2}}$	Snyder L^{12}	Ⓕ 10000	71-17	Borit'sBest,SntRosBell,Ruby'sDrm	12
30Jun83-2LaD	6f	$:22^2$	:47	$1:14^4$gd	43	114	$11^{9\frac{1}{4}}$	$11^{9\frac{1}{4}}$	9^{10}	$8^{6\frac{3}{4}}$	DlhossyDJ^8	Ⓕ[S] 12500	62-27	Tar'sJoy,CowboysnIndins,KrteLdy	12
10Jun83-9LaD	1^{70}	:47	1:13	$1:45^1$ft	$4\frac{1}{4}$	112	6^3	3^3	3^4	$2^{3\frac{1}{2}}$	Snyder L^7	Ⓕ 8000	67-17	ShufflnPly,TooMuchWork,Dbundy	12
30May83-2LaD	6f	$:22^3$	$:46^1$	1:12 ft	20	114	$8^{8\frac{3}{4}}$	9^{15}	7^{11}	9^{15}	Knapp K^{10}	Ⓕ[S] 12500	68-17	Isn'tShePrtty,DibolicHroin,KrtLdy	12
28Apr83-1JnD	$6\frac{1}{2}$f	$:23^3$	$:47^4$	1:22 ft	*1	113	$3^{2\frac{1}{2}}$	$4^{2\frac{1}{4}}$	$4^{1\frac{1}{4}}$	1^2	Torres M R^5	M15000	75-19	TooMuchWork,CrdinlWnds,JyHgh	10
20Apr83-4JnD	1^{40}	$:47^4$	$1:13^2$	$1:42^1$ft	$3\frac{3}{4}$	115	$2^{2\frac{1}{2}}$	$2^{2\frac{1}{2}}$	$4^{4\frac{1}{2}}$	$4^{8\frac{1}{2}}$	Torres M R^2	[S]Mdn	78-17	WorthyStyl,NoGoodChntr,BdcsSn	10
31Mar83-3FG	6f	$:23^1$	$:47^3$	$1:13^4$gd	$7\frac{3}{4}$	115	$6^{5\frac{3}{4}}$	7^6	$5^{5\frac{1}{2}}$	$5^{5\frac{1}{2}}$	Frazier R L^2	[S]M30000	70-27	HourOfReson,LongHd,HrComsSnt	11
25Mar83-3FG	$1\frac{1}{16}$	$:48^3$	$1:14^3$	$1:48^3$ft	4	112	1^2	$1^{2\frac{1}{2}}$	2^1	$4^{3\frac{3}{4}}$	Frazier R L^1	M25000	65-21	Alesund, Circulante, Sumit Talker	10
19Mar83-3FG	6f	$:22^3$	$:46^4$	$1:13^1$ft	$5\frac{3}{4}$	117	$6^{3\frac{3}{4}}$	4^5	$4^{4\frac{1}{2}}$	4^5	Frazier R L^2	ⒻMdn	74-19	Lt. Lite, Sea Squaw, Taffy Apple	8

Santa Rosa Belle

Own.—Hobeau Farm Ltd **109^5**

B. f. 4, by Bill Boland—Coup d' Etat, by Royal Vale
Br.—Hobeau Farms Ltd (Fla)
Tr.—Breashear Bill **$10,000**
Lifetime 9 0 1 0 $2,720

1983	9	M	1	0	$2,720
1982	0	M	0	0	

9Jly83-2LaD	1^{70}	$:47^2$	1:13	$1:43^4$ft	59	109^5	1^{hd}	1^{hd}	2^{hd}	2^6	Hiett K^4	Ⓕ 10000	72-17	Borit'sBest,SntRosBell,Ruby'sDrm	12
29Jun83-1LaD	6f	$:23^1$	$:48^2$	$1:16^4$m	34	116^5	$4^{1\frac{1}{4}}$	$4^{2\frac{3}{4}}$	$5^{2\frac{3}{4}}$	$5^{7\frac{3}{4}}$	Hiett K^6	ⒻM35000	51-36	MajesticMaid,JulietCapulet,Chadr	10
14May83-4LaD	$1\frac{1}{16}$	:49	$1:15^2$	$1:50^1$gd	37	116^5	7^5	$6^{7\frac{3}{4}}$	7^{16}	7^{22}	Valovich C J^8	ⒻMdn	39-25	LckyProspctor,CtyPrncss,WrPtrol	11
30Apr83-1LaD	$1\frac{1}{16}$	:48	1:14	$1:49^1$ft	20	116^5	2^{hd}	4^{nk}	7^{11}	7^{19}	Valovich C J^3	ⒻMdn	47-19	ClownAbout,MillPlsur,GunflintSis	10
23Apr83-4LaD	$6\frac{1}{2}$f	$:23^2$	$:47^4$	1:21 sl	61	116^5	7^6	$7^{7\frac{1}{2}}$	6^8	6^{11}	Sorrows AGJr^5	ⒻMdn	59-22	B.HppyGrl,ClownAbot,McnpyMgc	12
11Apr83-7OP	$1\frac{1}{16}$	:48	$1:14^2$	$1:47^2$ft	63	119^5	$2^{1\frac{1}{2}}$	$4^{4\frac{1}{2}}$	7^{19}	8^{34}	Sorrows AGJr^2	ⒻMdn	37-22	CyprssBrr,NvrTwst,SmmrConfssn	12
31Mar83-1OP	1^{70}	:48	$1:15^2$	$1:46^4$ft	14	119^5	$4^{4\frac{1}{2}}$	4^5	10^{16}	11^{31}	SrrwsAGJr^{10}	ⒻM25000	31-21	HiddnHony,Donn'sRvvl,PnutsDncr	12
25Mar83-4OP	6f	$:22^1$	$:46^3$	$1:13^1$ft	10	119	$5^{3\frac{3}{4}}$	$4^{5\frac{1}{2}}$	4^8	4^{13}	SorrowsAGJr^{11}	ⒻMdn	66-19	PssThMums,PrmnntWvy,MillPlsur	11
17Feb83-4OP	$5\frac{1}{2}$f	$:22^2$	$:47^1$	$1:07^1$ft	18	119^5	8^{11}	8^{12}	8^{10}	$6^{7\frac{1}{2}}$	Sorrows AGJr^6	ⒻMdn	74-19	SwpsMusc,DoublDdt,Pocktfulplsr	12

Jun 20 LaD 5f ft $1:04^1$ b

Bessie Ball
Dk. b. or br. f. 4, by Pleasure Castle—Thrice As Fair, by Fair Ruler
Br.—Ball Tom & Eva (La) 1983 5 0 0 1 $2,276
Own.—Ball T 111 Tr.—Romero Gerald $10,000 1982 19 3 1 2 $23,167
Lifetime 30 5 1 3 $30,843
13Jly83-2LaD 6f :223 :464 1:124ft 5¾ 1095 74¾ 76½ 67 44¾ Faul J H3 ⒻⓈ 8000 74-23 KrtLdy,SistrAnnYoung,EysonHvn 11
30Jun83-2LaD 6f :222 :47 1:144gd 34 1095 54 33 33 42¾ Faul J H10 ⒻⓈ 12500 66-27 Tar'sJoy,CowboysnIndins,KrteLdy 12
20May83-4LaD 6f :23 :474 1:153m 5½ 111 43½ 32 32 33½ Snyder L3 Ⓕ 8000 61-39 BonniBluJn,WhispringList,BssiBll 12
5May83-2LaD 6f :222 :46 1:123ft 53 114 54¾ 68½ 56½ 55¾ Court J K4 ⒻⓈ 12500 74-23 DbolcHron,Msctogoby,Chngymnd 12
30Jan83-4FG 6f :231 :474 1:133ft 19 111 62½ 63¾ 54¾ 76½ Ebanks R12 Ⓕ 10000 71-26 EerieLight,MissEthel,Royce'sDrm 12
11Dec82-3FG 6f :223 :471 1:14 sy 30 114 117¾121.11215 — Guidry RD10 ⒻⓈ 15000 — — Beztmyshke,DeltDmsel,Clire'sRule 12
11Dec82—Distanced
30Oct82-8JnD 7f :223 :474 1:254ft 4¾e112 1½ 3½ 611 714 Menard N2 25000 72-27 TexsJohnny,HighBoret,LeedsCreek 9
15Oct82-7LaD 6f :224 :464 1:132ft 57 111 76¾ 87 79½ 78½ Romero G4 Ⓢ 20000 73-21 Dip's Boy, TheRealOne,TonyCloud 12
6Oct82-6LaD 6f :221 :46 1:12 ft 27 1085 97¼ 96¼ 79½ 56½ Woodruff TB5 Ⓕ 20000 82-12 Effie's Doll, Honey Miles,LaToque 10
29Sep82-8LaD 1⅛:48 1:123 1:461ft 12 1055 2½ 21 35 69 Woodruff TB4 Ⓕ 20000 78-11 MissHmpn'sCim,VoydE.,BrightLIBll 7
Jun 17 LaD 4f ft :503 b Jun 10 LaD 5f ft 1:022 b May 29 LaD 4f ft :474 b

SMITH 11:1

Ruby's Dream
Dk. b. or br. f. 4, by Patti's Plaything—Miss Nez, by Fair Turn
Br.—Steed Earl B (Ark) 1983 12 1 4 2 $23,580
Own.—Steed E et al 114 Tr.—Steed Bobby J $10,000 1982 1 M 0 1 $1,200
Lifetime 13 1 4 3 $24,780
9Jly83-2LaD 170:472 1:13 1:434ft 5½ 114 32½ 33 44 36¼ Whited D E11 Ⓕ 10000 72-17 Borit'sBest,SntRosBell,Ruby'sDrm 12
25Jun83-1LaD 6f :224 :47 1:143sl 8 114 106¼ 96½ 86½ 58½ Whited D E2 Ⓕ 12500 61-30 DibolicHeroin,Hndynsty,PcificSpic 11
12Jun83-2LaD 6f :221 :452 1:122ft 11 114 1215111711141111 Romero G11 Ⓕ 16000 70-16 HyperL.,ThinkSwaps,MakeaSwitch 12
12Jun83—Stumbled at the start
29May83-3LaD 6f :222 :462 1:122ft 6 118 99 75½ 57½ 45½ Romero G9 Ⓕ 16000 75-14 HwSwtItWs,Eff'sDll,CwbysnIndns 12
22May83-2LaD 6½f :234 :49 1:224sy *2 118 1hd 2hd 46 418 Ardoin R3 16000 43-35 OffDuty,LaToque,SophisticatedMm 8
8May83-2LaD 6½f :233 :474 1:20 ft *2½ 121 31½ 3nk 3nk 22 Perrodin E J8 Ⓕ 16000 73-22 JustaTecuy,Ruby'sDrem,Effie'sDoll 9
29Apr83-9LaD 170:472 1:13 1:443ft 5 1165 52½ 62¾ 69½ 813 SrrwsAGJr4 ⒻAw11500 61-23 I'mDriven,SinghingGoose,BforA.M. 9
11Apr83-3OP 6f :223 :48 1:15 ft *1 124 64¾ 21½ 15 16½ Whited D E2 ⒻⓈMdn 70-22 Ruby'sDream,MorePetls,TrulyGry 12
4Apr83-3OP 170:483 1:154 1:482ft *1 1195 4nk 21½ 2½ 2½ Allen K K11 ⒻⓈMdn 53-23 OnMorDnc,Rby'sDrm,WrdlwOrphn 12
4Apr83—Drifted, stretch
21Mar83-10P 6f :224 :48 1:134ft *6-5 124 41 42 42 2¾ Day P5 ⒻⓈMdn 75-26 PrincessDi,Ruby'sDream,FriskyJn 12
Jun 21 LaD 4f ft :50 bg Jun 10 LaD 4f ft :494 b Jun 5 LaD 3f ft :362 b

9:2

Ask Me That
Dk. b. or br. f. 4, by Rajab—Susan's Best, by Bay Bloom
Br.—Karutz Dr W S (Fla) 1983 15 2 2 2 $7,591
Own.—Loyd & Shackelford Gail 114 Tr.—Shackelford Gail $10,000 1982 17 M 4 0 $5,255
Lifetime 37 2 7 2 $14,456 Turf 1 0 0 0
13Jly83-8JnD 6½f :233 :48 1:211ft *8-5 117 66 54 44½ 44½ Torres M R2 Ⓕ 7500 74-23 Southwick,UniquelyDone,Cndy'sHir 8
3Jly83-5JnD 6½f :233 :47 1:192ft 2¾ 115 65¾ 67 44 48½ Talley W T10 7500 79-13 RobRob,FoolsApril,AmyntorImage 10
15Jun83-5JnD 140:482 1:14 1:43 ft *9-5 120 11 1½ 1½ 23 Talley W T1 Ⓕ 7500 80-21 Summerline,AskMeTht,MystryDust 9
9Jun83-5JnD 6½f :224 :471 1:21 ft 3¼ 120 66 44½ 21 12 Talley W T6 Ⓕ 6500 80-18 AskMTht,AutumnFir,Hitchnr'sDoll 10
9Jun83—Angled out inf final yards
27May83-1JnD 140:482 1:141 1:43 ft *7-5 120 31 3nk 1hd 12 Talley W T7 ⒻM11000 83-13 AskMTht,CloudStppr,ProdstOfAll 10
10May83-2JnD 6½f :233 :48 1:214ft *2¼ 115 53½ 54¾ 41½ 2hd Talley W T1 M11000 76-20 LoftyJobber,AskMeThat,Lindfleet 10
10May83—Moved four wide for the drive
26Apr83-5JnD 6½f :232 :47 1:204ft 11 115 56½ 47 44 3¾ Torres M R3 Mdn 80-16 Mr.T.Tml,GrndSundncKid,AskMTht 9
21Apr83-2JnD 6½f :24 :483 1:214ft 6½ 115 64 52 54 31¼ Torres M R4 M12500 75-19 TheSyndictor,Southwick,AskMTht 10
3Apr83-6FG a7½f Ⓣ 1:33 fm 50e110 89½ 89 814 719 Rubbicco P7 Aw9200 65-14 DevilInHerEyes,GeTon,OldU.S.Mint 9
11Mar83-3FG 1$\frac{1}{16}$:483 1:143 1:481ft 19 115 34½ 58½ 710 724 Breen R2 M50000 47-23 SophistictdMm,SumitTlkr,Circulnt 9
● Jun 30 JnD 5f sl 1:05 b

FLETCHER 8:1

Beth R.
Ch. f. 4, by Stormy Will—Blaze D., by Our Pleasure
Br.—Biehl M A (Okla) 1983 5 M 0 0
Own.—Shirley L & Mrs et al 114 Tr.—Richards Ken $10,000 1982 2 M 0 0
Lifetime 7 0 0 0 Turf 1 0 0 0
Entered 22Jly83- 7 LAD
15Jly83-3LaD 1$\frac{1}{16}$:483 1:144 1:494m 18 114 109¾ 913 919 832 Whited D E11 Ⓕ 8000 31-32 TooMuchWork,Brth'sBby,TrcysGrl 11
29Jun83-1LaD 6f :231 :482 1:164m 34 118 1012109¼ 98¾ 68 Engle J3 ⒻM32500 51-36 MajesticMaid,JulietCapulet,Chadr 10
29Jun83—Was shuffled back after the start
27May83-8LaD 1 Ⓣ:4731:13 1:384fm 110 114 108 108¼10181020 Engle J6 ⒻAw11500 60-17 SinghingGoos,Sm'sFrstLdy,LToqu 11
6Apr83-6OP 6f :223 :473 1:142ft 73 120 1214121512171218 Melancon L6 ⒻM40000 55-26 GllntNurse,QueenNicole,BeutyPro 12
11Feb83-4OP 5½f :231 :493 1:10 gd 76 124 118¼111010131012 Engle J12 ⒻMdn 56-28 GaleoFolly,I'mDriven,Mlle.Lotluck 12
11Sep82-1LaD 1⅛:483 1:14 1:532ft 56 117 33 45½ 817 926 Rivas C7 ⒻMdn 57-06 LadyCollet,Milemrker,DtelessMiss 12
4Sep82-2LaD 6½f :223 :461 1:181ft 55 117 911 911 818 721 Rivas C1 ⒻMdn 70-09 TwoTrips,TffyApple,PiPhiOfCours 11
Jun 17 LaD 5f ft 1:023 b

ENGLE 35:1

Whispering List
Own.—Everett-White **114**
Ch. f. 4, by List—Whisper Pam, by Whisper Jet
Br.—Kroop John (Ky) **1983 9 1 3 0 $8,220**
Tr.—Dantin Lee **$10,000** **1982 0 M 0 0**
Lifetime 9 1 3 0 $8,220

2Jly83-1LaD	1 70	:464	1:13	1:462ft	8½	114	31½	22½	33	22	Croker C R1	Ⓕ 10000	63-19	Tmmy'sJyJ,WhsprngLst,QnfthTrb	12
3Jun83-5LaD	6f	:23	:463	1:114ft	7¾	114	1hd	31	23	26	Croker C R3	Ⓕ 8000	78-15	Von'sToy,WhispringLst,OWhtRlfts	12
20May83-4LaD	6f	:23	:472	1:153m	19	114	21½	21½	22	21½	Croker C R1	Ⓕ 8000	63-39	BonniBluJn,WhispringList,BssiBll	12
22Apr83-8LaD	6f	:221	:452	1:114ft	111	114	126¾	1114	1115	1213	Croker CR5	ⒻAw11000	71-16	Earl's Good Time,Lt.Lite,PollyLee	12
23Mar83-2OP	6f	:221	:463	1:134ft	48	116	59	612	815	1111	Lively J9	7500	65-20	Glenwood Ace, Mr.Fondy,RareCap	12
9Mar83-5OP	6f	:232	:49	1:151ft	14	112	53¼	85¼	1017	1020	Lively J8	Ⓕ 10000	49-29	Mid Morn, Snowbelle, Ritzy Rags	11
26Feb83-5OP	6f	:222	:471	1:131ft	22	119	97¼	1113	1128	1129	Lively J10	ⒻAw16000	50-23	SwapsMusic,EternllyYours,Librell	11
22Jan83-5Lat	6f	:232	:471	1:142sy	6½	122	12½	11½	13	14	Catalano W12	ⒻMdn	72-32	Whispering List, Posslq, Promised	12
2Jan83-5Lat	6f	:232	:47	1:141ft	8	121	21½	21½	34	611	Catalano W7	ⒻMdn	62-32	CorportDriv,SpnnkrSlly,MrsllsAnn	12

Jun 28 LaD 4f gd :51 b **Jun 20 LaD 6f ft 1:183 b** **Jun 14 LaD 5f ft 1:041 b**

Play for Bev
Own.—Dorignac J P Jr **114**
B. m. 7, by Playgoer—Sally Summers, by Salason
Br.—Durrett Mr-Mrs J W (Ark) **1983 11 2 1 2 $13,212**
Tr.—Dorignac J P III **$10,000** **1982 11 1 1 4 $7,762**
Lifetime 89 9 8 14 $58,258 **Turf 8 0 2 4 $7,154**

2Jly83-1LaD	1 70	:464	1:13	1:462ft	3¼	114	89¼	77	56	42¼	Ardoin R9	Ⓕ 10000	63-19	Tmmy'sJyJ,WhsprngLst,QnfthTrb	12
4Jun83-1LaD	1 70	:474	1:141	1:453ft	3	114	73½	71½	54	24½	Ardoin R6	Ⓕ 10000	64-18	Tmmy'sJyJy,PlyforBev,MissWrdlw	12
13May83-4LaD	1 70	:49	1:161	1:492m	2¼	114	44½	42	67	68½	Franklin R J7	Ⓕ 16000	41-37	Vega Fury, VoyedE.,StarPreformer	7
8May83-2LaD	6½f	:233	:474	1:20 ft	4¼	114	83¼	75½	74¾	67¼	Franklin R J4	Ⓕ 16000	68-22	JustaTecuy,Ruby'sDrem,Effie'sDoll	9
29Apr83-4LaD	1 70	:474	1:131	1:463ft	4	114	811	710	66½	611	Smith R A7	Ⓕ 16000	58-23	Alidate,Quickasakiss,StarPreformer	8
6Mar83-6FG	1 40	:482	1:134	1:412ft	6	113	83¾	64	76	69¼	Ardoin R8	A6000	77-20	Exotic King, Glenn D., Mr. F. J. D.	8
17Feb83-10FG	1 1/16	:481	1:143	1:48 ft	*8-5	116	710	64½	44	34	Franklin R J1	Ⓕ 16500	68-22	Tiffy K., Pucci'sPocket,PlayforBev	9
5Feb83-6FG	1 40	:473	1:132	1:423ft	2½	113	78½	64½	79¼	513	Franklin R J1	Ⓕ 27500	67-17	Claire'sRule,IfyTimes,TimelessMgic	7
27Jan83-6FG	1 40	:481	1:161	1:462sl	*8-5	117	48	44	11	14½	Franklin R J6	Ⓕ 16000	61-32	PlyforBev,TiffyK.,SondheimrSpcil	10
20Jan83-6FG	1 1/16	:49	1:16	1:512m	5	113	54	54½	11½	18	Franklin R J2	Ⓕ 15000	55-31	PlyforBv,Pcc'sPockt,SndhmrSpcl	11

May 27 LaD 5f ft 1:021 b

JULY 23—RACE 5 (Exacta Wagering)

Queen of the Tribe—1 for 32 lifetime. Although third last time only a 63 speed rating. Therefore, this horse is not giving notice. Not a contender.

Too Much Work—Won last time, and claimed, but moves up after losing ground. The week before it came fourth after a speed duel with **Santa Rosa Belle**. Not a contender.

Santa Rosa Belle—A maiden versus winners. *HOWEVER*, **Santa Rosa Belle** raced in this class at this distance last time out. Its race was superior for these horses. She ran second after a tough, tough race. Her pace and speed ratings are the highest at the distance. Last time she gave notice and today is the only speed in the race. That's why she was bet down to 9:1 after being 59:1 last time, but I'm not going to complain.

Bessie Ball—Wrong distance. Raise after a loss. No way.

Ruby's Dream—Beaten by **Santa Rosa Belle** last time with no excuse. Not a contender.

Ask Me That—Shipper from Jefferson Downs where the quality of racing is not as good as Louisiana Downs. If a horse can't beat $7,500 claimers there, it shouldn't beat $10,000 here. Throw it out.

Beth R.—Nowhere last time (or any other time) in $8,000 claimers. No way this time.

Whispering List—Second to **Tammy's Jay Jay** last time and ahead of **Queen of the Tribe**. However, only a 63 speed rating.

Play For Bev—The favorite, an unfavorable jockey switch, and fourth to **Tammy's Jay Jay**. You figure it out; I can't. If there ever was a false favorite. . .

THE BET: This is another race you really have to love. Sound fundamental handicapping and reading between the lines really pays off here. The favorite doesn't figure and the second choice is moving up after struggling against cheaper. **Santa Rose Belle** is the only speed with top figures for speed and pace. The only other possible horse to play in the exactas is **Whispering List**. I thought 90% of the M.B. for the race; 55% on **Santa Rosa Belle** to win because she is 9:1 and I don't want to blow the bet if I miss the exacta.

Exactas:

Santa Rosa Belle—Whispering List	25%
Whispering List—Santa Rosa Belle	10%

This time, most of the bet was on **Santa Rosa Belle** to win because I'm not that confident with **Whispering List**. Wheeling **Santa Rose Belle** may also be correct, but I just can't see anyone beating **Whispering List** for second. If I'm wrong about **Whispering List** I can live with myself because I bet 55% of the M.B. on a 9:1 shot. If correct, I collect big.

RESULTS: **Santa Rose Belle** got loose on the lead and won paying $21.20. **Whispering List** was second completing a $5 exacta that returned $279.50.

4th La. Downs

1 MILE 70 YDS
LOUISIANA DOWNS
START FINISH

1 MILE 70 YARDS. (1.39⅗) MAIDEN. SPECIAL WEIGHT. Purse $8,500. 2-year-olds. Weight, 120 lbs. (Preference to non-starters for a claiming price.)

Blue Carrie
Own.—Elkins F 117
Ch. f. 2, by Blue Times—Double Carrie, by Tronado
Br.—Taylor Made Farm (Ky) 1983 2 M 0 0
Tr.—Elkins Mike
Lifetime 2 0 0 0
29Sep83-6LaD 170 :492 1:153 1:483ft 109 117 93 1012 920 1027 Fletcher R6 Mdn 27-32 Pssion'sDlight,FullCourt,FoggnJm 12
14Sep83-6LaD 170 :484 1:152 1:463ft 72 119 119¾ 1113 1123 931 Adkins G10 Ⓕ Mdn 33-26 IntlIntnt,WstwoodCommnd,Shffld 12
Sep 3 LaD 6f ft 1:193 b Aug 23 LaD Tr. 6f ft 1:192 hg Aug 19 LaD 3f ft :39 hg Aug 11 LaD 3f ft :40 b.

Koliga
Own.—Hartley D O 120
Ch. g. 12, by Jato Ribot—Polly Step, by Never Cede
Br.—Hartley D O (Okla) 1983 2 M 0 0
Tr.—Broomfield Gerald 1982 0 M 0 0
Lifetime 2 0 0 0
28Sep83-6LaD 6f :222 :463 1:141ft 123 120 1219 1218 913 611 Engle J11 Mdn 61-27 J. A.'s United, Mito Hy,BoldJigger 12
5Sep83-3LaD 6½f :23 :464 1:204ft 74 120 108½ 1112 1112 1115 Engle J7 Mdn 56-28 Bold Greek, J. A.'sUnited,Dabayea 11
Aug 16 LaD Tr. 6f ft 1:19 hg

***Vilgora's Note**
Own.—Yeager D F lessee 115⁵
B. c. 2, by Vilgora—Brief Note, by Counsel
Br.—Southdown Stud (GB) 1983 1 M 0 1 $950
Tr.—Bergquist Wally A
Lifetime 1 0 0 1 $950
22Sep83-1LaD 170 :501 1:172 1:494gd 20 1155 62¾ 43½ 38 312 Milligan E R Jr3 Mdn 36-39 JudgMBst,Mr.Moonbm,Vlgor'sNot 12
Oct 1 LaD 7f ft 1:343 b Sep 17 LaD 6f ft 1:162 b Sep 13 LaD Tr. 6f ft 1:18 hg Sep 7 LaD Tr. 6f m 1:174 hg

Falcon Kingdom
Own.—Woods R 115⁵
Ch. c. 2, by Noble Kingdom—Eiderdown, by Momus
Br.—Woods R (Tex) 1983 4 M 0 0 $40
Tr.—Burwell Tom
Lifetime 4 0 0 0 $40
29Sep83-6LaD 170 :492 1:153 1:483ft 134 1155 82½ 910 819 926 Stroud S5 Mdn 28-32 Pssion'sDlight,FullCourt,FoggnJm 12
12Aug83-8LaD 6f :223 :462 1:13 ft 120 114 127¾ 1217 1120 1021 SorrwsAGJr11 Aw10000 57-23 Darby'sRaider,SafeCrcker,Swisher 12
30Jun83-5LaD 5½f :224 :473 1:073gd 46 120 77¾ 1114 — — Bianchini J5 Mdn — — Leonora'sGuy,FearlessNtive,LUno 11
30Jun83—Eased
15Apr83-9Sun 5f :221 :454 :583ft 35 120 77½ 76½ 511 519 Harless B J5 Mdn 70-14 GoExclsvGo,TrckLst,MghtyMmntm 9
Sep 27 LaD 5f ft 1:04 b

Full Court
Own.—Nickoff T 120
B. g. 2, by Full Out—Betty Beautiful, by Handsome Boy
Br.—Noonan H B (Ohio) 1983 8 M 1 1 $4,428
Tr.—Valdizan Fernando
Lifetime 8 0 1 1 $4,428
29Sep83-6LaD 170 :492 1:153 1:483ft 2¾ 120 1hd 1hd 1hd 2no Brown B W4 Mdn 54-32 Pssion'sDlight,FullCourt,FoggnJm 12
15Sep83-4LaD 170 :484 1:152 1:463ft 12 120 42¾ 32½ 26 38½ Brown B W3 Mdn 56-20 ConfidntLdd,FogginJim,FullCourt 12
3Sep83-3LaD 6f :231 :47 1:131ft 70 120 95¾ 78½ 57½ 58 Brown B W4 Mdn 69-20 A HardTen,MitoHy,ConfidantLadd 12
18Aug83-6LaD 6f :224 :461 1:124ft 49 120 94½ 810 714 912 Whited D E2 Mdn 67-18 GpOpnng,Consngunty,ConfdntLdd 12
21Jly83-6LaD 6f :222 :462 1:124sy 13 120 69 49½ 614 715 Hightower T W5 Mdn 64-21 SafeCracker,Andy'sMagic,Lnburg 12
18Jun83-9RD 5½f :224 :463 1:064ft 9½ 112 88½ 815 713 514 DelaguardiF5 Ⓢ Ohioan 67-38 TahDah,HighlandsNell,TllMedows 10
10Jun83-3LaD 5f :222 :464 :594ft 12 1155 53 44½ 36 57½ Valovich C J1 Mdn 84-17 WhtAWhistle,LUno,AbsoluteTrsur 10
20May83-8LaD 4½f :23 :474 :543m 12 1095 5 810 99¾ 810 Valovich C J1 Aw12000 77-14 WhrlngShttl,Mbry'sAx,PrIrshGold 10
Sep 11 LaD 4f ft :524 b Aug 11 LaD 5f ft 1:06 b Aug 6 LaD 3f m :374 b

Judge Forest
Own.—Hamrick A G 120
B. c. 2, by Judger—Forest Trail, by Rainy Lake
Br.—McCogden Stable (La) 1983 2 M 0 0
Tr.—Dantin Lee
Lifetime 2 0 0 0
30Sep83-3LaD 170 :494 1:16 1:47 ft 20 120 83 51¾ 610 821 Faul J H12 ⒻⓈ Mdn 41-26 LipanMagic,Vando,SpeedyTruxton 12
16Sep83-3LaD 6½f :232 :463 1:19 ft 56 120 1210 1115 818 620 Frazier R L2 Ⓢ Mdn 60-21 Kantiomara'sBoy,MrCTSad,Ttush 12
Aug 16 LaD 6f ft 1:20 hg Aug 11 LaD 4f ft :524 hg

LIVELY 29:1

I'm Tickled — B. c. 2, by Bold Debonair—Gaylord's Canoe, by Gaylord's Feather
Br.—Taylor D R (La) 1983 1 M 0 0 $600
Own.—Sunbelt Stable Lessee 120 Tr.—Hefner Hank
Lifetime 1 0 0 0 $600
30Sep83-3LaD 170:494 1:16 1:47 ft 46 1155 62¼ 62¼ 45½ 415 MillignERJr8 ⒻⓈMdn 47-26 LipanMagic,Vando,SpeedyTruxton 12
Sep 7 LaD Tr. 6f gd 1:193 hg Aug 30 LaD 4f ft :494 bg Aug 23 LaD 3f ft :38 bg

11:1

Rojo Magnifico — Ch. c. 2, by Goof John—Little Johns Joy, by Johns Joy
Br.—Duffied O F (Fla) 1983 3 M 0 0 $1,140
Own.—D T Farm 120 Tr.—Thomas William C
Lifetime 3 0 0 0 $1,140
29Sep83-6LaD 170:494 1:153 1:483ft 14 120 72¼ 42¾ 44½ 44½ Wacker D J2 Mdn 49-32 Pssion'sDlight,FullCourt,FoggnJm 12
22Sep83-1LaD 170:501 1:172 1:494gd 99 120 128¾ 108¾ 611 413 Brown B W11 Mdn 35-39 JudgMBst,Mr.Moonbm,Vigor'sNot 12
11Aug83-6LaD 6f :23 :471 1:133ft 47 120 1214 1215 1113 1114 DelahoussayeDJ2 Mdn 61-23 GrndpJssiBoy,Andy'sMgic,Lnburg 12

2:1

Costa Del Sol — B. f. 2, by L'Heureux—Centerfold Girl, by Decimator
Br.—Scott Mrs F & Scott Co Inc (Ky) 1983 3 M 0 2 $2,160
Own.—Scott Mrs F C 117 Tr.—Holthus P E
Lifetime 3 0 0 2 $2,160
Entered 5Oct83-4 LAD
23Sep83-1LaD 6½f :231 :472 1:22 ft 4 119 1214 1013 98½ 34 Franklin R J4 ⒻMdn 61-29 IncredibleDoll,MryFern,CostDlSol 12
19Aug83-6LaD 6f :224 :47 1:134ft 17 1145 97½ 89 49½ 33½ Valovich C J2 ⒻMdn 71-22 MenMimi,JoyWon'tTell,CostDlSol 11
29Jly83-1LaD 6f :222 :46 1:12 ft 23 1145 911 712 612 512 Valovich C J7 ⒻMdn 70-21 Quick Justice, Geevilla, Mary Fern 12
Sep 16 LaD 5f ft 1:03 b Aug 12 LaD 4f ft :511 b

50:1

Exotic Empery — Dk. b. or br. c. 2, by Empery—Exotic Visage, by Tom Rolfe
Br.—King Ranch Inc (Ky) 1983 1 M 0 0
Own.—Carden C T et al 120 Tr.—Soileau J Y
Lifetime 1 0 0 0
28Sep83-6LaD 6f :222 :463 1:141ft 22 120 1015 1014 1215 1016 Ardoin R7 Mdn 56-27 J. A.'s United, Mito Hy,BoldJigger 12
Sep 24 LaD 5f ft 1:05 hg Sep 17 LaD 4f ft :501 b Sep 5 LaD 5f ft 1:04 b Aug 23 LaD Tr. 6f ft 1:182 hg

Also Eligible (Not in Post Position Order):

9:2

Mito Hy — Dk. b. or br. g. 2, by Mnt Point—Hygro's Solution, by Peaceful Solution
Br.—Kelly H C (Tex) 1983 4 M 3 0 $5,400
Own.—Epperson Carolyn 120 Tr.—Reel Freddie L
Lifetime 4 0 3 0 $5,400
28Sep83-6LaD 6f :222 :463 1:141ft 5¼ 120 32½ 31 11½ 2½ White J R6 Mdn 71-27 J. A.'s United, Mito Hy,BoldJigger 12
3Sep83-3LaD 6f :231 :47 1:13 ft 8 120 11 11½ 1hd 21 White J R9 Mdn 76-20 A HardTen,MitoHy,ConfidantLadd 12
10Aug83-6LaD 6f :231 :471 1:14 ft 24 120 1hd 2hd 22 27 Court J K12 Mdn 65-27 Sneakinprince, MitoHy,BoldJigger 12
15Jly83-6LaD 6f :223 :47 1:14 m 16 120 76½ 78½ 68½ 716 White J R12 Mdn 55-32 Sustnnc,SovrignExchng,Snkinprnc 12
Aug 19 LaD 3f ft :38 b

OCTOBER 6—RACE 4

This is the kind of race you'd like to see every time you go to the track! You know you have the winner (or at least think so) *and* it's not the favorite.

Blue Carrie—Nowhere and no way.

Koliga—Nowhere and no way.

Vilgora's Note—Ran third on a good track, but beaten 12 lengths with a 36 speed rating. Not today.

Falcon Kingdom—Has never been close. No way.

Full Court—The favorite. Head and head all the way and only beaten a nose at the distance. Let's reserve further discussion until later.

Judge Forest—Never close. No way.

I'm Tickled—A state-bred filly moving up after losing by 15. No way.

Rojo Magnifico—Fourth at the distance, but beaten 4 1/2 lengths by Full Court.

Costa Del Sol—A closer stretching out and a female stepping up to face males. A weak contender.

Exotic Empery—Not close only start. Not a contender.

Mito Hy—Three seconds. A front runner stretching out. A contender.

DISCUSSION: Eight days ago **Mito Hy** was a length off the leader in a half that went in :46^3. Therefore, he went in :46^4. **Full Court**, the favorite, had to battle for the lead in a half that went in :49^2! Even though **Full Court** raced on a slower track, it wasn't that much slower. The difference in these two halves is thirteen fifths of a second—approximately 13 lengths. Most of the other horses haven't been close to the winner. It should be obvious by now that **Mito Hy** will have things his own way. He will be loose on the lead setting his own pace. If **Full Court** tries to keep up he will probably tire. **Mito Hy**, although tiring a bit at six furlongs, will have plenty of energy left to go the added distance because no one will push him to the half.

The only other horse to consider is **Costa Del Sol**, the closer stretching out. Always take the speed stretching out. If this isn't a satisfactory enough explanation, look closer. In sprints she runs nine lengths off a :47 half, or about :48^4. The half figures to go the same today but she'll have to go more than two furlongs extra. **Costa Del Sol** will, most likely, flatten out because of the distance. Remember, **Mito Hy** was going to the half faster in sprints. By going slower today he will have reserved energy. **Costa Del Sol**, by going in the same time to the half won't have any reserved energy for the added distance.

THE BET: 100% of the M.B. on **Mito Hy** to win.

RESULTS: **Mito Hy** got loose on the lead making the half in :48^2. Thereafter, he steadily increased his lead to win easily by about 5 lengths. He paid $11.00.

Full Court raced off the pace, but faded as expected. He finished fourth. **Costa Del Sol** was outrun, finishing sixth. She didn't have any energy left to close ground, also as expected. Sound handicapping and betting all the way.

Penn National

Penn National has a much smaller handle compared to Aqueduct and Louisiana Downs. From a bettor's standpoint, I think it is one of the best run tracks in the country and its employees are warm and friendly. Because the quality of racing is below that of Aqueduct (e.g. Penn runs $2,500 claimers), it is even more important to check the paddock. At all small tracks where many horses don't race to form because they are cheap or hurting, it is important to understand the trainer's winning pattern. There is no better indication of when the horse is fit and ready or when it is hurting. Cheaper horses do not keep their form as long as more expensive horses do. And the bettors are less sophisticated as those are in New York. It is possible to catch good prices, especially in the place and show pools (although show betting is recommended only for the casual race goer). Recently, the track has accepted off-track wagering. This may have also helped the overlays because these bettors obviously cannot check the paddock.

Remember, just because a trainer is at a small track doesn't mean that he doesn't know what he's doing. There are some big fish in these small ponds. Top trainers at small race tracks may know just as much as New York and California trainers, maybe even more. I don't know Mario Beneito personally, but based on what I've seen, I respect the way he manages his horses. He is a top trainer at Penn National and no doubt could hold his own anywhere, including New York and California.

3 PENN NATIONAL — 5 FURLONGS PENN NATIONAL

5 FURLONGS. (.56⅘) MAIDEN SPECIAL WEIGHT. Purse $7,500. Fillies. 2-year-olds. Weights, 118 lbs. (Pennsylvania Bred Preferred.) (If eight or more Pennsylvania Breds pass the entry box, the race shall become closed to all but Pennsylvania Breds.)

Coupled—Cathy's Bluff and Que Beam. SCR

7:5 **Speedy Tweetie** — Ch. f. 2, by Proud Birdie—Mighty Fit, by Cap Size — Br.—Schmidt A M (Fla) — Tr.—Mills M Edgar Jr — 118 — Lifetime 1 0 0 0 $250 — 1983 1 M 0 0 $250
Own.—S K C Stable
9Aug83- 4Tim fst 4f :23⅗ :46⅘ ⒻMd Sp Wt 2 8 5^7 $5^{5\frac{1}{2}}$ 4^6 Grove P b 119 3.10 85-07 The Hay You Say 119$^{1\frac{1}{2}}$ Run And Roll 119^2 Itch'sSis112$^{2\frac{1}{2}}$ Rallied 9

21:1 **Countess Tess** — B. f. 2, by Rollin Count—Behaving Sis, by Ambehaving — Br.—Bush W (Pa) — Tr.—Miller M Joe — 118 — Lifetime 0 0 0 0 — 1983 0 M 0 0
Own.—Ardin Stable
LATEST WORKOUTS ●Aug 13 Pen 4f fst :49 b

7:2 **Steen A Way** — B. f. 2, by Cathy's Prince—Citaway, by Abdul — Br.—Latsha E E (Pa) — Tr.—Curtin Richard T — 113^5 — Lifetime 4 0 1 0 $1,500 — 1983 4 M 1 0 $1,500
Own.—Latsha E E
20Aug83- 3Pen fst 5f :22 :47⅕ 1:00⅖ ⒻⓈMd Sp Wt 7 2 $3^{2\frac{1}{2}}$ 3^2 $2^{2\frac{1}{2}}$ $2^{\frac{1}{2}}$ Rozell R M^5 b 111 11.80 81-19 Silky Soony 116$^{\frac{1}{2}}$ Steen A Way 111$^{5\frac{1}{2}}$ Ranunculus 116$^{\frac{1}{2}}$ Rallied 7
12Aug83- 3Pen fst 5f :22⅗ :47⅗ 1:00 ⒻMd Sp Wt 4 6 $7^{6\frac{1}{2}}$ 7^8 7^{12} $6^{8\frac{1}{2}}$ Rozell R M^5 111 41.10 75-21 Jacolina 116$^{1\frac{1}{2}}$ Madame B. 116^3 Margogo 116^2 No factor 8
3Aug83- 3Pen fst 5f :22⅗ :47⅗ 1:00⅖ ⒻMd Sp Wt 4 9 10^{13} 10^{19} 10^{18} — Montoya R 116 19.60 — — Angel Steam 116$^{1\frac{1}{2}}$ SilkySoony116$^{1\frac{1}{2}}$RumbleStilts116$^{4\frac{1}{2}}$ Distanced 10
16Jly83- 3Pen fst 5f :23 :47⅕ :59⅗ Md Sp Wt 6 1 4^2 $6^{7\frac{1}{2}}$ 7^{13} 7^{16} Montoya R 111 6.60 71-13 SpinCycle116$^{3\frac{1}{2}}$MightyEchelon115$^{4\frac{1}{2}}$MightySword116$^{1\frac{1}{2}}$ Early foot 7
LATEST WORKOUTS Jly 9 Pen 4f fst :49⅘ hg

5:1 **Hai Cutie** — B. f. 2, by Ga Hai—Mad Cutie, by Rash Prince — Br.—Tesauro D (Pa) — Tr.—Henry Billy J — 118 — Lifetime 0 0 0 0 — 1983 0 M 0 0
Own.—Cinemod Stable
LATEST WORKOUTS Sep 2 Pen 5f fst 1:01⅗ hg

11:1 **Cathy's Bluff** — B. f. 2, by Cathy's Reject—Cabin Bluffer, by Big Bluffer — Br.—Katalpa Farm (Ky) — Tr.—Arnold Pamela — 118 — Lifetime 1 0 0 0 — 1983 1 M 0 0
Own.—Handford S & Wendy
30Aug83- 1Key fst 6f :22⅕ :45⅘ 1:12⅕ ⒻMd 22500 5 9 9^{12} 8^{13} 8^{14} 7^{13} Berry J 119 16.40 67-23 Langhorne 119$^{5\frac{1}{2}}$ Yeya 112^{nk} Mongo's Reflection119$^{1\frac{1}{2}}$ Slow start 9
LATEST WORKOUTS ●Aug 24 Pen 5f fst 1:02⅕ h

6:1 **Birthday Fling** — B. f. 2, by Northern Fling—Ovulator, by Rejected — Br.—Bergman R V (Pa) — Tr.—Clay George — 118 — Lifetime 0 0 0 0 — 1983 0 M 0 0
Own.—Talbot Cynthia
LATEST WORKOUTS Sep 3 Pim 3f fst :37 h Aug 11 Pim 3f fst :39 bg

4:1 **Takes Time** — Dk. b. or br. f. 2, by Double Edge Sword—Fleet Foot, by Globemaster — Br.—Frame R S (Md) — Tr.—Manchio Belinda — 118 — Lifetime 0 0 0 0 — 1983 0 M 0 0
Own.—Frame R S
LATEST WORKOUTS ●Aug 26 Pen 5f fst 1:01⅗ bg Aug 19 Pen 3f fst :35⅗ hg Aug 13 Pen 4f fst :51⅕ b Aug 4 Pen 3f fst :37 h

40:1 **Winnie's Edge** — Ch. f. 2, by Double Edge Sword—Winnie Roe, by Rash Prince — Br.—Brandt R L (Md) — Tr.—Stough William D — 118 — Lifetime 0 0 0 0 — 1983 0 M 0 0
Own.—Brandt R
LATEST WORKOUTS Aug 24 Pen 4f fst :51⅗ bg

PROUGH

Throwing out all first time starters (because previous starters have showed potential) leaves us with **Speedy Tweetie, Steen A Way** and **Cathy's Bluff**.

Speedy Tweetie—Lost ground at 4 furlongs and must go longer today. A false favorite.

Steen A Way—Ran second in state-breds but nowhere in open company like today. Throw her out.

Cathy's Bluff—Ships in from Keystone. Horses that ship in from Keystone do unusually well here. Favorable jockey switch. J. D. Prough always does well for Pamela Arnold. **Cathy's Bluff** has an alibi last race—a slow start. The only knock seems to be that she raced in a maiden claimer—*BUT*, this was at Keystone. A $22,500 maiden at Keystone almost always outclasses a state-bred maiden at Penn National. Additionally, she is 11:1 today!

THE BET: 30% of the M.B. on **Cathy's Bluff** to win and 20% wheeling her on top in the exactas. The bettor doesn't want to waste an 11:1 shot, but nothing sticks out for second. Wheeling **Cathy's Bluff** on top pays more than a win bet in 4 out of 7 of the possible exactas. The three other possible exactas should be bet a couple more times than the others because of the low payoff. More than 50% of the M.B. isn't possible. Although **Cathy's Bluff** ships in from Keystone after an alibi she was still beaten 13 lengths. The bettor cannot be sure if the jockey eased up on the horse afterwards. he can only assume it by reading in between the lines.

RESULTS: **Cathy's Bluff** won by 2 paying $24.20. **Hai Cutie** ran second completing a $2 exacta worth $173.40. A $2 wheel would have cost $14. Betting $14 on the winner would have returned $169.40.

7 PENN NATIONAL

6 FURLONGS
PENN NATIONAL

6 FURLONGS. (1.08⅘) CLAIMING. Purse $2,500. 4-year-olds and upward which have not won three races since March 12. Weights, 119 lbs. Non-winners of two races since July 18, allowed 3 lbs. Two races since June 18 6 lbs. Claiming Price $2,500.

Great Proprieter

ROZELLE 7:1

Own.—Idyll Acres Farm

Dk. b. or br. g. 4, by Great Sun—Proprietress, by Your Host
$2,500 Br.—Peckham W H (Ky)
Tr.—Beattie Thomas G

1115 Lifetime 22 3 1 2 $9,420 | 1983 9 2 1 2 $5,010 | 1982 13 1 0 0 $4,410 | Turf 1 0 0 0

2Sep83- 1Pen fst 6f :22⅘ :46 1:13⅗ Clm 2500 6 6 1½ 12 13 3½ Kaenel J M5 b 114 37.10 76-20 RulersJester116½Boniveinte114hdGreatProprieter114nk Weakened 10
24Aug83- 8Pen fst 6f :23⅕ :46⅗ 1:12⅗ Clm 2500 8 10 52½ 31 47 57½ Rozell R M5 b 114 14.80 74-21 Formal Diplomat119hdPrinceDarlington1192½Boniveinte1144 Tired 12
15Aug83- 8Pen fst 5½f :22⅕ :46⅖ 1:05⅗ 3+ Clm 3125 1 8 23½ 44 42 97 Rozell R M5 b 114 10.50 82-22 Takeoff Time 1133 Draconic's Boy 113nk Ms. SandraJ.1191½ Tired 9
1Aug83- 9Pen sly 6f :23 :46⅘ 1:13⅘ 3+ Clm 3500 8 10 52½ 2½ 2½ 1½ Rozell R M7 b 109 3.70 75-16 Great Proprieter 109½ AliasKahn116nkO'HaraBegorra116½ Driving 11
18Jly83- 5Pen fst 6f :23 :46⅘ 1:13⅗ Clm 2500 1 6 11½ 13 14 12 Rozell R M7 b 108 *1.10 76-22 GretProprieter1082Roby'sVentur113½PrincRcupr115no Ridden out 10
6Jly83- 9Key fst 6f :22⅗ :46⅘ 1:12⅘ Clm 3500 11 3 13 1½ 23 66½ Johnson V L5 b 108 6.80 70-20 Mukaluk 1123 King Legs 1072 Stage Gem 115no Tired 12
22Jun83- 9Key fst 6f :22⅖ :46 1:13⅖ Clm 3500 3 6 45 36 34½ 42 Johnson V L5 b 109 *2.20 72-23 KrimisBhvior117nkTimTimminy114½LghtnngBck1151 Lacked rally 12
8Jun83- 9Key fst 6f :22⅖ :46⅕ 1:12 Clm 3500 4 4 11½ 1hd 23 35½ Johnson V L5 b 108 3.60 76-22 StupidIsForvr1134½GonToHowrd's116½GrtPropritr1081 Weakened 12

Classy Mac

BAXIS 10:1

Own.—Ritchey T F

Dk. b. or br. h. 7, by Mickey McGuire—Xtra Classy, by Bethel
$2,500 Br.—Green G (Ky)
Tr.—Ritchey Tim F

113 Lifetime 82 9 10 6 $46,148 | 1983 19 2 2 2 $5,285 | 1982 14 1 5 1 $8,560 | Turf 9 2 1 1 $13,681

29Aug83- 6Pen fst 1 1/16 :49⅘ 1:13⅘ 1:48 3+ Clm 3000 1 3 2½ 11½ 11½ 41½ Aviles R B 114 19.40 65-22 Yankee Intruder 1161 Good Freedom 116nkProteus116hd Faltered 9
24Aug83- 8Pen fst 6f :23⅕ :46⅗ 1:12⅗ Clm 2500 5 4 119½ 1210 1013 99½ Aviles R B 113 8.10 71-21 FormalDiplomat119hdPrinceDrlington1192½Boniveinte1144 Outrun 12
14Aug83- 2Pen fst 6f :22⅗ :46⅖ 1:11⅘ Clm 2500 5 7 74½ 76½ 68 611 Kaenel J M7 106 9.50 74-13 NorthHaven1191½StolenCrown1144½FormalDiplomt1221½ Came in 8
5Aug83- 9Pen gd 6f :22⅗ :46 1:12 Clm 2500 4 5 86½ 84½ 35½ 26½ Kaenel J M7 106 7.00 77-19 Lou's Craft 1146½ Classy Mac 106½ Tooit 114no Gained place 10
27Jly83- 7Pen fst 5½f :22⅘ :46⅘ 1:06⅖ Clm 3125 4 1 53½ 63½ 43½ 5½ Kaenel J M7 106 27.20 83-21 Sumoto 108½ QuebecDancer113nkSundayDiplomat115no No factor 7
24Jun83- 5Pen fst 6f :22⅗ :46 1:12 Clm 3000 8 5 85½ 89½ 811 88 Montoya R 112 8.70 76-20 Flintsman 1192 Boniveinte 115½ Stolen Crown 1151 Outrun 11
6Jun83- 5Pen fst 5½f :23⅕ :47⅗ 1:06⅘ Clm 2500 7 6 64½ 64 41½ 1½ Montoya R 113 19.50 82-20 Classy Mac 113½ Flaming Day 119½ Patch O'Dust 116½ Driving 12
28May83- 9Pen fst 6f :22⅗ :46⅗ 1:13⅗ Clm 2500 8 12 1216 1217 1114 1113 Montoya R 113 5.80 63-22 Gun Dance 1141 Rogation 115nk Berserk 119½ Outrun 12

Harvey's Mission

FITZGERALD 5:2

Own.—Velter J

Dk. b. or br. g. 11, by Hansem Harve—More Omission, by Blue Jay
$2,500 Br.—Lewis Mrs E G & R L (W.Va)
Tr.—Beneito Marie

116 Lifetime 79 21 12 14 $82,097 | 1983 5 2 2 0 $3,980 | 1982 11 4 0 2 $10,862 | Turf 1 0 0 0

20Aug83- 1Pen fst 5½f :22⅗ :46⅖ 1:06 Clm 2500 7 2 21 1hd 1½ 1hd Winnett B G Jr b 116 *.80 86-19 Harvey's Mission 116hd Basic Buck 1142 Havluck 1141½ Driving 9
30Jly83-10Pen fst 5½f :22⅘ :47⅗ 1:06⅘ Clm 2500 7 5 1hd 1hd 13 2hd Fitzgerald R b 119 *2.40 82-22 SuperSerch113hdHrvey'sMission1194½ThundrBoy1141½ Just failed 11
9Jly83- 4Pen fst 5½f :22⅘ :46 1:05⅕ Clm 2500 7 2 12 12 13½ 13 Fitzgerald R b 114 *.80 90-14 Harvey's Mission 1143 Hy Powered 1141 Wang 1132 Driving 8
27Jun83- 9Pen fst 5½f :22⅕ :46⅕ 1:05⅗ Clm 2500 1 8 23½ 21½ 11½ 2hd Fitzgerald R b 116 3.80 88-20 BordeauxCount116hdHarvey'sMission1161½Strtled1165 Just failed 12
6Jun83- 5Pen fst 5½f :23⅕ :47⅗ 1:06⅘ Clm 2500 2 4 1½ 1½ 3½ 75½ Prough J D b 113 5.80 76-20 Classy Mac 113½ Flaming Day 119½ Patch O'Dust 116½ Tired 12
28Nov82- 9CT sly 4½f :22 :45⅘ :52⅕ 3+ Clm 3500 2 8 88 68 57 Munden M F b 116 *2.50 86-11 Fancy Ambition 1095 Cutladdy 108noCosmopolitan114½ No factor 9
6Nov82- 7CT fst 4½f :22 :46 :52⅖ 3+ Clm 5000 3 5 54½ 33½ 35 Munden M F b 117 3.80e 87-13 MightyBoozr1143TkingTmps1172Hrvy'sMission117½ Lacekd a bid 10
24Oct82- 3CT fst 4½f :22⅗ :46⅘ :53 3+ Clm 5000 6 2 51½ 64½ 711 Martinez F W b 117 *.90 78-13 TakingTemps1104½GreatChard1143Monrch'sFlight114no No factor 7

Con Ga Doro

3:1

Own.—Vitale J

B. g. 5, by Harasul—Decision Minded, by Melson
$2,500 Br.—Barchitta J (SC)
Tr.—Trivigno Mike

113 Lifetime 39 3 5 6 $18,225 | 1983 5 1 0 0 $1,895 | 1982 15 1 1 4 $6,024

3Sep83- 4Pen fst 170 :47⅘ 1:13 1:45 Clm 2500 8 6 57½ 24 1½ 12 Kotenko R b 116 3.10 75-17 ConGDoro1162Istri'sSon1161½TheGoodLife1163½ Bore in; driving 9
24Aug83- 6Pen fst 5½f :22⅕ :46⅕ 1:05⅘ 3+ Clm 3125 5 3 815 818 713 56½ D'Aleo K b 114 67.50 80-21 Magna Man 113no Capidoro 114hd Padraic 1143 No factor 8
15Aug83- 7Pen fst 170 :47⅘ 1:13⅖ 1:45⅘ Clm 2500 4 7 79 67 65½ 44 Kotenko R b 113½ 31.00 67-22 Roman Spear 119½ Catch Poppy 1142½ Men's Lad 113½ Mild gain 8
15Aug83-Dead heat
3Aug83- 5Pen fst 6f :22⅗ :46 1:12⅕ Clm 2500 1 8 917 918 917 815 Drury G E b 116 34.30 68-17 Capidoro 1161 Brelly 1113½ Chuck's Friend 1162½ Outrun 10
3Jly83- 7GBF fst *6½f 1:33⅖ 3+ Clm 3000 2 8 812 710 55 67½ Konan J M b 123 5.50 30-45 Icy Defender 1222½ Moody Bob 122nk Ruane 1224½ Outrun 8
16Oct82- 5FL gd 6f :22⅗ :46 1:13⅘ 3+ Clm 2500 6 3 57½ 611 1012 107½ Alejandro H M b 113 4.60 72-18 DBrevon 1161½ Little Distinction 119½ Savage Mac 1131½ Tired 10
28Sep82- 6FL gd 6f :22⅗ :47⅕ 1:13⅘ 3+ Clm 5000 8 2 65½ 64 74½ 87½ Faine C b 113 7.90 72-21 AGoodCounsel1152½JointheCavlry113hdOfCounsel109hd Fell back 8
25Jly82- 3Suf fst 6f :23 :46⅘ 1:13⅘ 3+ Clm 5000 2 5 57½ 613 615 621 Mercier N b 114 *2.60 52-26 Grey Minstrel 1175 Salt Lick 1151 Romolo 1141 Outrun 7

Cool Roller

AVILES 7:1

Own.—North American Thoroughbreds

Dk. b. or br. g. 5, by Cool Moon—Native Role, by Droll Role
$2,500 Br.—McGregor Ranch (Tex)
Tr.—Kravets Bruce M

113 Lifetime 54 3 5 7 $11,467 | 1983 15 2 1 2 $5,349 | 1982 5 0 0 0 $394 | Turf 4 0 0 1 $910

2Sep83- 1Pen fst 6f :22⅘ :46 1:13⅗ Clm 2500 10 2 2½ 22 23 72½ Aviles R B b 113 5.80 75-20 Rulers Jester 116½ Boniveinte 114hd Great Proprieter 114nk Tired 10
19Aug83- 9Pen fst 6f :22⅖ :45⅗ 1:11⅕ 3+ Clm 3200 4 2 11 2hd 79 715 Aviles R B b 117 6.30 73-18 Copper Reign 1102½ Lou's Craft 1104 Kasinoff 1221 Stopped 7
10Aug83- 4Pen fst 6f :22⅗ :46 1:12 3+ Clm 3200 4 5 2½ 1hd 12 32½ Aviles R B b 117 9.20 81-19 Kasinoff 119½ Boniveinte 1152 Cool Roller 1171 Weakened 6
31Jly83- 2Pen gd 6f :22⅗ :46⅕ 1:12⅘ Clm c-2500 5 5 2hd 2hd 31½ 53 Fitzgerald R b 119 6.60 77-20 North Haven 1192½ Stolen Crown 113no Brave Effort 113nk Tired 10
22Jly83- 8Pen fst 6f :23⅕ :46⅘ 1:12⅕ Clm 3200 8 1 12½ 1½ 22 47½ Gress D b 119 3.70 75-22 Drunken Tiger 1153 Boniveinte 1151½ Granite Run 1153 Tired 9
9Jly83- 1Pen fm 1 1/16 ① 1:43⅖ Clm 5000 7 1 11 12½ 1½ 44 Fitzgerald R b 114 3.40 69-27 Kasinoff 1131 Grand Emperor 1082½ Monoscope 113½ Tired 10
25Jun83- 9Pen fst 6f :22⅘ :46⅗ 1:12⅗ 3+ Clm 3500 10 2 13½ 1½ 12 12½ Fitzgerald R b 116 2.80 81-21 Cool Roller 1162½ Window Table1131½DoubleBusher1136½ Driving 11
18Jun83- 2Pen fm 1 1/16 ① 1:44 Clm 5000 8 2 1hd 1½ 3½ 44 Fitzgerald R 114 19.50 66-30 Gentle Guy 1151 Tight Shot 1131 Kasinoff 1132 Weakened 12

Eagle's Coin

WAGNER 13:1

Own.—Rising Sun Stable

B. g. 5, by Spring Double—Save The Eagle, by Bald Eagle
$2,500 Br.—Casey J W (Va)
Tr.—Minnich Clarence

113 Lifetime 50 9 4 2 $44,193 | 1983 20 3 2 1 $10,363 | 1982 17 2 1 1 $11,760

2Sep83- 7Pen fst 5½f :22⅕ :46 1:05⅗ 3+ Clm 3125 6 6 2hd 2½ 54½ 79½ Berry J b 113 11.30 78-20 Charlie's Bow 1142½ Red Zip Man 1141½ Raw Whiskey111hd Tired 7
20Aug83- 8Pen fst 5½f :22⅖ :46⅗ 1:05⅗ 3+ Clm 4000 8 4 31 43 76 86½ D'Aleo K b 113 25.80 81-19 Wheelivright 1131½ Sun Dial 114½ General Harper 113½ Tired 9
13Aug83- 8Pen fst 6f :22⅕ :45⅗ 1:12⅖ 3+ Clm 4000 1 6 21½ 11 54 77½ Baker C J b 114 7.80 74-18 Winging Through 1141 Polar Point 1131 Lou's Craft1162 Stopped 8
1Aug83- 8Pen sly 5f :22⅖ :45⅘ :58⅖ 3+ Clm 5000 1 2 2hd 1hd 33½ 512 Rozell R M7 b 109 3.50 80-16 Gridiron 1149½ One Great Native 119nk Wealthy Greek119hd Tired 9
23Jly83- 4Pen fst 5½f :22⅖ :46 1:05 Clm 4000 5 1 11½ 12 21 25½ Rozell R M7 b 109 3.80 85-17 Battle Train1165½Eagle'sCoin1092½CarlBernstein1141 Second best 7
16Jly83- 8Pen fst 6f :22⅗ :46 1:11⅕ Clm 4000 2 7 12 1hd 22 74 Colton R E b 116 5.90 84-13 Linaje I 114½ My Hot Dog King 116½ What A Captain 119½ Tired 8
6Jly83- 4Pen fst 6f :22⅗ :45⅗ 1:11 Clm 5000 1 6 1½ 2hd 44½ 511 Colton R E b 116 5.00 78-16 Flintsman 1163½ Beat the Bishop 116½ Bay Oaks 1161½ Tired 6
24Jun83- 8Pen fst 5f :22 :46 :58⅘ Clm 5000 4 3 32 32½ 32 64½ Colton R E b 113 *3.00 86-20 OneGreatNative1192½BoldGentry1091JohnBurney113hd Weakened 10

Rox It Easy

26:1

Own.—Fleming H

Ch. g. 4, by Rogrox—Easy Penny, by Penny Pincher
$2,500 Br.—Fleming H L (Tex)
Tr.—Fallwell Buck

1085 Lifetime 24 3 4 3 $8,376 | 1983 18 2 3 2 $5,309 | 1982 6 1 1 1 $3,067

2Sep83- 1Pen fst 6f :22⅘ :46 1:13⅗ Clm 2500 8 3 62½ 68 68½ 62½ Bender P H5 111 44.10 75-20 Rulers Jester116½Boniveinte114hdGreatProprieter114nk No threat 10
24Aug83- 8Pen fst 6f :23⅕ :46⅗ 1:12⅗ Clm 2500 11 2 86½ 75 58 46½ Bender P H5 113 54.10 75-21 FormlDiplomt119hdPrinceDrlington1192½Boniveint1144 Mild gain 12
5Aug83- 9Pen gd 6f :22⅗ :46 1:12 Clm 2500 10 3 75½ 55½ 56 69 Drury G E 116 51.80 75-19 Lou's Craft 1146½ Classy Mac 106½ Tooit 114no No factor 10
15Jly83- 2Pen fst 6f :23⅕ :46⅘ 1:13 Clm 2500 7 2 65 34 35 1hd Rozell R M7 108 10.10 79-17 Rox It Easy 108hd Canterbury's Ring1141SwapsDawn113½ Driving 10
1Jly83- 2Pen fst 6f :22⅖ :45⅗ 1:12⅗ Clm 2500 4 5 79½ 815 1013 105 Stanton N L7 109 10.90 76-17 Prince Solar 122hd Loudly 116hd Fast Watch 116½ Fell back 12
22Jun83- 8Pen fst 6f :22⅘ :47 1:12⅘ Clm 2500 7 1 97 75½ 36 36½ Stanton N L7 109 24.40 74-25 Layover 1131 Cook's Foxson 1115½ Rox It Easy 1093 Ducked out 10
8Jun83- 7Pen fst 6f :23⅕ :47⅗ 1:14⅕ Clm 2500 4 3 86½ 811 77½ 64½ Stanton N L10 108 4.00 68-23 RoughN'Boldly113hdCook'sFoxson1103DrmCbin1131½ No menace 9
28May83- 4Pen fst 6f :22⅘ :46⅕ 1:13⅕ Clm 2500 7 1 44½ 34 33 1nk Stanton N L10 108 3.90 78-22 Rox It Easy 108nk Cool Roller 1143 Prince Recupere115no Driving 9

***Boniveinte** B. h. 10, by Negro el Veinte—Bonidiba, by Bonicate
$2,500 Br.—Haras Los Fletes (Arg)
Tr.—McGreevy Thomas
Own.—McGreevy P
113 Lifetime 110 20 20 20 $62,836
1983 15 2 5 4 $8,117
1982 24 4 3 6 $13,014

BAKER 5:2

2Sep83- 1Pen	fst	6f	:22 4/5	:46	1:13 2/5	Clm 2500	3	5	8 3½	5 6½	5 6	2 ½	Wagner B R	114	4.30	76-20 Rulers Jester 116½ Boniveinte 114hd GreatProprieter114nk	Rallied 10
24Aug83- 8Pen	fst	6f	:23 1/5	:46 3/5	1:12 3/5	Clm 2500	10	1	7 4½	4 3	3 2	3 2¼	Baker C J	114	*1.80	79-21 FormlDplomt119hdPrncDrlngton1192¼Bonvnt1144	Lacked late bid 12
10Aug83- 4Pen	fst	6f	:22 3/5	:46	1:12	3↑Clm 3200	3	6	6 4	5 4	2 2	2 ½	Baker C J	115	3.90	83-19 Kasinoff 119½ Boniveinte 1152 Cool Roller 1171	Brshd,carried out 6
22Jly83- 8Pen	fst	6f	:23 1/5	:46 4/5	1:12 1/5	Clm 3200	7	2	6 5½	3 3½	3 2½	2 3	Aviles R B	115	5.10	80-22 Drunken Tiger 1153 Boniveinte 1151½ Granite Run 1153	Rallied 9
4Jly83- 4Pen	fst	6f	:22 3/5	:46 1/5	1:12	Clm 3200	5	5	4 3¾	4 2½	3 2½	3 1¾	Aviles R B	115	*1.20	82-19 North Haven 1191½ Super Search 115½ Boniveinte 1154	Bumped 6
4Jly83-Awarded second purse money																	
24Jun83- 5Pen	fst	6f	:22 3/5	:46	1:12	Clm 3200	2	10	9 6½	6 7½	3 2	2 2	Aviles R B	115	9.60	82-20 Flintsman 1192 Boniveinte 115½ Stolen Crown 1151	Gained place 11
12Jun83- 2Pen	fst	6f	:23	:46 4/5	1:13	Clm 2500	5	4	5 4¾	5 3¾	5 6	4 1¼	Berry J	113	5.80	78-20 King's Dominion 113¾ Stolen Crown 114hd Brelly 113¾	Steadied 11
27May83-10Pen	fst	6f	:22 3/5	:46 1/5	1:12 1/5	Clm 3200	5	6	8 5½	8 8	6 7	6 6¾	Aviles R B	115	*3.30	76-24 Kasinoff1121¼QuebecDancer1152¾TkeoffTime1151	Squeezed back 11

SEPTEMBER 12—RACE 7 (Quinella Wagering)

Great Proprietor—Right there at this level. A contender and an overlay.

Classy Mac—Unfavorable rider switch. Not a contender.

Harvey's Mission—Wins at 5 1/2 furlongs but always loses ground. Today this eleven year old must go longer. That extra half furlong is a tremendous difference to cheap claimers. This horse is also suspect because Mario Beneito doesn't move him up in class despite four big outings. Most likely those races have taken their toll on this old horse.

Con Ga Doro—Won last time, but bore in and therefore, may be hurting. Also, nothing at today's distance. Not a contender.

Cool Roller—Beaten by others in this field with no excuse. Throw him out.

Eagle's Coin—Drops, but is nowhere at this distance.

Rox It Easy—Also beaten by others in this field with no excuse. Not a contender.

Boniveinte—Made a nice late run to miss a half length for it all. Also beat **Great Proprietor** by a head.

THE BET: **Great Proprietor** and **Boniveinte** should run one, two, but who will win? Although **Boniveinte** beat **Great Proprietor** by a head it will have to make up more ground today because it is a closer with an outside post. Also, **Great Proprietor** drops three pounds. They really cannot be separated, but fortunately this is a quinella race. Therefore, 70% of the M.B. on these two in the quinella.

RESULTS: **Great Proprietor** beat **Boniveinte** by a neck paying $16.40. The $3 quinella returned $35.70. A really aggressive bettor might have played Great Proprietor to win besides playing the quinella, taking his chances on it because he was 7:1 whereas **Boniveinte** was only 5:2. There's nothing wrong with this if two horses are inseparable. If he wins 1 out of 2 he's still ahead of the game.

2 PENN NATIONAL

1 MILE 70 YDS
PENN NATIONAL
Start Finish

1 MILE 70 YARDS. (1.40) CLAIMING. Purse $2,900. 3-year-olds and up. Weights: 3-year-olds, 118 lbs.; older, 122 lbs.; non-winners of two races at one mile or over since September 18 allowed 3 lbs.; one such race, 6 lbs.; such a race since September 4, 9 lbs. Claiming Price $2,500.

Zange
LUCERO 23:1

B. c. 4, by Son Ange—Patty's Fault, by Bronze Babu
$2,500 Br.—Clay A G (Ky) Tr.—Lebarron Keith
Own.—Daniela Stable
113 Lifetime 42 5 5 5 $44,880 | 1983 14 3 1 2 $10,975 | 1982 20 1 4 2 $18,885 | Turf 2 0 0 0

25Sep83- 2Pen fst 1 1/16 :48 4/5 1:14 1:47 4/5 3+ Clm c-2500 8 11 10 15 11 14 11 16 910 3/4 Kotenko R b 113 5.40 56-16 Pukka Pukka 119 2 3/4 Dr. L'Amore 114 1/2 Quranta Bay 113 2 Outrun 11
26Aug83- 9Key fst 170 :47 3/5 1:13 1:44 3/5 3+ Clm 3500 3 3 6 9 8 16 78 1/2 78 1/4 Fernandez L Jr b 116 6.80 69-22 Eleven Shamrocks 106 1/2 Love Boldly 113 nk FieldService 112 1 3/4 Tired 9
3Aug83- 4Key fst 6f :21 4/5 :45 1/5 1:12 1/5 3+ Clm 5000 3 11 11 19 11 20 11 18 11 18 Fernandez L Jr b 117 36.40 72-17 Sauders Creek 112 1/2 KingOfTheCuff 115 1 RoyalSpinner 112 2 Trailed 11
12Jly83- 2Key fst 1 1/16 :48 2/5 1:13 4/5 1:46 2/5 3+ Clm c-3500 7 5 6 6 76 3/4 68 1/2 610 3/4 Johnson V L5 b 112 *2.40 61-21 Choice Friend 112 1 Stake 120 5 Graban Apple 117 nk Tired 9
25Jun83- 9Key fst 1 1/16 :47 2/5 1:13 1:46 3/5 Clm 5000 9 4 4 10 5 7 45 1/2 37 3/4 Johnson V L5 b 115 8.30 63-21 Mike J. S. 112 1 1/2 Leader Of The Pack 112 6 1/2 Zange 115 1 Rallied 9
7Jun83- 2Key fst 1 1/16 :48 1/5 1:13 3/5 1:46 4/5 Clm c-3500 7 4 35 1/2 2 hd 1 3 1 1/2 Johnson V L5 b 114 3.70 70-16 Zange 114 1/2 Rope Walk 113 3 1/2 Withershins 109 nk Driving 9
20May83- 9Key my 1 1/16 :49 3/5 1:15 3/5 1:48 3/5 Clm 3500 6 6 5 5 33 1/2 22 1/2 2 6 Johnson V L5 b 114 2.40 55-35 Graban Apple 119 6 Zange 114 nk North Star 119 8 1/2 Held place 8
8May83- 2Key fst 1 1/8 :48 3/5 1:13 2/5 1:54 3/5 Clm 3500 4 6 4 6 31 1/2 1 1/2 12 1/2 Pagano S R b 119 *2.80 62-25 Zange 119 2 1/2 Mr. Joe Morgan 113 hd Humoristico 116 nk Drew clear 8

Withershins
AGUIRRE 8:1

B. g. 5, by Crozelian Hero—Wigwag, by Admiral's Voyage
$2,500 Br.—Gamble S (SC) Tr.—Dumestre David A
Own.—Dellinger Nadine
113 Lifetime 38 9 4 8 $43,751 | 1983 8 2 1 1 $6,255 | 1982 20 5 3 2 $28,570

14Sep83- 9Key fst 1 1/16 :48 2/5 1:14 1/5 1:47 4/5 3+ Clm c-3500 5 7 4 8 57 1/2 7 20 817 1/2 Romaine V7 b 112 11.50 47-26 MistrBlds 119 1 1/2 CourtRuffin 119 4 AcdmicFrdom 119 3/4 Squeezed start 8
17Aug83- 2Atl fst 1 1/16 :47 1/5 1:12 4/5 1:47 2/5 3+ Clm 3500 10 3 2 1/2 3 2 8 9 88 3/4 Romaine V10 b 110 2.70 59-26 Spark Jet 115 1/2 Pepperstone 122 1/2 Jenawi 120 nk Tired 10
3Aug83- 6Atl fst 1 1/16 :47 2/5 1:12 1/5 1:46 1/5 3+ Clm 3500 2 1 1 1 1 3 1 4 1 4 Romaine V10 b 106 4.90 74-22 Withershins 106 4 Chevere 116 1 1/2 Jenawi 113 2 Driving 9
4Jly83- 9Key fst 1 1/16 :47 3/5 1:12 2/5 1:46 2/5 Clm 3500 2 2 21 1/2 36 1/2 4 13 913 3/4 Pagano S R b 117 *2.80 58-15 Number One Monk 117 1 1/2 Stake 120 5 AcademicFreedom 112 4 Tired 10
7Jun83- 2Key fst 1 1/16 :48 1/5 1:13 3/5 1:46 4/5 Clm 3500 2 1 1 5 1 hd 2 3 3 4 Romaine V10 b 109 4.80 66-16 Zange 114 1/2 Rope Walk 113 3 1/2 Withershins 109 nk Weakened 9
17May83- 9Key fst 170 :47 2/5 1:13 4/5 1:46 3/5 Clm 3500 5 1 1 2 1 5 1 3 1 3/4 Deibler C E III b 114 3.20 67-26 Withershins 114 3/4 Willie Chopper 114 4 Barefoot Boy 110 1 Driving 12
6May83- 9Key fst 1 1/16 :48 2/5 1:13 1/5 1:48 4/5 Clm 3500 7 2 21 1/2 1 1/2 1 3 2 1/2 Wade R M Jr5 b 107 6.70 59-25 Mason Creek 113 1/2 Withershins 107 2 WillieChopper 113 1 1/2 Weakened 11
23Apr83- 1Key fst 7f :22 3/5 :45 4/5 1:26 1/5 Clm 3500 6 12 12 11 12 22 12 21 12 24 1/2 Pagano S R b 113 8.60 52-22 Archie Does 114 nk Mr. Achiever 113 1 1/2 Little Bit Too 113 2 Trailed 12

Hardy's Starr
2:1

Dk. b. or br. g. 5, by Fusion III—Queen of Hearts, by Gentle Art
$2,500 Br.—Hardy J S (Ind) Tr.—Beneito Mario
Own.—Coto R
119 Lifetime 46 4 6 6 $19,406 | 1983 19 2 0 4 $6,397 | 1982 11 1 2 2 $5,280 | Turf 1 0 0 1 $370

22Oct83- 7Pen fst 1 1/8 :48 1:12 1/5 1:52 3/5 3+ Hcp 4000s 3 10 10 14 66 1/2 56 1/2 67 3/4 Winnett B G Jr b 105 23.10 81-20 March To Peace 111 3 SpanishBeat 113 3 RahRahNaskra 119 1 1/2 Outrun 10
14Oct83- 8Pen fst 170 :48 3/5 1:14 1:45 2/5 Clm 2500 1 7 66 3/4 31 1/2 1 1/2 1 1 Winnett B G Jr b 119 3.90 73-22 Hardy's Starr 119 1 Mesabi Range 113 1 Sir Christian 109 2 Driving 7
8Oct83- 10Pen fst 1 1/16 :47 2/5 1:13 1:47 Clm 2500 7 10 10 16 79 1/2 3 2 11 1/2 Winnett B G Jr b 116 6.40 71-20 Hardy's Starr 116 1 1/2 All for Magic 116 2 1/2 Havluck 116 2 Driving 12
2Sep83- 4Atl fst 1 1/16 :49 1:14 3/5 1:47 1/5 3+ Clm 2500 7 5 56 1/2 67 3/4 6 13 821 3/4 Saumell L b 116 3.20 47-22 Importance 113 3 Pepperstone 122 2 1/2 Full In 111 4 Ret. bleeding 8
19Aug83- 4Atl fst 1 1/16 :47 4/5 1:13 2/5 1:46 4/5 3+ Clm 2500 11 11 9 11 64 1/2 31 1/2 33 1/2 Chavez S N5 b 111 2.80 67-21 Alamer 120 2 Roulette Joe 116 1 1/2 Hardy's Starr 111 2 Rallied 12
16Jly83- 2Crc fst 1 1/16 :49 3/5 1:14 4/5 1:48 2/5 3+ Clm 5000 10 11 116 1/2 98 1/2 65 1/2 43 1/2 Ramos A b 114 55.40 73-18 Olympic Answer 118 1/2 King Quail 122 1 1/2 Amalot 118 1 1/2 Caused foul 11
16Jly83-Disqualified and placed eleventh
4Jly83- 2Crc fst 1 1/16 :48 4/5 1:14 4/5 1:49 1/5 Clm 4000 3 8 10 16 9 11 5 4 44 1/2 Solis A b 112 12.40 68-16 Run For Rick 117 hd Koru 115 2 Noble Blue 112 2 1/2 Rallied 11
25Jun83- 1Crc fst 7f :23 3/5 :47 1/5 1:27 Clm 4000 6 11 11 19 11 19 7 11 4 8 Solis A b 112 6.60 73-17 Highclass Sport 112 6 1/2 ClassyHap 112 1 CabinCaptain 106 1/2 Mild rally 11

LATEST WORKOUTS Sep 1 Atl 3f fst :37 b

O'Hara Begorra
12:1

B. g. 4, by O'Hara—Gay Staddie, by War Age
$2,500 Br.—Bullock A J (Md) Tr.—Trivigno Michael
Own.—Scietz Joanne
116 Lifetime 40 4 6 4 $16,869 | 1983 22 3 4 4 $11,213 | 1982 16 1 2 0 $5,656 | Turf 1 0 0 0

14Oct83- 6Pen fst 1 1/16 :48 3/5 1:14 1:47 3/5 3+ Clm 3000 9 3 4 3 54 1/2 68 1/2 711 1/2 D'Aleo K b 116 8.00 56-22 Major Tell 113 4 Whisper A Bit 116 nk Promotional 116 4 Tired 9
1Oct83- 10Pen sly 1 :48 1:14 1:41 3/5 Clm 2500 6 6 56 1/2 3 2 2 hd 12 1/2 D'Aleo K b 119 10.00 73-23 O'Hara Begorra 119 2 1/2 Promotional 119 3/4 BeastyTales 116 2 Driving 9
19Sep83- 1Pen fst 1 :47 3/5 1:13 2/5 1:41 Clm 2500 4 2 2 1 54 1/2 7 13 816 1/2 Kotenko R b 119 3.70 60-17 Socko 116 1/2 Catch Poppy 119 hd Hotly 116 3 1/2 Tired 9
5Sep83- 4Pen fst 1 :48 2/5 1:13 2/5 1:40 1/5 3+ Clm 3500 1 1 11 1/2 11 1/2 1 2 1 3 Kotenko R b 116 3.30 80-23 O'Hara Begorra 116 3 Mr. Milton 116 nk Last Charade 114 2 3/4 Driving 7
10Aug83- 1Pen fst 6f :23 :46 1/5 1:12 3+ Clm 3500 5 3 74 1/2 76 1/2 6 8 6 7 Kotenko R b 116 7.80 77-19 Shurwinner 116 no Hagley Bagley 116 1 Alias Kahn 116 5 Outrun 9
1Aug83- 9Pen sly 6f :23 :46 4/5 1:13 3/5 3+ Clm 3500 10 1 95 3/4 7 5 4 4 3 3/4 Kotenko R b 116 *3.00 74-16 Great Proprieter 109 1/2 Alias Kahn 116 nk O'HaraBegorra 116 1/2 Rallied 11
20Jly83- 8Pen sly 1 :48 1:13 4/5 1:41 2/5 3+ Clm 3500 7 4 2 1/2 2 hd 1 hd 21 1/2 Keller R L b 116 2.90 72-26 AntiStrike 116 1 1/2 O'HaraBegorra 116 1/2 HveTheProof 116 1 1/2 Weakened 10
1Jly83- 8Pen fst 170 :46 3/5 1:12 1/5 1:42 1/5 Clm 5000 6 3 2 1 2 1 6 12 718 1/2 Kotenko R 116 8.60 70-17 Majestic Leader 116 8 1/2 ToHailNasrullah 116 5 BennyKazats 116 1 Tired 9

FIATO 10:1

Valedictorian — Dk. b. or br. rig. 9, by Mr Leader—Space Craft, by Crafty Admiral
$2,500 Br.—Lawes Mr-Mrs W (Ont-C); Tr.—Shevelove Lawrence B — **114^5**
Own.—Nilson Arthur E
Lifetime 157 16 25 19 $84,470 — 1983 13 3 2 1 $7,021; 1982 12 2 0 1 $3,524; Turf 13 1 2 3 $7,966

9Oct83- 2Pen fst 1 1/16	:49⅕ 1:14⅗ 1:48⅕	3+Clm 2500	2 1 31 1hd 4¾ 52	Baker C J	b 119	6.70	63-21	Win Some Back 122½ Three Setter 113½ Sub Goal 113nk	Tired	12
26Sep83- 1Pen fst 1	:47⅘ 1:13⅕ 1:40⅘	Clm 2500	6 4 52¾ 44½ 33 1no	Baker C J	b 116	*2.10	77-18	Valedictorian 116no Hotly 113nk Classy Mac 1131½	Driving	10
17Sep83- 1Pen fst 1 1/16	:48⅕ 1:13 1:46⅕	Clm 2500	6 1 1½ 21½ 25 26½	Bender P H5	b 111	9.00	68-18	Oyez 1096½ Valedictorian 1113 Dormelletto 114½	Weakened	8
7Sep83- 1Pen fst 1 1/16	:48⅘ 1:14 1:47⅗	Clm 2500	3 1 1hd 21½ 21 2no	Bender P H5	b 114	11.90	68-21	Win Some Back 119no Valedictorian 1141½ Oyez1144¼	Just missed	8
29Aug83- 8Pen fst 170	:47 1:13 1:44⅘	Clm 2500	7 1 22 43 45 56½	Bender P H5	b 114	7.40	70-22	Roman Spear 1192¾ Binc 1141½ Sub Goal 113nk	Fell back	8
12Aug83-10Pen fst 170	:48⅕ 1:13⅗ 1:46	Clm 2500	2 1 1hd 1hd 13 11½	Bender P H5	b 114	8.40	70-21	Valedictorian 1141½ Power Mood 1132 Fellow Heir 1192	Driving	9
3Aug83- 1Pen fst 1	:47⅘ 1:14 1:41⅗	Clm 2500	1 1 1hd 1hd 2½ 31½	Stanton N L7	b 112	6.40	72-17	Rulers Jester1191½VictoryPlay114nkValedictorian1122¼	Weakened	10
21Jly83- 6CT fst 1 1/16	:49⅕ 1:14⅘ 1:48⅘	3+Clm 2500	1 1 11 11 11 11¾	Stanton N L7	b 107	6.90	78-30	Valedictorian1071¾SurgicalTouch1143½Brown'sFncy1144½	Driving	9

9:1

Archie Does — B. h. 5, by Cabin—Foreign Spy, by Vertex
$2,500 Br.—Lasater Farm (Ky); Tr.—Sokolski Michael — **113**
Own.—Sokolski M C
Lifetime 52 6 8 6 $41,795 — 1983 19 3 5 1 $13,610; 1982 10 0 1 1 $3,130

23Oct83- 4Pen sly 1 1/16	:49⅕ 1:14⅗ 1:48⅕	3+Clm 2500	2 1 11 1½ 21½ 22	Gress D	b 113	4.80	63-22	RulersJester1162ArchieDoes1134½SaveTheWhales113nk	Weakened	6
16Oct83- 3Pen fst 170	:48⅕ 1:14 1:46	3+Clm 2500	5 5 51½ 4nk 21½ 2hd	Burton J E	b 114	28.60	70-22	Fabulist 119hd Archie Does 1141 Sub Goal 113hd	Rallied	7
9Oct83- 2Pen fst 1 1/16	:49⅕ 1:14⅗ 1:48⅕	3+Clm 2500	11 7 62¾ 106¾ 109½ 98	Burton J E	b 114	17.50	57-21	Win Some Back 122½ Three Setter 113½ Sub Goal113nk	No threat	12
24Sep83- 9Pen fst 5½f	:22⅗ :46 1:05	3+Clm 4000	2 8 910 910 813 710½	Berry J	b 113	45.80	80-19	Membrino 1131½ Speedy George 1142½ Superfoxtrot 1081½	Outrun	9
17Sep83- 5Pen fst 6f	:23 :46⅖ 1:12⅘	3+Clm 4000	4 8 116¾ 911 99¼ 98½	Berry J	b 113	14.40	73-18	Mike's Gent 113½ Jasper J. 113nk [D]Lou's Craft 113¾	Outrun	11
4Sep83- 2Key fst 6f	:22⅘ :46⅖ 1:12	3+Clm 5000	8 1 86¾ 89½ 710 78½	D'Agusto J G	b 114	18.00	72-21	Speedy George 119¾ Freedom Won 1141 Mukaluk1141½	No factor	9
10Aug83- 9Key fst 6f	:22⅗ :46 1:11⅗	3+Clm c-3500	4 5 42½ 53½ 35 44¾	Shurtz W R	b 112	8.60	78-23	Balakiev 1173 Sparkling Blue 1171 Island Drive 115¾	Rallied	11
24Jly83- 4Key fst 6f	:22⅗ :46⅗ 1:12⅘	3+Clm 3500	8 6 96¾ 86¾ 78 75½	Lee R F	b 115	*3.20	71-19	GoneToHowrd's120nkGlitterWig1172½AlpinVillg117nk	Squeezed st.	11

LATEST WORKOUTS Sep 13 Pen 4f fst :51⅗ h

5:1

Win Some Back — Dk. b. or br. g. 7, by Carry Back—Win Some Devil, by Royal Living
$2,500 Br.—Wiersum F W (Fla); Tr.—Ritchey Tim F — **113**
Own.—Ritchey T F
Lifetime 112 17 14 21 $72,385 — 1983 17 6 0 4 $13,729; 1982 25 5 7 1 $18,560

9Oct83- 2Pen fst 1 1/16	:49⅕ 1:14⅗ 1:48⅕	3+Clm 2500	10 9 95¾ 52½ 5¾ 1½	Aviles R B	122	7.60	65-21	Win Some Back 122½ Three Setter 113½ Sub Goal 113nk	Driving	12
2Oct83- 1Pen gd 170	:48⅕ 1:14 1:44⅗	3+Clm 2500	5 7 610 67¾ 57½ 511	Aviles R B	119	5.10	66-21	Cliff Chesney 1197¾ GallantSong1131½Dr.L'Amore1141¾	No threat	7
26Sep83- 9Pen fst 1 1/16	:48 1:12⅗ 1:46⅖	3+Clm 3200	9 11 1218 1224 916 813¾	Winnett B G Jr	116	5.10	60-18	Sound Advice 116½ Sir Scotty 1111½ Barney Ree 1163¾	Outrun	12
7Sep83- 1Pen fst 1 1/16	:48⅘ 1:14 1:47⅗	Clm 2500	8 7 77 55 33 1no	Aviles R B	119	*1.60	68-21	Win Some Back 119no Valedictorian 1141½ Oyez 1144½	Driving	8
31Aug83- 3Pen fst 1 1/16	:48 1:13⅗ 1:47	Clm 2500	4 6 59 42½ 12 16	Aviles R B	116	*1.00	71-23	WinSomeBack1166BanappleGs1131½Csnov'sCup1132½	Ridden out	6
21Aug83- 2Pen fst 1¼	:47 1:39 2:05⅕	3+Clm 3200	8 8 78 78½ 812 78	Fiato P G5	110	4.60	84-15	Berserk 1102 North Haven 1151 Lambie Boy 1193½	Outrun	9
7Aug83- 1Pen fst 1¼	:47 1:39 2:05	3+Clm 3200	2 6 56 64 32 53	Fiato P G7	108	3.10	90-14	VlentineSurprise1191LmbieBoy119nkGoodFrdom110nk	Weakened	8
24Jly83- 2Pen gd 170	:47⅗ 1:13⅗ 1:45	Clm 2500	3 8 912 76¼ 65 32½	Aviles R B	119	4.10	72-19	Hall Monitor119noMesabiRange1132½WinSomeBack1192	Steadied	9

27:1

Track Admiral — B. g. 7, by Navy Brass—Middle Of The Day, by Middle Brother
$2,500 Br.—Liselotte Farm & Stefanek Lisa (Ohio); Tr.—Hoffa Rich W Jr — **113**
Own.—Hoffa Connie L
Lifetime 68 5 10 4 $24,806 — 1983 18 1 5 1 $5,523; 1982 4 0 0 0; Turf 2 0 0 0 $318
Entered 29Oct83- 8 PEN

22Oct83- 4Pen fst 1	:48⅗ 1:14 1:41	3+Clm 2500	10 4 43½ 67 813 915½	Baker C J	b 116	5.90	60-20	Con Ga Doro 1194 Bless This Mess 1171 Dr. L'Amore 1142	Tired	10
14Oct83- 8Pen fst 170	:48⅗ 1:14 1:45⅖	Clm 2500	2 4 43½ 41¾ 42½ 44	Baker C J	b 114	5.80	69-22	Hardy's Starr 1191 Mesabi Range 1131 Sir Christian 1092	Evenly	7
5Oct83- 8Pen fst 1 1/16	:48 1:13 1:47⅖	3+Clm 3000	2 8 99¾ 911 87¾ 65¾	Berry J	b 113	7.10	63-24	Oyez 1111½ Roman Spear 116nk Binc 1161¾	Outrun	10
24Sep83- 5Pen fst 170	:47⅘ 1:13 1:43⅗	Clm 2500	3 6 75 64½ 2½ 23	Berry J	b 113	12.80	78-19	Whtsthedifference1193TrckAdmirl113hdMsbiRng1131½	Held place	9
11Sep83- 3Pen fst 1 1/16	:49⅗ 1:14⅘ 1:47⅕	3+Clm 2500	3 4 41½ 42 33 28	Baker C J	b 114	6.80	62-18	Cliff Chesney 1148 Track Admiral 1142 Hotly 113¾	Rallied	6
4Sep83- 1Pen fst 170	:47 1:12⅗ 1:44⅕	Clm 2500	5 4 44½ 44 35 37	Baker C J	b 114	9.50	72-17	Pukka Pukka 1194 Ultra Lark 1123 Track Admiral 1142	Mild Bid	8
27Aug83- 9Pen fst 1 1/16	:48 1:13 1:47	Clm 2500	3 5 54 55 79 79¾	Deibler C E III	b 113	18.00	61-25	Oyez 1141¾ Barney Ree 1163 The Good Life 113nk	No factor	8
19Aug83- 2Pen fst 1	:48 1:14 1:41⅖	Clm 2500	6 5 52¼ 43 3½ 21¾	Baker C J	b 114	4.90	72-18	Rough N' Boldly 1131¾ TrackAdmiral114nkFellowHeir1195	Rallied	8

ROZELLE 25:1

Lord's Image — Ch. g. 7, by Hard Work—Boob Tube, by T V Lark
$2,500 Br.—Woodford B (Ky); Tr.—King Larry — **108^5**
Own.—Frankhouser S
Lifetime 62 16 10 7 $57,797 — 1983 12 2 2 1 $5,440; 1982 10 3 1 3 $9,104; Turf 1 0 0 0 $174

19Aug83- 3Pen fst 1 1/16	:48⅗ 1:13⅕ 1:46⅘	3+Clm 3000	1 1 3½ 56¼ 512 511¼	Lloyd J S	b 114	4.00	61-18	Camscall 111no Hot Steel 1161¾ Power Mood 1162½	Tired	5
24Jly83- 2Pen gd 170	:47⅗ 1:13⅗ 1:45	Clm 2500	8 6 78½ 99½ 911 99¼	Seefeldt A J	b 119	8.50	66-19	Hall Monitor 119no Mesabi Range1132½WinSomeBack1192	Outrun	9
17Jly83- 3Pen fst 1 1/16	:48⅕ 1:13⅗ 1:46⅘	Clm 2500	5 3 1hd 1hd 1½ 32½	Seefeldt A J	b 119	9.60	69-15	Win Some Back 113hd Nomad 1142½ Lord's Image1193	Weakened	8
17Jun83- 2Pen fst 1	:48⅗ 1:14 1:41⅖	Clm 2500	6 1 1hd 21½ 2hd 11½	Lloyd J S	b 119	*3.20	74-19	Lord's Image 1191½SpreadThin116noGallantSong1161½	Drew clear	9
1Jun83- 4Pen fst 1 1/16	:49 1:15⅕ 1:49⅗	Clm 2500	6 1 1hd 1½ 1½ 2nk	Colton R E	b 119	5.70	58-28	Hav A Brook 119nk Lord's Image 119nkFreedomBell1136½	Gamely	7
21May83- 5Pen sly 1 1/16	:48⅗ 1:14⅖ 1:49⅕	Clm 2500	7 1 11 11 13 14½	Colton R E	b 116	5.80	60-25	Lord's Image1164½Wumble111hdFlashingConsort116nk	Drew clear	10
22Apr83-10Pen fst 170	:46⅘ 1:13⅗ 1:46⅗	Clm 3200	5 6 715 815 711 714	Wagner B R	b 116	13.50	53-26	Young Dream 116¾ Pistoleer 1163½ Seeds and Stems113hd	Outrun	9
5Apr83- 2Key fst 1 1/16	:47⅘ 1:14⅖ 1:48⅗	Clm 3500	5 1 1½ 1hd 511 814¾	Wagner B R	b 115	6.00	46-30	Choice Friend 114no Retama 1178½ Montana Eagle 1141½	Tired	12

3:1

Rulers Jester — Ch. g. 4, by Court Ruling—Thumb Tack, by Poker
$2,500 Br.—Redson J H (Ark); Tr.—Roberts B Dean — **119**
Own.—Roberts B D
Lifetime 42 8 7 5 $32,070 — 1983 12 5 2 1 $10,593; 1982 7 1 2 1 $8,510; Turf 1 0 0 0 $110

23Oct83- 4Pen sly 1 1/16	:49⅕ 1:14⅗ 1:48⅕	3+Clm 2500	4 2 21 2½ 11½ 12	O'Donnell E E	116	*1.00	65-22	Rulers Jester 1162 Archie Does1134½SaveTheWhales113nk	Driving	6
16Oct83- 5Pen fst 6f	:22⅖ :46 1:12⅖	3+Clm 2500	6 8 76½ 1015 89½ 75½	Slaven M	119	4.20	76-22	Penowa Secret 1142 Lucky Motive 1151 Padraic 114no	Outrun	12
2Oct83- 4Pen gd 170	:47⅖ 1:13⅕ 1:44	3+Clm 4000	1 2 22 21½ 23 24	O'Donnell E E	113	*1.60	76-21	Sir Scotty 1134 Rulers Jester 1137½ Smooth Key 1093	Tired	7
18Sep83- 1Pen fst 170	:46⅗ 1:12 1:44	3+Clm 4000	1 3 25 23 24 25	O'Donnell E E	113	3.60	75-17	Topian1135RulersJester1133¾VlentineSurprise1193	Best of others	6
11Sep83- 9Pen fst 170	:46⅗ 1:13 1:45	3+Clm 3000	8 4 46½ 32 1½ 12½	O'Donnell E E	112	5.20	75-18	Rulers Jester 1122½ Pukka Pukka 115½ Smooth Key1142½	Driving	8
2Sep83- 1Pen fst 6f	:22⅘ :46 1:13⅖	Clm 2500	7 1 31½ 46 45½ 1½	O'Donnell E E	116	2.60	77-20	Rulers Jester 116½ Boniveinte 114hdGreatProprieter114nk	Driving	10
19Aug83- 9Pen fst 6f	:22⅗ :45⅗ 1:11⅕	3+Clm 3200	1 5 54 53½ 55 47¼	O'Donnell E E	115	7.40	81-18	Copper Reign 1102½ Lou's Craft 1104 Kasinoff 1221	Rallied	7
3Aug83- 1Pen fst 1	:47⅘ 1:14 1:41⅖	Clm 2500	7 6 54¾ 2hd 1½ 11¼	O'Donnell E E	119	*3.80	74-17	Rulers Jester 1191¼ Victory Play 114nkValedictorian1122¼	Driving	10

LATEST WORKOUTS Sep 29 Pen 4f fst :52 b

OCTOBER 30—RACE 2

This race is a good example of a 90–100% bet.

Zange—Nothing last time. Although claimed, returns to the same level after it is out of jail (claimed horses in most states must be raised in class if they race within thirty days of being claimed). Keith Lebarron thinks this horse isn't good enough now to run against better. Not a contender.

Withershins—David Dumestre's winning pattern, if you remember, is first time after a claim and putting Aguirre in the irons. *HOWEVER*, this time he drops the horse the first time after the claim as soon as it gets out of jail. Even the best trainer can't always claim champions. Remember, too, all handicapping rules/fundamentals are only guidelines. Not a contender.

Hardy's Starr—This is the horse! In New Jersey, at Atlantic City, he returned bleeding on September 2. Mario Beneito gets a hold of him and he wins at first asking. Remember, Mario wins with shippers and he did with this one too, paying $14.80 that day. The next race, on October 14th, this horse wins again versus $2,500 claimers. After the trainer corrected the problem (i.e. bleeding), **Hardy's Starr** went 2 for 2. Beneito then races this horse in a $4,000 starter handicap. $4,000 claimers is a raise of two classes. A $4,000 handicap is an even bigger raise. **Hardy's Starr** ran sixth, but still beat four horses. Today, he returns to an undefeated level after his trainer thought it might beat a lot tougher. Any horse can lose a race, but this one is a 100% of the M.B.!

O'Hara Begorra—An in and outer who tires at today's distance. Not a contender.

Valedictorian—Unfavorable jockey switch. Throw it out.

Archie Does—Two nice races. This horse woke up in its last two. A contender.

Win Some Back—Wins in routes.

Track Admiral—Nowhere last time and beaten by Hardy's Starr the time before. Not a contender.

Lord's Image—Not close recently and poor speed ratings at the distance.

Ruler's Jester—Remember him? He wins at the $2,500 level and shows so here. The public thinks so, too, making him the second choice. BUT, we know rules are only guidelines. This horse is suspect and not a contender for three reasons:

1. 119 pounds—never carried it to victory at this distance or longer.

2. Dean Roberts, the trainer, didn't raise him after a win, as is his pattern. This may indicate the horse isn't ready for his top effort.

3. The most important reason—post position #10. With his weight and this post it's doubtful he'll be pushed very hard. Why waste the horse's energy in a losing effort?

THE BET: 60% of the M.B. on **Hardy's Starr** to win. 15% each on exactas with **Archie Does** and **Win Some Back**, and 5% each on the reverse exactas. Betting 60% to win insures that this horse, this "lock," is not wasted even if the exactas lose. At 2:1 he's a real overlay.

RESULTS: Hardy's Starr didn't disappoint. He won and paid $6.20. **Archie Does** ran second and **Win Back Some** was third. The exacta was worth $57.20.

7 PENN NATIONAL

6 FURLONGS
PENN NATIONAL

6 FURLONGS. (1.08⅘) ALLOWANCE. Purse $6,900. 3-year-olds and up which have not won $4,200 twice since July 30 other than maiden, claiming, optional or starter. Weights 3-year-olds, 119 lbs.; older, 122 lbs.; non-winners of $4,200 since September 30 allowed 3 lbs.; $3,600, 6 lbs.; $3,300 since August 30, 9 lbs. (Maiden, Claiming and Starter races not considered in estimating allowances).

Coupled—Aspy and Dear Commander. SCR

L'Araignee 21:1

Ro. f. 4, by Par Excellent—Crystal Spider, by Davis II
Br.—Morlock J L (Md)
Tr.—Sheveleve Lawrence B
Own.—Weisleder H

110 Lifetime 30 7 5 2 $31,159 | 1983 16 4 3 1 $19,762 | 1982 14 3 2 1 $11,397 | Turf 2 0 0 0

Date-Race	Cond	Dist	Fractions	Class	Running line	Jockey	Wt	Odds	Speed	Finishers	Comment	Fld
10Oct83- 6Pen	fst	6f	:23⅕ :47 1:12	3↑ⒻClm 20000	7 1 12½ 1½ 11 1½	Baker C J	b 115	15.90	84-21	L'Arignee115½SometimeTomorrow1091½StreyenAnn1101½	Driving	7
1Oct83- 7Pen	sly	6f	:23 :46⅕ 1:11⅘	3↑ⒻAlw 7200	5 1 65 67 611 612¾	Baker C J	b 114	16.60	74-23	Here Comes Patsy 1141½ Bushy's Babe 1132 MayBay113nk	Trailed	6
17Sep83- 6Pen	fst	6f	:22⅖ :46 1:12⅖	3↑ⒻClm 15000	1 3 55 32 31 1hd	Baker C J	b 115	6.10	82-18	L'Araignee 115hd Hasty Sarah 1151½ Miss Mirabel 117hd	Driving	6
3Sep83- 6Pen	fst	5½f	:22⅕ :46 1:05	3↑ⒻClm 15000	5 6 66 56 56 43	Baker C J	b 115	9.00	88-17	Lady Twink 119nk Miss Mirabel 1191¾ Hasty Sarah1151	Mild gain	8
14Aug83- 7Pen	fm	1⅛ Ⓣ	1:42⅕	3↑ⒻHandicap	8 8 911 921 928 —	Aguirre E C	b 112	42.10	— —	Glimmer Glass1174GoldenStatue1213½GloryAlleluia114½	Distanced	9
25Jly83- 7Pen	fst	6f	:22⅖ :45⅘ 1:11⅘	ⒻClm c-15000	4 8 77½ 78 86¾ 85½	Daniels W H	b 119	*1.80	79-18	Miss Mirabel 1122 Hasty Sarah 119hd Streyen Ann 1151½	Outrun	8
15Jly83- 9CT	fst	6½f	:22⅘ :45⅕ 1:19⅗	3↑ⒻAlw 5200	6 5 47½ 412 35 21½	Daniels W H	b 120	3.60	85-23	Surprise Visit 1141½ L'Araignee 1202 Nalees Blues 1141½	Rallied	7
6Jly83- 6Pen	fst	6f	:22⅖ :45⅘ 1:11⅘	ⒻClm 15000	1 6 55 44½ 32 22¼	Montoya R	b 119	3.50	86-16	Marchamp 1192¼ L'Araignee 119½ Hasty Sarah 1191½	Slow early	6

Immigrant HUTTON 6:5

B. g. 5, by Ambernash—New Virginian, by Diatome
Br.—O'Brien Bros (Md)
Tr.—Verlay Filemon
Own.—Hill Top Stable

122 Lifetime 13 5 0 1 $40,680 | 1983 3 1 0 0 $6,000 | 1982 10 4 0 1 $34,680 | Turf 2 0 0 0

Date-Race	Cond	Dist	Fractions	Class	Running line	Jockey	Wt	Odds	Speed	Finishers	Comment	Fld
9Oct83- 9Suf	fst	6f	:22⅖ :45⅗ 1:10⅘	3↑Alw 10000	3 1 1hd 11½ 14 11¾	Petro N J5	b 117	4.60	87-23	Immigrant 1171¾ Crocketts Bluff 1224½ Aurbar 119¾	Ridden out	6
15Jan83- 8Bow	fst	7f	:22⅕ :45 1:23⅘	3↑ⓈStr De Nsk H	2 2 13 13½ 55¾ 811¼	McCarthy M J	b 109	11.20	76-23	Lord Duck 1161¾AMagicSpray1152WhatAMichael1201	Drifted out	10
8Jan83- 8Bow	fst	6f	:22⅖ :45⅗ 1:11⅘	3↑S Maryland H	4 6 45½ 814 813 813½	Miller D A Jr	b 113	5.00	70-26	What A Michael 117noPrinceValid1141WithCaution1181½	Stopped	8
23Dec82- 8Aqu	fst	6f	⊡:22⅖ :45⅘ 1:12⅕	Alw 37000	5 5 11½ 12½ 12 43½	McCarron G	b 119	1.40	81-27	MortgageMan113nkFleetSaber117noSonny'sHoss1152	Speed, tired	5
9Dec82- 8Aqu	fst	6f	⊡:23⅖ :47 1:12⅘	3↑Alw 27000	2 4 12½ 13 13 12¾	McCarron G	119	3.60	82-30	Immigrant 1192¾ DaveTheDude1204½OurEscapade119¾	Ridden out	9
25Nov82- 6Key	fst	7f	:22⅕ :45 1:24	3↑Alw 10000	1 4 14 16 18 17½	Hutton G W	b 116	*1.00	87-29	Immigrant 1167½ Buck Jump1208½SeaweedNSand109½	Ridden out	6
28Oct82- 8Lrl	fst	1	:45⅗ 1:11⅗ 1:38	3↑Alw 11000	1 1 16 1½ 23½ 57	Miller D A Jr	b 118	*1.80	75-25	Mister Al 1123½ Did We Win 1071½ Wet Socks 115hd	Used in pace	9
19Oct82- 6Lrl	fm	1	Ⓣ:46⅖ 1:11⅘ 1:37⅘	3↑Alw 11000	6 1 15 13 1½ 64½	Miller D A Jr	b 116	*.90	77-19	Davrick 112½ Going Aground 115½ Did We Win 1071½	Gave way	12

LATEST WORKOUTS ●Oct 27 Bow 3f gd :35⅘ h   Oct 3 Bow 3f gd :36 hg   ●Sep 24 Bow 6f fst 1:14⅘ h   ●Sep 14 Bow 5f sly 1:00 h

Aspy MONTOYA 10:1

Ro. h. 6, by Swerve—Spinach, by Count Of Honor
Br.—Mecom J W (Ky)
Tr.—Whitehair George M
Own.—F J C Stables

113 Lifetime 60 8 15 9 $78,459 | 1983 20 5 4 5 $38,947 | 1982 15 0 5 2 $10,904 | Turf 2 0 0 0 $3,315

Date-Race	Cond	Dist	Fractions	Class	Running line	Jockey	Wt	Odds	Speed	Finishers	Comment	Fld
16Oct83-10CT	fst	7f	:23⅗ :47⅘ 1:26⅘	3↑Handicap	1 3 66½ 57 55 44	Small S	b 126	3.30	82-21	Mighty Ben 1252 J. B.'s Dynamite 1222 Leetuck 117no	No mishap	6
25Sep83- 7Pen	fm	1⅛ Ⓣ	1:41	3↑Pa Gov Cup H	5 3 33½ 48½ 414 423½	Daniels W H	b 114	17.00	62-17	John's Gold 1212½ Trevita 1183 Classic Steed 11318	Tired	5
10Sep83- 9CT	fst	1⅛	:47⅗ 1:13⅘ 1:53⅘	3↑Geo Dickel	7 3 32½ 31½ 21 21	Daniels W H	b 118	5.40Ⓓ	83-23	Forceful Intent 1211 ⒹAspy 118hd Mighty Ben 1157	Drifted wide	10
10Sep83-Disqualified and placed third												
31Aug83- 8CT	my	1⅛	:48⅘ 1:14 1:54⅕	3↑Alw 6500	2 2 32 21 2hd 11½	Daniels W H	b 120	*.80	80-31	Aspy 1201½ Eli Dreamt 117no Leetuck 1173	Driving	6
21Aug83-10CT	fst	1 1/16	:47⅕ 1:13⅗ 1:47⅕	3↑Alw 5500	1 2 32 31½ 2hd 14	Daniels W H	b 120	*1.10	84-24	Aspy 1204 Bordello 1201 Lt. Lee 114½	Ridden out	5
7Aug83-10CT	fst	1 1/16	:47⅗ 1:12⅗ 1:46⅕	3↑Alw 5500	3 2 22 2hd 1hd 1¾	Daniels W H	b 120	*1.30	89-21	Aspy 120¾ Lt. Lee 1172 Crown Roast 11421	Driving	5
16Jly83- 9CT	fst	1 1/16	:46⅖ 1:11⅗ 1:45	3↑Mountainer H	6 5 56½ 55 57 69½	Daniels W H	b 117	2.10	86-18	Lawful Melody 110¾ Amber's Riddle 1205 Mighty Ben117½	Outrun	7
3Jly83- 8CT	fst	7f	:23 :46⅘ 1:26⅕	3↑Alw 5200	7 5 44½ 33 21 11	Daniels W H	b 114	*.80	89-22	Aspy 1141 Jove In Motion 1142 Mayo's Touch 114hd	Driving	8

LATEST WORKOUTS ●Oct 14 CT 3f hy :38 b

Dr. Kroy LEASURE 9:5

B. g. 5, by Jolie Jo—Miss Myra, by Ambehaving
Br.—Giangiulio P (Pa)
Tr.—Stough William D
Own.—M J M Stable

116 Lifetime 41 8 11 4 $63,595 | 1983 16 3 4 3 $31,979 | 1982 20 4 5 1 $26,376 | Turf 1 0 0 0

Date-Race	Cond	Dist	Fractions	Class	Running line	Jockey	Wt	Odds	Speed	Finishers	Comment	Fld
8Oct83- 7Key	fst	6f	:21⅘ :44⅖ 1:10	3↑Alw 16000	4 6 64½ 74½ 65½ 43	D'Agusto J G	b 113	13.80	88-17	Hail to Leader 117hd Big Monarch 117no Eliodoro 1123	Mild bid	7
25Sep83- 7Key	fst	6f	:22⅖ :45⅕ 1:09⅘	3↑Alw 16000	1 3 3½ 32 34 37	Cole A K	b 114	6.20	85-18	Sarah N Lou's Boy 1152 Big Monarch 1195 Dr. Kroy 1143	Evenly	6
11Sep83- 7Pen	fst	6f	:22⅗ :45⅘ 1:10⅘	3↑Alw 7200	5 1 21½ 2hd 1hd 11½	Gress D	b 116	*.40	90-18	Dr. Kroy 1161½ Double Trance 1142½AdmiralWhiskers1147	Driving	6
4Sep83- 8Key	fst	6½f	:22⅗ :45⅗ 1:16⅘	3↑Labor Day	5 1 42 32½ 23 31½	D'Agusto J G	b 112	6.70	88-21	Wananish1151½GlintGentlemn122noDr.Kroy1125¾	Frcd wide, brshd	5
20Aug83- 8Key	fst	7f	:22⅗ :45⅖ 1:22⅘	3↑Addy Boy H	6 4 62¾ 63½ 45½ 56½	D'Agusto J G	b 112	15.80	86-17	Brother George114hdBoldRelic1163Overdeposited1132½	No factor	9
6Aug83- 7Key	fst	6f	:22⅕ :45 1:10	3↑Alw 15000	1 5 54½ 79½ 58½ 45½	D'Agusto J G	b 112	5.60	85-17	Geron 116½ Hail to Leader 1175 Big Monarch 113no	Rallied	8
23Jly83- 7Pen	fst	6f	:22⅗ :45 1:09⅘	3↑Alw 7200	6 2 55½ 42½ 21 12	D'Agusto J G	b 113	*1.20	95-17	Dr. Kroy 1132 Northern Games 1184 Little Slalom122½	Drew clear	7
4Jly83- 6Key	fst	7f	:22⅕ :44⅗ 1:21⅘	3↑ⓈAlw 14000	4 6 51½ 53 24 24½	D'Agusto J G	b 114	11.60	93-15	Addy Miss 1124½ Dr. Kroy 114nk Little Slalom 1131½	Game try	8

LATEST WORKOUTS Oct 28 Pen 3f gd :35⅘ h   ●Oct 3 Pen 3f gd :35⅘ h   Sep 23 Pen 3f fst :36⅘ h   ●Sep 2 Pen 3f fst :36 h

Water Piston AVILES 7:1

B. h. 6, by Gunflint—Water Princess, by Beau Gar
Br.—Hobeau Farm Inc (Fla)
Tr.—Kravets Bruce M
Own.—New Concepts Stable

113 Lifetime 67 16 8 9 $89,986 | 1983 15 5 2 1 $23,676 | 1982 17 5 2 3 $23,370

Date-Race	Cond	Dist	Fractions	Class	Running line	Jockey	Wt	Odds	Speed	Finishers	Comment	Fld
9Oct83- 6Pen	fst	6f	:22⅖ :45⅗ 1:12	3↑Clm c-15000	1 7 46 49½ 67½ 65¾	Colton R E	119	*1.50	78-21	Ima Spook 119hd Sicilian Jet 1152¾ Phivor 1151	Tired	8
23Sep83- 7Key	fst	6f	:22⅖ :45⅘ 1:11⅕	3↑Clm 18000	1 4 31 36 39 46	Colton R E	120	3.50	79-24	Catchawink 1162½ Jara 1163¾ Scarlet Invader 116no	Tired	8
11Sep83- 6Pen	fst	6f	:22⅖ :45⅖ 1:10⅗	3↑Clm 15000	3 1 2hd 12 13 15¾	Colton R E	115	*1.30	91-18	Water Piston 1155¾ Native Cup 115¾ Equil Liberty 119nk	Driving	6
28Aug83- 7Pen	fst	6f	:22⅕ :45⅕ 1:10⅖	3↑Clm 15000	6 5 41½ 2½ 21½ 22½	Colton R E	115	5.10	90-15	Double Trance 1132½WaterPiston1152ElegantandBold115¾	gamely	7
17Jly83- 6Pen	fst	6f	:23 :45⅗ 1:09⅘	Clm 18000	1 7 31 32½ 56 57½	Colton R E	112	3.00	87-15	Hijo Plato 119nk Tribal Ceremony 1153 Sir Winsum 1124	Tired	7
17Jly83-Placed fourth through disqualification												
8Jly83- 8Key	fst	6½f	:22⅗ :45⅗ 1:17⅗	3↑Clm 18000	4 1 31 43½ 48 44½	Baker C J	120	2.90	81-21	Manny T. 1111½ Zoning Appeal 1161½ Contofer 1121½	Lacked bid	6
19Jun83- 4Pen	fst	6f	:22⅗ :46 1:10⅘	Clm 20000	5 2 44 32½ 41½ 41½	Lloyd J S	119	*1.40	88-17	Up Is O. K. 115hd Sir Scan 115½ Jara 1161	Weakened	8
8Jun83- 8Key	fst	6f	:22⅗ :45⅘ 1:10⅘	Clm 22500	3 5 43 53 42 42½	Lloyd J S	120	8.30	85-22	Dr. Kroy 116nk Jest Sam 1221 Mr. Fancy Face 1161	Came out st.	7

Bordello 58:1

B. g. 4, by Shy Native—Hot Time, by Rambunctious
Br.—O'Sullivan Farms (WVa)
Tr.—Pankewicz Donald
Own.—Pankewicz & Thomas

113 Lifetime 23 4 6 3 $22,242 | 1983 12 2 3 2 $12,398 | 1982 9 2 3 1 $9,714 | Turf 2 0 0 0 $675

Date-Race	Cond	Dist	Fractions	Class	Running line	Jockey	Wt	Odds	Speed	Finishers	Comment	Fld
9Oct83- 7Pen	fm	1 Ⓣ	1:35⅗	3↑Alw 7500	6 5 64½ 63½ 54¾ 44½	Burton J E	114	27.50	84-14	Dr. Tipton 1162½ Admiral Whiskers 1141¾ ASureHit114nk	Mild bid	7
18Sep83- 7Pen	fm	170 Ⓣ	1:39⅕	3↑Alw 7500	6 3 44½ 67½ 57 57	Kaenel J L	116	11.40	83-19	Little Slalom 1131½ Cookie 1133½ Buttered Grits 1132	Early foot	7
4Sep83- 6Pen	fst	1 1/16	:48 1:12⅖ 1:45⅕	3↑Clm c-15000	3 1 1hd 11 1hd 2½	Fitzgerald R	117	*2.10	79-17	Rotary Bit 114½ Bordello 1174½ Hello Pal 1151½	Weakened	7
21Aug83-10CT	fst	1 1/16	:47⅕ 1:13⅗ 1:47⅕	3↑Alw 5500	3 5 57 43½ 31½ 24	Shaw N W	120	3.00	80-24	Aspy 1204 Bordello 1201 Lt. Lee 114½	Rallied	5
7Aug83- 7Key	fst	1 1/16	:47⅖ 1:12⅕ 1:45⅖	3↑Clm 18000	4 4 42½ 55 45 43½	Edwards J W	120	16.30	73-20	Rattle the Keys 1161 Balongo 1161 Rigid 1161½	No excuse	11
23Jly83- 9CT	my	1 1/16	:46⅕ 1:11⅘ 1:46⅘	3↑Alw 5500	1 3 25 25 2½ 13½	Daniels W H	120	7.80	86-16	Bordello 1203½ Kiss Chris 114hd Lt. Lee 1171½	Going away	6
9Jly83- 9CT	fst	7f	:23⅗ :47⅕ 1:28	3↑Alw 4800	8 4 510 58½ 31 13½	Shaw N W	120	3.90	80-22	Bordello 1203½ Roark 1201½ Thornbush 1091	Driving	8
26Jun83-10CT	fst	1 1/16	:47⅗ 1:12⅘ 1:46⅖	Alw 5500	1 3 34½ 34 43½ 57	Shaw N W	114	6.40	81-22	Amber's Riddle 1201 Lt. Lee 1203½ Mamas Hill 114½	Tired	7

LATEST WORKOUTS ●Oct 22 Pen 4f fst :50 h   Oct 5 Pen 4f fst :49⅘ h

***Sharply** — Dk. b. or br. h. 5, by Sharp-Eyed Quillo—Good Girl, by Bristol
Own.—Markowitz E — Br.—Haras Geoffrey Bushell (Chile) — Tr.—Boniface J William — 113
Lifetime 17 4 1 6 $34,504 — 1983 3 0 0 1 $2,760 — 1982 7 3 0 4 $15,804 — Turf 2 0 0 1 $819

6May83- 8Pim fst 1 1/16 :47 1/5 1:11 3/5 1:44 3/5 Alw 15000 3 4 4^8½ 4^9½ 5^4¾ 4^2¼ Edwards J W 115 20.70 80-22 Count Misty 109^nk Eurodancer 119^1¾ Ixatapa 114^nk Mild rally 8
27Apr83- 8Pim fst 1 1/16 :46 3/5 1:11 1:44 2/5 Alw 15000 4 3 3^10 4^11 5^7½ 3^6 Edwards J W 115 27.20 78-22 Once Twice 114no Pol Luka 114^5 Sharply 115no Rallied 6
12Apr83- 8Pim fst 6f :23 :45 2/5 1:09 3/5 Alw 14500 6 7 7^8½ 7^15 7^22 7^18¼ Edwards J W b 115 25.20 80-19 Jordana's Count 114^7 Antiash 114^1 Shifty Sheik 115¾ Tired 7
30Jun82 ♦ 10H'podromo(Chile) fst*7f 1:24 1/5 Handicap(Index 55 & down) 3 112 -- -- Further Information Not Available 7
2Jun82 ♦ 7H'podromo(Chile) fst*7f 1:25 2/5 Handicap(Index 55 & down) 3 115 -- -- Further Information Not Available 7
15May82 ♦ 10H'podromo(Chile) fst*7½f 1:30 4/5 Clasico Rep. ArentinaHcp 3 117 -- -- Salinidad 108^4½ Nino Moro 134^nk Sharply 117^3 10
1May82 ♦ 11H'podromo(Chile) fst*7f 1:26 Handicap(Index 43 to 31) 1 119 -- -- Further Information Not Available 11
4Apr82 ♦ 4ClubHipico(Chile fm*7½f 1:32 2/5 Ⓣ Handicap(Index 38 to 30) 3 117 -- -- Further Information Not Available 9
LATEST WORKOUTS Oct 27 Lrl 6f fst 1:18 2/5 b

Piedmont Pete — Dk. b. or br. h. 7, by Son of Bagdad—Agnes Ashley, by Uncle Percy
Own.—Little & Royse — Br.—Harris W R (Md) — Tr.—Vowell Dwayne — 113
Lifetime 68 17 18 9 $257,371 — 1983 8 0 4 2 $11,227 — 1982 1 1 0 0 $21,385 — Turf 1 0 1 0 $1,936

23Sep83-10Alb fst 6f :22 2/5 :46 2/5 1:12 1/5 3+ Alw 8000 4 2 1^1 1½ 1^1 4^3½ Burgos S b 117 *1.00 78-23 Delightful Battle 111^2½ Annihilater 116½ Bet On Me 116¾ 9
15Sep83-12Alb fst 5f :22 :44 2/5 :58 2/5 3+ Sandia H 2 5 6^3¾ 6^4½ 5^4½ 5^7¾ Powell J P 115 2.80 85-24 Special Hank 121^1 Pride Of Loom 114^2¼ Captense 117^1¾ 8
5Sep83-11Rui fst 5½f :22 1/5 :45 4/5 1:05 3/5 3+ Alw 6000 2 3 4^1¾ 3^2 2^hd 2^nk Martinez O A Jr 116 *.70 97-10 Pride Of Loom 113^nk Piedmont Pete 116¾ Jack The Knife 118^9 5
28Aug83-10Rui fst 6½f :22 3/5 :46 2/5 1:18 2/5 3+ Handicap 6 1 1^1 1^2 1^hd 3^1½ Martinez O A Jr 115 4.30 94-09 Fill Mackis Cup 121¾ Double B Express 119¾ PiedmontPete115^no 6
7Aug83-10Rui fst 6f :22 3/5 :46 1:12 2/5 3+ Spr Champ 3 1 3^1½ 2½ 1^hd 2^1¾ Martinez O A Jr 113 3.10 94-15 Fill Mackis Cup 119^1¾ Piedmont Pete 113^hd Special Hank 118^1½ 7
29Jly83-11Rui fst 6f :22 3/5 :46 3/5 1:12 3/5 3+ Alw 4600 3 1 2½ 2^hd 1^hd 2^3 Asmussen S M 117 *.30 92-20 Captense 118^3 Piedmont Pete 117^3½ Bourbon And Blues 116^3½ 7
17Jly83-11Rui my 6½f :23 1/5 :47 2/5 1:19 4/5 3+ S Blanca 3 2 1^1 1^2 1^1 2no Asmussen S M 116 *2.50 89-19 Fill Mackis Cup 118no Piedmont Pete 116½ Curribot 120½ 6
2Jly83-11Rui fst 4f :21 3/5 :45 1/5 3+ Alw 4500 10 3 5^4½ 5^4 3^5¾ Asmussen S M^5 117 4.60 91-03 Special Hank 121^1 Real Speculation 121^4¾ Piedmont Pete 117^1 10
LATEST WORKOUTS Oct 27 Pen 5f gd 1:03 1/5 b

OCTOBER 30—RACE 7 (Exacta Wagering)

A classic situation. The local residents have read all the press on **Dr. Kroy** and think the world of him. No doubt he's a nice horse, winning at Penn National at 2:5, but beware of the shipper.

L'Araignee—Claimer who lost ground last time, stepping up into an allowance race. Not a contender.

Immigrant—This is the horse. On December 23, this horse set the fractions against **Mortgage Man** as the highweight in a $37,000 allowance race. He tailed off after that and was freshened. On October 9th he returned like a champ, winning easily. An 87 speed rating at Suffolk on a track rated 23 is too much for these to handle. In addition, **Immigrant** wasn't pushed that race, is the only real speed today, and should improve in his second start after a 9-month layoff. In this race **Piedmont Pete** may show some "l's" in his past performance lines, but he doesn't go to the half in :45 like Immigrant.

Aspy—Wrong distance. Not a contender.

Dr. Kroy—The competition, but can't compete with **Immigrant** who wins in New York against tougher.

Bordello—Wrong distance. Throw it out.

Sharply—Not close at the distance. Not a contender.

Piedmont Pete—Ships in from Albuquerque, New Mexico, and doesn't last at the distance. The ship alone is enough to defeat most horses. Not a contender.

THE BET: For the rest of the world 100% of the M.B., probably 80% on an exacta with **Immigrant** on top and **Dr. Kroy** second and 20% on the reverse. There are times to be aggressive and this is one of them. I can't see anyone beating these two and I'm convinced **Immigrant** is better. For me, however, not a dime. Why? The race occurred when I was a seeded finalist at Penn National's World Series of Handicapping contest, along with John Pricci, Russ Harris, Andy Beyer, Ray Kerrison and John Piesen, among others.

In recent years various race tracks around the country have been promoting handicapping contests. Sometimes there is even an entry fee of as much as $200 or $300 for a chance to win thousands. Some contests are worth $90,000 to $150,000 to the winner.

The best handicappers do not always win contests, however. At Penn National, for instance, each participant starts out with an imaginary $1,000. They bet a minimum of $2 per race on as many horses as they wish per race. Win, Place and Show betting only. At the end of three days, the contestant with the most money wins. In my mind, it is 30% handicapping, 60% money management, and 10% luck. These contests are usually make or break. Most people, especially at smaller tracks where horses may not hold their form as well, are not willing to grind it out—picking solid horses and a lot of them. Rather, the winning philosophy is to take the big chance. Bet all or most of your money on one race. If it wins you are well ahead of everyone. Then just sit on the lead unless someone comes within reach.

Since its inception in 1976, none of approximately 25 professional handicappers have won the contest at Penn National. I'm sure that in each of their big races something happened—usually poor racing luck. From about 125 amateurs and media people, one has been lucky or skilled enough to get the money. Before the sixth race, I told John Pricci (racing columnist for *Newsday* on Long Island, and president of the N.Y. Turf Writers Association), that I bet everything on a 9:1 shot in that race. After it won I was going to parlay everything on **Immigrant**. After **Immigrant** won, with only three races left in the contest, I would have opened up too many lengths on the field for anyone to catch me. The $90,000 first prize would be all mine. **Handsome Doc R.**, my bet in the sixth, was all over the track and missed by a neck at 9:1!

Pricci came up to me after the race and said we should tap out on **Immigrant**, otherwise it would win just to rub it in that I lost $90,000 by a neck. I told John that never in my life did I want a horse to lose so badly.

RESULTS: Naturally, **Immigrant** shot out of the gate making the first quarter in :21^3 and the half in :45. The race was over out of the gate. They couldn't catch him. He paid $4.40. **Dr. Kroy** got up for second. The exacta returned $8.20. Pricci came up to me after the race and just shook his head. There was just nothing left to say.

A top handicapper for one of the New York newspapers watched his big bet stumble out of the gate losing all chance. Probably the top seed in the contest got wiped out before the end of the first day. So, I rationalized my poor racing luck.

The winner of the New York Racing Association contest, in 1983, told me he listened to Tony DeMucci talking on television about a 10:1 shot. Due to Tony he played the horse and won that contest. Superior handicappers have an edge, especially those who do their homework. Sometimes, though, it's better to be lucky than smart.

The Final Steps

The final steps in the betting process are the paddock check, post parade, and making the bet itself. It is here that the bet is adjusted for the last time—either increased, decreased, or changed.

The general public overlooks the paddock, but the serious bettor must check the paddock every race—without exception. Spotting hurting animals or changes in an animal's condition can be important. When visiting the paddock, jot down not only which animal has what injury, but also the severity of the problem. Write "left front ankle 1" for shouldn't be racing or hurting badly, "left front ankle 2" for one that looks bad and seems bothersome and so on.

The eight most important things to look for in the paddock are:

1. *Washiness*—The bettable horse should be alert, notice his surroundings, attentive to what is going on around him. A little excited or anxious is fine—even desirable. Experienced horses have been in the paddock often enough to know that the next step is the race itself. After years and years of inbreeding, the thoroughbred has become a high strung animal. A little sweat is fine—an indication of alertness, excitement, and a willingness to run. During the summer months almost all horses sweat visibly. As post time draws near, the sweat remains the same or even disappears. If a horse is washy, however, the sweat worsens and the skin appears to get darker. At his worst, a washy horse breaks into a lather that looks like soap. Sweat is visible on the neck and underneath the girth (belly) in particular. Sometimes one can literally see the sweat dripping underneath its belly. This animal should be thrown out from consideration completely.

2. *Kidney Sweat*—The horse's kidneys are located on top of his back toward the end on each side. This is similar to washiness and the severity is measured by the amount of

sweat. It's almost always a bad bet when an animal exhibits kidney sweat. This judgment, like all others in the paddock area, is subjective. It comes only with experience.

3. *Knees*—Horsemen detect knee problems by heat in the area or by the horse's action (stride). In the paddock, a horse with obvious knee problems will either have his legs spread apart or its head turned to one side (opposite of the hurting knee) to take weight off the bad knee. If the knee is bothering it badly enough for the horse to favor it, do not waste money backing it. Knee problems are serious and can end a horse's career.

4. *Ears*—Positive signs in the paddock include ears that turn in the direction of a noise. This horse is alert and curious about his surroundings. However, ears that flicker constantly indicate a nervous animal.

   Never bet a horse with airplane ears—those almost parallel to the ground. This horse is depressed and/or hurting.

   Depending on your point of view, a horse whose ears are rigid can be either exhibiting positive or negative signs. Many horsemen will agree this is a sure sign that the horse has been drugged. The ears don't react to noises. If you ever find such an animal and are convinced that a trainer is trying to illegally win a race here, there is no reason not to take advantage of the situation and cash a winning ticket. Let the race track officials enforce the rules. For such action, however, the penalties against the trainer should be severe!

5. *Bandages*—Support bandages and run down bandages are used for protection against clipping heels and gritty track surfaces. They do not indicate a hurting horse. On the other hand, the bigger bandages point out infirmities—whether it be muscles, tendons, or suspensories. If a horse has only rear bandages and otherwise checks out OK don't hesitate to play him. The front legs are a different story. They take

the pounding. At bigger race tracks never bet horses with front bandages. Sometimes they win, but not often enough. At smaller race tracks it is less important. This depends more on the odds and the level of competition. At 7:1 why not? At even money—no! A horse stepping up, meeting much tougher competition, can overextend himself. Very often a once classy horse, one with heart, will let his heart take control and try to do more than it can. It is not unusual for an infirm horse to break down in such a case.

6. *Coat*—A horse's coat is a good indication of his general well being. Most healthy horses have nice shiny coats—sprinters even more so than routers. When a horse is really on edge there is dappling—the coat is spotted. Furthermore, if the horse is "dancing on his toes," besides being dappled, one can take this as a sure sign of the horse being fit, ready, and more importantly, eager to run. A router up on his toes is an even bigger play.

   A particularly good circumstance to back dappled animals up on their toes is in a field of first-time starters. This is a strong indication that the trainer has his horse ready to win at first asking. As further confirmation of this, look for a horse "on the muscle." This is similar to a muscle man on the beach. The horse's muscles will be very pronounced and he will have the racing dimple. This is the long line on each side of his rear indicating powerful muscles.

7. *Eyes*—As stated previously, horses should be alert and attentive to their surroundings. One can see this alertness and curiosity in a horse's eyes. However, at least one or two times a day, one encounters the "white-eye." This horse's eyes are so wide open they bulge and the whites of the eyes become clearly visible. This animal is ready to rear up or bolt at the drop of a pin. If no incidents occur in the paddock or post parade, it should not affect the horse's chances. From a bettor's viewpoint it's preferable for a horse to be a little frightened than a little dull.

8. *Ankles*—Look for swollen ankles. If you're not sure what a normal ankle looks like, examine the rest of the horses in the paddock. Write down, in a notebook, which ankle is swollen and how badly (either a 1, 2 or 3). The next time this horse runs refer back to your book. Many times after a layoff, such an injury improves greatly. Usually, you can catch a good price in this situation.

The Post Parade

The post parade is your last check-point before betting. Briefly, positive signs here include reduced sweat (not increased), being up on its toes even more so than in the paddock, and being tightly held with its head behind the lead pony as if very eager to run if let loose. During the gallop, notice horses that like the mud (i.e. when the track is off). They will firmly plant both rear feet on the ground almost simultaneously. Those that don't will plant one foot at a time – as if they prefer not to land at all. It's simple to spot and the dividends can be tremendous. On the negative side, never play a horse that gets loose wasting its energy for the stretch drive.

The Walk To The Windows

Now that you've put it all together, there's only a little soul searching left. Discipline (discipline, discipline, discipline) is the key here. The bet should be decided upon before the pari-mutuel clerk looks you in the eye. If still not sure, and time is running out, the smart bettor decreases his bet substantially, or passes the race entirely.

When you have done all of your homework, are truly confident in your selections and bets, and can't wait for the race to go off, then you are ready for the final step – the walk to the windows. Good luck!

Acknowledgements

The author and the publisher express gratitude to the Daily Racing Form, Inc. for the use of their copyrighted materials.

Additional information about the *Daily Racing Form* newspaper may be obtained by contacting:

Daily Racing Form
10 Lake Drive
P.O. Box 1015
Hightstown, N.J. 08520

or

Daily Racing Form, Inc.
170 South Bimini Place
Los Angeles, CA 90004

Index

adjusted speed figures 89–100
ankles 161
Aqueduct examples 113–145

bandages 159
biases, track 81–83
blinkers 50
breeding 60–65

coat 159
chalk horse 105
"cheating" 33, 36
"class" 36
confidence 22

daily doubles 28, 104
  betting 108
dedication 12
discipline 19

ears 159
equipment 50
exactas 28
  betting 110
exotics 28–29, 102
  betting 108
eyes 160

first-time starters 60

handicapping basics 73–78
"heart" 33

intelligence 10

jockey switches 56, 59
jockeys 54–60

key race 14
kidney sweat 158
knees 159
knowledge 18

long shots 107
"loose on the lead" 65, 66
Louisiana Downs examples 132–145

math skills 21
maximum bet 106
memory 13
money management 21
"money man" 53
"mudders" 62

objectivity 18
odds 24
overlay 105

pari-mutuel betting, fundamentals of 23–30
Penn National examples 145–157
pick-six betting 29, 111
place betting 25
place pool 25
post parade 161
problem-solving 11

quinellas 28
  betting 109

rating a horse 86
reading between the lines 78

savers 107
show betting 27
show pool 27
"sour" horses 71, 72

trainer patterns 43
trainers 40–54
trip handicapping 83
triples or trifectas 28
  betting 110

underlay 105

washiness 158
win bet 23
win pool 24